A Gospel for a New People

A Gospel for a New People
Studies in Matthew

GRAHAM N. STANTON

Westminster/John Knox Press
Louisville, Kentucky

Copyright © T&T Clark Ltd, 1992

T&T Clark Ltd, 59 George Street, Edinburgh EH2 2LQ, Scotland

This edition published under license from T&T Clark Ltd by
Westminster/John Knox Press
100 Witherspoon Street, Louisville, Kentucky 40202-1396

First American edition 1993

PRINTED IN GREAT BRITAIN

9 8 7 6 5 4 3 2 1

Library of Congress Cataloging-in-Publication Data
Stanton, Graham.
  A gospel for a new people : studies in Matthew / Graham N.
Stanton.
        p.   cm.
  Includes bibliographical references and indexes.
  ISBN 0-664-25499-3

  1. Bible. N.T. Matthew—Criticism, interpretation, etc. I. Title.
BS2575.3.S738 1993
226.2'06—dc 20   93-7233

To my parents

Gladys and Norman Stanton

CONTENTS

Part II: The Parting of the Ways

Part III: Studies in Matthew

Preface

Several years ago one of my students asked me about my research and writing projects. As soon as I mentioned Matthew's gospel, her face fell and she said with a wry grin, 'Matthew is my least favourite gospel'. I did not need to ask why she had reached that conclusion, for it is a typical modern reaction. For the serious reader, however, Matthew's gospel is rewarding, even if it is also demanding and often puzzling. I have certainly found plenty of historical, exegetical and theological issues to interest and challenge me.

As I complete this book I am aware that in spite of all that I have learnt from other scholars and all that I have discovered for myself, important issues remain unresolved, and individual verses still baffle me. On the other hand, my appreciation of the evangelist's literary and theological achievement has grown steadily. Matthew may lack the subtlety and profundity of several other New Testament writers, but the more fully one appreciates the theological and social tensions he faced in relating 'new' and 'old', the greater one's admiration. The evangelist wrote his gospel for a 'new people' in quite specific circumstances, but his breadth of vision and his literary skill encouraged others in later generations and later centuries to use his gospel to enrich the life of the church. Down through the centuries Christians have always set some parts of Matthew aside (at least temporarily) and tried to appropriate the parts which they have understood. And so it is today, though we would do well not to ignore passages which run against the grain of our current church and cultural life; if we take them seriously, they may surprise us.

I began my work on Matthew during a period of six month's study leave in the University of Tübingen. I am most grateful to the Alexander von Humboldt Stiftung for the award of a research fellowship. Professor Martin Hengel took a keen interest in my work while I was in Tübingen, as he has done ever since. At that time I began to study the social world of first century Antioch, long before such studies became fashionable. But as I could not persuade myself that Matthew wrote for Christians in Antioch, I abandoned the project and eventually found other paths to explore.

My debt to other scholars who have been working on Matthew in recent years is enormous. Many have generously sent me copies of their books and offprints of their articles. The seminars on Matthew which have been led by Professors Ulrich Luz and Jack Dean Kingsbury at recent annual meetings of *Studiorum Novi Testamenti Societas* have been very influential.

Early versions of several parts of this book have been given as lectures or seminars in Leuven, Basel, Toronto, Melbourne, as well as in a number of Universities in the United Kingdom and in New Zealand. The sharp questions of many have forced me to think further about many points. A dozen of my doctoral students from almost as many countries have worked with me on parts of Matthew's gospel from several different angles: they have taught me a great deal.

My work on Matthew has been carried out while I have been committed to major editorial, teaching and administrative responsibilities, as well as to other writing projects. Hence the support (and patience) of my colleagues in Biblical Studies at King's College London has been invaluable. Ronald Clements, Richard Coggins, Michael Knibb, Leslie Houlden, Judith Lieu, and Francis Watson have been generous with their help and advice. Their warm friendship has been a constant delight, and their own scholarly work a continual stimulus.

My father read the proofs of most of the chapters of this book in Christchurch, New Zealand; Bridget Upton (London) and David Sim (Melbourne) kindly read the proofs of several chapters and made a number of helpful suggestions. My wife has had to endure a great deal – any expression of gratitude would be inadequate. This book is dedicated to my parents, Gladys and Norman Stanton, who first pointed me to the way of righteousness.

Abbreviations

Matthew	*The Interpretation of Matthew. Issues in Religion and Theology* 3; ed. G.N. Stanton, Philadelphia and London 1983.
Matthieu,	*L'Evangile selon Matthieu. Rédaction et Théologie,* ed. M. Didier, BETL 29, Gembloux 1972.
NovT	*Novum Testamentum*
NovTSup	Supplements to *Novum Testamentum*
NTAbh	Neutestamentliche Abhandlungen
NTD	Das Neue Testament Deutsch
NTS	*New Testament Studies*
RB	*Revue Biblique*
REB	Revised English Bible (1989)
RSR	*Religious Studies Review*
SBLDS	Society for Biblical Literature Dissertation Series
SBS	Stuttgarter Bibelstudien
ScEccl	*Sciences Ecclésiastiques*
ScEs	*Science et esprit* (Montreal)
SNTSMS	Society for New Testament Studies Monograph Series
ST	*Studia Theologica*
SUNT	Studien zur Umwelt des NT
TB	*Tyndale Bulletin*
TD	*Theology Digest*
ThB	*Theologische Beiträge*
ThHK	Theologischer Handkommentar zum NT
ThLZ	*Theologische Literaturzeitung*
ThR	*Theologishe Rundschau*
Tradition	Bornkamm, G., Barth, G., and Held H.J., *Tradition and Interpretation in Matthew,* E.tr. London, 1963.
TS	*Theological Studies*
TU	Texte und Untersuchungen zur Geschichte der altchristlichen Literatur
VC	*Vigiliae Christianae*
WJT	*Westminster Theological Journal*
WUNT	Wissenschaftliche Untersuchungen zum Neuen Testament
ZThK	*Zeitschrift für Theologie und Kirche*

Chapter One

Introduction

A large number of fascinating historical and theological questions soon confront the reader of Matthew's gospel. By no means all of them are tackled in this book. I am primarily concerned with the relationship of the Christian communities for whom Matthew writes to contemporary Judaism. Was Matthew an apologist who attempted to set out for his Christian readers a 'response' to some of the Jewish teachers of his day? From the evangelist's perspective, what were the main issues at stake between Christians and Jews? Does Matthew's gospel reflect inner-Jewish disputes within a very tolerant Judaism? Or did the communities to whom the evangelist wrote see themselves as a distinct entity over against Judaism?

Was Matthew himself a Jew, or was he a Gentile who drew on earlier traditions which had been shaped by tensions between Christians and Jews? Were the communities to whom he wrote still facing hostility (whether real or merely perceived) from local Jewish leaders? Or was Jewish persecution of Christians a matter of past history? Why are apocalyptic motifs borrowed from Jewish writings and utilised so much more extensively in this gospel than in the other three? Did Matthew still hope that some Jews would accept Christian claims concerning Jesus? Or was missionary activity in the evangelist's day largely confined to Gentiles? And finally, perhaps the most puzzling question of all: why

1

is this gospel both profoundly Jewish and profoundly anti-Jewish?

It is by no means easy to answer these and many related questions. They are tackled from a number of different angles in the chapters which follow, half of which have been published as articles in journals, essays in *Festschriften*, and contributions to symposia; details are given at the end of this Introduction.

This chapter sketches briefly my views on the setting and purpose of Matthew's gospel; they lie behind the chapters which follow and are expounded and defended in many of them. The remainder of the book is then introduced and summarised; like Matthew's gospel itself, most parts (but not quite all) are inter-related.

At the end of this chapter the title I have chosen for this bc ok is discussed. I shall try to show that although the evangelist did not provide his writing with a title, he does refer to it as 'this gospel' (24. 14 and 26. 13); the communities to whom he wrote are considered to be a 'new people' (21. 43).

I am convinced that Matthew wrote following a period of prolonged dispute and hostility with fellow-Jews. He and his opponents are heirs to the same Scriptures and share many religious convictions, but differences run deep. Mutual incomprehension has led to mutual hostility and, eventually, a clear parting of the ways.

With considerable literary, catechetical and pastoral skill Matthew has composed a gospel for a new people – fellow-Christians (both Jews and Gentiles) in a cluster of Christian churches which are defining themselves over against local synagogues. The Christian communities with which the evangelist is in direct or indirect contact have grown rapidly: shallow faith and dissension are much in evidence.

The evangelist writes with several strategies in mind. He intends to set out the story and significance of Jesus as a 'foundation document' for his readers: his primary aims are Christological and catechetical. In some passages he responds to the criticisms and jibes which he knows are the stock in trade of his readers' Jewish opponents. In other passages he tries to account for the parting of the ways: he does this partly by laying the blame squarely on the Jewish leaders, partly by explaining the reasons for Israel's continuing and almost total rejection of her Messiah, and partly by defending the emergence of the 'new people' as a distinct religious entity over against Judaism. As often happens in conflict between closely related groups, whether they be political or religious, the 'new people' carefully differentiates itself from the parent body. But since Matthew believes that disciples of Jesus in his own day are heirs to God's promises of old, he also takes pains to stress continuities and similarities with Judaism.

Although many books on early Christianity still state or imply that Judaism gradually withered away following the fall of Jerusalem in A.D. 70, this is a mistaken assumption. The Christian churches to whom Matthew writes are minority groups still living in the shadow of thriving local Jewish communities. For this reason the evangelist encourages group solidarity in the face of perceived hostility from external sources.

Matthew is concerned about the failings of many of his fellow-Christians, their 'lawlessness', but he is not engaged in an 'inner-Christian' doctrinal dispute. The widely held view that the evangelist is struggling not only with Jewish opponents, but also with libertine, antinomian or 'Pauline' Christians is not well founded. Matthew does stress much more strongly than Mark the continuing importance of the law (as it has been interpreted by Jesus). However, he does this out of a general concern about 'lawlessness' within Christian communities and in response to Jewish jibes that that Christians are 'lawless', rather than in order to refute the 'heretical' views of a faction within the communities for whom he is writing.

The evangelist does not have one over-riding concern which provides the key to his gospel. The more narrowly his purposes are defined, the less compelling are the explanations offered. Matthew writes with broad catechetical and pastoral concerns: he sets out the story and significance of Jesus in order to assist Christians to come to terms with their identity as communities distinct from Judaism.

3

In this sketch of Matthew's purposes I have deliberately refrained from referring to the evangelist as a theologian. Of course many of his concerns are profoundly theological, but he does not set them out in a systematic or a coherent way, as a modern theologian is expected to do. In the wake of the development in the 1950s and 1960s of redaction criticism as the dominant method used in serious study of the gospels, it became customary to refer to the evangelists as theologians. In order to bestow this honour on Matthew, some writers have forced awkwardly into the same theological mould rather disparate traditions. Others have assigned to 'pre-Matthean tradition' passages which did not cohere with what they have taken to be the evangelist's theology. I think it is preferable to accept that Matthew is not always as consistent as many of his modern interpreters would like. His skills are those of a pastor and gifted communicator rather than those of a theologian.

The three chapters in Part I take up an issue which has become more and more pressing in Matthean studies in recent years: the appropriate methods for scholarly study of this gospel. Matthean scholarship is in some disarray at present, largely as the result of the use of quite diverse methods. The development of fresh approaches to study of the gospels has been welcomed warmly by many scholars, but as yet there has been little critical discussion of the new methods and of their relationship to one another. Writers on Matthew who have used the new methods have not attempted to integrate them with the methods which have been tried, tested, and carefully honed over many decades.

Three recently published books on Matthew illustrate my point. In their stimulating book, *Calling Jesus Names: the Social Value of Labels in Matthew*, Sonoma Calif. 1988, B.J. Malina and J.H. Neyrey draw on insights from cultural anthropology in their discussion of 'name-calling' in Matthew. Although the authors claim that they have used 'social science models closely in conjunction with the findings of the historical critical method' (p. 137), they make hardly any use of redaction criticism. Several of the accusations against

Jesus which they assign to 'early Matthean tradition' (by which they mean Q) have in fact been sharpened and extended considerably by the evangelist himself.

In the main text of his *The Gospel according to Matthew: A Structural Commentary on Matthew's Faith*, Philadelphia 1987, Daniel Patte expounds Matthew lucidly from the particular structuralist approach he favours, but his notes could have been written by any competent redaction critic and are largely unrelated to the main body of the commentary. In his *Matthew as Story*, Philadelphia 2nd ed. 1988, Jack Dean Kingsbury, at present one of the most prolific and influential writers on Matthew, offers a narrative critical exposition of this gospel. In effect Kingsbury has changed sides, since in his earlier work on Matthew he used redaction criticism. However in the final chapter of his most recent book on Matthew, narrative critical insights give way to comments on the intended readers of the gospel which are based on redaction critical studies. Neither Patte nor Kingsbury adopts a fully-fledged ahistorical stance, but their partial concessions to traditional historical methods seem grudging.

Without broad agreement on the appropriate methods for serious study of Matthew and of their relationship to one another, scholarly discussion of the evangelist's distinctive emphases and of his main purposes in writing is impossible. Since I am convinced that careful consideration of questions of method is overdue, I hope that the three chapters in Part I will stimulate discussion in this area: I do not imagine for one moment that I have said the last word on this controversial topic.

Over the last forty years redaction criticism has been the dominant method used in serious study of the synoptic gospels, but recently it has fallen on hard times. Some scholars have expressed doubts about its basic premises, while others have been bewitched by alternative methods, especially various forms of literary criticism. In Chapter 2 the strengths and limitations of redaction criticism are assessed. I argue that while some aspects of this method do need to be reconsidered, it is an essential tool for serious study of

Matthew's gospel. The chapters in Parts II and III offer numerous examples of the use of this method.

Chapter 3 discusses literary critical methods which are being used in Matthean studies at present. While some have been used to good effect for a long time, others have been developed recently with mixed results. I make an important distinction between literary methods which take seriously the first century setting of Matthew's gospel, and those which do not. While some literary techniques are 'timeless', and can be found in ancient as well as in modern writings, others are not. Insights drawn (for example) from study of the literary techniques used by modern novelists and short story writers may not be appropriate for a careful 'reading' of Matthew's gospel. As we shall see, from a literary critical perspective the genre of Matthew is a quite fundamental question. Once this is recognized, the relationship of Matthew to Mark is back on the agenda, since in terms of genre (as well as of content) Matthew is heavily dependent on Mark. Rather unexpectedly, literary criticism turns out to raise redaction critical questions. In this chapter I emphasize the importance of the responses of the first recipients of the gospel, and I argue that in a number of passages Matthew has used the literary strategy of comparison which was almost a commonplace in the Graeco-Roman world of his day.

In Chapter 4 I try to show the value of sociological perspectives for discussion of the various aspects of Matthew's relationship to contemporary Judaism which are the focal point of this book. In recent years sociological insights have been used with profit in study of several New Testament writings. But up until now few scholars have considered Matthew from this vantage point. I try to show that Matthew's gospel is a sophisticated writing which legitimates the painful separation of sectarian Christian communities which have been in prolonged conflict with Judaism. Studies of the behaviour and attitudes of sectarian communities, of conflict theory, and of strategies which are often used to legitimate new movements enable us to read Matthew's gospel more sensitively. These three sociological models help to account for several of its most distinctive features.

Many sociologists are convinced that particular patterns of behaviour recur in otherwise diverse societies. Hence they raise no basic objections to the cautious use in the study of ancient writings of sociological models based on studies of 'partings of the ways' of modern religious movements. However, in view of my insistence in the previous chapter that ancient and modern literary techniques should not be confused, the case for the use of sociological models in study of Matthew's gospel would obviously be strengthened if, from a sociological perspective, a comparable ancient writing could be shown to exhibit similar features. I suggest that the *Damascus Document*, a foundation document of the Qumran community, provides a helpful analogy: like Matthew, it was intended to legitimate the stance of a sectarian community which perceived itself to be in sharp conflict with the parent body from which it had parted company.

At the end of Part I some suggestions are made concerning appropriate methods for study of Matthew's gospel, and their relationship to one another. I am convinced that redaction criticism must remain as the basic tool for serious study of Matthew, but its results are more compelling when they are complemented by some (but not all) literary critical approaches and by the careful use of sociological insights. Like the evangelist himself, the well-trained modern 'scribe' must learn to bring out of his treasure what is new and what is old (Matt 13. 52).

The seven chapters in Part II are all concerned, either directly or indirectly, with the parting of the ways between the Christians for whom Matthew wrote and Judaism. The four views of the relationship of Matthew to contemporary Judaism which have been held by modern scholars are set out and discussed in some detail in Chapter 5. I show why three of them are untenable and why my own view (which is shared by a number of other scholars) accounts for the evidence more satisfactorily. In this chapter I set out the reasons why I am convinced that at the time Matthew wrote 'church' and 'synagogue' had parted company.

Chapter 6 takes discussion of the setting and purpose of Matthew further by linking two of this gospel's distinctive features which are not usually considered to be related: the sharper anti-Jewish polemic and the increased use of apocalyptic motifs. In this chapter some sociological considerations are developed.

The only major Christological theme in Matthew which provokes direct opposition from the Jewish leaders is discussed in Chapter 7: the claim that Jesus is the Son of David. Why does this particular claim provoke hostility? Perhaps we are in touch with claims and counter-claims being made by Christians and Jews at the time Matthew wrote. This possibility is strengthened by the observation that in Matthew there are only two hostile comments about Jesus from his opponents which seem to have been of particular interest to the evangelist himself: the accusation that the exorcisms have been carried out 'by the prince of demons' (9. 34; 10. 25; 12. 24, 27) and the reference in 27. 63 to Jesus as 'that deceiver'. I suggest that these two criticisms are related to the double accusation against Jesus which is found in a wide range of early Christian and Jewish writings: Jesus is a magician and a deceiver.

In Matt 24. 20 two phrases, 'your flight' and 'nor on a Sabbath', are added to Mark 13. 18; the reason for the addition has long puzzled exegetes. The various explanations which have been advanced are discussed in Chapter 8. I argue that since Matthean Christians did not keep the Sabbath strictly, they would not have hesitated to try to escape from their persecutors on a Sabbath. However Matthew feared (rightly or wrongly) that flight on a Sabbath would provoke further hostility from some Jewish leaders; hence he insisted that it was to be avoided if at all possible.

With the exception of the Beatitudes and the Lord's Prayer, probably no passage in Matthew's gospel is appealed to more frequently by contemporary theologians, preachers and writers than 25. 31-46. Yet the apocalyptic discourse of the sheep and the goats has been interpreted in several very different

8

ways ever since the third century. In the last two decades or
so the various exegetical options have been debated even
more keenly – and several new options have been canvassed.

Who will be judged 'when the Son of man comes in his
glory'? Will all men, or just Christians, be judged on the basis
of their attitude to the poor and needy? Or were Matthew's
intentions very different? If 'the least of these my brethren'
(25. 40, 45) refers to Christian disciples, then the whole passage is an encouragement to hard-pressed disciples who are
lamenting the apparent triumph of the enemies of God's
'new people': they are being assured that in due course the
nations will be judged on the basis of their acceptance or
rejection of Christian disciples, for in so doing they will have
accepted or rejected the Son of man himself. In Chapter 9 I
have set out some fresh considerations which seem to me to
support this interpretation. In particular I appeal to a number
of passages in apocalyptic writings in which readers are
assured that their despair at the apparent triumph of their
oppressors will be heard and answered by God.

If this interpretation is correct, this passage strongly
supports my suggestions about the setting and purpose of
Matthew's gospel. Hence I have tried to meet the objections
which have been raised against this explanation of what is,
on any view, an enigmatic passage. If, however, one of the
alternative interpretations is preferred, my proposals
concerning the origin and purpose of the whole gospel
would not thereby be falsified; they would simply lose one of
the many pillars which support them.

Chapters 10 and 11 set the 'parting of the ways' between
Matthean Christianity and contemporary Judaism in a wider
context. Although these chapters are primarily concerned
with passages in Justin Martyr's *Dialogue with Trypho*, the
Testaments of the Twelve Patriarchs, *5 Ezra*, and the Nag
Hammadi *Apocalypse of Peter*, several verses and themes in
Matthew are discussed and, I hope, set in a fresh light.

The five chapters in Part III are rather more disparate, but
they are partly related to some of my main concerns in Parts I
and II. Chapters 12 and 13 discuss the Sermon on the Mount.

The former, which was originally prepared for non-specialists, sets out the main theological and exegetical questions which are at stake in interpretation of Matthew 5–7. This chapter is followed by a detailed discussion of H.D. Betz's novel proposal that the Sermon on the Mount was originally composed long before the evangelist Matthew's day as an epitome of the teaching of Jesus. I try to show that even in these three chapters the evangelist uses vocabulary and develops themes which are prominent in redactional passages elsewhere in the gospel.

In Chapter 14 I discuss a number of passages in which the evangelist himself has created sayings of Jesus. The evangelist's creativity turns out to have been in the service of the traditions at his disposal: Matthew is bound by them and yet he felt free to expound and extend them in the light of his own emphases elsewhere. Redaction critical study of these passages confirms that Matthew is an expositor *par excellence* and that his concerns are frequently catechetical.

Matthew's use of the Old Testament, which is one of the most striking features of his gospel, is discussed in Chapter 15. In no fewer than ten passages the Old Testament is cited with an introductory formula. The evangelist does this in order to comment on the story of Jesus and so draw out its deeper significance by stressing that all its main features are in fulfilment of Scripture. I argue that Matthew himself is responsible for the wording of the introductory formulae and for the choice and adaptation of many of the Old Testament passages he cites.

The final chapter opens with a brief discussion of the use of Matt 11. 28-30 in liturgies. I then try to show that this passage is less clearly related to Sirach 51 than most exegetes have supposed. It contains 'comfortable words' (the phrase Cranmer used in his 1549 Prayer Book) for hard-pressed disciples rather than an invitation to crowds in need of acceptance or forgiveness.

I must now comment on the title I have chosen for this book. My use of the phrase 'for a new people' is much less controversial than the implication in my title that Matthew saw his writing as 'a gospel'. So we shall start with the more straight-forward term. 'A new people' refers to followers of Jesus (both Jews and Gentiles) in the evangelist's day who see themselves as a distinct religious group over against both Judaism and the Gentile world. Some writers have referred to the evangelist's readers as the 'new Israel' or the 'true Israel',[1] but there are strong reasons for not using these phrases with reference to Matthew's gospel. Although the later widely held Christian view of the church as the 'new' or 'true' Israel has roots which go back as far as Gal 6. 16, some thirty years before Matthew wrote, the evangelist does not use either of these terms. As far as we know, they did not become current until Justin Martyr's *Dialogue with Trypho*, written about A.D. 160.[2] I do not think that either term accurately sums up the evangelist's view: both imply a greater degree of continuity between 'church' and 'Israel' than does Matthew.

In the light of Matt 21. 43, the term 'new people' is prefer-able. The evangelist adds this whole verse, which is thoroughly Matthean in its phraseology, to Mark's parable of the wicked husbandmen. The verse is addressed to the Jewish leaders: as a result of their rejection of the son of the owner of the vineyard, the tenants themselves will be rejected. 'The kingdom of God will be taken away from you, and given to a people (ἔθνος) who do yield its proper fruit.' This redactional verse expresses clearly the self-understanding of the Christians to whom Matthew is writing. The evangelist considered his readers to be a 'new

---

[1] For use of the term 'new Israel', see R. Hummel, *Die Auseinander-setzung zwischen Kirche und Judentum im Matthäusevangelium*, Munich 2nd ed. 1966, 156 n.72 and 160f.; W.D. Davies, *The Setting of the Sermon on the Mount*, Cambridge 1964, 290. The use of 'true Israel' is especially associated with W. Trilling who used the phrase as the title of his important book on Matthew: *Das wahre Israel*, Leipzig 2nd ed. 1961; Munich 3rd ed. 1964.

[2] The phrase 'true Israel' is found in 11. 5; 123; 135. 3; the term 'new Israel' is implied in 119. 3 and 138. 2. Cf. the use of Gen 25. 23 and Gen 48. 19 in Barnabas 13 to develop a 'two peoples' theology: the 'greater' (elder, i.e. Israel) shall serve the 'lesser' (younger, i.e. Christians).

people' – in effect a 'third race' (*tertium genus*) over against both Jews and Gentiles.[1] The evidence which supports this conclusion is discussed in Chapter 4 and from many angles in the chapters in Part II.

Christians today refer without hesitation to Matthew's written work which sets out the teaching and actions of Jesus as a 'gospel'. But did Matthew see his writing as a 'gospel'? Or did he intend his opening sentence, βίβλος γενέσεως Ἰησοῦ Χριστοῦ υἱοῦ Δαυὶδ υἱοῦ Ἀβραάμ, 'book of the genealogy of Jesus Christ, the son of David, the son of Abraham', to be the title of his writing? The latter view, which goes back to Jerome, has recently been revived by W.D. Davies and D.C. Allison in the first volume of their International Critical Commentary (1988). It has had some modern support, most notably in Theodor Zahn's commentary (1903).[2] If Matt 1. 1 is taken as the title of the whole writing rather than as the introduction to the genealogy in 1. 2-17, then it must be translated either as 'Book of the History of Jesus Christ. . .' (so Zahn) or as 'Book of the New Genesis (Creation) brought about by Jesus Christ. . .' (so Davies and Allison).[3] If either of these two interpretations is correct, I should have used 'book' rather than 'gospel' in my own title.

Most modern scholars have insisted that Matt 1. 1 must be translated as 'record', or 'book' of the 'genealogy' or 'origin' of Jesus Christ. Thus the opening line refers either to the genealogy which follows in 1. 2-17, or, just possibly, to the whole of chapter 1. The only two examples of the phrase βίβλος γενέσεως in the Septuagint, Gen 2. 4 and 5. 1, together with the use of ἡ γένεσις in Matt 1. 18 (where it must refer to

---

[1] So too G. Strecker, *Der Weg der Gerechtigkeit*, FRLANT 82, Göttingen 3rd ed. 1971, 33.

[2] W.D. Davies and D.C. Allison, *Matthew I*, ICC, Edinburgh 1988, 150 n.6 list other modern scholars who support this view; see also J.D. Kingsbury, *Matthew: Structure, Christology, Kingdom*, London 1975, 10 n.54.

[3] See their detailed defence in *Matthew I*, 149-55; see also W.D. Davies, *Setting*, 67-72.

the birth of Jesus) are usually considered to rule out the view that 1. 1 is a title which refers to the whole book.

The recent attempt by W.D. Davies and D.C. Allison to take Matt 1. 1 not only as a title, but also as a reference to the 'new creation' brought about by Jesus Christ is interesting but unconvincing. While Paul (and perhaps John 1. 1) sees the coming of Jesus as the counterpart of the creation account narrated in Genesis, there is no evidence which suggests that Matthew did so. Davies and Allison concede that Gen 5. 1 and Matt 1. 18 incline one 'to think that βίβλος γενέσεως has special reference to the story of Jesus' origin.' They then suggest that 1. 1 has 'more than one evocation': it refers to the genealogy, to the birth of Jesus, to his life story, and to the whole new creation which begins at his conception. This seems to me to be over-subtle.[1]

The closest parallels to Matt 1. 1 and 1. 18 are undoubtedly Gen 2. 4 and 5. 1; these two verses confirm that the opening line of Matthew refers either to the genealogy which follows or to the account of the 'origin' of Jesus in 1. 2-25.[2] If Matt 1. 1 is not a title, how would Matthew and his first readers have referred to the whole writing? Is it possible that they may have referred to it as a 'gospel'?

There is general agreement that in earliest Christianity the term 'gospel', εὐαγγέλιον, refers to oral proclamation of the significance of the death and resurrection of Jesus, not a written account of the story of Jesus. There is also general agreement that in the second half of the second century

---

[1] Some of the detailed points made by Davies and Allison support the view that 1. 1. refers to the whole of chapter 1, rather than just to the genealogy. Their claim that 1. 1 is a general title for the whole book rests largely on an appeal to the introductory use of *seper* or βίβλος or βιβλίον in ancient Jewish and Christian literature. But later Christian usage is hardly relevant. Of the Jewish examples cited, only Tobit 1. 1 seems to be a close parallel.

[2] So also, for example, U. Luz, *Matthäus* I, EKK, Zürich et al 1985, 88; R.H. Gundry, *Matthew: a Commentary on his Theological Art*, Grand Rapids 1981, 13; and R.E. Brown, *The Birth of the Messiah*, Garden City, NY 1977, 58-9.

εὐαγγέλιον was used to refer to a 'gospel-book'.[1] From the end of the second century and the first half of the third century there is clear evidence from papyri, the Old Latin and the Coptic versions, and from Irenaeus, Clement of Alexandria, and Tertullian, that the titles εὐαγγέλιον κατὰ Ματθαῖον, Μάρκον κτλ, 'the gospel according to Matthew, Mark, etc', were widely used.[2]

But precisely when were Matthew, Mark, Luke, or John first referred to as 'gospels' ? Two very different answers have recently been given to this question. H. Koester has claimed that Marcion introduced this usage in the middle of the second century as a 'revolutionary novelty'.[3] If this view is correct, Matthew's written work was not understood as a 'gospel' by the 'new people' for whom he wrote, and as a corollary, the title I have chosen for this book would be inappropriate. M. Hengel has given a very different answer. He sees Mark, who wrote some eighty years earlier than Marcion, as the innovator, and cautiously suggests that there may have been even earlier 'Petrine' roots.[4] I think that the evidence, taken cumulatively, points more clearly to the evangelist Matthew than either to Marcion or to Mark.

Within a generation or so of the writing of Matthew's gospel (and some forty years before Marcion designated his version of Luke as 'the Gospel') τὸ εὐαγγέλιον was used in the Didache and by Ignatius to refer to a book which is most probably Matthew.[5]

---

[1] Justin, *I Apol.* 66. 3 (about A.D. 150-55) provides the first example of the plural εὐαγγέλια to refer to 'gospel books'.

[2] See M. Hengel, 'The Titles of the Gospels' in his *Studies in Mark*, E.tr. London 1985, 66f. Hengel argues convincingly against the widely held view (which is reflected in the titles of the four gospels in the 26th edition of the Nestle-Aland text) that a shorter form (κατὰ Ματθαῖον etc) of the later titles was original.

[3] 'From the Kerygma-Gospel to Written Gospels', *NTS* 35 (1989) 361-81, here 381. See now his *Ancient Christian Gospels: their History and Development*, London and Philadelphia 1990, 1-48.

[4] See 'Titles', 82-3, also 53-4.

[5] U. Luz, *Matthäus*, 182, notes that the identification of εὐαγγέλιον with a book is first made in Didache 8. 2; 11. 3; 15. 3f., a writing closely

As soon as an individual or a community had access to more than one narrative account of the life of Jesus, it would have been necessary to distinguish between them by means of a title, especially in the context of readings at worship. That first happened as soon as Matthew had completed his writing, for the evangelist (and perhaps some of the communities to whom he wrote) then had two accounts of the story of Jesus: his own, and Mark's. Koester partly undermines his own case by conceding a similar point in a final note. He allows that even before Marcion's day liturgical readings from the written gospels may well have been introduced as 'the gospel'.[1]

If Marcion was not the first to use the term εὐαγγέλιον to refer to a written account of the story of Jesus, was Mark the innovator, some eighty years earlier? Mark uses the noun seven times: 1. 1, 14, 15; 8. 35; 10. 29; 13. 10; 14. 9. With the exception of 1. 1 and 1. 14, the noun is used without any modifying word or phrase. For Mark τὸ εὐαγγέλιον is the proclaimed message about Jesus Christ. His usage is close to Paul's, even though Mark, unlike Paul, sets out a narrative of the teaching and actions of Jesus as a 'sermon' on, or expression of, the gospel.[2] This is how Mark's opening line ἀρχὴ τοῦ εὐαγγελίου Ἰησοῦ Χριστοῦ, 'the beginning of the gospel of

---

related to Matthew. H. Koester, 'Kerygma-Gospel' 371f., assigns these passages rather arbitrarily to the final redaction of the Didache which he dates to the end of the second century. This late dating and his denial of the dependence of the Didache on Matthew are accepted by few other scholars.

In some passages in Ignatius εὐαγγέλιον probably refers to oral proclamation, but in *Smyrn.* 5. 1 and 7. 2 (and perhaps in some other passages) a book is referred to, most probably Matthew.

[1] 'Kerygma-Gospel', 381 n.1. Koester acknowledges the force of this suggestion made by Henry Chadwick in the discussion which followed his 1988 SNTS paper. M. Hengel had made the same point in some detail earlier. See his 'Titles', 74-81.

[2] W. Marxsen's discussion of Mark's use of τὸ εὐαγγέλιον has been influential. See his *Mark the Evangelist*, Nashville E.tr. 1969, especially 126-38. For similar views, see (among many others) E. Best, *Mark: the Gospel as Story*, Edinburgh 1983, 37-43; R. Guelich, *Mark* I, Word Biblical Commentary, Dallas 1989, 8-10.

Jesus Christ', should be interpreted. Whether τοῦ εὐαγγελίου is taken as a subjective or as an objective genitive, 1. 1 refers to 'proclamation', not a 'written report'.[1] While it is true that Mark's development of Paul's use of εὐαγγέλιον paves the way for later reference to the story of the life of Jesus as a εὐαγγέλιον, Mark did not take that step himself.

Matthew, however, did so. In order to show this, we must examine closely the differences between the use of εὐαγγέλιον in Matthew and in Mark. Matthew omits some of Mark's uses of εὐαγγέλιον and expands others. In Matt 4. 17 the evangelist draws on Mark 1. 14b and 15 but omits Mark's two uses of εὐαγγέλιον. At Matt 16. 25 and 19. 29 Matthew is following Mark, but in both passages εὐαγγέλιον is omitted. Why does Matthew make these four omissions? Unlike Luke, who does not use the noun at all in his first volume (and only twice in Acts), Matthew is not averse to the noun. He uses it in two key passages, 4. 23 and 9. 35, to summarize the proclamation of Jesus as 'the gospel of the kingdom'. From the context it is clear that in both passages he has the teaching of Jesus in mind. 26. 13, which refers to the woman's act of anointing the head of Jesus with costly oil, shows that for Matthew 'this gospel' includes not only the teaching of Jesus, but also accounts of his actions.[2]

Matthew omits the four Marcan uses of εὐαγγέλιον just referred to because he has a very different understanding of this word. Mark 8. 35 and 10. 29 confirm that for Mark 'the gospel' is something distinct from Jesus himself: in both

[1] W. Marxsen suggests that it is almost accidental that something in the way of report also appears, *Mark the Evangelist*, 131. R. Guelich argues strongly that 1. 1 is not a title for the whole work since syntactically it must be linked with the sentence which follows. See his *Mark*, 9, and more fully in 'The Gospel Genre', *Das Evangelium und die Evangelien*, ed. P. Stuhlmacher, Tübingen 1983, 183-219, esp. 204-8.

[2] So also U. Luz, *Matthäus* I, 182. W. Marxsen, *Mark the Evangelist*, 124, claims that for Matthew the 'gospel is of a piece with his speech complexes', but 26. 13 surely rules that out. On p. 141 he concedes that there is 'a kernel of truth' in the hypothesis that Matthew's addition of τοῦτο is intended to set up a connection between the gospel as such and the book of Matthew.

verses we read '. . . for my sake and the gospel's.' Matthew, however, saw the earthly Jesus, his teaching and actions, as 'gospel' and so omitted the Marcan passages.

The two passages in which Matthew retains Mark's use of εὐαγγέλιον are equally revealing. In 24. 14 Matthew expands Mark's absolute use of the noun to τοῦτο τὸ εὐαγγέλιον τῆς βασιλείας, 'this gospel of the kingdom'. In 26. 13 Matthew has τὸ εὐαγγέλιον τοῦτο; once again Mark's absolute use of the noun is modified. In both passages the addition of τοῦτο is very striking. The redactional phrase ὁ λόγος τῆς βασιλείας, 'the word of the kingdom', at Matt 13. 19 is clearly closely related to 24. 14 and 26. 13.

What is 'this gospel of the kingdom' (or 'word of the kingdom', 13. 19) with which the readers of Matthew are to confront the whole world? No definition or explanation is given in any of these three passages. As J.D. Kingsbury notes, the evangelist simply assumes that his readers will know what 'this gospel' is on the basis of their acquaintance with his written document.[1] We may conclude with Kingsbury that the phrase 'the gospel of the kingdom' is Matthew's own capsule-summary of his work.[2]

Matthew did not provide a title for his writing, but he intended his full account of the teaching and actions of Jesus to set out for his readers the content of 'this gospel of the kingdom'. As we noted above, a title would have been needed soon after the writing was completed, and this phrase, or, as is perhaps more likely, an abbreviation of it, would have been an obvious choice.

We may conclude then, that long before Marcion's day 'gospel' was used for a written account of the story of Jesus.

[1] J.D. Kingsbury, *Structure*, 130, and also 163.

[2] *Matthew*, 131. Kingsbury refers to several earlier writers who have supported the same conclusion. R.H. Gundry, *Matthew*, 480, accepts this view, as does U. Luz, *Matthäus* I, 181, who quotes Kingsbury's conclusion with approval. See also W. Schenk, *Die Sprache des Matthäus*, Göttingen 1987, 265. H. Koester rather rashly claims that all modern commentaries agree that 'this gospel' in Matt 26.13 cannot refer to Matthew's gospel, thus overlooking not only the scholars just mentioned, but also the commentaries of J. Schniewind and W. Grundmann.

17

But since Mark's usage is closer to Paul's and is very different from Matthew's, Mark is not the 'radical innovator'.[1] Need we look any further than the evangelist Matthew?[2] By his insistence that the teaching and actions of Jesus are 'gospel' and by his addition of τοῦτο to Mark's τὸ εὐαγγέλιον in 24. 14 and 26. 13, he indicates clearly to his readers that his writing is 'a gospel'.[3]

While Matthew does not use the phrase 'a new people', he did see Christians in his own day as a distinct entity over against Judaism. This is confirmed by the important redactional verse 21. 43 and, as we shall see in several chapters below, numerous other passages. My title, 'A Gospel for a New People', does not correspond precisely to the evangelist's own terminology, but it does sum up his intentions.

Chapters 1–5, 7, 9, and 12 have not been published before.[4] Apart from a handful of minor changes, the correction of errors, and, in the case of Chapters 11 and 16, the inclusion of

---

[1] M. Hengel, who sees Mark as the innovator, does not discuss the differences between Matthew and Mark in 'Titles'.

[2] U. Luz, *Matthäus* I, 182, is a little more cautious: 'the identification of εὐαγγέλιον with the Matthean work is not yet drawn directly, but it already ushers it in.' He suggests that the identification of εὐαγγέλιον with a book is first made in the Didache, which is strongly influenced by Matthew's gospel. I am unable to see a major difference between Matthew and the Didache in the usage of εὐαγγέλιον.

[3] For a very different view, see H. Frankemölle, *Jahwebund und Kirche Christi*, Münster 1974, who claims that Matthew is a literary work, a *Buch der Geschichte* modelled on Jewish history writing such as Deuteronomy and Chronicles. This is an exaggerated claim which does not do justice to the importance for Matthew of the OT prophetic writings and of Mark .

[4] Some paragraphs in Chapters 2 and 5 are taken from § II.1 and III. 2 of G.N. Stanton, 'The Origin and Purpose of Matthew's Gospel: Matthean Scholarship from 1945 to 1980', *ANRW* II, 25.3, Berlin 1984, 1889-1951. With these exceptions, I have not included in this book my lengthy survey of Matthean scholarship. As my survey was completed in 1979 (with just a few small additions in 1981), it would have been a major task to bring it up to date. In addition, I decided that the inclusion of this survey would not leave enough room for my own views on Matthew.

a note on more recent literature, the remaining chapters are printed here as they were first published.

Chapter 6 was given as the 1983 Manson Memorial Lecture in the University of Manchester; it was published in *BJRL* 66 (1984) 264-84. Chapter 8 was included in a special issue of *JSNT* in honour of David Hill, *JSNT* 37 (1989) 17-30. An earlier draft of Chapter 4 (unpublished) was given in Oxford as a lecture to the 1990 meeting of the British Association of New Testament Scholars; the original version of Chapter 9 (also unpublished) was given in Hull to the 1981 meeting of the same society. Chapter 10 was delivered as a Main Paper at the 39th General Meeting of *Studiorum Novi Testamenti Societas* in Basel in August 1984; it was published in *NTS* 31 (1985) 377-92. Chapter 11 was published in *JTS* 28 (1977) 67-83. Chapter 12 will be included in *A Dictionary of Jesus and the Gospels,* eds. J.B. Green, S. McKnight, I.H. Marshall, Downers Grove, Illinois 1992. Chapter 13 was published in a Festschrift in honour of E. Earle Ellis, *Tradition and Interpretation in the New Testament* eds. G.F. Hawthorne and O. Betz, Grand Rapids and Tübingen 1987, 181-94. Chapter 14 was included in a symposium on the gospels, *Das Evangelium und die Evangelien,* ed. P. Stuhlmacher, Tübingen 1983, 273-87; E.tr. Grand Rapids 1991. Chapter 15 was published in a Festschrift in honour of Barnabas Lindars, SSF, *It is Written: Scripture Citing Scripture,* eds. D.A. Carson and H.M.G. Williamson, Cambridge 1988, 205-219. Chapter 16 was published as part of a series of articles entitled 'Salvation Proclaimed' in *ExT* 94 (1982) 3-9. I am grateful to the various publishers for permission to include these articles.

Part I

Methods New and Old

Every scribe who has been trained
for the kingdom of heaven
is like a householder
who can produce from his store
things new and old.

Matthew 13. 52

Chapter Two

Redaction Criticism: the End of an Era?

For three decades or so after the end of World War II redaction criticism was the dominant method – indeed almost the only method – used in study of the synoptic gospels. Many of the results have been most impressive. In the last decade or so, however, enthusiasm for this method of gospel criticism has waned. Scholarly study of Matthew has been part of this general pattern. Are we reaching the end of the redaction critical era? Or have some scholars been bewitched by the twin goddesses, Novelty and Fashion?

In this chapter I shall argue that while many redaction critics have been over confident in some of their claims, there are no sound reasons for spurning this method of gospel criticism. The central pillars of redaction critical study of Matthew need to be inspected carefully: by and large they are in good condition. However, as the two chapters which follow will show, the results of redaction criticism are more compelling when they are complemented by other methods.

While there have been some piecemeal appraisals of aspects of redaction criticism, there has been very little critical discussion of the method as such.[1] Given the almost universal acceptance of this method until quite recently, this is a curious state of affairs. Most redaction critical studies of Matthew have been based on three assumptions whose adequacy now needs to be assessed. Can we still be confident

---

[1] One exception is Morna Hooker's article, 'In his own Image', in *What about the New Testament?* (FS *Christopher Evans*) eds. Morna Hooker and Colin Hickling, London 1975, 28-44.

that Matthew has drawn on Mark, Q, and additional traditions to which he alone had access (the so-called 'M' material)? Do the changes made by the evangelist to these sources reflect his distinctive theological concerns? Does the redactional work of the evangelist put us in direct touch with the history, needs, and the particular circumstances of his own Christian community?

Before these questions are taken up one by one, I wish to show that the roots of redaction criticism are much deeper than is usually supposed. Hence careful reconsideration of its basic premises is all the more important.

The dawn of an era

The redactional critical era is usually said to have been opened by the publication in 1948 of Günther Bornkamm's brilliant short study, 'Die Sturmstillung im Matthäusevangelium'. Bornkamm assumed that Matthew had used Mark's account of the stilling of the storm (Matt 8. 23-7 = Mark 4. 35-41). He paid close attention to the additions, modifications and omissions which Matthew made, as well as to the different context in which the pericope had been placed. Bornkamm concluded that Matthew was not merely handing on the Marcan story but was expounding its theological significance in his own way: Matthew was the first exegete of the Marcan pericope. In passing, Bornkamm noted that whereas in the form critical era scholarly attention had been focused upon the single pericope, the single saying and the single deed of Jesus as the primary data of tradition, in future it would be necessary 'to enquire also about the motives in the composition of the individual Gospels'.[1]

Although the importance of Bornkamm's essay for the development of modern Matthean scholarship can hardly be overestimated, it is worth noting that earlier scholars had anticipated redaction critical work on Matthew to a much

[1] G. Bornkamm, 'The Stilling of the Storm in Matthew', *Tradition*, 52-8; the quotation is from 58.

greater extent than is usually appreciated. Two years earlier in 1946 G.D. Kilpatrick had published quite independently *The Origin and Purpose of the Gospel according to St Matthew*, the first major study in English since B.W. Bacon's *Studies in Matthew*, 1930. Kilpatrick's discussions of the relationship of Matthew to Judaism, and of the genre of Matthew, have influenced scholarship considerably. While it is true that on the whole he worked on a much larger canvas than later redaction critics were to do, in some parts of his book he anticipated the development of redaction criticism. For example, he analyzed Matthean vocabulary and style (pp. 14-36) and even spoke of the 'editorial activity of the evangelist' (p.25). Right at the outset of his book (p.2) Kilpatrick set out an important principle that was to become a pillar of redaction criticism:

> The context or 'Sitz im Leben' of a new gospel was as important a feature in its production as it was in the shaping and carrying on of unwritten tradition. While we may not say that the Gospel (of Matthew) was created by a community, yet it was created in a community and called forth to meet the needs of a community.

In 1930 B.W. Bacon entitled one chapter in his book, 'Traits of the Redactor' and on pp.132-3 he wrote as any redaction critic in the 1960s and 1970s might have written:

> Much can be determined concerning the general characteristics of our first canonical evangelist by the mere observation of the structure and salient traits of his compilation, and in particular his treatment of Mark. . . Our relatively late and wholly unknown evangelist is more than a skilful compiler and editor. He has blended diverse elements together into a unit, a whole which is more than a mosaic.

In his major commentary on Matthew which was first published in 1929, A. Schlatter also anticipated some aspects of redaction criticism: he saw the evangelist as an author in

25

his own right and attempted to deduce from Matthew a picture of the evangelist's church; he claimed that quite bitter enmity between the primitive Palestinian community and Judaism can be detected. Schlatter adopted this approach even though he rejected Marcan priority and form criticism, both of which were to become axiomatic in all the early redaction critical work on Matthew.[1]

The roots of redaction criticism can be traced back even earlier.[2] A century before redaction critics began to discern behind Matthew tensions or polemic among Christians and to locate the gospel within a particular understanding of the development of early Christianity, F.C. Baur and his younger colleagues began to apply 'Tendenzkritik' to the gospels.[3] G. Volkmar, for example, accepted Marcan priority (unlike Baur who utilised the Griesbach hypothesis) and saw Mark as a representative of Pauline Christianity.[4] Then came the conservative 'Petrine' Jewish Christian reaction which Luke attempted to counter by showing that Paul is not inferior to Peter. And finally, Matthew, who is seen as a Jewish Christian, sympathetic to Paulinism, accepts the Gentile mission but stresses the motif of the fulfilment of the Old Testament in the ministry of Jesus. Volkmar's sketch of Matthew's purposes is not far removed from the views set out in this book.

There is a sense, then, in which redaction critical studies of Matthew since World War II can be seen as a natural

---

[1] See, for example, 410, 501, 665, 672.

[2] In his chapter on the date and local origin of Mark and Matthew B.H. Streeter anticipated some of the methods and observations of later redaction critics. In one particularly significant paragraph he suggested that many of the traditions peculiar to Matthew were, in a way, parasitic on Mark: 'they stand to Mark as the mistletoe to the oak'. See *The Four Gospels*, 488 - 528, esp. 502. I owe this reference to Mr David Sim.

[3] F.C. Baur, *Kritische Untersuchungen über die kanonischen Evangelien*, Tübingen 1847.

[4] G. Volkmar, *Die Religion Jesu*, Leipzig 1857. For further details, see C.M. Tuckett, 'The Griesbach Hypothesis in the 19th Century', *JSNT* 3 (1979) 29-60; R.H. Fuller, 'Baur versus Hilgenfeld: A Forgotten Chapter in the Debate on the Synoptic Problem', *NTS* 24 (1978) 355-370.

development of earlier work.[1] Its roots go right back to the widespread acceptance in the middle of the nineteenth century of Matthew's dependence on Mark's gospel. But even though some aspects of redaction criticism were anticipated long before Bornkamm's 1948 essay, in retrospect his study of Matthew's account of the stilling of the storm marks a most important turning point in Matthean scholarship. This is borne out by contrasting Bornkamm's essay with his teacher Rudolf Bultmann's comments on Matthew, written twenty years earlier. Bultmann accepts that Matthew reshaped his sources, especially Mark, but then writes as follows: 'Matthew's portrayal is not so consciously motivated by the Christian church's outlook as was Mark's. It is much more an unconscious influence in Matthew, and that is why the literary form of his work is not to the same extent as Mark's dependent on this outlook.'[2]

Bornkamm, on the other hand, sees Matthew as not only a hander-on of the Marcan narrative, 'but also its oldest exegete, and in fact the first to interpret the journey of the disciples with Jesus in the storm and the stilling of the storm with reference to discipleship, and that means with reference to the little ship of the Church.' The evangelist shows 'proof of definite theological intentions' (pp.55-7).

In the first flush of redaction criticism after 1945 a number of studies of Matthean themes or sections of the gospel appeared, all of which drew attention to Matthew's distinctive theological viewpoint. The first redaction critics all simply assumed without discussion that the evangelist used Mark, Q, and 'M' traditions. They insisted that Matthew's gospel is not simply an anthology of the teaching of Jesus.

---

1 For further discussion of the precursors of redaction criticism, see J. Rohde, *Rediscovering the Teaching of Jesus*, E.tr. London 1968, 31-46. Unfortunately Rohde overlooks not only the work of F.C. Baur and G. Volkmar, but also P. Wernle, *Die synoptische Frage*, Fribourg 1899, and R.H. Lightfoot's two books, *History and Interpretation in the Gospels*, London 1935, and *The Gospel Message of St. Mark*, Oxford 1950; G.D. Kilpatrick's work is given insufficient attention.

2 I have quoted from the revised English translation, *The History of the Synoptic Tradition*, Oxford 1972, 357.

The evangelist's modifications and rearrangement of his sources were examined in detail; they were alleged to be consistent and to reveal Matthew's own theological stance and to shed light on the history, convictions and structure of the Christian community from which the gospel stems. These assumptions must now be considered one by one: they can no longer be taken for granted.

Source criticism

1. Marcan priority

When Bornkamm first published his study of Matthew's redaction of the stilling of the storm pericope in 1948, Marcan priority and the Q hypothesis had not been challenged seriously for many decades. Just three years later, however, B.C. Butler launched a full-scale attack on Marcan priority. He attempted to revive Augustine's conclusion that Mark was the follower and abbreviator of Matthew (tamquam pedisequus et breviator). His solution of the synoptic problem, however, has not attracted support and it has not been influential on Matthean scholarship.[1]

In 1964 W.R. Farmer revived the Griesbach hypothesis (in a modified form) and he has continued to champion it vigorously ever since. On this hypothesis (which Farmer now refers to as the 'two gospel hypothesis') Matthew's gospel was the first to be written, Luke used Matthew, and Mark used both Matthew and Luke. Although Farmer has found few supporters, he has been successful in reopening serious discussion of the synoptic problem.

Why should Mark wish to abbreviate Matthew so drastically? That question has been pressed repeatedly by critics of the 'two gospel' hypothesis. Replies have taken two forms. Some have suggested that Mark was attempting to produce a

---

[1] H.B. Green notes that the inheritors of Butler's Benedictine tradition of Matthean priority in the United Kingdom have now gone over to the Griesbach hypothesis: 'The Credibility of Luke's Transformation of Matthew' in Synoptic Studies, ed. C.M. Tuckett, Sheffield 1984, 131.

'neutral' gospel in order to reconcile supporters of Matthew with supporters of Luke. Others have sought to provide a more sophisticated response by setting out comparable examples of abbreviation and reconciliation in antiquity.[1] Although the examples from ancient writings which have been produced so far have not been convincing, one has to concede that for Augustine abbreviation of Matthew by Mark was not such an absurd proposition as it appears to most modern scholars. Augustine's acceptance of Matthean priority, however, was based on the conviction that, unlike Mark, the author of Matthew was a disciple of Jesus.

The Achilles' heel of the 'two gospel' hypothesis is the observation that on this solution Mark has not only produced an epitome of Matthew and Luke, but he has also added an enormous number of details which are quite irrelevant in a summary. I shall give only one example to make the point clear. Matthew uses the verb διδάσκω, 'teach' nine times with reference to Jesus, Mark (in his much shorter gospel) sixteen times. So Mark clearly has a special interest in the teaching activity of Jesus. Why then (on the 'two gospel' hypothesis) does he *omit* so much of Matthew's impressively organised account of the content of the teaching of Jesus, and yet in narrative contexts regularly *add* words and phrases which on any view are purely incidental?

A general consideration, to which we shall return below, is also of some importance. If we take Mark's gospel simply as it stands, there is striking literary power and theological depth; on the 'two gospel' hypothesis Mark becomes a ham-fisted summariser.[2]

---

[1] See, for example, D.L. Dungan, 'Reactionary Trends in the Gospel Producing Activity of the Early Church: Marcion, Tatian, Mark', in *L'Évangile selon Marc*, ed. M. Sabbe, Louvain 1974, 179-202; T.R.W. Longstaff, *Evidence of Conflation in Mark? A Study in the Synoptic Problem*, Missoula 1977. See C.M. Tuckett's thorough discussion of Longstaff's proposals, *The Revival of the Griesbach Hypothesis*, Cambridge 1983, 41-51.

[2] Here I am in agreement with H.B. Green's assessment of the 'two gospel' hypothesis. See his 'Luke's Transformation', in *Synoptic Studies*, 132.

29

The Augustinian and Griesbachian solutions of the synoptic problem both see Mark as dependent on Matthew. Several other proposed solutions of the synoptic problem claim that although Matthew and Mark have some traditions in common, they are independent of one another. Perhaps the most notable proposals (which differ considerably in details) are those of A. Gaboury,[1] J.M. Rist,[2] and M.-E. Boismard.[3]

Matthew's independence of Mark is, however, very difficult to defend. Most scholars have concluded that the agreements between Matthew and Mark in both content and order are so striking that there must have been some form of literary dependence. In pericope after pericope the two gospels are broadly similar in content; the differences form a consistent pattern. Literary dependence is almost inescapable: either Matthew has abbreviated Mark and added traditions he shares with Luke (Marcan priority and Q – the two source hypothesis) or Mark has omitted a large number of Matthew's traditions and yet at the same time he has added to Matthean traditions he retained purely incidental details

---

[1] *La structure des évangiles synoptiques*, Leiden 1970. Gaboury isolates those passages in the triple tradition which are found in the same order in all three gospels and claims that this 'gospel' is the foundation on which all three synoptic gospels have been built. As a basic premise he assumes that an evangelist would be reluctant to alter the order of his primary source. But would this necessarily be so, however highly the source was valued? For a thorough discussion of Gaboury's hypothesis, see F. Neirynck, 'The Gospel of Matthew and Literary Criticism', *ETL* 29 (1971) 37-69; now reprinted in his collected essays, *Evangelica*, Leuven 1982, 690-723.

[2] *On the Independence of Matthew and Mark*, Cambridge 1978. Rist is unaware that his hypothesis was anticipated by E. Lohmeyer, whose source critical proposals were considered by most scholars to be the least satisfactory part of his incomplete commentary on Matthew. Rist is also unaware of Neirynck's thorough discussion (see the preceding note) of Matthew's modifications of the Marcan order.

[3] See M.-E. Boismard, *Synopse des quatres évangiles* II, Paris 1972, and also M.-E. Boismard, 'The Two Source Theory at an Impasse', *NTS* 26 (1979) 1-17. For a recent discussion, see E.P. Sanders and Margaret Davies, *Studying the Synoptic Gospels*, London 1989, 105-11.

(both the Augustinian and the Griesbach or 'two gospel' hypotheses).

At first sight, however, the differences in order between Matthew and Mark do not point quite so clearly to literary dependence as do the similarities in content. In Matt 4. 12 – 13. 58 there are considerable divergences of order from Mark. These variations contrast sharply with the striking similarity of order in the second half of the gospel. If Matthew has used Mark, then he seems to have done so in two quite different ways in the two halves of his gospel: in the second half Mark's order is followed most carefully, but in the first half of the gospel Matthew alters the Marcan order very considerably.

Is it possible to offer a plausible explanation of Matthew's inconsistency? If not, Matthew's dependence on Mark would seem to be called in question. F. Neirynck has faced the problem squarely and has examined carefully Matthew's rearrangements of Mark's order. He shows that it is only in Matt. 4. 12 – 11. 1 that a problem is posed by a departure from Mark; indeed Matt 4. 12-22 is closely related to Mark 1. 14-15, 16-20 and these verses are, as it were, the title of this section of Matthew. Within the section 4. 23 – 11. 1 Matthew's liberty of order is only relative, for Mark's order can still frequently be traced; where the Marcan order is changed by Matthew, he can be shown to have been inspired by his sources. In short, on the hypothesis of Matthean use of Mark, the evangelist's changes to Mark's order are not arbitrary but consistent and coherent.[1]

There is no need to repeat here the case for Marcan priority. In the preceding paragraphs I have tried to show that some of the more substantial challenges and proposed alternative explanations of the evidence are far from convincing. None of the rival hypotheses offers a more

---

[1] See F. Neirynck, 'La rédaction matthéenne et la structure du premier évangile' in *De Jésus aux évangiles*, ed. I de la Potterie, Gembloux-Paris 1967, 41-73; now reprinted in his *Evangelica*, 3-36. See also C.M. Tuckett, 'Arguments from Order', in *Synoptic Studies*, ed. C.M. Tuckett, 208-11.

31

satisfactory explanation of the relationship between Matthew and Mark.

2. The Q Hypothesis [1]

If the recent challenges to Marcan priority do not pose a threat to the central pillar of redaction critical study of Matthew, can the same conclusion be drawn in the case of the Q hypothesis? In the last decade or so debate over Q has been as intense as discussion of Marcan priority. Since abandonment of Q usually carries as a corollary Luke's use of Matthew, acceptance or rejection of Q leads to very different assessments of Luke's methods and distinctive emphases.

With Matthew, however, matters are different. Most redaction critics have accepted that Matthew used Q and have been able to show that the evangelist has reshaped Q traditions in ways consistent with his redaction of Mark. If, instead of using Q, Matthew drew on a substantial set of traditions of the teaching of Jesus which Luke knew only via Matthew's gospel,[2] some redaction critical conclusions would have to be modified and some stated more cautiously, but the method itself would not be called in question. Hence we need not attempt to assess in detail recent discussion of the Q hypothesis.

The most sustained attack on Q has been that mounted by Michael Goulder. He has recently followed up earlier articles with a full-scale attempt to show that Luke has used Matthew.[3] In my view Goulder has not been able to overturn the objections to this theory which have been made by several scholars. In spite of Goulder's eloquent exposition of Luke's alleged methods and intentions, I still find it impossible to believe that Luke has re-written Matthew's five

---

[1] For the literature see W.D. Davies and D.C. Allison, *Matthew* I, 115 n.68.

[2] In his *Midrash and Lection in Matthew* M.D. Goulder claims that apart from Mark, Matthew had virtually no other traditions at his disposal; the non-Marcan material in Matthew is the result of Matthew's elaborations of Mark. Few scholars have taken this theory seriously; most of those who have conclude that it is far-fetched.

[3] *Luke, a New Paradigm*, I and II, Sheffield 1989.

carefully organised discourses and ignored almost all Matthew's various modifications of Mark.

Goulder recognizes that Matthew's fifth discourse poses particular difficulties for his hypothesis. He has to concede that Luke has carefully separated the Marcan and non-Marcan parts of Matt 24–25. The former are included in Luke 21, the latter are isolated (by marking a copy of Matthew with a pen!) and included in Luke chapters 12–13, 17, and, we may add, 19.

But this concession is crucial, for on Goulder's view we may now suppose that Luke has compared Mark and Matthew most carefully. Why, then, does Luke omit so many of Matthew's numerous expansions of Marcan material?[1] This point has often been pressed by those who deny that Luke has used Matthew. Goulder is aware of the difficulty and replies as follows. Luke has a 'block policy': 'when he (Luke) is treating Marcan matter he has Mark in front of him, and he has made it his policy not to keep turning up Matthew to see what he has added. . . Luke does not include the additions because he had decided on a policy which involved letting them go.'[2] This leads Goulder to suggest that once a Marcan block has been dealt with, Luke sometimes comes back to Matthew's additions to Mark: some of the additions are transferred to other contexts, some are ignored unintentionally, some are re-written. This is a tortuous explanation of Luke's methods, to say the least.

Even if we could accept that Luke has used Matthew in this way, there is a further phenomenon which seriously erodes the plausibility of Goulder's hypothesis: the minor agreements of Matthew and Luke against Mark. Goulder appeals to the minor agreements in order to undermine the Q hypothesis and also to offer clear-cut support for Luke's use of Matthew.[3] The minor agreements, however, can be turned against his own hypothesis.

[1] See J.A. Fitzmyer's commentary on Luke, I, 73-4 for lists of such passages.

[2] *Luke, a New Paradigm*, I, 44.

[3] In addition to *Luke, a New Paradigm*, I, 47-50, see his 'On Putting Q to the Test', *NTS* 24 (1978) 218-43 where he discusses twelve minor

On Goulder's explanation of the minor agreements, in Marcan contexts Luke sometimes prefers Matthean words or phrases. But three pages earlier we have been assured that in Marcan contexts Luke makes it his policy *not* to keep turning up Matthew to see what he has added![1] There is clearly an important flaw in his case against Q. Goulder must either abandon his claim that the minor agreements undermine the Q hypothesis, or he must accept that in passage after passage Luke has had Matthew in front of him and has redacted Matthew quite perversely. For on Goulder's view, Luke has repeatedly retained quite tiny modifications Matthew has made to Mark (the minor agreements); at the same time Luke has ignored numerous major Matthean additions or modifications to Mark which would have suited his purposes, and transferred or re-written only some of them.

Enough has been said to show that it is by no means easy to suppose that Luke has used Matthew. However, it is as difficult to falsify this hypothesis as it is to establish conclusively that Matthew and Luke both used Q.[2] At the end of the day we are left to balance probabilities. Redaction criticism does in fact offer a way forward, for the results which rival theories offer at the redactional level can be compared. For example, on the assumption that Matthew's source was Luke's gospel, it would be possible to examine the modifications made by Matthew and then to consider whether this

---

agreements in detail. See C.M. Tuckett's point by point reply, 'On the Relationship between Matthew and Luke', *NTS* 30 (1984) 130-42.

[1] See 47-50 and 44.

[2] For careful defences of the Q hypothesis, see (for example) the following: J.A. Fitzmyer, 'The Priority of Mark and the "Q" Source in Luke', in *Jesus and Man's Hope* I, ed. D. G. Miller et al., Pittsburgh 1970, 131-170 (this article is summarized in Fitzmyer's *Luke* I, 1982, 73-82); M. Devisch, 'Le document Q, source de Matthieu', in *Matthieu*, 71-98; W.D. Davies and D.C. Allison, *Matthew* I, 115-121, with a good bibliography on 115 n.68. Unfortunately the otherwise stimulating book by J. Kloppenborg, *The Formation of Q*, Philadelphia 1987, does not consider the objections which have been raised against the Q hypothesis.

hypothesis offers a more coherent explanation of Matthean redaction than the assumption that Matthew's sources were Mark and Q.[1]

The Augustinian and Griesbach solutions of the synoptic problem can be tested along these lines, as can the proposal that Luke has used Matthew. While it is possible to offer some explanation of Mark's abbreviation and redaction of Matthew on the Augustinian hypothesis, and some explanation of Lucan and Marcan redaction of Matthew on the Griesbach hypothesis, in both cases Marcan priority offers a much more plausible and coherent account of the origin and distinctive purposes of Matthew and Luke.[2]

The same point can be pressed against the claim that Luke has used Matthew. This hypothesis is not, as Goulder insists, the simplest solution of the synoptic problem. On this view, Luke has used his sources in an extremely complex set of ways; his redaction of Matthew and of Mark cannot readily be explained as the result of his own theological preferences.

The success of redaction criticism in clarifying the literary methods and distinctive theological emphases of Matthew and Luke on the assumption of dependence on Mark and Q is an important argument in favour of the two-source hypothesis.[3] While some of the arguments which were used in the past to support the two-source hypothesis have now been shown to be reversible, or in one or two cases, untenable, no more satisfactory account of the phenomena

---

[1] C.M. Tuckett, 'The Griesbach Hypothesis in the 19th Century', *JSNT* 3 (1979) 48.

[2] See J.D. Kingsbury's interesting study, 'The Theology of St Matthew's Gospel according to the Griesbach Hypothesis', in *New Synoptic Studies*, ed. W.R. Farmer, Macon 1983.

[3] In the Introduction to their ICC commentary on Matthew (I, 98) W.D. Davies and D.C. Allison stress that they began their exegetical work with open minds. They wished 'to discover just why the standard theory was suffering so much at the hands of so many'; they found that they were more than ever persuaded of the priority of Mark, a hypothesis which 'consistently brought illumination'. See also J.M. Robinson, 'On the Gattung of Mark (and John)', in *Jesus and Man's Hope* I, ed. D.G. Miller et al, Pittsburgh 1970, 101f.

presented to us by the text of the three synoptic gospels has yet been produced.

The synoptic problem has been discussed for so long and from so many angles that many scholars feel that we have reached an impasse. However, progress is still possible! One quite fresh consideration has recently been introduced into the discussion. In a set of careful articles F.G. Downing has examined the ways ancient writers handled the sources on which they were dependent.[1] He has shown that the redactional methods involved in the two-gospel hypothesis and in the claim that Luke used Matthew are quite unlike the ways ancient writers handled their sources. On the other hand, Matthew and Luke use Mark and Q in ways which do bear comparison with well-established conventions in antiquity. This observation strengthens still further the conclusion that the claims of the two source hypothesis are far stronger than those of any of its rivals.

3. *Grounds for caution*

Most redaction critics accept without further ado that all the differences between Matthew and Mark in a modern critical edition of the Greek text stem from the hand of the evangelist Matthew, as do all the modifications made to Q. But there are a number of reasons which are rarely noted for suggesting that a more cautious approach is appropriate.

(i) Redaction critics assume too readily that the original text of the synoptic gospels has now been established.[2] In the case of Matthew, for example, it is very difficult to decide whether or not Matt 9. 34; 13. 14-15; 16. 2b-3; and 21. 44

---

[1] F.G. Downing, 'Compositional Conventions and the Synoptic Problem', *JBL* 107 (1988) 69-85; 'Redaction Criticism: Josephus' *Antiquities* and the Synoptic Problem', I, *JSNT* 8 (1980) 46-65; II, *JSNT* 9 (1980) 29-48; 'A Paradigm Perplex: Luke, Matthew and Mark', *NTS* 38 (1992), forthcoming.

[2] W.D. Davies and D.C. Allison, *Matthew* I, 113-4, are a notable exception.

formed part of the original text.[1] At 21. 29-31, a crucial point in the 'story line' of the whole gospel, the text is in disarray. And in addition, assimilation of one gospel to another is such a widespread phenomenon that in a number of passages there is continuing uncertainty about the original text.[2] These considerations need to be borne in mind in all forms of redaction critical study. When this is done, some results will need to be stated more tentatively; in particular, some forms of statistical analysis which are used to establish Matthean vocabulary and style need to be refined.

(ii) How do we know that Matthew used Mark's gospel as we now have it? The version of Mark used by Matthew may have undergone minor revision (or even major redaction) *after* it became available to Matthew or his community. Many scholars accept (correctly in my view) that Q traditions may have been used by Matthew and by Luke at different stages in their development. So why is there reluctance to concede that once Mark was written, no further development of the Marcan tradition took place? But the transition from oral tradition to an exclusively written tradition may have been much more gradual than most students of the gospels have supposed.[3]

A thorough-going *Ur-Markus* theory has not been canvassed for some time.[4] There are sound reasons for this, but it is difficult to rule out the possibility that canonical Mark may be a lightly revised version of the text of Mark which Matthew and Luke used.

---

[1] In his interesting study, 'Conjectural Emendations in the Gospel of Matthew', *NovT* 31 (1989) 1-15, D.A. Black refers to several recent studies of the text of Matthew.

[2] See J.K. Elliott, 'Textual Criticism, Assimilation and the Synoptic Gospels', *NTS* 26 (1980) 231-42.

[3] For a fuller discussion, see G.N. Stanton, 'Form Criticism Revisited', in *What About the New Testament?* (FS *Christopher Evans*) eds. Morna Hooker and Colin Hickling, London 1975, 13-27.

[4] See W.G. Kümmel's *Introduction,* 61-3 for a brief discussion and references. I have not seen the revival of the 'deutero-Mark' hypothesis by Andreas Ennulat, *Die "Minor Agreements". Untersuchungen zu einer offenen Frage des synoptischen Problems*, Tübingen 1991.

In a number of passages where the later evangelists are following Mark, Marcan sentences or phrases are missing. In many cases the agreement of Matthew and Luke against Mark can be readily accounted for. However there are exceptions. In only one case does Kümmel allow that a phrase may have been added later to the version of Mark known to Matthew and Luke: the phrase 'and Andrew with James and John' in Mark 1. 29.[1] I think there are several more passages where an equally strong case can be made out. (a) 'The sabbath was made for man, and not man for the sabbath' (Mark 2. 27); (b) 'And he said to the sea, "Silence! Be still!" ' (Mark 4. 39); (c) 'And the Jews', a phrase linked awkwardly to 'the Pharisees' in Mark 7. 3; (d) 'By saying this he declared all foods clean' (Mark 7. 19b); (e) 'The son of Timaeus, Bartimaeus' (Mark 10. 46); (f) 'For it was not the season for figs' (Mark 11. 13c).[2]

(iii) The sources on which Matthew drew may have been modified or conflated prior to the compilation of the gospel. In his important study of Matthew's passion narratives, N.A. Dahl concedes that this may have been so, but few redaction critics have taken account of this possibility.[3] E. Schweizer is an exception: in his commentary he suggests that the three Q beatitudes contained in the Lucan sermon on the plain (Luke 6. 20-49) were already supplemented in the Matthean community and altered for the purposes of catechism prior to the composition of Matthew's gospel; a pattern based on 'seven' appears to crop up occasionally in the pre-Matthean

---

[1] *Introduction*, 63, n.46

[2] (d) (e) and (f) are explanatory comments, a feature of Marcan style. But this does not rule out possible further later explanatory additions to the text of Mark which Matthew and Luke used.

B.H. Streeter, *The Four Gospels*, London 1936, 171, suggests as a serious possibility that Mark 4. 26-9 may have dropped out of the copy of Mark used by one or both of the other evangelists owing to 'homoioteleuton'. U. Luz suggests (plausibly in my view) that Mark may well have circulated in several slightly different versions; *Matthäus* I, 30.

[3] 'The Passion Narrative in Matthew', in *Matthew*, ed. G.N. Stanton, 42-55.

tradition. In his recent commentary U. Luz defends a similar view and claims that Q circulated in different recensions.

Many of the examples of pre-Matthean redaction of Mark, Q, or even 'M' which have been proposed are plausible.[1] But once again it is difficult to establish criteria by which pre-Matthean redaction can be differentiated from the evangelist's own modification of the sources on which he drew. To take one example: if we accept that the version of the Lord's prayer found in Matt 6. 9-13 is an expansion of an originally shorter Q version similar to Luke 11. 2-4, were the additional words and phrases all added by Matthew himself, or are we to think of liturgical revision over a long period of time? Was Matt 6. 14 added to the Lord's Prayer by the evangelist himself? If he did so, why did he fail to bring τὰ παραπτώματα (trespasses) into line with τὰ ὀφειλήματα (debts) in 6. 12? Or was this Marcan logion associated with the prayer long before Matthew wrote and therefore simply included by him without change?

(iv) Redaction critics also need to consider the possibility that the text of our Matthew includes some redaction which took place *after* the gospel left the hand of the individual or group primarily responsible for it. Many scholars concede that this happened to the Fourth Gospel, so why not to Matthew? In my judgement it is highly likely that Matt 13. 14-15 was added to the original text at an early stage in its transmission.

While it is difficult to rule out a priori the possibility of other later additions, it is not easy to see how one could hope to establish criteria by which later additions to the evangelist's text could be spotted. There will rarely be sufficiently clear stylistic evidence, so a decision would need to be based either on an alleged 'awkwardness', or on an 'unMattheanism' in the text – and that assumes that the evangelist was always logical and consistent in the redaction of the sources at his disposal.

---

[1] H.D. Betz goes very much further. He claims that Matt 5–7 is a pre-Matthean epitome of the teaching of Jesus. For a critical assessment of this intriguing theory, see Chapter 13 below.

It is all too easy to claim that a word or phrase which does not square with one's own proposals is a gloss added at a later point to the text the evangelist wrote. For example, in 23. 3 readers and listeners are urged to carry out the teaching of the scribes and Pharisees; this seems to contradict 23. 16-22, where the teaching of these same leaders is repudiated. 23. 3a is usually seen as an 'unassimilated' pre-Matthean tradition, but it might equally well be taken as a post-Matthean 're-judaizing' gloss.

(v) In a number of passages the differences between Matthew and his two major sources, Mark and Q, may be the result of the continuing influence of oral tradition rather than the evangelist Matthew's own modifications. The phrase 'who struck you', which Matt 27. 68 and Luke 22. 64 add to Mark 14. 65, is a good example. There has been a greater willingness in recent years to allow for the continuing influence of oral tradition. If this possibility is taken seriously, redaction critical conclusions need to be correspondingly more tentative.

Taken cumulatively, these various considerations suggest that the formation of Matthew's gospel may have been the result of a much longer and a much more complex process than the 'one-stage' redaction commonly envisaged. Even though it is very difficult indeed to isolate with confidence changes made to Mark, Q, or 'M'[1] traditions by redactors other than Matthew, there are good grounds for urging caution: not every difference between Matthew and the sources on which he drew represents a modification introduced by the evangelist Matthew himself.

But even when all the above considerations are taken to heart, in the vast majority of cases the differences between Matthew and Mark, Q, and 'M' form such a consistent pattern

---

[1] The so-called 'M' traditions raise special problems. Here it is much more difficult than in the case of Mark and Q to disentangle the evangelist's own redaction (or creation of material) from earlier stages of the tradition. See the discussions of Matt 25. 31-46 in Chapter 9 and of Matt 11. 28-30 in Chapter 16 of this book. See also S.H. Brooks, *Matthew's Community*, JSNTSS 16, Sheffield 1987, *passim*.

that we may reasonably suppose that they stem from the evangelist himself. The more examples of a particular set of changes which can be adduced, the stronger the case for Matthean redaction.

Matthew's theology

The second pillar of redaction critical study of Matthew has been the conviction that the modifications the evangelist makes to his sources reflect his own distinctive theological emphases. I accept that in numerous passages this is so, and that impressive results have been achieved on the basis of this assumption. Once again, however, there are grounds for caution.

Discussion of Matthew's theological convictions is usually based on the presupposition that his gospel reflects a logically coherent theology. As a result, there is a real danger that the redaction critic's zeal to establish Matthew's theological emphases will gloss over inconsistencies. It is all too easy to set aside one strand of the evidence as 'pre-Matthean tradition' and accept another as the contribution of the evangelist himself. The evangelist was rather less consistent than some of his modern students.[1]

Several further considerations are relevant at this point. In the first phase of redaction criticism it was customary to suppose that Matthew's theological concerns were reflected only in the modifications he has made to his sources. That assumption was mistaken: if we concentrate on the changes introduced by the evangelist, we fail to appreciate that he frequently uses his traditions with little or no modification simply because he accepts them and wishes to preserve them and make them part of his portrait of Jesus and of his

[1] J. Jeremias's claim (*New Testament Theology* I, London 1971, 307 n.1) that unconcerned juxtaposition of conflicting traditions was almost a characteristic of Matthew, and that this is one of the fundamental reasons why redaction critical analysis of the first gospel cannot achieve success, is unnecessarily pessimistic.

41

message to his own Christian communities. Earlier traditions reflect Matthew's theological convictions just as much as his redactional modification; Matthew uses material from his tradition in the service of his own major themes and purposes.[1]

The titles or sub-titles of several influential redaction critical studies of Matthew's gospel refer to the evangelist's 'theology'.[2] While it would be unfair to claim that some of the authors concerned expound Matthew's theology in the light of their own pre-conceived theological systems, some have assumed that the evangelist's concerns were primarily theological. As a result, Matthew's theological emphases are sometimes discussed in a framework which owes more to systematic theology than to the gospel itself.

Redaction critics have frequently given insufficient attention to the possibility that some of the evangelist's modifications are stylistic rather than theological. Matthew's accounts of the feeding of the five thousand and of the four thousand are good examples. Whereas Matt 14. 19 and 15. 36 have been said to reflect more clearly than Mark 6. 41 and 8. 6 the institution of the eucharist, on closer inspection Matthew's alterations of Mark turn out to be completely consistent with purely stylistic modifications he makes elsewhere.[3]

Was the evangelist a theologian? In Paul's epistles, in the epistle to the Hebrews, and in the Fourth Gospel, we see theologians at work. But we do not do so in Matthew's

---

[1] This point has frequently been made. See, for example, A. Kretzer, *Die Herrschaft der Himmel und die Söhne des Reiches*, Stuttgart 1971, 303.

[2] For example, note the sub-titles of the following: G. Strecker, *Der Weg der Gerechtigkeit. Untersuchungen zur Theologie des Matthäus*, 1st ed. Göttingen, 1962; 3rd ed. 1971; W. Trilling, *Das wahre Israel: Studien zur Theologie des Matthäus-Evangeliums*; A. Sand, *Das Gesetz und die Propheten: Untersuchungen zur Theologie des Evangeliums nach Matthäus*; M. Didier, ed., *L'évangile selon Matthieu, Rédaction et Théologie*, Gembloux 1972.

[3] For the details, see F. Neirynck, 'La rédaction matthéenne et la structure du premier évangile', *ETL* 43 (1967) 50f., now reprinted in *Evangelica*, 12f.

gospel. Matthew's primary concerns were pastoral and catechetical.[1]

The five discourses which the evangelist has composed
himself illustrate this point well. It is possible to see some
broad theological concerns in the arrangement of the five
discourses: the mission discourse of chapter 10 precedes the
community discourse of chapter 18, for example, and the
eschatological discourse in chapters 24 and 25 completes the
set.

But on closer inspection there are numerous loose ends if
we assume that the evangelist sets out the traditions at his
disposal with a coherent theology in mind. Is the Sermon on
the Mount to be seen as 'proclamation of good news' or as
instruction for committed followers – as 'grace' or as
'demand'? Are some of the parables in chapter 13 intended to
reflect on 'mission' (sower, pearl, treasure), while others
reflect on 'congregational discipline' (tares, dragnet)?[2] Does
the Sermon on the Mount set out commands which, if
violated, require the disciplinary procedures laid out in
chapter 18? And how, in turn, is this action related to chapter
13, according to which wheat and tares are to be separated
only at the End?[3]

Matthew writes with several Christological, ecclesiological
and eschatological concerns. But in all three areas themes are
juxtaposed, sometimes awkwardly, rather than related
carefully to one another. J.D. Kingsbury has shown convincingly that 'Son of God' is the most prominent Christological
title in Matthew.[4] In a number of passages this title is
introduced redactionally; in others it is retained from earlier
traditions and its importance is underlined. But Kingsbury's
further claim that Matthew's other Christological themes are

---

[1] R. Thysman, *Communauté et directives éthiques: la catéchèse de
Matthieu*, Gembloux 1974, 6f., correctly notes that the term 'theologian'
does not accord well with the evangelist's pastoral orientation.

[2] I owe this point to my colleague, J. Leslie Houlden.

[3] I owe the latter two questions to L.E. Keck, 'The Sermon on the Mount', in
Jesus and Man's Hope, ed. D.G. Miller et al., II, Pittsburgh 1971.

[4] *Matthew: Structure, Christology, and Kingdom*, London 1976.

subsumed under his 'Son of God' Christology is much more difficult to substantiate.

M.J. Suggs has insisted that whereas in Q Jesus is the representative of personified Wisdom – Sophia, as a result of Matthean redaction Jesus himself becomes Sophia. 'It would not greatly overstate the case', Suggs writes, 'to say that *for Matthew* Wisdom "has become flesh and dwelled among us" (John 1. 14).'[1] Even if we accept Suggs's exegesis of the key passages, Matt. 11. 19, 25-30; 23. 34-9, questions remain. How is this bold Christological claim related to the evangelist's other Christological themes? And why is such a radically innovative theme found (with the possible exception of 11. 28-30) only in two Q passages?

Matthew can hardly be said to have a coherent doctrine of the church. Some passages imply that Matthew's communities were egalitarian (e.g. 18. 17; 23. 6-12), while others suggest a rudimentary hierarchy (e.g. 10. 41-2; 23. 34). In 16. 16-19 Peter is singled out as the rock on which the church (of Jesus) will be built; he alone is given the authority to 'bind and loose'. However, in 18. 18 that same authority is given to all the disciples; in this so-called ecclesiological discourse Peter plays no more than a marginal role (18. 21-2).

All five discourses end with eschatological teaching, but just how do the varied eschatological traditions relate to one another? What is the relationship between the judgement of the 'wicked' outside the community and the judgement of the 'wicked' or the 'lawless' within the community? Does Matthew expect two quite separate judgements – and if so, in what order?[2] Why is it difficult in some passages to decide which group is in view?

I do not doubt for one moment that distinctive theological emphases can be discerned in Matthew's account of the story and significance of Jesus. However, if we assume that Matthew is primarily a theologian, more questions than

[1] *Wisdom, Christology and Law in Matthew's Gospel*, Cambridge, Mass. 1970, 57.

[2] See D. Marguerat, *Le Jugement dans l'Évangile de Matthieu*, Geneva 1981, 504-6.

44

answers quickly emerge, for the evangelist does not reshape his sources in the light of a carefully thought-out coherent theology: his gifts and concerns are primarily catechetical and pastoral.

Matthew's communities

The third pillar of redaction criticism is the conviction that the modifications made by the evangelist to his sources reflect the needs and circumstances of his readers or listeners. Is this assumption valid? May we take a further step and reconstruct the history of the Matthean community or communities? Is it possible to distinguish between the evangelist's views and the contrary views of some of those to whom he writes – in other words, is Matthew writing (at least in part) to correct 'heretical' views?

It is possible to discern from the text of Matthew's gospel the circumstances of the evangelist's readers. Several chapters in Part II of this book take this as axiomatic. But as with the two pillars of redaction criticism we have just examined, there are some general grounds for caution.

My first point is a simple one, but it has been overlooked surprisingly frequently. Matthew is writing a gospel, not a letter. The literary genre chosen by Matthew indicates to his readers or listeners the expectations they should have. The evangelist's primary aim is to set out the story of Jesus. That he does so from a particular perspective is undeniable. What is less clear is the extent to which that perspective is *directly* related to the views and circumstances of the addressees. How do we know which parts of Matthew are intended to challenge or change the views of the readers or listeners? In the New Testament letters it is difficult enough to make this distinction; the genre Matthew has chosen makes this doubly difficult.

My second point draws on my insistence earlier in this chapter that Matthew's own views are reflected, not only in the changes he makes to his sources, but also in his choice of

45

the traditions he incorporates. Similarly, the whole gospel must be used in any quest for the needs, circumstances, and history of the community or communities to whom Matthew writes. This may seem obvious, but it has often been ignored. J. Rohde, for example, claims that the material peculiar to the evangelist is particularly unsuitable for an investigation of the theological conceptions of the evangelist and the 'Sitz im Leben' of his gospel.[1] This is surely a short-sighted approach: a careful study of Matthew's infancy narratives will soon show just how closely they are related to the evangelist's emphases elsewhere.

S.H. Brooks makes exactly the opposite decision: he insists that a clear delineation of tradition and redaction in the 'M' sayings is essential to an accurate portrait of Matthew's readers and of the history of Matthew's community.[2] Brooks uses redaction criticism with considerable skill to isolate the 'M' sayings (which he does not consider to have come from a written source), but it is rash to use these sayings as the sole base on which to build a reconstruction of the history of Matthew's community.

1. *History?*

Even if all the various strands of Matthew's gospel are used alongside the evangelist's modifications of his sources, it is not easy to reconstruct with any confidence the history of the Matthean community or communities.[3] Assignment of traditions to two or more stages in the life of the community is difficult, but it is not impossible.

Given that on some central Matthean themes the evangelist has recorded sayings which diverge considerably, is it possible to link such variations with different stages in the history of Matthew's community? For example, some sayings imply a positive attitude towards Gentiles and

[1] *Rediscovering the Teaching of the Evangelists*, E.tr. London 1968, 91.

[2] *Matthew's Community*, Sheffield 1987.

[3] For an interesting sophisticated attempt to set out the history of the Matthean community, see Schuyler Brown's set of articles listed in the Bibliography and also his *The Origins of Christianity: a Historical Introduction to the NT*, Oxford 1984, 107-14.

missionary activity among them (e.g. 2. 1; 4. 15-16; 5. 14; 8. 11-12; 10. 18; 12. 18-21; 24. 14; 28. 18-20); others are hostile to Gentiles (6. 7; 6. 32; 18. 17), and some imply that missionary activity is to be confined to Israel (10. 5-6, 23).

How do we account for such variations? There are only two plausible explanations. Perhaps Matthew was a rather naïve anthologist who simply juxtaposed divergent traditions. But since we know from Gal 2 that the Gentile mission was a sensitive and divisive topic within earliest Christianity, this seems rather unlikely. Or perhaps the evangelist expected that his readers would discern from the thrust of his gospel as a whole, and from their own experience and self-understanding, that some sayings belonged to an earlier stage of their history. The latter view is surely more plausible.

If so, then as a corollary we must allow that it is possible to set out in broad terms the historical development of the communities for whom the evangelist wrote. I have used the phrase 'in broad terms' quite deliberately. The paragraphs which follow will confirm that redaction critics have often drawn over-hasty conclusions about the circumstances and the development of Matthean communities. Any attempt to reconstruct their history must inevitably look beyond the meagre evidence of the gospel itself and draw heavily on other considerations concerning the origins of earliest Christianity.

2. *Antinomian heretics?*

Many redaction critics have accepted G. Barth's view that the evangelist is 'fighting on two fronts': he is concerned to oppose both the leaders of contemporary Judaism and Christian antinomian heretics who threaten the true life of the congregation.[1] Barth claims that Matthew's emphasis on

---

[1] In his influential essay, 'Enderwartung und Kirche' (1956), Bornkamm hinted that Matthew was opposing antinomians; Matt 5. 17-19 are directed against a tendency to abandon the law. Bornkamm's pupil, G. Barth also took 5. 17-19 as his starting point, but he went much further: see *Tradition*, 62-76; 159-64. Barth's view was accepted by R. Hummel, *Auseinandersetzung*, 64-6, but Hummel did not offer any fresh

47

the abiding validity of the law in 5. 17ff.; 7. 15ff.; and 24. 11 ff. is directed at antinomian opponents who can best be described as Hellenistic libertines; they are the false prophets of 7. 15 and 24. 11. 'Matthew opposes a group who appeal in support of their libertinism to the fact that Christ has abolished the law; these opponents rely on their *charismata*, their spiritual gifts, but not on their πίστις. . . .The knowledge of this battle-front is important for the understanding of Matthew's Gospel'. (p.164)

In numerous passages Matthew levels harsh criticisms at his Christian readers. Is he attacking one particular 'heretical' group? In his composite picture of the opponents Barth appeals to several passages and themes. But the evangelist may have in mind several different groups, or he may be addressing his readers in very general terms. Matthew uses ἀνομία three times to refer to Christians (7. 23; 13. 41; 24. 12). G. Strecker rightly insists that these are general references to disobedience to the 'will of the Father'. He also notes that 24. 10-12 is to be taken as a general reference to disobedience to the 'will of the Father'; it is not to be limited to antinomians. Matthew's warnings about false prophecy do not go beyond the similarly indefinite comments about heresy which we find in passages such as 1 Tim 6. 3ff.; Titus 1. 16 and Didache 11. 1-8.[1]

Barth uses the opening phrase of Matt 5. 17, μὴ νομίσητε, 'don't think', to support his hypothesis: the antinomians believe that Jesus has come to abolish the law and the prophets (p. 67). Strecker (and many other interpreters) takes

considerations. Other scholars who have accepted Barth's hypothesis include E. Schweizer, 'Observance of the Law and Charismatic Activity in Matthew', *NTS* 16 (1969-70) 216ff.; A. Sand, 'Die Polemik gegen "Gesetzlosigkeit" im Evangelium nach Matthäus und bei Paulus', *BZ* 14 (1970) 112ff.; E. Cothenet, 'Les prophètes chrétiens', *Matthieu*, 300; M.D. Goulder, *Midrash and Lection*, 308; G. Künzel, *Studien zum Gemeindeverständnis des Matthäus-Evangeliums*, Stuttgart 1978, 163. The most thorough exposition of this hypothesis is by J. Zumstein, *La condition du croyant*, 171-200. He refers to Matthew's 'struggle against heresy'.

[1] *Der Weg*, 137 n.4. See also J.E. Davison, 'Anomia and the Question of an Antinomian Polemic in Matthew', *JBL* 104 (1985) 617-35.

this clause, and the identical one in 10. 34 (where it is redactional) as a rejection of a theoretical possibility – i.e., as a very general comment which might be paraphrased, 'Don't even be tempted to think'. This is certainly a plausible interpretation, but I think that a third possibility is even more likely.

We know that Jewish opponents of Christianity frequently alleged that Jesus and his followers had abandoned the law,[1] and we know that in several passages Matthew is responding to Jewish counter-propaganda. So is it not probable that the scribes and Pharisees who are in view in 5. 20 at the end of this pericope are also in view at the beginning of 5. 17? In this verse the evangelist opens his sustained exposition of his case concerning the Scriptures: 'Don't think, as the scribes and Pharisees allege, that I have come to destroy the law and the prophets. . . ' For Matthew the law and the prophets continue to be authoritative for Christians – with the proviso that they are interpreted in the light of the teaching of Jesus, especially the love-commandment.

Our discussion of G. Barth's hypothesis has shown just how difficult it is to identify particular opponents Matthew may have had in mind. Given these difficulties, the proposal that ἐλάχιστος in 5. 19 ('the least in the kingdom') is a veiled reference to Paul's own self-designation in 1 Cor 15. 9 ('the least of the apostles') is implausible.[2] Use of the text of New Testament epistles to 'mirror' opponents and their arguments is fraught with difficulties.[3] We do well to be even more cautious in our use of redactional passages in Matthew to identify groups who are being opposed. Hypotheses based on a possible interpretation of one verse, or even of a cluster of verses, are likely to be insecure. The only opponents who are in view from the beginning to the end of Matthew's gospel (from 2. 1 to 28. 15) are the Jewish leaders.

---

[1] For the details see Chapter 10 below.
[2] This view, which goes back to J. Weiss, has recently been revived by H.D. Betz. See Chapter 13 below.
[3] See J. Barclay's careful discussion, 'Mirror Reading a Polemical Letter: Galatians as a Test Case', *JSNT* 31 (1987) 73-93.

3. Community or Communities?

Since the advent of redaction criticism it has been customary to refer to the recipients of Matthew's gospel as the Matthean *community*. Numerous attempts have been made to identify the geographical location of that community, but they are all based on flimsy evidence.[1] The early, rapid, and widespread circulation of Matthew suggests that the first recipients lived in or near a major city with good communications to other cities;[2] Matthew's preference for πόλις offers some further support for this view.[3]

But did Matthew write for one group of Christian believers? Many redaction critics have assumed that Matthew's relationship with his readers was rather like Paul's intimate relationship with the Christian communities to whom he wrote. That view needs to be reconsidered. I have already emphasized that Matthew is writing a gospel and not a letter, and we have just seen that it is most unlikely that Matthew intended to counter the views of a particular group.

A further consideration suggests that the Pauline analogy is inappropriate. First century Christians met in houses; it would have been difficult for many more than 50 or so

---

[1] See G.N. Stanton, 'Origin and Purpose', 1941-2, and U. Luz, *Matthäus* I, 73-5. Luz suggests that Antioch is 'not the weakest hypothesis'!

[2] The classic study is E. Massaux, *Influence de l'Évangile de St. Matthieu sur la littérature chrétienne avant St. Irénée*, Louvain 1950; revised ed. BETL 75, Leuven 1986. There have been several recent important discussions: W.-D. Köhler, *Die Rezeption des Matthäusevangeliums in der Zeit vor Irenäus*, Tübingen 1987; Otto Knock, 'Kenntnis und Verwendung des Matthäus-Evangeliums bei den Apostolischen Vätern', *Studien zum Matthäusevangelium* (FS W. Pesch) ed. Ludger Schenke, Stuttgart 1988, 157-77; H.B. Green, 'Matthew, Clement, and Luke: their Sequence and Relationship', *JTS* 40 (1989) 1-25.

[3] G.D. Kilpatrick, *Origins*, 124-5, noted that whereas Mark used πόλις eight times, πόλις is used twenty six times in Matthew. Four of these additional references are redactional, but are less striking than Kilpatrick implies: 8. 34; 9. 35; 21. 10, 18. More significant are the references to the flight of disciples from city to city in 10. 23 and 23. 34.

people to crowd into even a quite substantial house.[1] Is it likely that Matthew would have composed such an elaborate gospel for one relatively small group? Is it not much more likely that Matthew, like Luke, envisaged that his gospel would circulate widely? If so, then it is no surprise to find that his criticisms of his readers are severe but imprecise. Matthew is well aware of the tensions and pressures his readers faced, but we must not read his gospel as if it were Galatians, I or II Corinthians, or even Romans.

In this chapter I have drawn attention to some of the issues and questions redaction critics have often ducked. If my observations are valid, some of the basic assumptions which have been made in redaction critical study of Matthew do need to be reconsidered. But there are no grounds for abandoning a method which has been very fruitful. The three pillars of redaction criticism need to be repaired in some places, but not replaced.

After a century of discussion of the synoptic problem, Matthew's dependence on Mark is the single most assured result. The extent of that dependence is astonishing. Matthew reproduces the substance of over 600 of Mark's 661 verses; it is not difficult to account for the omissions.[2] Mark's order is followed very closely from Matt 11. 1 to the end of the gospel; the variations in order from 4. 12 to 11. 1 are the result of the way Matthew has carefully designed this part of his gospel. As we shall see in most of the later chapters in this book, nearly all Matthew's prominent themes and distinctive emphases are the result of his development of his sources. The genre of Matthew is determined by the genre of Mark.[3] In short, F.C. Burkitt's seventy year old formulation can hardly

---

[1] I do not know of any studies of the size of first century houses in Syrian cities. On the basis of archaeological excavations in Corinth, J. Murphy-O'Connor suggests that between 40 and 50 Christians belonged to the house-church there: 'The Corinth that Saint Paul Saw', *Biblical Archaeologist* 47 (1984) 157.

[2] B.H. Streeter, *The Four Gospels*, 159.

[3] This point is discussed in Chapter 3.

be bettered: 'Matthew is a *fresh edition* of Mark, revised, rearranged, and enriched with new material. . . .'[1]

Given this close correspondence between Matthew and Mark, interpretation of Matthew cannot proceed satisfactorily without careful consideration of all the changes the evangelist has made to his major source – i.e. without responsible use of redaction criticism. Consistent patterns in Matthew's redaction of Mark can be observed: Matthew's distinctive vocabulary, style, structure, and emphases can be readily discerned. On the basis of these secure results, it is possible to show that Matthew has developed his Q and 'M' traditions in the same ways.[2]

In the first phase of redaction criticism the *modifications* made by the evangelist to his sources were taken to be indicative of his theological concerns. More recent redaction critical study of Matthew has quite rightly emphasized that in addition, attention must be given to the traditions which are incorporated with little or no changes, for by accepting them Matthew makes them his own.

Matthew's gospel must be read and interpreted as a whole. Even when the evangelist incorporates earlier traditions without significant modification, re-interpretation takes place by dint of the immediate context in which they are placed, and also by dint of the framework and distinctive thrust of the whole gospel. So it is important to consider the sweep of the whole gospel; the first redaction critics often misguidedly adopted an atomistic approach.

However, if we wish to understand Matthew's distinctive contribution to earliest Christianity, we must give careful attention to the ways he has developed the traditions at his disposal. Matthew is not simply an expansion of Mark, and the differences do matter.

The Pauline writings offer a useful analogy. Students of Paul's letters must consider every word they contain. But if we wish to elucidate Paul's thought and to determine how his mind worked, his own terms and turns of phrase must

---

[1] *The Earliest Sources for the Life of Jesus*, London 1922, 97.
[2] See Chapter 14 below for an extended illustration of this principle.

take priority over the pre-Pauline formulae, the Scriptural citations, and the conventional Jewish and Graeco-Roman ethical traditions he has incorporated. In his use of these earlier traditions, Paul makes them his own. But since he rarely draws on earlier traditions without modifying them, the changes he makes are of particular interest. So too with Matthew.

Chapter Three

Literary Criticism: Ancient and Modern

Ever since Matthew's gospel was written, the evangelist's literary skills have contributed to its widespread use and popularity. The evangelist's prose has rhythmic and poetic qualities unequalled by the other evangelists.[1] For example, Matthew's versions of the Beatitudes, the Lord's prayer, and the parable of the house built on the rock are all much more memorable than the parallel passages in Luke; to this day they are regularly preferred in the context of worship.

In recent years literary approaches to Matthew have taken quite new forms as many scholars have found fruitful insights in the work of modern literary critics.[2] Literary studies of Matthew have followed rather belatedly on the

[1] See especially M.D. Goulder's valuable chapters on Matthew's poetry and imagery in his *Midrash and Lection*, 70-115.

[2] The pioneers have been J.D. Kingsbury and R.A. Edwards. Since 1984 Kingsbury has written extensively on Matthew from the point of view of narrative criticism. His first writings from this perspective were 'The Figure of Jesus in Matthew's Story: a Literary-Critical Probe', *JSNT* 21 (1984) 3-36, and *Matthew as Story*, Philadelphia 1986; 2nd ed. 1988. Two of his former doctoral students, David R. Bauer and Dorothy Jean Weaver, have now published narrative critical studies of Matthew. R.A. Edwards's *Matthew's Story of Jesus*, Philadelphia 1985, partly anticipated more recent interest in reader response criticism; see also his 'Uncertain Faith: Matthew's Portrait of the Disciples' in *Discipleship in the New Testament*, ed. Fernando F. Segovia, Philadelphia 1985. David B. Howell uses 'selected aspects of narrative criticism and a type of reader response criticism' in his *Matthew's Inclusive Story. A Study in the Narrative Rhetoric of the First Gospel*, JSNTSS 42, Sheffield 1990.

heels of rapidly increasing interest in literary critical approaches to the other three gospels, and to the Biblical writings in general.[1] Since 1984, however, perhaps as many as half the scholarly books and articles published in English on Matthew have been written from literary perspectives.

The reasons for this new development within Matthean scholarship are complex. Some have turned to literary approaches convinced that source critical uncertainties have undermined redaction criticism. Other scholars have become frustrated with traditional historical methods which seem to be subject to a law of diminishing returns: more scholarly endeavour leads only to an increased awareness of the gaps in our knowledge. Others find literary approaches less threatening than historical criticism to their conservative views of the Bible and their traditional Christian theological convictions. Still others have turned from historical to literary criticism with more positive hopes: they sense that literary criticism will produce more and better religious fruit.[2] Such hopes (which in my view are too optimistic) are bolstered by the conviction that literary criticism will bridge the gap between antiquity and the end of the twentieth century, whereas historical criticism merely draws attention to its breadth. Others have found – as I have myself, but with an important proviso on which I shall insist – that modern literary theory is an attractive dancing partner: although theoretical studies are bewildering in their rich and varied profusion, with eclectic use many Biblical writings may be read more sensitively and with a new appreciation of the 'final form' of the text.

A whole series of fascinating and mostly fresh issues have been raised in recent literary approaches to Matthew. How-

---

[1] David Rhoads and Donald Michie's *Mark as Story: An Introduction to the Narrative of a Gospel*, Philadelphia 1982, has been influential, as has R.A. Culpepper's *Anatomy of the Fourth Gospel: A Study in Literary Design*, Philadelphia 1983. In his survey, *Literary Criticism and the Gospels: the Theoretical Challenge*, New Haven 1989, Stephen D. Moore refers to Matthew much less frequently than to the other gospels.

[2] On this point see R. Morgan with J. Barton, *Biblical Interpretation*, Oxford 1988, 202-63.

ever, the assumptions behind their use need to be scrutinised as rigorously as the assumptions of redaction critical studies. Since several helpful guides and surveys have now been published,[1] I shall not attempt to expound recent literary approaches to the gospels.

In this chapter I shall set out some proposals relevant for the interpretation or 'reading' of Matthew from a literary perspective. I shall argue that although modern literary theory is stimulating and helpful, precedence must be given both to the literary conventions which influenced the evangelist and to the expectations of his first century readers. This point, which I take to be axiomatic, has been overlooked in much recent literary critical discussion of Matthew.

In my insistence that interpretation of a text cannot be carried out in isolation from consideration of the social setting of its readers (whether ancient or modern), I shall seem to many literary critics to be knocking at an open door, for New Criticism with its 'text immanent' perspective was buried some time ago. For example, the influential literary critic Jerome J. McGann – and he is not a lone voice – has argued forcefully that 'literature is a human product, a humane art. It cannot be carried on (created), understood (studied), or appreciated (experienced) outside of its definitive human context. The general science governing that human context is socio-historical.'[2]

---

[1] See especially Stephen D. Moore, *Literary Criticism*; Mark Alan Powell, *What is Narrative Criticism?* Philadelphia 1990; Burton L. Mack, *Rhetoric and the New Testament*, Minneapolis 1990. The articles in *A Dictionary of Biblical Interpretation*, eds. R.J. Coggins and J.L. Houlden, London 1990, are also invaluable.

[2] 'Keats and Historical Method' in *The Beauty of Inflections. Literary Investigations in Historical Method and Theory*, Oxford 1988, 63. McGann claims that New Criticism began to be called in question about 1965. See also his *Social Values and Poetic Acts. The Historical Judgement of Literary Work*, Cambridge, Mass. 1988. Frank Kermode has recently made a similar point in his *Poetry, Narrative, History*, Oxford 1990, 49: '. . .more and more people are turning away from the idea that literary works should be treated as autonomous and without significant relation to the world in which they are produced and read.'

The shades of New Criticism, however, still seem to haunt some New Testament scholars who insist on reading the gospels in isolation as far as possible from their socio-historical setting.[1] J.D. Kingsbury, for example, wants to approach Matthew 'as a unified narrative . . . .to attend to the very story it tells. When one reads Matthew. . . (one) enters into another world that is autonomous in its own right.' (p.2) These comments are strongly reminiscent of New Criticism's insistence on a 'close reading' of texts solely in terms of the text itself. Kingsbury's approach, however, is not as radically ahistorical or 'text immanent' as that of many New Critics. Although socio-historical considerations are largely absent from his exposition of Matthew's story world, he includes a final chapter on the community of Christians for which Matthew's story was originally written, and he concedes that what can be inferred from the text about the intended readers may be supplemented by 'occasional glances at Mark or Luke or at other historical data. . .' (p.147).

Similarly, Daniel Patte's exposition of Matthew from a structuralist perspective is less radically ahistorical than most structuralist studies.[2] Although the main text of his commentary is written strictly from a 'text immanent' structuralist stand-point, he includes redaction critical and even occasionally socio-historical notes at the end of each section

---

[1] My strong emphasis on ancient literary conventions is shared by several recent studies of Mark and John (but not yet of Matthew): Mary Ann Tolbert, *Sowing the Gospel. Mark's World in Literary - Historical Perspective*, Minneapolis 1989; Mary Ann Beavis, *Mark's Audience. The Literary and Social Setting of Mark 4.11-12*, JSNTSS 33, Sheffield 1989; M.A. Stibbe, *John as Story Teller. Narrative Criticism and the Fourth Gospel*, SNTSMS 73, Cambridge 1992. See also W. Riley, 'Situating Biblical Narrative: Poetics and the Transmission of Community Values', *Proceedings of the Irish Biblical Association*, 9 (1985) 38-52; M. Sternberg, *The Poetics of Biblical Narrative*, Bloomington 1985. The tide also seems to have turned within Old Testament scholarship: see J. Barton, *Reading the Old Testament. Method in Biblical Study*, London 1984.

[2] *The Gospel According to Matthew. A Structural Commentary on Matthew's Faith*, Philadelphia 1987.

of his commentary. The main text and the notes, however, are not integrated.

Kingsbury's and Patte's very different 'text immanent' studies of Matthew both leave the impression that the socio-historical setting of the original readers is secondary, 'milk', not 'meat'. With McGann and other literary critics I want to insist that it is primary – whether we are considering the intended readers (the authorial audience) or modern readers.

At this point the terminology used in this chapter (and elsewhere in this book) must be clarified. I am using the term 'literary criticism' to refer to literary studies of the gospels which utilise the work of modern literary theorists and which concentrate attention on the text as it now stands and the responses of readers, whether ancient or modern.[1] I have chosen this general term quite deliberately. I am concerned to stress that 'narrative criticism' (which is primarily text centred), 'reader response criticism', and 'rhetorical criticism' (which considers the *means* through which a work achieves a particular effect on its readers) should not be considered in isolation from one another. Although 'narrative criticism' has been widely used in recent discussion of Matthew, I am uneasy about the term. It is not used by scholars in other disciplines, and its use has encouraged a rather narrow approach to the gospels which sometimes eschews both 'reader response criticism' and 'rhetorical criticism'.[2]

The term 'ancient literary criticism' (and similar phrases) is used to refer to the literary and rhetorical conventions which were known in antiquity and which may have influenced (however indirectly) both the evangelist's

---

[1] This usage is now gaining general acceptance among Biblical scholars, even though it may be said to mark a complete break with earlier practice; until quite recently 'literary criticism' was used by Biblical scholars to refer to *historical* inquiry into the sources and the history of the traditions behind the gospels, as well as their original historical settings. These are the very issues which are studiously ignored or devalued in some current literary studies of the gospels.

[2] In his exposition of 'narrative criticism' M.A. Powell differentiates it from both these other approaches. See his *What is Narrative Criticism?* especially 14-15.

methods of composition and also the ways his first readers and listeners understood his gospel.

First of all I shall discuss the genre of Matthew. Although this question has not been prominent in recent literary studies of Matthew,[1] I take it to be of paramount importance for any study which claims to be literary critical. Following discussion of the original audience, I shall suggest that Matthew uses σύγκρισις, 'comparison', as a rhetorical strategy in order to make his story of Jesus more persuasive.

Genre

The first step in the interpretation of any writing, whether ancient or modern, is to establish its literary genre.[2] The reader usually does this instinctively by comparing the writing with other similar writings with which he or she is familiar; occasionally further acquaintance with the text may lead to a revised assessment of its genre, and so of its interpretation. A decision about the genre of a work and the discovery of its meaning are inextricably inter-related; different types of text require different types of interpretation.[3]

A literary genre is not a strait-jacket either for an author or for her or his readers. Authors regularly adapt or extend existing genres which are familiar to their readers. But they are able to do this only if they are confident that communication with their readers will still be possible. If an author were to invent a totally new genre, readers would be baffled and communication would be impossible. In this way genre acts

---

[1] There are exceptions. See P.L. Shuler, *A Genre for the Gospels. The Biographical Character of Matthew*, Philadelphia 1982, which is discussed below. J.D. Kingsbury includes a brief survey of scholarly discussion of the genre of Matthew in the second edition of his *Matthew*, Proclamation Commentaries, Philadelphia 1986, 9-13.

[2] Cf. E.D. Hirsch, *Validity in Interpretation*, New Haven 1967, 76: 'All understanding of verbal meaning is necessarily genre-bound.'

[3] On this see A. Fowler, *Kinds of Literature*, Oxford 1982, 38; E.D. Hirsch, *Validity in Interpretation*, 113.

as a constraint on an author, even though it offers readers an initial framework for the determination of meaning.

Recognition of the importance of the genre of the Biblical writings for their interpretation has been almost universal in modern Biblical scholarship.[1] It is surprising, therefore, to find that the importance of genre has not always been appreciated by scholars who have recently discussed Matthew from a literary perspective,[2] even though several influential literary critics have recently re-emphasized the importance of literary genre for interpretation.

The literary critic Alastair Fowler, who has extended and given greater sophistication to his mentor E.D. Hirsch's work on genre, writes as follows: 'Genre is ubiquitous in literature, as the basis of the conventions that make literary communication possible.'[3] Fowler notes (surely correctly) that genre 'is a communication system for the use of writers in writing, and readers and critics in reading and interpreting.'[4] These comments underline the close relationship of author, text, and readers, the very point I am emphasizing in this chapter.

The importance of genre is not the discovery of modern literary critics: its crucial role in interpretation was noted and discussed by Aristotle and the ancient rhetoricians.[5] In

---

[1] As an interesting recent example, see the opening chapter of John S. Kloppenborg, *The Formation of Q. Trajectories in Ancient Wisdom Collections*, Philadelphia 1987.

[2] Stephen Moore, *Literary Criticism*, completely by-passes genre; the term does not even appear in his Index which covers virtually every other aspect of literary criticism.

[3] Fowler, *Kinds of Literature*, 36.

[4] Fowler, *Kinds of Literature*, 256. See also E.D. Hirsch's extended discussion of the paramount importance of genre, 68-126; see especially 74: 'An interpreter's preliminary generic conception of a text is constitutive of everything that he subsequently understands, and . . . this remains the case unless and until that generic conception is altered.'

[5] See Stanley F. Bonner, *Education in Ancient Rome*, London 1977, 202; Hirsch, *Validity*, 100f., and Fowler, *Kinds of Literature*, 38, 219. See also D.A. Russell, *Criticism in Antiquity*, London 1981. Some of the main texts are collected in D.A. Russell and M. Winterbottom, *Ancient Literary Criticism: the Principal texts in Translation*, Oxford 1972; revised edition published as *Classical Literary Criticism*, Oxford 1989.

antiquity conventions concerning genre were rather rigid. In his *Ars Poetica*, lines 86-9, 92, Horace writes:

> If I have neither the ability nor the knowledge to keep the duly assigned functions and tones of literature, why am I hailed as a poet? Why do I prefer to be ignorant than to learn, out of sheer false shame? A comic subject will not be set out in tragic verse. . . Everything must keep the appropriate place to which it was allotted. [1]

Cicero makes the same point: 'In tragedy the comic is a fault, and in comedy the tragic displeases.' (*De Optimo Genere Oratorum* 1).[2] And as a third example we may note Quintilian, *Institutio Oratoria*, 10. 2; 21-2:

> One thing to avoid (many fall into this trap) is thinking that we should imitate poets and historians in oratory, or orators and declaimers in poetry and history. Each genre has its own rules and proprieties.[3]

Modern literary critics have a less rigid understanding of genre. Fowler, for example, lays particular emphasis on literary genres as families which are subject to change.[4] Authors frequently modify genres which are familiar to their readers. Once this point is taken seriously, it is obvious that the state of the genre at the time when the work was written must be established.[5]

So if we are to take the genre of Matthew seriously (as we must), an important corollary follows: Matthew's gospel must be set in its first century literary context and the literary

---

[1] I have cited D.A. Russell's translation from *Ancient Literary Criticism*, 281.

[2] I have cited M. Winterbottom's translation from *Ancient Literary Criticism*, 250.

[3] M. Winterbottom's translation, 403.

[4] See Fowler's opening chapter, especially 18, and also 42: 'family resemblance theory seems to hold out the best hope to the genre critic.'

[5] Fowler, *Kinds of Literature*, 259ff.

conventions of the most closely related ancient writings must be considered carefully.

1. *Matthew as a biography*

What, then, is the literary genre of Matthew? What were the expectations of the first readers and listeners? In the case of ancient writings, there are three considerations which help us to answer these questions. (i) A title or a preface may indicate the genre of the writing; occasionally an ancient author even includes explicit comments on the genre of his work. (ii) Early readers' comments on the genre of the writing in question may prove helpful, but one must bear in mind the possibility that its genre was misunderstood. (iii) The form and the content of the writing must be considered together.[1] It must then be compared and contrasted with its closest relatives. Here we need to recall Fowler's point (noted above) that genres are families which are subject to change.[2]

(i) The first consideration is of little help in the case of Matthew. The traditional title is a later addition to the original text, and there is no formal preface.[3] The evangelist does not include any direct statements about either the genre he has used or his purposes. If my suggestion in Chapter 1 that Matthew was the first writer to refer to his written work as a 'gospel' is correct, we still need to discover the genre of a 'gospel'.

(ii) Consideration of early readers' comments on Matthew, however, is more fruitful and points us in the right direction. Writing about A.D. 155, Justin Martyr referred to the gospels as ἀπομνημονεύματα τῶν ἀποστόλων – 'memoirs of the apostles' (*Apology* 66. 3; 67. 3; *Dialogue with Trypho*

---

1 Fowler, *Kinds of Literature*, 55f., notes that Aristotle ('and the best of the older theorists') kept external and internal forms together in discussing genre; 'and the best modern criticism concurs'. See R.A. Burridge's valuable discussion, *What are the Gospels?*, 126-7; also R. Wellek and A. Warren, *Theory of Literature*, New York 3rd ed. 1956, 231.

2 I have adapted Fowler's list of four kinds of evidence for earlier states of genres. See *Kinds of Literature*, 52-3.

3 See above, 11-13.

thirteen times; note especially 103. 8 and 106. 3). Justin's use of this phrase is almost certainly intended to recall Xenophon's *Memorabilia* (= ἀπομνημονεύματα), a 'biography' of Socrates.[1]

While the evidence is a little less clear, it is probable that three decades earlier Papias viewed Mark as ἀπομνημονεύματα, which he understood as 'memoirs' which were 'not artistically arranged'. However Papias seems to have believed that Matthew had gathered together the sayings of Jesus in a more polished or finished form. Hence within two generations of the composition of Matthew's gospel (or three, if we exclude Papias), at least some readers of the gospels considered them to be a type of biography.[2]

(iii) Was this early assessment of the genre of the gospels correct? That question can only be answered by comparing the form and content of Matthew with its closest relatives. For several decades earlier this century it was generally accepted that Justin was mistaken; some even suggested that Justin had been misled by his education in the Greek rhetorical tradition.

Rudolf Bultmann and several other influential form critics insisted that in terms of their genre the gospels are *sui generis*: they are not to be read as biographies, whether ancient or modern. Bultmann firmly denied that Hellenistic biographies provide an analogy to the genre of the gospels. However, his assessment of ancient biographical writing was surprisingly inaccurate.

Some years ago I drew attention to the ways in which the conventions of ancient and modern biography differ; the details (which have been generally accepted) need not be

---

[1] Peter Pilhofer, 'Justin und das Petrusevangelium', *ZNW* 81 (1990) 60-78, has recently revived the view that Justin used the Gospel of Peter; he also suggests that Justin's use of ἀπομνημονεύματα is to be traced directly to his use of the Gospel of Peter.

[2] See D.E. Aune, *The New Testament in its Literary Environment*, Philadelphia 1987, 66-7. I am less confident than Aune that the comments of Papias reveal a knowledge of technical rhetorical terms and conventions.

repeated here.[1] I concluded that while the gospels were much closer to ancient biographical writings than most scholars at that time were prepared to concede, there are important differences which mark them off from ancient biographies. I have rightly been criticised for failing to see that the logic of my own evidence confirmed that the gospels do belong to the Graeco-Roman biographical tradition.[2] At that time I did not appreciate fully either the extent to which genres may be adapted or the fact that the evangelists may have been influenced (even if only indirectly) by the Graeco-Roman literary tradition.[3] However, I now accept that the gospels are a type of Graeco-Roman biography. In a careful and thorough study which will remain the standard discussion for a long time to come, R.A. Burridge has recently shown that while the gospels do diverge from Graeco-Roman βίοι in some respects, they do not do so to any greater extent than βίοι do from one another.[4]

2. An encomium biography?

I do not think that it is possible to link Matthew closely with any one particular strand of the Graeco-Roman biographical

---

[1] See G.N. Stanton, *Jesus of Nazareth in New Testament Preaching*, SNTSMS 27, Cambridge 1974, 117-36.

[2] See C.H. Talbert, *What is a Gospel? The Genre of the Canonical Gospels*, Philadelphia 1977, 131 n.44; P.L. Shuler, *A Genre for the Gospels. The Biographical Character of Matthew*, Philadelphia 1982, 89-90; R.A. Burridge, *What are the Gospels? A Comparison with Graeco-Roman Biography*, SNTSMS 70, Cambridge 1992.

[3] More recently in *The Gospels and Jesus*, Oxford 1989, 19-20, I noted that the gospels can be linked with the Graeco-Roman biographical tradition only with very considerable qualifications: 'Many features of Mark's gospel would have puzzled readers familiar with the techniques of ancient biographical writing: the evangelist's concentration on the death of Jesus; his enigmatic opening which sets out "the beginning of the gospel" as the fulfilment of prophecy and which seems to assume that his readers know something about Jesus; his curiously abrupt ending; and his avoidance of entertaining anecdotes.' In his *What are the Gospels?* (see above) R.A. Burridge has shown that this assessment is too cautious.

[4] *What are the Gospels?* So also D.E. Aune, *Literary Environment*, 46-76.

tradition.[1] Philip L. Shuler has argued that Matthew is an encomium or laudatory biography, 'a *bios* genre of considerable importance in antiquity, whose primary purpose was to present a portrait of a person in such a way as either to elicit praise from an audience or to persuade an audience of the subject's praiseworthiness.' Shuler sets out examples of laudatory biography selected from the works of Isocrates, Xenophon, Philo, Tacitus, Lucian, Josephus and Philostratus.[2] But the writings which are alleged to belong to the same sub-genre, laudatory biography, are much more varied in both form and content than Shuler allows.[3] Some of the features (e.g. use of the techniques of amplification and comparison) which seem at first sight to indicate that they belong to the same sub-genre, are in fact shared by other kinds of biography. Conversely, many of the features of Matthew to which Shuler draws attention can be found in biographies which are not laudatory.

There are further difficulties with this proposal, the most important of which concerns the response Matthew intended to elicit from his readers and listeners. Shuler concedes (p.105) that Matthew writes in order to elicit a response of faith from his readers. 'Faith' however, is very different from 'praise', the response elicited in an encomium biography. Matthew does not present Jesus as a hero, a striking individual whose feats and character traits were intended to evoke adulation.

I am puzzled by Shuler's failure to note that in terms of their genre Matthew and Mark have a strong family resem-

---

[1] For a thorough critical discussion of C.H. Talbert's claims that the gospels conform to ancient lives of philosophers, see D.E. Aune, 'The Problem of the Genre of the Gospels: a Critique of C.H. Talbert's *What is a Gospel?*' in *Gospel Perspectives: Studies of History and Tradition in the Four Gospels*, eds. R.T. France and D. Wenham, vol. 2, Sheffield 1981, 9-60.

[2] Philip L. Shuler, *A Genre for the Gospels*; the quotation is from 86.

[3] Shuler himself concedes (85) that a comparison of any of the works which he has linked together (with the possible exception of Isocrates and Xenophon) would yield almost as many differences as similarities.

blance.[1] Shuler claims that source critical considerations are irrelevant in the determination of genre.[2] This is only partly true. If we accept that Matthew has incorporated most of Mark into his gospel, then an important corollary follows: Matthew has accepted and modified the genre of Mark. But the case for linking Mark with encomium biography is even weaker than it is for Matthew, for many of the features which led Shuler to link Matthew with encomium biography are not present in Mark.

Matthew is undoubtedly closer to Mark than to any other ancient biography. Quite apart from the evidence which leads most scholars to conclude that Matthew has incorporated a revised and abbreviated version of almost the whole of Mark's gospel, consideration of the genre of Matthew encourages us to compare the two gospels closely. At this point I may seem to be labouring the obvious. I do so because some scholars who use literary approaches to Matthew claim that the relationship of the two gospels is irrelevant to a 'reading' of Matthew.

Once we accept that Matthew has included most of Mark's gospel, then it is clear that he has adapted the genre of Mark. As noted above, adaptation of a literary genre is more common than its close imitation. By his addition of infancy narratives and his fuller passion and resurrection narratives, Matthew links his gospel even more closely to the ancient biographical tradition.

3. *Adaptation of the genre of Q*

If Matthew has adapted the genre of Mark, what has he done with his second major source, Q? I think it is possible to show that in his incorporation of Q Matthew has adapted and extended its literary genre. Since this is less obviously the case than with Matthew's adaptation of the genre of Mark, I must support this claim.

---

[1] Shuler claims that he has chosen Matthew for special study because it has received the least attention from scholars who have discussed the relationship of the gospels to ancient biographies (92).

[2] See 92 and 121 n.13.

At this point J. Kloppenborg's study, *The Formation of Q*, is helpful. He notes that Q is a collection of wisdom sayings, a genre which is widely attested in ancient Near Eastern writings, and also in collections of Hellenistic gnomia and chreiae. Near Eastern wisdom collections often include a prologue which is narrative and biographical in form; in some cases the prologue includes the motif of the 'testing' or ordeal of the sage. Kloppenborg cites Ahikar as the best example and notes that some of the titles given to the collection in later versions confirm that some later editors regarded it as primarily biographical in intent. 'The line between instruction and biography is not easily defined but easily crossed.'[1]

Collections of chreiae in Greek also often have a biographical interest. Lucian's *Life of Demonax* is a good example: it opens with a preface in which Lucian explains his biographical purposes and then sets out a brief biographical sketch of Demonax. Kloppenborg is able to show that within the Hellenistic tradition, 'the distinction between the chreiae collection and the *bios* is a fine one'.[2]

From these observations it is but a small step to the conclusion that the temptation story (which was probably the latest addition to Q) functions as a biographical-narrative preface; its 'testing' theme is found widely in ancient collections of sayings of an individual. 'The movement of Q from instruction to proto-biography simply exercised options available within sayings genres in general.'[3]

Although Kloppenborg says very little about Matthew's gospel, his observations are relevant to discussions of its literary genre. At first sight Matthew seems to have 'destroyed' Q, both by incorporating it into the Marcan biographical framework, and also by re-arranging its order and by weaving Q with other traditions of the teaching of

---

[1] J. Kloppenborg, *The Formation of Q*, 280.
[2] J. Kloppenborg, *The Formation of Q*, 316. Kloppenborg cites A. Momigliano, *The Development of Greek Biography*, Cambridge Mass., 1971, 72-3.
[3] J. Kloppenborg, *The Formation of Q*, 328.

Jesus. But in his development of the genre of Q (and in many other respects[1]) Matthew is not a radical innovator. In terms of their literary genre, Mark and Q are not as far apart as might be supposed, for as we have just seen, in antiquity biography and collections of the sayings of an individual were closely related.[2]

In his five discourses Matthew has preserved (at least in part) the genre of Q. Luke may have retained the original order of Q much more faithfully than Matthew, but the five Matthean discourses not only extend the contents of parts of Q, they have the same external literary form and internal structural organization as Q itself.

The evangelist himself draws attention to the discourses as collections of the sayings of Jesus. In his conclusions (or transitional comments) at the end of three of them, he writes ὅτε ἐτέλεσεν ὁ Ἰησοῦς τοὺς λόγους τούτους, 'when Jesus had finished these sayings' (7. 28; 19. 1; 26. 1; slightly different wording is used at 11. 1 and 13. 53). At the end of the fifth discourse πάντας, 'all', is added, thus confirming that all five belong together as λόγοι τοῦ Ἰησοῦ, 'sayings of Jesus', a phrase which recalls the use of similar phrases in collections of sayings such as Proverbs 22. 17 – 24. 22; Proverbs 30 and 31; the Testaments of the Twelve Patriarchs; 'Abot; Didache 1. 3 – 2. 1; the Gospel of Thomas.[3]

The Matthean discourses, like Q itself, are collections of sayings of Jesus which are linked together sometimes by catchwords, sometimes by the literary form of the individual units, sometimes by theme. Kloppenborg claims that Q ranks

---

[1] See below, Chapter 14.

[2] The general point being made in this section would not be effected if M. Sato's understanding of the genre of Q were to be preferred to J. Kloppenborg's. Whereas for Kloppenborg prophetic traditions in Q are subsidiary to wisdom traditions, for Sato precisely the reverse is the case. Collections of prophetic traditions, just like collections of wisdom traditions, tended to develop biographical traits. See M. Sato, *Q und Prophetie*, Tübingen 1988.

[3] This was first noted by J.M. Robinson, 'LOGOI SOPHON: On the Gattung of Q', in J.M. Robinson and H. Koester, *Trajectories through Early Christianity*, Philadelphia 1971, 71-113.

with the most highly organized and structured of the chreiae collections, even though in neither case are they rhetorically structured to lead to a conclusion.[1] The same is true of the five Matthean discourses, though there is scope for further research at this point.

We may conclude, then, that Matthew has extended the literary genres of both his main sources. For all their obvious differences, both Mark and Q have biographical features. In his combination, revision, and extension of them Matthew has written a gospel which is even closer than Mark to the Graeco-Roman biographical tradition.[2]

Like many ancient biographers, Matthew sets out the life of Jesus in order to persuade readers of his significance. Matthew takes pains to emphasize that the disciples of Jesus (and his later followers) proclaim the same message as Jesus (10. 7, cf. 4. 17; 28. 20) and act in the same ways (10. 8, cf. chs. 8 and 9); there is a strong implication that they will share the

---

[1] *The Formation of Q*, 325.

[2] In her excellent study, *Sowing the Gospel*, Mary Ann Tolbert has recently proposed that the genre and literary strategies of Mark are closer to the ancient novel than to ancient biographies (59-70). In my view the differences in form and content between the gospels and ancient novels are much more striking than the similarities. Unlike the gospels, ancient novels were intended primarily to provide entertainment (which often included titillation), for in antiquity there was little appreciation of the modern commonplace that fiction is instructive about the human condition. Tolbert shows that Mark and the ancient romances do share some literary conventions. Most of them, however, are also found in biographical writings. Tolbert's reasons for setting biography aside in discussion of the genre of Mark (58-9) are inadequate and apply even less to Matthew than to Mark. Mary Ann Beavis also considers Mark against the background of ancient novels, but correctly links Mark more closely with the biographical tradition; see her *Mark's Audience*, 35-9. In addition to the literature on the Greek romances cited by Tolbert, see P.G. Walsh, *The Roman Novel. The Satyricon of Petronius and the Metamorphoses of Apuleius*, Cambridge 1970; E.L. Bowie, 'The Greek Novel' in *The Cambridge History of Classical Literature* I, eds. P.E. Easterling and B.M.W. Knox, Cambridge 1985, 683-98; Graham Anderson, *Ancient Fiction. The Novel in the Graeco-Roman World*, London and Totawa, NJ. 1984.

same fate as Jesus (5. 11; 10. 18, 25; 23. 34). There is a sense in which even though Jesus as Son of God is clearly set apart from his followers, his story is their story.[1]

Since ancient writers frequently wrote with apologetic and polemical aims,[2] we shall not be surprised to find in Part II of this book that Matthew also does so. D.E. Aune perceptively notes that 'the unconscious functions of Greco-Roman biography involve the historical legitimation (or discrediting) of a social belief / value system personified in the subject of the biography.'[3] This is precisely the social function I envisage for Matthew's biography of Jesus.

The conclusion that Matthew is an ancient biography is important for current discussion of the appropriate methods for study of the gospels. Since the ancient biographers gave prominence to character portrayal for blame or praise, the recent interest of narrative critics in Matthew's character portraits is certainly not out of place. However they have looked to modern literary theorists for insight into the evangelist's methods of characterization and have failed to note that some of the techniques used by modern writers were unknown in antiquity.

In ancient biographical writing (including Matthew) there is a deeply-rooted convention that a person's actions and words sum up the character of an individual more adequately than the comments of an observer.[4] In his own direct

---

[1] A.T. Lincoln stresses that readers of Matthew are encouraged to emulate the disciples rather than Jesus the Son of God. See his valuable study, 'Matthew – a Story for Teachers', in *The Bible in Three Dimensions*, eds. D.J.A. Clines, S.E. Fowl, and S.E. Porter, Sheffield 1990, 103-26. Although Matthew's Jesus is undeniably unique, there are nonetheless many ways in which his followers are encouraged to emulate him. See also D.B. Howell, *Matthew's Inclusive Story*, 249-59.

[2] See R.A. Burridge, *What are the Gospels?* 151 and 187-8 for examples.

[3] *The New Testament in its Literary Environment*, London 1988, 35.

[4] See, for example, Xenophon, *Memorabilia*, I, iii, 1; Isocrates, *Evagoras* 76; Aristotle, *Rhetoric*, I.ix.33, 1367b. For a fuller discussion, see G.N. Stanton, *Jesus of Nazareth in New Testament Preaching*, 122ff. For recent studies, see *Characterization and Individuality in Greek Literature*, ed. C.B.R. Pelling, Oxford 1990.

comments to the reader Matthew does occasionally link carefully the actions and words of Jesus (4. 23 and 9. 35), but by and large they are simply juxtaposed and allowed to speak for themselves. Psychological analysis of character traits and interest in the development of an individual's personality are commonplace in modern biographies and in modern novels, but both are largely missing in ancient writers.

Matthew's use of extended discourses and his frequent topical arrangement of material are both found in many ancient biographies. Lucian's *Life of Demonax* and Plutarch's *Life of Cato the Elder* 7-9 are good examples. However, as a result of paying more attention to the story-telling techniques of modern novelists than to the methods of ancient biographers, narrative critics have emphasized the 'story-line' and plot of Matthew at the expense of doing justice to his five extended discourses.[1] Like many ancient biographers, Matthew was concerned to give particular prominence to the sayings of Jesus (28. 20a).

The first audience

Contemporary reader response critics insist that the meaning of a text cannot be understood apart from the response of its readers.[2] Although they all emphasize strongly the close relationship of text and reader, that relationship is understood in several quite different ways.

---

[1] In the first edition of his *Matthew as Story* (1986), J.D. Kingsbury had little to say about the five discourses. In the second edition (1988) he added a chapter on them, 106-14. Although several helpful observations are made, their importance is underplayed. In his *Matthew's Inclusive Story*, Sheffield 1990, D.B. Howell pays scant attention to Matthew's discourses; the Sermon on the Mount receives only two paragraphs, the other four a paragraph each.

[2] See Jane P. Tompkins' introduction to the seminal essays she has edited, *Reader-Response Criticism. From Formalism to Post-Structuralism*, Baltimore and London 1980, ix-xxvi. See also James L. Resseguie, 'Reader-Response Criticism and the Synoptic Gospels', *JAAR* 52 (1984) 307-24.

These on-going theoretical discussions provide welcome stimulus to Biblical scholars concerned with the appropriation today of writings deemed by communities of faith to be authoritative. The jargon used by literary critics is new, but many of the issues are not. Those who have wrestled with Bultmann's insistence on the crucial role played by the presuppositions and the pre-understanding of the interpreter will feel that they have been here before.[1]

Although some Biblical scholars who have taken an interest in reader response criticism have failed to distinguish between the response of the original recipients of Matthew and the response of modern readers, I am convinced that it is important to do so.[2] My primary concern is to insist on the importance of the socio-historical setting of the original audience for the interpretation of Matthew. I take it for granted that their responses offer invaluable guidance to modern readers, but I do not accept that the meaning of a text for modern readers is *determined* either by the author's original intention or by the response of the original audience.

I now wish to discuss briefly three general issues which are important in any consideration of the responses to Matthew of the first recipients.

(i) My insistence on the circumstances of the original readers is not the blind prejudice of a Biblical scholar wedded solely to traditional historical scholarship. Many contemporary literary theorists also emphasize the extent to which meaning is determined by the particular social context of readers.[3]

---

[1] See G.N. Stanton, 'Presuppositions in New Testament Criticism' in *New Testament Interpretation*, ed. I.H. Marshall, Exeter 1977, 60-74.

[2] So Stephen Moore, *Literary Criticism and the Gospels*, 99. In her *Mark's Audience*, 16f., Mary Ann Beavis rightly criticizes R.M. Fowler's influential study *Loaves and Fishes: The Function of the Feeding Stories in the Gospel of Mark*, SBLDS 54, Missoula 1981, for setting aside the question of what the original (historical) reader of Mark was like. 'His 'reader' is a sort of trans-historical entity, unaffected by factors of place, time, and culture. . .'

[3] See Jane Tompkins, *Reader-Response Criticism*, and the references given by M.A. Beavis, *Mark's Audience*, 16.

If we insist on the importance for interpretation of the socio-historical circumstances of the readers of a text, how are they to be determined? The text itself will provide some clues, but the text alone is inadequate. In the case of Matthew, a close reading of the text alone will not take us very far. In order to uncover the conventions and assumptions shared by the evangelist and his readers, it is necessary to use all the historical, philological and social-scientific tools at our disposal in order to set Matthew's gospel as firmly as possible in the context of earliest Christianity in the first century Graeco-Roman and Jewish worlds. Here is a further reminder that a 'text immanent' approach is a blind alley for interpreters of ancient texts.

This important point may be illustrated by a specific example. Close attention to the 'story world' of Matthew alone will not enable us to appreciate why and how he uses apocalyptic imagery. Many individual sayings and incidents will baffle us unless they are set in the context of first century Jewish (or Christian) teaching. In Part II of this book I hope to show that by elucidating the social setting of Matthew as fully as possible – and I do not underestimate the difficulty of that task – we are able to read the gospel with greater sensitivity and appreciation.

(ii) I turn now to a quite different aspect of the relationship of the first recipients to the text. Classical scholars have noted for some time that reading in the Graeco-Roman world was 'predominantly reading aloud, performance in fact.'[1]. Since the evangelists wrote in Greek, they shared the general literary conventions of their day, conventions which were by no means confined to the upper strata of society. Hence the gospels were almost certainly intended for *oral performance*, not silent personal study. Biblical scholars have rarely

---

[1] B.M.W. Knox in *The Cambridge History of Classical Literature* I, Cambridge 1985, 7-10. See also Knox's important article, 'Silent Reading in Antiquity', *GRBS* 9 (1968) 421-35. Knox has challenged the assumption of some classicists that *all* reading in antiquity was reading aloud; hence his use of 'predominantly' in the quotation above.

appreciated this fact.[1] When the first recipients are under discussion, we need to bear in mind that there were many more listeners than readers.

This observation raises two further issues, though more research is urgently need. (a) Attention has regularly been drawn to the distinctive stylistic features of Matthew: his repetition of favourite words, phrases, formulas, and even whole sentences; his use of triads of different kinds; his fondness for *inclusio, chiasmus,* and foreshadowing; his collections of similar material (e.g. miracle stories, parables, sayings of Jesus).[2] Why did Matthew use all these (and other) stylistic techniques so extensively? This question is rarely asked; when it is, attention is usually drawn to parallels in Old Testament narratives. There may be another answer: the evangelist may have used them because he considered that they were all appropriate for the oral delivery of his story of Jesus. Indeed it is hard to think of a single Matthean stylistic technique which would be more appropriate for silent study than for reading aloud.

(b) My suggestion that Matthew probably intended his gospel to be read aloud may provide an answer to another enigma. A great deal of scholarly energy has been invested in

---

[1] M.A. Tolbert, *Sowing the Gospel,* has recently drawn attention to this important point. She quotes Quintilian to good effect (45 n.36): 'It is one and the same thing to speak well and to write well: and a written speech is merely the record of a delivered speech.' (*Institutio oratoria* 12.10.51). What Werner Kelber (*The Oral and the Written Gospel,* Philadelphia 1983) calls the 'oral legacy' of Mark, Tolbert correctly sees as Mark's rhetorical intention. See also M.A. Beavis, *Mark's Audience,* 19-20.

Both Tolbert and Beavis assume that 'reading aloud' was universal in antiquity. The claim (to which Tolbert refers, 44 n.35) that the first person in antiquity who is reported to have read aloud without sound was St Ambrose has been called in question by B.M.W. Knox. Tolbert is unaware of Knox's careful discussion referred to in the previous note; Beavis lists it in her Bibliography, but does not discuss it.

[2] See the commentaries of W.D. Davies and D.C. Allison (I, 72-96) and U. Luz (I, 37-41) for thorough discussions with references to examples in Matthew and scholarly studies.

discussion of the overall structure of Matthew.[1] Several very different proposals enjoy strong support; there is still no agreement.[2]

There are numerous 'structural markers' in shorter sections of the text of Matthew, but it is difficult to discern which of these (if any) are intended to mark the major divisions of the gospel as a whole. Perhaps this phenomenon is the outcome of the composition of the gospel for oral delivery. Since it would take about three hours to read the whole gospel aloud, it was probably read in shorter sections, the length of which varied from time to time.[3] Both readers and listeners would appreciate the care the evangelist took with the structure of shorter sections, but the division of the whole gospel into three, four, or five major sections was less important. Readers and listeners both knew the overall 'story line'; on any given occasion the story could be resumed at many different points.

Further research is clearly needed into the differences between stylistic techniques appropriate for oral delivery of a narrative text and those appropriate for silent personal study of a written text.[4] The reception of Matthew in the early

---

[1] See D.B. Bauer's appraisal of the proposals in *The Structure of Matthew's Gospel. A Study in Literary Design*, JSNTSS 31, Sheffield 1988, 21-56; also G.N. Stanton, 'Origin and Purpose', *ANRW* II.25.3, 1903-6.

[2] J.D. Kingsbury's claim that Matt 4. 17 and 16. 21 are the primary structural markers and an important key to the evangelist's overall purpose has now won significant support. See his *Structure*, 7-25, and more recent writings. U. Luz (*Matthäus*, I, 18 n. 12) shrewdly notes that there are as many similar verbal similarities in 5. 17 and 10. 34 as there are in 4. 17 and 16. 21, but noone has yet proposed that these verses introduce the main sections of the gospel. Luz divides the gospel into three sections: 1. 1 – 4. 22; 4.23 – 11. 30; 12. 1 – 28. 20.

[3] This is exactly how the 'memoirs of the apostles' were used in Justin's day (*I Apology* 67): sections were read 'as long as time permits'.

[4] See H. Parunak's important article, 'Oral Typesetting: Some Uses of Biblical Structure', *Biblica* 62 (1981) 153-68. I owe this reference to Ms Bridget Upton.

church has been studied intensively,[1] but the *ways* the gospel was used will repay further study. For example, there are divisions and structural markers in some uncial manuscripts of Matthew. Are any of them intended to assist those who read the gospel aloud? In what settings is the gospel likely to have been used? Many have claimed that Matthew was used primarily in worship, but its use in formal and informal instruction is just as likely.

(iii) Reader response critics often set out a close reading of a work of modern fiction from the standpoint of a first-time reader. Several attempts have now been made to read the gospels from this perspective, in the case of Matthew most notably by R.E. Edwards.[2] But once we consider the ways Matthew's gospel was encountered for the first time by the first recipients, this becomes an exercise of doubtful value. Christians (or non-Christians for that matter) are unlikely to have become acquainted with Matthew by means of an oral performance of the whole gospel. They are much more likely to have heard shorter sections. They may well have been acquainted with Mark's gospel before Matthew's. In other words, for most of the first recipients, Matthew's gospel was an extended commentary on what the original readers and listeners already knew. Hence the story-line and the plot contained few surprises.

Once again the question of genre is important. The initial expectations and responses of the first *listeners* to Matthew's biography are likely to have been very different from the 'virginal responses' of a first-time *reader* of a modern novel, short story, or poem.

---

[1] See E. Massaux, *Influence de l'Évangile de St. Matthieu sur la littérature chrétienne avant St. Irénée*, Louvain 1950; W.-D. Köhler, *Die Rezeption des Matthäusevangeliums in der Zeit vor Irenäus*, Tübingen 1987.

[2] *Matthew as Story*. See also J.L. Staley, *The Print's First Kiss: A Rhetorical Investigation of the Implied Reader in the Fourth Gospel*, SBLDS 82, Atlanta 1988; Stephen Moore, *Literary Criticism and the Gospels*, 79ff.

Rhetorical strategies

Matthew uses a large number of rhetorical strategies in order to persuade his readers and listeners of the significance of both the story of Jesus and of his teaching. Many stylistic techniques were recognized by exegetes long before the advent of recent literary approaches. Most of them can be paralleled without difficulty in narrative and biographical traditions in Old Testament and later Jewish writings, and also in Graeco-Roman writings.[1]

Recent narrative critical studies of Matthew have drawn attention to several further literary techniques: the point of view of the implied author; his direct 'asides' to the implied reader; the ways the implied reader is encouraged to associate herself or himself with some characters in the story, but not others; and the use of an even wider range of compositional patterns than had been recognized earlier. Discussions of these rhetorical strategies have greatly enriched our appreciation of the gospel. Although I am arguing that recent narrative critical studies of Matthew have paid insufficient attention to ancient narrative and biographical traditions, in these cases consideration of ancient stylistic techniques would refine but not undermine their observations.[2]

I now wish to draw attention to Matthew's use of σύγκρισις, 'comparison', a rhetorical strategy which has

---

[1] For recent studies of the use of Graeco-Roman rhetorical strategies by NT writers, see B.L. Mack and V.K. Robbins, *Patterns of Persuasion in the Gospels*, Sonoma Calif. 1989; Burton L. Mack, *Rhetoric and the New Testament*, Minneapolis 1990; Duane Watson, ed., *Persuasive Artistry: Studies in NT Rhetoric in Honour of George A. Kennedy*, Sheffield 1991.

[2] For example, see Tomas Hägg, *Narrative Technique in Ancient Greek Romances. Studies of Chariton, Xenophon Ephesius, and Achilles Tatius*, Stockholm 1972. Hägg notes that in their search for characteristics common to all narratives, some modern literary critics have given attention to ancient narratives. Hägg himself draws attention to some of the ways in which the techniques and conventions of ancient and modern writers differ. See his 'preliminary remarks' which preface most of his chapters.

largely been overlooked in recent discussion.[1] Although this technique is not unknown in modern writings, by comparison with the ancient world its use is rare.[2]

Instruction and practice in σύγκρισις formed part of the προγυμνάσματα, 'preliminary exercises', in education in rhetoric. Thorough expositions of σύγκρισις are found in the rhetorical handbooks.[3] For example, in a very detailed treatise Aelius Theon (who probably wrote at the end of the first century A.D.) notes that comparison is a form of speech which contrasts the better and the worse; comparisons are drawn between people, and between things; comparisons are not drawn between people who are vastly different.[4]

[1] My predecessor at King's College, Christopher Evans, first drew my attention to the importance of σύγκρισις for students of the New Testament many years ago. See now his fine study, 'The Theology of Rhetoric: the Epistle to the Hebrews', a lecture given to the Friends of Dr. Williams's Library, published by Dr. Williams's Trust, 1988. See also C. Forbes, 'Comparison, Self-Praise and Irony: Paul's Boasting and the Conventions of Hellenistic Rhetoric', NTS 32 (1986) 1-30.

[2] As far as I am aware, only two writers have drawn attention to Matthew's possible use of σύγκρισις. In 'Vilifying the Other and Defining the Self. Matthew's and John's Anti-Judaism in Focus' in 'To see ourselves as others see us'. Jews, Christians, 'Others' in Antiquity ed. J. Neusner and E.S. Frerichs, Missoula 1985, 130-1, S. Freyne comments in one paragraph on the evangelist's use of unfavourable comparison in order to distance himself and his community from Jewish opponents. P. Shuler has a more extended discussion in A Genre for the Gospel, 99-103; he refers to the comparison between Jesus and John the Baptist, and Jesus and his opponents, but not to the other passages discussed below. Shuler's discussion of the role of σύγκρισις in encomium biography is helpful, but he does not note its widespread use in other kinds of writings.

D.R. Bauer includes a chapter on Matthew's repetition of comparisons (comparisons between the mission of Jesus and the mission of the disciples; and between the ethical behaviour of Jesus and the ethical expectations for the disciples), but he does not seem to be aware of the importance of σύγκρισις in antiquity. See The Structure of Matthew, JSNTSS 31, Sheffield 1988, 57-63.

[3] For a full discussion, see S.F. Bonner, Education in Ancient Rome, London 1977, 250-76. σύγκρισις is discussed on 267.

[4] See the lengthy quotation from Theon cited by C. Forbes, 'Paul's Boasting', NTS 32 (1986) 6.

The origins of the προγυμνάσματα are disputed, but there is little doubt that by the first century B.C. the standard set of exercises was fairly complete; by then they were being used by teachers of rhetoric in Latin.[1] At the time Matthew wrote, it is not clear whether instruction in the techniques of 'comparison' was part of general secondary education, or whether it was reserved for the more advanced instruction given by rhetoricians.[2] But there is no doubt at all about the pervasive influence of rhetorical conventions. 'The rhetorical theory of the schools found its immediate application in almost every form of oral and written communication: in official documents and public letters, in private correspondence, in the law courts and assemblies, in speeches at festivals and commemorations, and in literary composition in both prose and verse.'[3]

σύγκρισις was widely used in encomia and in other types of biography, but it was not confined to this form of writing. The formal comparisons at the end of many of Plutarch's parallel lives of famous Greek and Romans provide good examples of the widespread convention.[4] A carefully constructed short comparison is used to establish the difference between them, or the superiority of one over the other.

It is highly likely that Matthew would have known about the uses of 'comparison', even if he did not receive formal instruction in rhetoric. Even if the evangelist's early education in a Jewish setting was followed by training as a scribe, the standard of his Greek suggests that he was well-educated and that he was probably familiar with at least the basic principles of rhetoric.[5] Since rhetoric permeated all

---

1 S.F. Bonner, *Education*, 250-1.
2 S.F. Bonner, *Education*, 251; C. Forbes, 'Paul's Boasting', *NTS* 32 (1986) 7.
3 G.A. Kennedy, *New Testament Interpretation Through Rhetorical Criticism*, Chapel Hill, N.C. 1984, 13. See also H.I. Marrou, *A History of Education in Antiquity*, New York 1956; Mentor edition 1964, 297-300.
4 S.F. Bonner, *Education*, 267, suggests that the comparisons at the end of the *Lives* would have been useful for school exercises, though evidence is lacking.
5 M. Hengel notes that even the master-pupil relationship in the rabbinate, with its dialectical form of instruction, may have been

levels of society, it is likely that the evangelist's readers and listeners would have been far more attuned to and impressed by comparisons than are modern readers.

I shall now discuss the main comparisons the evangelist draws in order to show that he has used this technique carefully and deliberately as a rhetorical strategy.

(i) For Jews there was no greater individual than Moses. Philo had even called him a θεός; his 'story' was widely known in the Gentile world. Matthew's repeated allusions to the similarities between Jesus and Moses would have been of considerable interest to a first century audience. Of course the superiority of Jesus is made clear by the claim that he is the Son of God. But that claim is underpinned by the sustained comparison with Moses: Jesus is strikingly similar to Moses, yet greater.[1]

The allusions to the story of Moses are clear in Matt 2. 13-23. They become clearer still in the phraseology of 5. 1 (and 8. 1): like Moses, Jesus 'went up on the mountain' in order that God might speak to his people through him (cf. Exod 19. 3, 12; 24. 15, 18; 34. 1-4). The so-called antitheses in 5. 21-48 clarify the relationship of Jesus to Moses. In these passages the teaching of Jesus is not antithetical to the teaching of Moses. The new commandments given authoritatively by the new Moses to the new people do not repudiate the law of Moses: they *extend* both the scope and the principles of the law. The sayings of Jesus are 'greater than' the law (cf. 7. 24-9; 28. 20).

influenced by the model of the Greek rhetorical schools. *Judaism and Hellenism* I, E.tr. London 1974, 81; see his full discussion of Greek education in Palestine, and of the development of the Jewish school, 70-83; also 104-5.

C. Forbes, 'Paul's Boasting', NTS 32 (1986) 4 and 25-6, notes that Philo uses comparison 26 times and stresses that comparisons require a basis of similarity before they can be legitimate comparisons.

[1] Dale C. Allison notes that many exegetes have drawn the opposite conclusion and claimed that obvious differences between Jesus and Moses suggest that the evangelist was not interested in the similarities. Allison rightly asks, 'What more could be said of a man than that he was like Moses? Given Moses' unrivalled stature . . . the parallels between the two figures were not just there for the sake of the differences.' 'Gnilka on Matthew', *Biblica* 70 (1989) 532.

80

(ii) The evangelist pays much more attention than Mark or Q to the similarities between Jesus and John the Baptist. Jesus and John preach the same message (3. 2 and 4. 17; 3. 10 and 7. 19). Together they are carrying out God's saving plan (3. 15). Like Jesus, John came to Israel 'in the way of righteousness' and was welcomed by tax collectors and sinners but not by 'this generation' (11. 19 and 21. 32). Like John, Jesus too will suffer and die at the hands of evil men (17. 12b and 13); in these two redactional sentences Matthew makes explicit a comparison which is barely hinted at in Mark (17. 12b: οὕτως καί, 'so also').

Why are the similarities between Jesus and John stressed so strongly? A first century audience accustomed to comparisons between two worthy individuals would draw the obvious conclusion from this sustained comparison. John is the one who is more than a prophet (11. 9), who is unrivalled by those born of women (11. 11a), and who is the promised returning Elijah (11. 14; 17. 12-13). In many respects Jesus is strikingly similar to John – but he is even greater.

(iii) In 5. 20, an important redactional verse, disciples of Jesus are told that their righteousness must 'surpass by far' (περισσεύσῃ πλεῖον) that of the scribes and Pharisees. In 5. 46 and 47 the comparison is extended to include tax collectors and Gentiles. In the latter verse the comparison is made more explicit than it is in the corresponding Q tradition (Luke 6. 33) and the phraseology of 5. 20 is recalled (περισσόν - περισσεύσῃ). In 6. 1-18 there is a comparison between the hypocrites' ways of carrying out almsgiving, prayer, and fasting, and the practices expected of disciples. Direct comparison between the behaviour of disciples and that of Jewish religious leaders is made once again at 23. 5-12.

These comparisons are all intended to establish that the ethical conduct of disciples must be superior to that of their opponents.

(iv) In Matt 10 the evangelist compares Jesus and the disciples. They preach the same message (cf. 4. 17 and 10. 7) and carry out the same healings and exorcisms (cf. chapters 8 - 9 and 10. 8). At 10. 24 Matthew extends a Q comparison (Luke 6. 40) between a pupil and his teacher. He makes the Q logion into a double comparison by adding a comparison between a servant and his master. This is done in order to prepare for the important redactional saying added at 10. 25b: 'If they have called the master of the house Beelzebul, how much more (πόσῳ μᾶλλον) will they malign those of his household.' In the preceding verses the disciples have been warned that they are to expect rejection and persecution. Now they are told that they are to expect *even greater* abuse than that heaped upon Jesus himself, abuse which has been referred to explicitly at 9. 34.[1]

(v) In Matt 12 no fewer than four direct comparisons are made. In v. 40 Matthew extends the Q logion about the sign of Jonah and he draws out (redactionally) the striking similarity between Jesus and Jonah: 'as Jonah was three days and three nights in the belly of the whale, so will the Son of man be three days and three nights in the heart of the earth.' For Matthew this comparison is extremely important: this is the only reference Jesus makes to his death and resurrection in the presence of Jewish leaders. It foreshadows the strongly ironical (and redactional) 27. 63 where the Pharisees inform Pilate that Jesus had told them about his resurrection while he was still alive.

The two Q comparisons between Jesus and Jonah, and between Jesus and the queen of the south follow (12. 41 and 42; cf. Luke 11. 31-2). They lead to the same conclusion: something greater than Jonah, and greater than Solomon is here. In each case the neuter comparative πλεῖον, 'something greater than', is used. But since these sayings are immediately preceded by a direct comparison between the person of Jesus and the person of Jonah (v. 41), it is clear that in Matthew (though probably not in Q, where they are in the reverse order) direct comparisons are made between Jesus on the one hand, and Jonah and Solomon on the other: Jesus is greater than both.

Earlier in chapter 12 the evangelist himself extends the pattern of 12. 41-2 and makes an even more striking comparison in his addition to a Marcan tradition: λέγω δὲ ὑμῖν ὅτι τοῦ

---

[1] For a fuller discussion of Matt 9. 34 and 10. 25, see below, Chapter 7.

ἱεροῦ μεῖζόν ἐστιν ὧδε, 'something greater than the temple is here' (12. 6). Exegetes have puzzled over the neuter comparative μεῖζόν, 'something greater than'. In view of the similar direct personal comparisons drawn in 12. 41 and 42, a reference to Jesus himself seems probable. Matthew's audience would have been well-acquainted with the greatness of the temple. There is no anti-temple polemic here. Matthew uses the comparison to make a striking Christological claim: Jesus himself is greater than the temple.

σύγκρισις seems to us today to be an unsophisticated rhetorical strategy. But its widespread use in all kinds of writings in the Graeco-Roman world and its prominence in education confirm that it was one of the more important techniques writers used to persuade their audiences. The use of comparisons in Matthew can hardly be compared with their use in Hebrews, where, as C.F. Evans has noted, 'the theme of comparison may be said to be stamped on the epistle at the start, and to control its argument.'[1] Nonetheless their use in Matthew is striking, the more so when we bear in mind that unlike the author of Hebrews, the evangelist was deeply dependent on two major sources.

Matthew has developed considerably comparisons he found in a handful of Q logia. In some cases he has extended or sharpened a Q saying, in others he has developed a comparison *de novo* in Marcan or Q passages he is using. Once again redaction criticism has proved to be a useful ally in our literary critical discussion.

Matthew's usage reflects that found in Graeco-Roman writings. The evangelist uses σύγκρισις to establish the difference between disciples and Jewish leaders by making unfavourable comparisons. More usually, as is the case generally in Graeco-Roman writings, his comparisons are favourable: Jesus is superior to Moses, to John the Baptist, to the temple, to Jonah, and to Solomon. The comparisons are not used in order to denigrate the lesser of the two, but in order to enhance the greater in the eyes of the audience.

---

[1] 'The Theology of Rhetoric', 9, as cited above, 78.

Perhaps the most striking comparison is at 10. 25b: disciples (and followers of Jesus in the evangelist's day) are warned that they are to expect even greater abuse than Jesus himself received. That saying surely reflects not only the first century literary setting of Matthew I have proposed in this chapter, but also the social setting which is explored in the chapters which follow.

In this chapter I have discussed a wide range of issues which arise as soon as Matthew is considered from a literary perspective. Recent literary studies mark a significant advance in our appreciation of Matthew's gospel. I have insisted on the importance of giving close attention to the literary genre of Matthew, to the literary conventions of antiquity, and to the rhetorical strategies the evangelist used in order to communicate with his first century readers and listeners. When this is done, several of the observations of scholars who have written on Matthew from a literary perspective are called in question, but the value of many of their other observations is enhanced further.

Chapter Four

Matthew's Gospel and the Damascus Document in Sociological Perspective

Over the last two decades or so the New Testament writings have been studied fruitfully from several social-scientific perspectives. Studies of Matthew's gospel from these new vantage points, however, have been few and far between. The contrast with the numerous literary critical studies which were referred to in the previous chapter is striking.[1]

In this chapter I hope to show that Matthew's gospel is particularly well-suited to careful use of sociological insights; they complement redaction critical and literary critical approaches. I accept that in studies of ancient writings social history should normally take precedence over sociological insights. Matthew's gospel, however, does not lend itself readily to a social historical approach. Whereas many details in Paul's correspondence with the Corinthians, for example, can be set firmly in the social setting of Corinth in the middle of the first century, we do not know for certain where Matthew wrote. Although many writers accept that Matthew

---

[1] An exception, however, is B.J. Malina and J.H. Neyrey, *Calling Jesus Names. The Social Value of Labels in Matthew*, Sonoma Calif. 1988. The authors utilize the anthropological models of witchcraft societies to interpret the accusations levelled against Jesus in chapter 12. In the second part of the book they draw on labelling and deviance theory in a study of Matthew's passion narratives in chapters 26 and 27. Although I think that Malina's and Neyrey's case would have been strengthened by more rigorous use of redaction criticism, their book is stimulating and perceptive.

was written in Antioch, the evidence is far from conclusive.[1]
We know a good deal both about earliest Christianity in
Antioch,[2] and also about the city itself.[3] But even if we could
be certain about the geographical setting of the gospel, a
further problem would remain. The social historian's eye
often alights on incidental details, but it is difficult to know
whether such details in Matthew reflect the social setting of
the earlier traditions used by the evangelist, or his own social
setting.

In spite of occasional objections, many Biblical scholars
now accept that careful use of sociological insights is an
invaluable complement to traditional historical methods.[4]
Although as yet there have been few studies of Matthew
from this perspective, I am convinced of its potential.[5]

---

[1] See G.N. Stanton, 'Origin and Purpose', in *ANRW* II. 25.3, 1941-2 for
discussion of the geographical setting of Matthew. U. Luz accepts that
Antioch 'is not the worst hypothesis', but leaves the question open: the
gospel originated in a large Syrian city whose *lingua franca* was Greek.
Matthäus I, 73-5.

[2] See R.E. Brown and J.P. Meier, *Antioch and Rome. NT Cradles of
Catholic Christianity*, London 1983. In their preface (p. ix) the authors
concede that their attempt to set Matthew within the history of
earliest Christianity in Antioch is speculative.

[3] See especially, G. Downey, *A History of Antioch in Syria from Seleucus
to the Arab Conquest*, Princeton 1961.

[4] See, for example, chapter 5, 'Theology and the Social Sciences', in R.
Morgan with J. Barton, *Biblical Interpretation*, Oxford 1988, 133-66. In
his *Community and Gospel in Luke-Acts*, SNTSMS 57, Cambridge 1987,
12-16, P.F. Esler includes discussion of objections raised by E.A. Judge to
the use of the social sciences in study of the NT writings.

[5] For my own earlier attempt to use sociological considerations with
reference to Matthew, see Chapter 6, which was first published in 1984.
See also J. Riches, 'The Sociology of Matthew: Some Basic Questions
Concerning its Relation to the Theology of the New Testament', *SBL
Seminar Papers* (1983) 259-71; W.A. Meeks, 'Breaking Away: Three
New Testament Pictures of Christianity's Separation from the Jewish
Communities', in *"To see Ourselves as Others See Us": Christians, Jews,
"Others" in Late Antiquity*, eds. J. Neusner and E.S. Frerichs, Chico
Calif 1985, 93-116; J.A. Overman, *Matthew's Gospel and Formative
Judaism*, Minneapolis 1990; B.T. Viviano, 'Social World and Community
Leadership: the Case of Matt 23. 1-12', *JSNT* 39 (1990) 3-21.

I do not think that it is possible to use sociological models to fill gaps in our historical knowledge, although some writers have done so, either consciously or unconsciously.[1] As sociologists in the tradition of Max Weber have repeatedly emphasized, sociological studies do not provide us with 'laws' which are applicable to all situations.[2] They are heuristic: they enable us to notice things about the evidence which we might otherwise overlook. They enrich historical study; at best, they may provide support for particular historical hypotheses or reconstructions. In short, they enable us to read Matthew's gospel more sensitively by clarifying its social setting.

In this chapter I shall use two complementary approaches. Sociological theory regularly makes use of 'models' which are constructed on the basis of cross-cultural studies of a wide range of phenomena from different historical periods.[3] These 'distant comparisons' are based on sets of similarities in the behaviour of individuals, groups and communities in a range of cultural settings. In spite of obvious differences, striking recurrent patterns can be observed which are not specific to a particular culture or historical setting. They offer the student of first century writings possible fresh ways of reading the text by encouraging one to keep a keen look-out for further relationships, analogies and resemblances.[4]

Our limited knowledge of first century communities, however, is a serious constraint on the use of sociological theory. For example, at many points our knowledge of the first recipients of Matthew's gospel is based on disciplined imagination rather than 'hard facts'. Inevitably, there will be

[1] See, for example, John Gager, *Community and Kingdom: The Social World of Early Christianity*, Englewood Cliffs 1983, 4.

[2] See Max Weber, *The Methodology of the Social Sciences*, New York 1968, 90.

[3] P.F. Esler defines a model as 'a conceptualization of a group of phenomena, a simplified and schematized picture of reality, which is capable of generating a set of hypotheses which, once verified, may either found or substantiate a theory.' *Community and Gospel in Luke-Acts*, 9.

[4] The term 'distant comparisons' is taken from M. Duverger, *Introduction to the Social Sciences*, London 1964, 226.

a temptation to fill out the picture with the use of sociological theory.

Sociological models built up on the basis of 'distant comparisons' of cross-cultural social settings will rarely be sharply defined. 'Close comparisons', however, provide a useful complement to 'distant comparisons'. Careful consideration of communities which have similar cultural and historical settings is often instructive. Here the differences (which are rarely significant when 'distant comparisons' are used) cry out for explanation. The similarities in the social phenomena may provide confirmation of assumptions about a particular writing or community, and also a check against the obvious dangers in transferring insights drawn from studies of modern societies into first century settings.

In Chapter 6 I shall draw attention to some similarities Matthew's gospel shares with I Thessalonians, the Fourth Gospel, the Didache, and 5 Ezra. In the present chapter I shall set out a more extended 'close comparison' of Matthew's gospel with the Damascus Document from Qumran as a complement to the 'distant comparisons' sociological theory offers.[1] Matthew's gospel and the Damascus Document come from strikingly similar settings: they were both written for 'sectarian' communities which were in sharp conflict with parent bodies from which they had recently parted company painfully. Both writings functioned as 'foundation documents' for their respective communities; they used several strategies to 'legitimate' the separation.

The complementary use of 'distant' and 'close' comparisons which I have just sketched is analogous with my own views on the ways literary critical methods may be used in a 'reading' of an ancient writing such as Matthew's gospel. This is no coincidence. In both cases 'distant comparisons' (i.e. modern theoretical considerations) need to be complemented

---

[1] Matthew and the Damascus Document have been compared and contrasted from a very different perspective by T.R. Carmody, 'Matt 18: 15-17 in Relation to Three Texts from Qumran Literature (CD 9: 2-8, 16-22; IQS 5: 25 – 6:1)', *To Touch the Text* (FS J.A. Fitzmyer) eds. M.Y. Horgan and P.J. Kobelski, New York 1989, 141-58. Carmody claims that Matthew wrote 18. 15-17 as a rebuttal of the Essene view of law.

with 'close comparisons' from the first century A.D. Modern literary and sociological theory both fire the imagination of the jaded redaction critic. But as I stressed in the preceding chapter, modern literary conventions are not necessarily those of antiquity. And as we shall see in the present chapter, some of the most striking features of first century Jewish and Christian communities are *not* found in other historical and cultural settings.

My use of the Damascus Document as a 'close comparison' with Matthew will seem to some to be built on a circular argument. A particular interpretation of both writings is used to reconstruct the social settings from which they came. That reconstruction is then used to elucidate the writings themselves. I openly acknowledge the danger, but it is a danger which is inherent in all forms of redaction critical work – indeed in all forms of historical reconstruction and even of interpretation. It can be mitigated (but not avoided entirely) by scrutinizing the assumptions and presuppositions with which one is working and by considering alternative explanations of the evidence of the texts.

Sectarian communities

Ever since Ernst Troeltsch's work was published in 1911, the notion of sectarianism has been prominent in sociological discussion. It has been of particular interest to students of earliest Christianity, and to students of modern Christian 'denominationalism'. Although the studies of Troeltsch and later of Max Weber were based on an inadequate understanding of first century Judaism as the 'national church', a static and monolithic institution over against which Jesus arose as a charismatic reformer, the notion of sectarianism which they developed is still fruitful in discussion of some early Jewish and Christian writings.[1]

---

[1] For fuller discussion, see L.M. White, 'Shifting Sectarian Boundaries in Early Christianity', *BJRL* 70 (1988) 7-24, especially 7-9.

What is a sect? L.M. White has recently offered the following helpful cross-cultural definition of a 'sect' a 'deviant or separatist movement within a cohesive and religiously defined dominant culture. Thus despite expressed hostilities and exclusivism, the sect shares the same basic constellation of beliefs or 'worldview' of the dominant cultural idiom.'[1]

J. Blenkinsopp, who notes that sociologists of religion have found it extraordinarily difficult to come up with a definition, writes as follows:

> A sect is not only a minority, and not only characterized by opposition to norms accepted by the parent-body, but also claims in a more or less exclusive way to be what the parent-body claims to be. Whether such a group formally severs itself, or is excommunicated, will depend largely on the degree of self-definition attained by the parent-body and the level of tolerance obtaining within it.[2]

Although Blenkinsopp modestly notes that his comments should not be taken as a definition of a sect, they sum up admirably the characteristics of many groups in second temple Judaism and in earliest Christianity. Blenkinsopp goes on to stress that once they have begun to go their own

---

[1] 'Shifting Sectarian Boundaries', 14. White notes that Bryan Wilson's influential studies of sects are based almost entirely on pluralistic tendencies within the cultural framework of contemporary Christianity; his typology does not fit so neatly all the types of splinter groups one sees in first century Judaism; much less to the complexities of religious life in the larger Roman Empire.
For Bryan Wilson's views, see, for example, *Religion in Sociological Perspective*, Oxford 1982; *The Social Dimensions of Sectarianism: Sects and New Religious Movements in Contemporary Society*, Oxford 1990. See also *Patterns of Sectarianism*, ed. B.R. Wilson, London 1967.

[2] 'Interpretation and the Tendency to Sectarianism: An Aspect of Second Temple History', in *Jewish and Christian Self-Definition* II, ed. E.P. Sanders, London 1981, 1-2.

way, sects can change their character very quickly, especially when they are successful.[1]

L.M. White's definition corresponds to the 'distant' comparisons I referred to above, while Blenkinsopp's comments are helpful for 'close comparisons'; together they provide a good base-line for our study of the Damascus Document and of Matthew.

1. The Damascus Document

There can be no doubt at all that the Damascus Document comes from a sectarian community. Most scholars accept that it was treasured by an Essene community which had parted company with the temple authorities in Jerusalem.

This conclusion, however, is called in question by the yawning gulf between Josephus's presentation of the Essenes and the self-understanding of the Qumran community which is presupposed by the Damascus Document. In the former there is not so much as a hint that the Essenes distanced themselves by sharp polemic from the Jerusalem authorities and saw themselves as minority sect hounded by the parent body. But this is precisely how the Qumran community saw itself. The gulf between the two views is usually bridged by claiming that for apologetic reasons Josephus presents the Essenes as a party with some quaint views rather than as a sect deeply at odds with its parent body.[2] While there may be some truth in this explanation, it does not account satisfactorily for the two very different portraits of Essenes.

---

[1] See also R. Scroggs, 'The Earliest Christian Communities as Sectarian Communities', in *Christianity, Judaism, and other Graeco-Roman Cults*, II, ed. J. Neusner, Leiden 1975, 1-23. Scroggs notes seven ways in which the earliest Christian movement fits the 'ideal type' of sect. See also R. Scroggs, 'The Sociological Interpretation of the New Testament: The Present State of Research', *NTS* 26 (1979-80) 164-79.

[2] For the relevant texts, see Todd S. Beall, *Josephus' Description of the Essenes Illustrated by the Dead Sea Scrolls*, SNTSMS 58, Cambridge 1988. Beall lists apparent discrepancies between Josephus and Qumran (129), but fails to list or discuss the most glaring difference noted above.

A more persuasive hypothesis has recently been set out by García Martínez who suggests that the origins of the Qumran group should be traced to a split produced within the Essene movement in consequence of which the group loyal to the Teacher of Righteousness was finally to establish itself in Qumran.[1] García Martínez suggests that some of the Qumran writings reflect Essene thought; some which stem from a period shortly after the parting of the ways with Essenism contain a characteristic halakhah but not a vision which is clearly differentiated from the Essenism which is its ultimate source; some are sectarian works which represent the thought and halakhah of Qumran in its most developed and typical form.

An important corollary follows: writings such as the Damascus Document and IQS which were treasured most highly as 'foundation documents' of the Qumran community incorporate elements from different periods in its history. The Damascus Document, for example, contains an Essene nucleus and a series of halakhic prescriptions from the formative period; both were reinterpreted once the community had been formed, and at a date certainly after the death of the Teacher of Righteousness.[2]

A partly published letter from Qumran seems to offer historical confirmation of this new explanation of Qumran origins. 4Q394-399, now usually abbreviated as MMT (derived from a phrase taken from its epilogue, 'some of the precepts of the Torah') is assumed by its editors to be a letter from a leader of the Qumran sect to the leader of its opponents.[3] Fragments of six copies of the work have been found; this suggests that the Qumran community considered this letter to be extremely important. The letter includes discussion of

---

[1] F. García Martínez, 'Qumran Origins and Early History: a Groningen Hypothesis', *Folia Orientalia* 25 (1988) 113-36.

[2] This particular suggestion is a refinement of a widely held view.

[3] See Elisha Qimron and John Strugnell, 'An Unpublished Halakhic Letter from Qumran', in *Biblical Archaeology Today: Proceedings of the International Congress on Biblical Archaeology, Jerusalem 1984*, Israel Exploration Society, Jerusalem; Israel Academy of Sciences and Humanities; with ASOR, 1985, 400-7.

about twenty halakhic topics on which the two communities differed and an appeal to the opponents that they should return to the 'true way'. As is usually the case with a sectarian community, its halakah was more strict than that of its opponents. (We may note Matt. 5. 20 and the antitheses in 5. 21-48 as a significant parallel.) The epilogue includes this comment: We have separated ourselves from the majority of the peo[ple...] from intermingling in these matters and from participating with them in these [matters].

Although García Martínez does not draw on sociological insights, they provide some confirmation for his hypothesis. On this view, the Damascus Document stems from a renewal or protest movement within Essenism which became a sect with a quite separate identity and tightly drawn boundaries. As often happens in sectarian communities, much of the 'worldview' of the parent body is retained, in spite of the development of the distinctive views which led to the parting of the ways. The new sectarian community has hijacked the claim of the parent body to be 'the true way'. The ferocious polemic directed at the parent body is part of the distancing process. In its final form the Damascus Document is a foundation document for the new community: it functioned as legitimation of the separation from Essenism.

I hope to show below (with examples from the text) that this way of reading the Damascus Document is illuminating and that it provides interesting insights for the student of Matthew's gospel. My comments will be based on acceptance of the García Martínez – Groningen hypothesis. However, a number of the sociological observations would still be of interest on the basis of alternative explanations of the origins of the Qumran community.

2. Matthew's gospel

Does Matthew's gospel also betray a sectarian outlook? For some this possibility is ruled out simply on the basis of knowledge or experience of inward looking or even bigoted modern sects. But in the light of the two descriptions of sects noted above, the issue is not settled quite so easily.

For some the openness of Matthew's gospel (especially to the Gentiles in 28. 18-20) and the breadth of the evangelist's theological vision seem far removed from the outlook of a sectarian. However, since sects need to recruit in order to survive, partly open community boundaries are typical. And the evidence which suggests a broad theological vision is counter-balanced, as we shall see, by contrary evidence; a similar juxtaposition of a broad theological vision and a sectarian outlook is found in John's gospel. Since sects often change their character quickly, especially when they are successful, the rapid dissemination and wide acceptance of Matthew within early Christianity do not tell against its sectarian origins.

The cumulative evidence from a sociological perspective for reading Matthew as a sectarian writing is strong. The evangelist and his readers have parted company with other strands of first century Judaism, especially Pharisaism (21. 43). They perceive themselves to be under threat of persecution from their opponents (5. 10-12; 10. 17f.; 21. 41-5; 22. 6f.; 23. 31-5), a somewhat beleaguered minority at odds with the parent body, and, to a certain extent, with the Gentile world (5. 47; 6. 7, 32; 10. 18, 22; 18. 7; 24. 9).[1] These are well-known features of sectarian groups, as are Matthew's emphasis on very stringent moral requirements (5. 20, 48; 18. 8-9; 19. 11-12) and the strong internal discipline of 'churches' (18. 5-19).[2] I shall set out in later sections of this chapter several further ways in which Matthew's gospel betrays its sectarian origins.

3. *Distancing from the parent body*

The opening lines of the Damascus Document use Biblical history, phraseology, and imagery to set out an account of the origins of the Qumran community. The very first line distinguishes sharply between the readers of the writing, 'those

---

[1] These themes and passages are discussed more fully in Chapters 5 – 11 of this book.

[2] See, for example, L.M. White, 'Shifting Sectarian Boundaries', and the writings of B.R. Wilson noted above.

who know what is right' and 'those who despise God'.[1] It soon becomes clear that the latter are the parent body, i.e. the Essenes who have 'turned aside from the way' and from 'the paths of righteousness' (CD I. 13, 16).

The Damascus Document opens with several positive references to the Essenes. Their origin is described as a 'root of (God's) planting' (I. 7) and by implication they are the heirs of the remnant preserved by God at the time of the exile (I. 4). They recognized their guilt before God and 'groped for the way for twenty years' (I. 8-10a); 'they sought God with a whole heart' (I. 10b). They were, however, 'like blind men' (I. 9).

The teacher of righteousness, who is raised up by God to declare his will, is contrasted sharply with the leader of the Essenes, 'a scoffer who dripped over Israel (from the context this is a reference to the Essenes) waters of lies, and led them astray in a trackless waste' (I. 14-15).[2] A highly rhetorical set of statements then catalogue the short-comings of the parent body: they have even transgressed God's covenant. The parent group has even opposed and persecuted 'all those who walked perfectly' (I. 20-1), i.e. the Qumran community which here perceives itself to be the faithful but beleaguered minority. The opening section of the Damascus Document concludes with a declaration of judgement on the parent body (I. 21b–II.1).[3]

---

[1] Unless indicated otherwise, I have cited M.A. Knibb's translation, *The Qumran Community*, Cambridge 1987.

[2] The scoffer is almost certainly to be identified with the individual referred to elsewhere in CD (and in other Qumran writings) as 'the liar' (XX. 15), 'the preacher of lies' (VIII. 13 = XIX. 25b-26a). See M.A. Knibb, *Qumran*, 23-4 and García Martínez, 'Qumran Origins', 124-5 for further details.

[3] The precise reasons for the parting of the ways between the Qumran community and the Essene movement are not important for my present purposes. García Martínez's summary is striking: 'The Teacher of Righteousness's consciousness of having received through divine revelation the correct interpretation of the Law led him to propound a series of ideological and legal positions (imminence of the last days, a particular festive calendar, the imperfection of the existing Temple and cult compared with what they should be, etc.) and of particular halakhoth conditioning daily life (MMT, 11QTemple) and to wish to

This sharp distancing of the minority group from the parent body is also found in several other sections of the Damascus Document, and also in several other passages in the Qumran writings. Similar 'distancing' strategies can be observed in other early Jewish and early Christian writings;[1] they can be paralleled, at least in general terms, in the writings of many sectarian communities in very different cultural settings.

From a sociological perspective the parallels between the opening sections of the Damascus Document and Matthew's gospel are striking. In both writings the parting of the ways is initiated by God thorough an individual 'charismatic leader' (CD I. 11; Matt. 21. 43). The leaders of the parent body (for Matthew they are primarily the Pharisees) are portrayed positively in 23. 2: they sit on Moses' seat; but as in the Damascus Document, the positive portrayal is soon swamped by a catalogue of criticisms. Like the Essenes, the Pharisees are blind guides (CD I. 9; Matt 15. 14; 23. 16, 17, 19, 24, 26). Like the Essenes, they are a planting (CD I. 7; Matt. 15. 13 [MtR] φυτεία); however, they have not been planted by the heavenly Father, and will be rooted up. In both writings there is a perceived threat of persecution from the parent group (CD I. 20-1; Matt 5. 10-12; 10. 17f.; 21. 41-5; 22. 6f.; 23. 31-5), but a strong conviction that judgement will ultimately be pronounced against the opposing leaders (CD I.2 1b-II. 1; Matt. 3. 7-10; 8. 12; 12. 37; 15. 13; 23. 33-6).

In both writings the polemic directed at the leaders of the dominant group is one way the minority community distances itself. As is frequently the case, polemic is part of

---

impose on all members of the Essene community this understanding of the Law. The failure of this attempts (sic) was due, according to the sectarian texts, to the influence of the Liar, the leader of the Essene movement who "led many astray with deceitful words, so that they chose foolishness and hearkened not to the Interpreter of Knowledge" (IQ171 I, 18-19). The result was to be the break between the adepts of the Teacher of Righteousness and the rest of the Essenes who remained faithful to the Liar.' 125.

[1] See J. Blenkinsopp's helpful study, cited above.

the sect's self-understanding as a distinct entity over against the parent body.

In Matthew there are several further more subtle ways in which 'the new people of God' distances itself or differentiates itself from the parent group. Disciples of Jesus are urged to exceed the righteousness of the scribes and Pharisees (5. 20; cf. 6. 1-18). The scribes and Pharisees enjoy being called 'rabbi', but disciples of Jesus are not to allow others to call them 'rabbi' (23. 7-8); it is no coincidence that only Judas refers to Jesus as 'rabbi' (26. 25, 49).

Matthew's careful distinction between ἐκκλησία and συναγωγή is striking. In six passages (4. 23; 9. 35; 10. 17; 12. 9; 13. 54; 23. 34) the evangelist has either modified an earlier tradition or has used his own words to emphasize the distance between the ἐκκλησία founded by Jesus by divine revelation (16. 18 and cf. 18. 17) and the συναγωγή which is seen as the self-identification of the parent group. What is implicit in the five passages in which αὐτῶν is used with συναγωγή becomes explicit in 23. 34. At the conclusion of the sustained sharp polemic directed at the scribes and Pharisees in chapter 23, Jesus rounds on them: 'I am sending to you (Christian) prophets and wise men and scribes, some of whom you will kill and crucify, and some you will scourge in your synagogues (ἐν ταῖς συναγωγαῖς ὑμῶν) and persecute from town to town.' At Matt. 9. 18 Matthew changes Mark's description of Jairus as εἷς τῶν ἀρχισυναγώγων to ἄρχων εἷς in order to avoid linking Jesus with the synagogue.[1] These passages confirm that the 'new people' has chosen a new self-identification in order to distance itself from the parent body: ἐκκλησία and συναγωγή are separate rival institutions.[2]

As we have seen, in a number of ways the Qumran community takes pains to distance itself from the Essenes. But whereas Matthew sharply differentiates the rival groups by his use of ἐκκλησία and συναγωγή, there is no comparable use of different terms for community self-identification in the Damascus Document. The same term 'Israel' is used for

---

[1] See further below 127.
[2] See further evidence and discussion in Chapter 5 below, 126-31.

'the people of God whose story is told in Scripture', for the Essenes, and for the Qumran community. In III. 12b-19, for example, 'Israel' seems to be used in all three ways.

Both the Damascus Document and Matthew's gospel reflect the self-understanding of groups which have parted company reluctantly with parent groups. From a sociological perspective, both bear many of the hall-marks of sectarian writings. In spite of shared traditions, and to a large extent shared goals, both new communities carefully distance themselves from their respective parent groups.

These conclusions are confirmed by studies of social conflict theory, to which I shall now turn. Once again I shall appeal both to 'distant comparisons' (sociological theory) and to a 'close comparison' of the Damascus Document and Matthew's gospel.

Social conflict theory

In this section I propose to draw on the studies of the behaviour of groups in conflict carried out by the distinguished sociologist Lewis Coser.[1] In his widely acclaimed book, Coser does not confine himself to the study of the behaviour of sects. However many of his observations are applicable to sects in conflict with parent bodies. Three are particularly illuminating for students of the Damascus Document and of Matthew's gospel.

1. Close relationships: intense conflict
Lewis Coser notes that the closer the relationship, the more intense the conflict. 'A conflict is more passionate and more radical when it arises out of close relationships. The coexist-

---

[1] *The Functions of Social Conflict*, London 1956. Coser expounds and sometimes modifies the classic work by the German sociologist George Simmel who was a contemporary of Max Weber, *Conflict*, E.tr. Glencoe, Ill. 1955. In his *Continuities in the Study of Social Critics*, New York 1967, 5-14, Coser responds to the accusation of some of his critics that he over-emphasized the *positive* results of social conflict.

ence of union and opposition in such relations makes for the peculiar sharpness of the conflict. Enmity calls forth deeper and more violent reactions, the greater the involvement of the parties among whom it originates.'[1]

These observations can be readily supported from the two writings we are comparing. In both there are claims that the 'new people' are the true people of God and the true interpreters of Scripture: their own history marks the fulfilment of the prophecies of Scripture. Both groups grudgingly acknowledge that at an earlier stage the parent group was acceptable – indeed it was a 'planting by God' (cf. CD 1. 7; cf. Matt 15. 13; 23. 2).

Matthew's gospel provides many further examples of 'closeness'. Disciples of Jesus share the goal of the scribes and Pharisees, righteousness, but they are to surpass their rivals in attainment (5. 20). They do not reject the three central religious practices of their rivals, alms, prayer, fasting, but they carry them out with different motivation (6. 1-18). They also have 'prophets, wise men, and scribes' (23. 34; 10. 41; 13. 52) and seek 'to make disciples of all nations' (cf. 23. 15 and 28. 18-20).

The 'closeness' of the two groups to their respective parent bodies partly explains the ferocity of the polemic. Perhaps the single most striking feature of the invective is the claim found in both writings that the rival group is under the sway of Belial or Satan. The Damascus Document claims that the Essenes (or Israel as a whole) have been ensnared by 'the three nets of Belial which appear to them as three kinds of righteousness: fornication, wealth, and making the sanctuary unclean' (CD IV. 12-19).

By making redactional changes to the Q tradition about the returning unclean spirit, Matthew intends his readers to see the unclean spirit as a figure of the evil that characterizes the generation of the scribes and Pharisees (12. 43-5). R.H. Gundry correctly notes that in Matthew 'the period of the unclean spirit's absence ceases to be a period of temporary relief for a demoniac and becomes a figure of the apparent righteousness

---

[1] *Social Conflict,* 71.

of the scribes and Pharisees; and the return of the unclean spirit with seven others worse than himself . . . comes to represent an outburst of multiplied evil on the part of the scribes and Pharisees.'[1] The immediate context strongly suggests that this passage is a rebuttal of the claim of the Pharisees that Jesus casts out demons by Beelzebul (12. 24; cf also 9. 34 and 10. 25): *they* (not Jesus) are possessed by evil spirits.[2]

The sustained invective directed at the parent group both in the Damascus Document and in Matthew puzzles modern readers. This bewilderment is increased when note is taken of the close ties which still bind the 'new people' to the parent group, in spite of the parting of the ways. But from a sociological perspective this pattern of behaviour is not unexpected: as Lewis Coser has shown, the closer the relationship between rival groups, the more intense the conflict.[3]

2. Social conflict, boundaries, and dissent

Sects and groups in conflict have much in common. Both establish tight boundaries and both are intolerant of dissent. Lewis Coser notes that 'group boundaries are established through conflict with the outside, so that a group defines itself by struggling with other groups.'[4] Elsewhere he observes that the sect is exclusive. 'Exclusion is attained through conflict with the outside and the maintenance of this exclusive standing requires the sect to be an internally cohesive conflict group.'[5]

These observations have an important corollary which is of particular interest to the reader of the Damascus

---

[1] R.H. Gundry, *Matthew*, 246. It is possible that a similar point is made in Matt 13. 38: the 'sons of the evil one' may include the Jewish religious leaders. Most commentators interpret this phrase as a reference to unfaithful Christians; in his *Parables*, 102-4, J.D. Kingsbury allows that the leaders of Judaism may also be in mind in a secondary sense.

[2] See the fuller discussion of 9. 34; 10. 25; 12. 24, in Chapter 7.

[3] *Social Conflict*, 95.

[4] *Social Conflict*, 87.

[5] *Social Conflict*, 91.

Document and of Matthew. Coser notes that in groups in conflict, the sharpness of the reaction to the 'inner enemy' is in proportion to the sharpness of the conflict with the outer enemies. A group in conflict will react with even more hostility to a heretic than to an apostate, for a heretic still shares many of the goals of his former fellow-members.[1] Hatred is directed, not in the first place against opponents of its own view of the world order, but against dreaded rivals who are competing for the same end.[2]

In both the Damascus Document and Matthew, there is strong condemnation of erring or unfaithful members of the community; their rejection and judgement is referred to in several passages. But since restoration is at least possible, in Coser's terminology both writings refer to 'heretics' rather than to 'apostates'. I doubt whether 'apostates', i.e. those who reject totally and finally the 'worldview' of the community, are in view in either writing.

The final sections of the exhortation in the Damascus Document contain repeated warnings to unfaithful members of the community. In one section restoration of unfaithful members is ruled out for the period between the death of the 'teacher of the community' and the 'appearance of the messiah from Aaron and from Israel' (CD Ms B XIX. 33–XX. 1a). The paragraph which follows, however, implies that expulsion from the community is temporary (XX. 1b-8). A later paragraph (XX. 22-7) declares that unfaithful members 'will be punished in the same way (by death) as wrongdoers who had never joined the movement.'[3] Loosely related material seems to have been stitched together a little awkwardly. The precise ways in which erring members have been unfaithful is unclear; the reference in XX. 2 to the one

---

[1] *Social Conflict*, 169 n.4 and 70-1. See also H. Himmelweit, 'Deviant Behaviour', in *A Dictionary of the Social Sciences*, eds. J. Gould and W.L. Kolb, New York 1964, 196.

[2] *Social Conflict*, 70. Coser refers to the work of Robert Michels in order to establish this point. Michels is primarily concerned with political rivalries, but his observation has wider relevance.

[3] So M.A. Knibb, *Qumran*, 76.

who 'shrinks from carrying out the precepts of the upright' is typical.

Several passages in Matthew also pronounce judgement on unfaithful members of the community. In 7. 19 those who do not bear good fruit will be cut down and thrown into the fire. In the pericope which follows judgement is pronounced on those whose deeds are evil (7. 23). In the explanation of the parables of the weeds (Matt 13. 36-43), a passage in which the evangelist's own hand is clearly evident, the 'sons of the evil one' are evildoers who will be thrown into the furnace of fire at the close of the age. In 24. 51 the evangelist makes a redactional change to the Q tradition he is using and stresses that unfaithful Christians will share judgement with 'the hypocrites', i.e. with the scribes and Pharisees on whom judgement is pronounced in chapter 23.

In both the Damascus Document and Matthew the 'inner enemy' is rejected as vigorously as the 'outer enemy'. Both writings illustrate the hostility a group in conflict shows towards internal dissent. In neither writing is the precise nature of the failing of the 'evildoers' indicated, but the failure of 'erring members' to accept or carry out the principle tenets of the community clearly poses a serious threat to its cohesiveness and stability. Hence their rejection.

3. Group cohesion and centralized control

Lewis Coser notes that strong group cohesion as a consequence of outside conflict does not necessarily carry with it the need for centralized control. 'Indeed, a sect, engaged in intense conflict with the surrounding world of the "damned", may have such strong cohesion that each member of the group participates in the exercise of control tasks and that there is no need for centralization of these tasks in the hands of a few.'[1]

The Damascus Document says very little about the structure of the community. Several passages imply an

---

[1] *Social Conflict*, 91. Coser stresses that once sects engage in *warfare* the situation changes and they develop differentiated structures and centralized organization (91-5).

egalitarian structure. At XX. 18, for example, we read that following the death of the Teacher of Righteousness members of the community are to engage in mutual support: 'they will then speak to one another to turn one another to righteousness that their step may hold firmly to the way of God.'

A very different picture of community life at Qumran emerges as soon as we turn to the Community Rule, in which regulations for a highly structured community are set out in great detail. Are the two writings in this respect incompatible? Perhaps they relate to different stages in the life of the community.

One passage in the Community Rule (IQS VIII. 1-10a) sets out a pattern for the future community without even hinting at the detailed rules and structures which are referred to in other passages. Partly on the basis of the way the manuscript is set out, and partly on the basis of traditio-historical considerations, this passage is often said to be the oldest in the Rule.[1] If so, then the Qumran community may not at first have been highly structured.

Sociological theory offers some confirmation for this hypothesis. A sectarian community which perceives itself to be at odds with the parent body from which it has parted will have strong group cohesion and be much more likely to be egalitarian than to have a rigid internal structure. With the death of the charismatic leader, 'routinization of charisma' gradually takes place and eventually structures are developed.

The Qumran community may well have followed this pattern. Following the initial parting of the ways at the instigation of the Teacher of Righteousness, the community did not have a strong internal structure (CD in its penultimate form – columns IX–XVI have a different tradition history; IQS VII. 1-10a). In the course of time, and perhaps as sharp conflict with the Essenes diminished, a highly organized community was developed with its own distinctive self-understanding (IQS). This is no more than a

[1] So M.A. Knibb, *Qumran*, 129.

hypothesis which needs to be tested by detailed study of the texts.

Perhaps the communities for whom Matthew wrote developed in similar ways. Some passages suggest that there was little or no structure (e.g. 18. 17-18; 23. 8-12), while others suggest rudimentary structures (16. 19, but cf. 18. 18; 10. 41-2; 23. 34). While the Matthean communities may have been egalitarian in theory, there are some signs of leadership roles.[1] This ambivalence concerning institutional structures conforms to the pattern Coser has noted: sharp conflict with an 'outer enemy' encourages strong group cohesion, but the group does not necessarily develop internal structures. In the course of time the communities which used Matthew's gospel did develop structures. Perhaps it is no coincidence that at the same time the ferocity of conflict with the parent body diminished.

At this point it is important to recall that at the outset of this chapter I emphasized that sociological observations must not be allowed to fill in gaps in our knowledge. But as we have seen, they do provide some interesting fresh questions and stimulus for further rigorous historical study.

Legitimation

Legitimation is the collection of ways a social institution is explained and justified to its members. Study of this social phenomenon is associated particularly with P.L. Berger and T. Luckmann.[2] Their observations have been used to good effect by P.F. Esler with reference to Luke-Acts and by F.B.

---

[1] See E. Krentz, 'Community and Character: Matthew's Vision of the Church' and D.C. Duling's response to this paper in the *SBL Seminar Papers 1988*.

[2] *The Social Construction of Reality: a Treatise in the Sociology of Knowledge*, New York and London 1966. See also P.L. Berger, *The Social Reality of Religion*, London 1969.

Watson in his study of the Pauline writings.[1] The Damascus Document and Matthew can also be considered with profit in the light of the work of Berger and Luckmann.

Legitimation includes the use of polemic to denounce the parent group and to differentiate the new group; both have been discussed above. Legitimation also includes for the internal consumption of the new group responses to the hostile allegations of the parent group; some important examples from Matthew are discussed in Chapter 7 of this book.

Two further aspects of legitimation are illuminating. First, legitimation includes the claim of the new group that it is *not* innovatory: it is the parent group which has gone astray. The new group is the legitimate heir to shared traditions which are now reinterpreted in the light of new convictions.

The Damascus Document sets out an explanation of the parting of the ways precisely along these lines. The rival group (on the García Martínez hypothesis, the Essenes) is said 'to have turned aside from the way' (CD I. 13); i.e. *they* are responsible for the separation. The parent group has been led astray by 'the scoffer' and has 'pulled up the boundary stone which the men of former times had set up in their inheritance' (CD I. 14-16).

The parting of the ways has divine sanction; the new group is the true heir of God's covenant with Israel. 'But with those who held fast to the commandments of God, who were left over from them, God has established his covenant with Israel (i.e. the true Israel, the Qumran community), revealing to them the hidden things in which Israel (the parent group, the Essenes, or perhaps Israel as a whole) had gone astray: his holy sabbaths and his glorious feasts, his righteous testimonies and his true ways . . . .' (CD III. 12-15).

The evangelist Matthew has a similar explanation for the parting of the ways. It is not the new community which is responsible for the separation. Israel has failed to respond to

---

[1] P.F. Esler, *Community and Gospel in Luke-Acts*; F.B. Watson, *Paul, Judaism and the Gentiles: a Sociological Approach*, SNTSMS 56, Cambridge 1986.

Jesus her Messiah, the Son of God, because she has been led astray by her stubborn, blind, and evil leaders. The new people has deep roots (1. 1-17) and is the true heir of God's promises and kingdom (21. 43). The parting was foreseen by Jesus and carried out on God's initiative (21. 43).

Secondly, Berger and Luckmann note that legitimation formulas must be repeated in a social institution's explanation and justification of itself to its members. The Damascus Document contains several slightly differing accounts of the origin of the Qumran community, some of which may have had an independent existence. In CD I. 1-12, for example, the role of the Teacher of Righteousness is stressed, but in III. 12b–IV. 12a, which is a similar explanation of the community's origin, his role is not mentioned. In its present form the Damascus Document is made up of a series of explanations of the origin and raison d'être of the community.

Matthew's gospel also contains several legitimation formulas. Israel's rejection of Jesus and God's acceptance of Gentiles are adumbrated clearly in chapter 2; both are referred to repeatedly as the story unfolds. Matthew's ten uses of formula quotations to stress that the story of Jesus is indeed the fulfilment of Scripture function as a legitimation formula.

Both the Damascus Document and Matthew's gospel explain and sustain the separate identity of communities which have parted company painfully with parent bodies. It is no surprise to learn that Cave 4 manuscripts of the Damascus Document include at the end of the writing a liturgy for the renewal of the covenant.[1] Its regular use in worship suggests that it functioned as a 'foundation document', a legitimation of the community's very existence. I am convinced that Matthew's gospel was intended to have a similar function: to explain to its readers how ἐκκλησία and συναγωγή came to be separate institutions and to sustain the on-going life of the former.

In this chapter I have tried to show that sociological observations can enrich our appreciation of ancient writings.

---

[1] M.A. Knibb, *Qumran*, 14.

Sociological models which are based on cross-cultural studies ('distant comparisons') often raise fresh insights and fresh questions. Close comparison of two ancient writings from a sociological perspective is a useful complement and a check on unwarranted assumptions. Read from this perspective the Damascus Document and Matthew's gospel are mutually illuminating.[1] If my observations on the social setting and purpose of these two writings seem simply to confirm what we already knew from historical and redaction critical studies, so much the better.[2]

---

[1] An earlier version of this chapter was given in Oxford in September 1990 as a paper to the annual conference of the British Society for NT Studies. In the discussion which followed my paper, and in subsequent correspondence, Ernest Best kindly drew my attention to differences between the Qumran community and Matthew: whereas the Qumran community became a closed group separated from Israel, the Matthean community became a sub-group of the general Christian group, and was therefore very different. However, I think there are sufficient similarities to sustain my main points. Following partings from 'parent bodies', both the Qumran and the Matthean communities clung to the optimistic hopes which are typical of sectarian groups: they both hoped that the 'parent bodies' would eventually join them, for they both saw themselves as the true heirs of God's promises. I do not think that immediately following a 'parting' with Israel, Matthew's communities joined a wider Christian movement. That was a later development, though we do not know exactly when and how it took place. At the time the evangelist wrote, his Christian communities were as much 'on their own' as Qumran. I do not think that in the mid-80s there was yet an entity, 'Christianity', for them to join. Matthew and the communities to whom he wrote may have been aware of further groups of Christians which had also 'parted' from Judaism, but they were not consciously linking up with them.

[2] I am grateful to two sociologists, Professor David Martin and Dr Peter Clarke for their advice and assistance. My colleague Professor Michael Knibb has given invaluable help with my study of the Qumran writings.

Conclusions to Part I

In Part I of this book I have emphasized that the assumptions which are made in the use of redaction criticism, and of literary and sociological approaches must all be kept under rigorous critical scrutiny.

In my appraisal of these three methods I have stressed strongly that they must all be anchored firmly in the first century world. Redaction critics need to attend to the ways ancient writers reshaped earlier traditions. In the elucidation of first century texts, modern literary theory must be underpinned by a keen awareness that ancient and modern literary conventions are not always congruent. Some literary strategies are common to ancient and modern narrators, but some are not, and we ignore the differences at our peril. Sociological considerations based on comparisons with similar ancient societies will be more compelling than 'distant comparisons' with societies and groups in very different cultural, religious and historical settings. A healthy scepticism about claims of cross-cultural continuity is in order.

These methods new and old all have their place: they can be used effectively to complement one another, for they are inter-related. In my view recognition of the value of all three methods and of their mutual inter-dependence is crucial for scholarly discussion of the gospels. This is the way forward from the current disarray which has arisen in Matthean scholarship as the result of the use of diverse methods. I must now comment further on this claim.

The roots of redaction criticism are much deeper than has usually been supposed. Although this approach to the gospels quickly gained supremacy in the years following the end of World War II, ever since the rise of modern historical scholarship close attention has been given to the differences between Matthew and Mark. With such deep and secure roots redaction criticism can be expected to continue to produce good fruit. There is no reason why it should not do so, especially since the dependence of Matthew on Mark is the single most assured result of gospel criticism, and the Q hypothesis continues to survive all onslaughts against it.

Matthew has re-shaped earlier traditions in two ways: some have been modified extensively, while others have been taken over with very little adaptation. In the latter case re-interpretation inevitably takes place as Marcan, Q and other traditions are set in a new framework. Once this is recognized, it is obvious that careful attention must be given to the structure and argument of the gospel as a whole. And in order to do this effectively, appropriate literary methods must be embraced with enthusiasm.

Literary criticism confirms that interpretation is a delicate balancing act: the author's intention, the text itself, and the expectations of recipients are equally important. Matthew shaped his gospel in order to elicit particular responses from his readers and listeners, responses which were strongly influenced by the social and historical context which author and recipients shared. The more we know about that context, the more keenly we shall appreciate the evangelist's achievement and the expectations of the first recipients.

Our inability to locate the city in which the evangelist Matthew wrote is a serious constraint on the use of the tools of the social historian. Partial compensation is possible, however, by drawing on the insights of the sociologist, especially when 'close comparisons' with writings from broadly similar first century groups are made.

The three methods should be seen as friends, not enemies. I see no reason why Matthew's gospel should not be considered in the first instance from any one of these three vantage points. Since the stance of the interpreter is crucial, however, we shall need to know precisely where we are taking our initial stance, and why. And we shall see further and more clearly if we accept that these three methods are complementary: each one can be used more effectively with the support of the other two.

'By their fruits you will know them (Matt 7. 16).' This Matthean dictum is as applicable to the appraisal of methods new and old, as it is to the discernment of true and false prophecy. Hence in the preceding chapters I have deliberately given as much space to discussion of the text of the gospel as to theoretical considerations.

Whether Matthew's gospel is considered from a redaction critical point of view, or from literary critical or sociological perspectives, the conflict of Jesus and his followers with the Jewish leaders is a central feature. The chapters which follow in Part II will explore this theme primarily from a redaction critical stand-point, but with the assistance of literary and sociological considerations. At many points our horizons will be broadened still further by setting Matthew's gospel in the context of early Christianity and early Judaism.

Part Two

The Parting of the Ways

Therefore, I tell you,
the kingdom of God will be taken away from you,
and given to a people
who will produce the proper fruit.

Matthew 21. 43

Chapter Five

Synagogue and Church

Did Matthew write his gospel for Christian communities which saw themselves as part of diverse Judaism, in spite of the strains which their claims about Jesus inevitably brought? Or did the evangelist and his readers see themselves as a distinct entity over against Judaism – small local churches set in the midst of numerous stronger local synagogues? Or was Matthew himself a Gentile who wrote for Christian communities dominated by Gentiles, communities for whom the tensions between Christians and Jews were merely a matter of past history?

Few questions have been debated more keenly by students of Matthew's gospel. They cannot be evaded, for our appreciation of the evangelist's purposes and the interpretation of numerous passages both depend on our understanding of the relationship of 'synagogue' and 'church' when the evangelist wrote. The four ways that relationship has been understood by modern scholars will be considered in this chapter. The four approaches are quite distinct, even though some scholars who adopt the same general stance differ considerably in their emphases, and some have managed to incorporate aspects of two of the four approaches I shall identify.

· I shall discuss first of all the traditional view that Matthew wrote before A.D. 70 for Jewish Christians in Palestine. I shall then turn to the claim that although Matthew wrote after 70 and used Mark's gospel, he and his readers saw themselves as *intra muros*, still within diverse Judaism. As the earlier

chapters of this book have already shown, I myself prefer the
third view: Matthew's gospel was written in the wake of a
recent painful parting from Judaism; the evangelist's readers
are *extra muros*. I shall then discuss the proposal that the
evangelist himself was a Gentile Christian for whom the
relationship of church and synagogue was not a primary
concern. Scholars who adopt this fourth approach claim that
in Matthew's view, Israel's complete and final rejection by
God was a *fait accompli* since she had rejected Christian
claims about Jesus. Passages in the gospel which suggest that
the author must have been a Jew are all pre-Matthean
traditions which do not put us in touch with the evangelist's
own views. In the final section of this chapter I shall discuss
the relationship of Matthew's gospel to the alleged introduction of the *birkath ha-minim* into the synagogue liturgy as
part of the reconstruction of Judaism which took place at
Jamnia.

The traditional view

From the middle of the third century right up to modern
times, Matthew was almost universally considered to be the
most 'Jewish' of the four canonical gospels: it was the first
gospel to be written; the evangelist was a disciple of Jesus
who wrote in Hebrew or Aramaic for a Palestinian Jewish
Christian community. Origen seems to have been the first to
state explicitly that Matthew was written before the other
gospels, though he claims that his comments are based on
earlier tradition. In his commentary on Matthew, which
dates from about A.D. 250 and which was the most extensive
written in the early church, Origen wrote as follows:

With reference to the only gospels which are accepted. . .
without controversy in the Church of God, I have learned
from tradition: The gospel according to Matthew, who was
first a tax collector and later an apostle of Jesus Christ, was

the first to be written; it was written in the Hebrew language for the believers from Judaism.

Only about half of Origen's commentary has survived. His comments on the origin of Matthew are not found in his commentary, but are preserved in a quotation in Eusebius of Caesarea (*H.E.* VI. 25. 4), who wrote in the early years of the fourth century.

Eusebius himself adds only one further point of interest for our present purposes. He claims that Matthew wrote his gospel for Jewish believers in order to compensate them for his impending departure 'for other peoples' (*H.E.* III. 24. 6). From the wider context it is clear that Eusebius envisages that Matthew was written just before the evangelist left Palestine for a ministry among Gentiles. This comment partially anticipates the influential modern view that Matthew wrote for Jews who had become Christians in order to defend a mission among Gentiles. We do not know on what basis Eusebius reached his quite specific view about the origin of Matthew. Perhaps he concluded on the basis of Matt 28. 19 that Matthew the apostle must surely have obeyed the command of Jesus to go and make disciples of all nations.

The comments of Origen and Eusebius strongly influenced later opinion; the traditional view was not challenged seriously until the final decades of the eighteenth century. It was still defended, albeit with considerable sophistication, and (as we shall see) important modifications, by A. Schlatter in his large commentary on Matthew, first published in 1929 and reprinted in a sixth edition as recently as 1963. Schlatter also assumed that Matthew was the first gospel to be written and insisted that its author was a disciple of Jesus who was bilingual in Aramaic and in Greek, and who wrote for Jewish Christians in Palestine before 70.[1]

---

[1] See his *Der Evangelist Matthäus, passim.* Since Schlatter's day the 'traditional' view has rarely been defended. One exception is P. Gaechter. In his commentary (1963) and his *Die literarische Kunst im Matthäus-Evangelium* (1965) he claimed that the gospel was written by the apostle in Hebrew.

The traditional view of the origin and purpose of Matthew and of its relationship to contemporary Judaism is untenable for the following reasons:

(i) The comments of early Christian writers on the origin of Matthew became more specific in the course of time.[1] While the earliest form of the tradition may contain a historical kernel, later forms of the tradition are elaborations and deductions which tell us little or nothing about the origin and purpose of the gospel.

This can be shown by comparing Papias's terse comment with the views of Origen and Eusebius noted above. About A.D. 130 Papias wrote as follows: 'So Matthew composed the oracles (τὰ λόγια) in the Hebrew style (or language) ('Εβραΐδι διαλέκτῳ) and each person interpreted them as best he could' (Eusebius, H.E. III. 39. 16).

It is important to note that Papias does not say that Matthew was the first gospel to be written. That view, which was well established by the time of Origen a century later, seems to have been based on two deductions. (a) Unlike Mark and Luke, Matthew was one of the twelve disciples of Jesus; thus he was therefore likely to have written his 'memoirs' before they did. (b) Since Matthew's gospel was thought to have been written originally in Hebrew, it must have been written before the other gospels which were written in Greek.

The tradition that Matthew wrote in Hebrew may have been based on a misunderstanding of Papias's phrase 'Εβραΐδι διαλέκτῳ. J. Kürzinger has produced strong philological evidence which suggests that 'Εβραΐδι διαλέκτῳ was intended by Papias to mean 'in Jewish forms of expression'.[2] If so, the later tradition that Matthew wrote in Hebrew may have arisen partly as a misunderstanding of this phrase and partly

---

[1] For a full discussion of early church traditions about the origins of Matthew, see P. Nepper-Christensen, *Das Matthäusevangelium – ein judenchristliches Evangelium?* Aarhus 1958, 37-75.

[2] 'Irenäus und sein Zeugnis zur Sprache des Matthäusevangeliums', *NTS* 10 (1963-4) 108-15.

as a result of confusion with traditions about the apocryphal gospel of the Hebrews.

Although the origin of the attribution of the gospel to 'Matthew' is an unresolved puzzle, there is no doubt about the prominence of 'Jewish forms of expression'. Papias's comments have often been dismissed out of hand, but they are probably based on an even earlier (and partly reliable) tradition which stems from 'the elder' at some point towards the end of the first century – i.e. not long after Matthew was written.[1]

Papias's comments are the earliest form of the traditional view. They tell us little about Matthew's purposes. Their later elaboration tells us much more, but the additional material is not based on reliable information about the evangelist's purposes and his relationship to Judaism.

(ii) Once Marcan priority is accepted, the main arguments which support the full form of the traditional view all collapse. Since Matthew's primary source was Mark's gospel, written in Greek, Matthew cannot have been written originally in Hebrew or Aramaic as the first gospel. If Matthew has drawn heavily on Mark, he is unlikely to have written before 70. And if he wrote after 70, his gospel is unlikely to have originated in Palestine.

(iii) With the possible exception of Eusebius's note concerning the evangelist's mission to Gentiles, which we discussed above, the traditional view does not do justice either to Matthew's strong emphasis on the Gentile mission or to the numerous passages in the gospel which reflect tension with contemporary Judaism.

---

[1] Eusebius's account of Papias's comments about Matthew is preceded immediately by Papias's comments on Mark. Since the latter are attributed by Papias to 'the elder', it is likely that his comments on Matthew come from the same source.

In his use of τὰ λόγια (the oracles), was Papias referring to Q (which is made up almost entirely of sayings of Jesus) or to the whole gospel of Matthew? The latter view is more likely, especially since Papias uses τὰ λόγια to refer both to Mark's account of the actions as well as the sayings of Jesus, and also to his own writings which certainly included narratives.

Although Schlatter may be seen as the final major representative of the traditional view, in his writings on Matthew he repeatedly draws attention to the conflicts between Jesus and the religious leaders of his day and freely acknowledges that these passages in Matthew also reflect later tensions between the church and the synagogue at the time the evangelist wrote.[1] In this respect, though not in his insistence that Matthew is our earliest gospel written by the apostle in Palestine before 70, Schlatter anticipates the second way the relationship between Matthew and contemporary Judaism has been understood.

It is worth noting, however, that in his large and learned commentary on Matthew which discusses nearly every verse in some detail, Schlatter completely bypasses 21. 43. This verse, which is the evangelist's redactional addition to his Marcan source, notes that the kingdom of God will be taken away from the Jewish leaders and given to a new people 'who will produce its fruit'. 21. 43 is as important as any other verse in the gospel for our understanding of the relationship of Matthew's community to Judaism. Schlatter's insistence on the priority of Matthew seems to have blinded him to its significance.

An internal dispute within Judaism?

Once Marcan priority was widely accepted in the final decades of the nineteenth century, it became very difficult to equate the 'Jewishness' of Matthew with an early date and a setting in Palestine. The strongly Jewish character of the gospel had to be explained in other ways. In 1918 B.W. Bacon claimed that chapters 3–25 are a Matthean imitation of the Pentateuch designed to show to Jews that Jesus is a greater lawgiver than Moses.[2] Ten years later E. von Dobschütz argued that the

---

[1] In addition to his commentary, see also *Die Kirche des Matthäus*, Gütersloh 1930.

[2] 'The "Five Books" of Moses against the Jews', *The Expositor* 15 (1918) 56-66.

author was a converted rabbi who had probably been trained in the school of Johanan ben Zakkai immediately after the fall of Jerusalem in 70.[1] Both scholars linked the 'Jewishness' of Matthew's gospel to the Judaism of the decade or so after 70, rather than to the preceding decade, as Schlatter had done.

G.D. Kilpatrick developed this general approach to Matthew very considerably. He examined Matthew against the background of relations between Christianity and Judaism between A.D. 70–135 and contrasted Mark and Matthew sharply. 'Mark reflects Jewish Palestine before the War of A.D. 66–70, while Matthew is more akin to the Rabbinism which worked out its programme at Jamnia and subsequently became dominant in Judaism.'[2] The 'Jewish' features of Matthew are not necessarily to be explained as retention of original features, for they could be 'rejudaization'.

Kilpatrick argued that the phrase 'their synagogue(s)' (συναγωγὴ αὐτῶν, especially the pronominal genitive) is uniquely Matthean.[3] It is to be linked with the insertion of the birkath ha-minim into the eighteen benedictions of the synagogue liturgy; the additional clauses were composed by Samuel the Small at Jamnia in about A.D. 85. As a result, Christian Jews were excluded from the synagogues of the Pharisaic party. But this observation did not lead Kilpatrick to conclude that the evangelist and his readers had parted company decisively with Judaism. He suggested, but just in passing, that the opposition between Christians and Pharisaism is for the evangelist an opposition 'within Judaism'.[4]

As we shall see below, it is not possible to make a direct link between the introduction of the birkath ha-minim into the synagogue liturgy and Matthew's use of the phrase 'their synagogue(s)' (συναγωγὴ αὐτῶν). However, Kilpatrick's

---

[1] 'Matthäus als Rabbi und Katechet', ZNW 27 (1928) 338-48; E.tr. in Matthew, 1-18.

[2] The Origins of the Gospel According to St. Matthew, Oxford 1946, 106.

[3] Origins, 110ff. See further below.

[4] Origins, 122.

observations on the evangelist's redactional addition of αὐτῶν (and ὑμῶν at 23. 34) to συναγωγή at 4. 23; 9. 35; 10. 17; 12. 9; 13. 54 are very important; indeed, as we shall see, they can be extended considerably.

Kilpatrick concluded that Matthew's gospel came into being in an essentially Jewish Christian community, where the building up of a church life in independence of Judaism was in progress. 'It is significant', he wrote, 'that the attitude to Judaism displayed by the book enabled this community to take over so much from Judaism and at the same time it radically distinguished the Church from the Synagogue.'[1]

In an early essay G. Bornkamm, who became one of the most influential Matthean specialists in the twentieth century, accepted and developed Kilpatrick's view that Matthew's Jewish Christian community had not yet broken its links with Judaism.[2] Bornkamm referred to the pericope about the Temple tax (17. 24-27): 'It shows that the congregation which Matthew represents is still attached to Judaism and that it in no way claims for itself exemption from the taxation of the diaspora congregations, but accepts it, though clearly conscious of its own special position: the disciples of Jesus pay the Temple tax as free sons, merely in order not to give offence.'[3] In the final section of this essay Bornkamm insisted that the gospel confirms throughout that the congregation which the evangelist represented 'had not yet separated from Judaism. . . . .The struggle with Israel is still a struggle within its own walls.'[4]

R. Hummel defends a similar position: Matthew did not write for Judaism, but nonetheless a controversy with Judaism runs like a scarlet thread through all twenty eight chapters.[5] Hummel, who acknowledges his debt to

---

[1] *Origins*, 123.
[2] 'End-Expectation and Church in Matthew', E.tr. in *Tradition*, 22 n.1. This essay was first published in 1954.
[3] *Tradition*, 19f.
[4] *Tradition*, 39.
[5] *Die Auseinandersetzung zwischen Kirche und Judentum im Matthäusevangelium*, BEvT 33, Munich, 1963; 2nd ed. 1966.

Bornkamm and Kilpatrick, also believes that the gospel reflects controversy with Judaism after 70, rather than in the lifetime of Jesus. But he insists, against Kilpatrick, that it was written before the *birkath ha-minim* was inserted into the synagogue liturgy. For Hummel the reference in 17. 27 to payment of the temple tax is decisive: it confirms that Matthew's community still belongs to the association of Jewish synagogues even though it is clearly developing a life of its own.[1]

W.D. Davies also accepts that the struggle with Judaism took place *intra muros* and uses Bornkamm's very phrase.[2] Davies provides a lengthy study of the reconstruction of Judaism which took place at Jamnia following the fall of Jerusalem in 70. The so-called Jamnian period, A.D. 70–100, is to be seen as a many-sided response to the need for unity and for adaptation to changed conditions. Davies claims, with due caution, that Jamnian Judaism was consciously confronting Christianity, and then goes on to ask whether the developments within Pharisaism at Jamnia were known to Matthew and whether they affected his Church. He suggests that a number of passages in the gospel and chapters 5–7 in particular, may be seen as the Christian answer to Jamnia. 'Using terms very loosely, the Sermon on the Mount is a kind of Christian, Mishnaic counterpart to the formulation taking place there.' Matthew's manifesto is best explained as arising from the desire and necessity to present a formulation of the way of the New Israel at a time when the rabbis were engaged in a parallel task for the Old Israel.[3]

In reply, however, K. Stendahl notes that if Matthew is the Christian answer to Jamnia, it is in a completely different

---

[1] See, for example, 32 and 159.

[2] *The Setting of the Sermon on the Mount*, Cambridge 1966, 290 and 332. In the lengthy Introduction in Vol. I of their ICC commentary, 1988, Davies and Allison do not discuss this point directly.

[3] *Setting*, 286; 315. In a lengthy review of Davies's book, G. Strecker accepted Davies's account of what happened at Jamnia, but is not convinced that there is a direct link with Matthew. The review is printed in the 3rd ed. 1971, 257ff. of *Der Weg der Gerechtigkeit*, FRLANT 82, 1st ed. Göttingen 1962; and also in *NTS* 13 (1967) 105f.

key, for it contains ethics and exhortation rather than halaka. He also insists that the influence of Palestinian Judaism on Matthew can hardly be as direct as Davies's study presupposes, for the evangelist works in Greek, primarily with Greek traditions, Mark and Q. [1]

As we shall see below, many scholars now accept that Matthew should be linked in some way to the Judaism of the Jamnian period, but reject the view that the struggle of Matthew's community with 'the synagogue across the street' was *intra muros*. Even G. Bornkamm, with whom the phrase *intra muros* is especially associated, modified his position between his 1956 essay quoted above and a study of Matthew 18 published in 1970. In the latter he noted, with reference to 18. 19f., that Matthew's community 'knows itself to be cut off from the Jewish community; gathered no longer about the Torah, but in the name of Jesus, in faith in him and in confession of him, and as such to be assured of his presence.'[2]

But Bornkamm's earlier position is still defended. M.D. Goulder argues that Matthew was written just before the crisis caused by the introduction of the *birkath ha-minim* into the synagogue liturgy: 'he belongs to Jewry and expects to be persecuted for his heterodoxy.'[3] Schuyler Brown suggests that the Gentile mission may have been an object of current controversy within the evangelist's community.[4] He claims, with Hummel, that the distinctively Matthean phrase συναγωγὴ αὐτῶν need imply no more than that Matthew's Jewish Christians were holding separate religious assemblies. 'The absence in the gospel of any explicit reference to excommunication, even where such a reference is present in a Lucan parallel (Luke 6. 22; cf. Matt 5. 11), suggests a date

---

[1] K. Stendahl, *The School of St Matthew*, 2nd ed. 1968, xii. On Jamnia, see further below, 142-3.

[2] 'The Authority to "Bind"and "Loose"', *Jesus and Man's Hope* I, ed. D.G. Miller et al., Pittsburgh 1970, 41.

[3] *Midrash and Lection*, 152.

[4] 'The Matthean Community and the Gentile Mission', *NovT* 22 (1980) 216.

before the decision at Jamnia. Furthermore, it is difficult to believe that Matthew would have allowed a recommendation of Pharisaic teaching (Matt 23. 2f.) to stand in his gospel if his community had definitely separated from Judaism.' [1]

J.A. Overman has recently emphasized that many of the issues which are prominent in Matthew were also of great concern to other first century Jewish groups and 'sects'. He shows that the social developments within the Matthean community frequently parallel and are analogous to the social and institutional developments within Judaism. But in insisting that Matthew 'takes his stand within Judaism' and that 'Matthew does not allow formative Judaism to go one way and his community to go another', he does not draw the conclusion to which most of his own perceptive observations point.[2]

This second view rightly stresses that in many ways Matthew's gospel is thoroughly Jewish, and it rightly accepts that many of the changes which Matthew has made to Mark are related to the circumstances in which Matthew was written. But this approach fails to do justice to some of the most important features of Matthew's gospel. In particular it

---

[1] *'Gentile Mission'*, 216. On the basis of his reading of Matt 13. 1-52, D.J. Harrington has recently argued that Matthew and his community remained within the framework of Judaism; 'they did not yet view themselves as practising a separate religion as the "church versus Israel" approach suggests.' 'The Mixed Reception of the Gospel: Interpreting the Parables in Matthew 13. 1-52', *NTS* 38 (1992) forthcoming.

[2] *Matthew's Gospel and Formative Judaism*, Minneapolis 1990, 157. Overman is not always consistent. Some of his general comments on Matthew's relationship to contemporary Judaism suggest that his view is similar to my own. In the final paragraph of chapter 3, for example, he insists that Matthew 'has set the beliefs and life of his community over against those of formative Judaism in such a way that the people of his community would have had to make a choice between the two. One could not support or be loyal to both. Lines of separation had been drawn, in a manner that appears to offer no way back.' (149) But just two paragraphs earlier he claims that Matthew and his community 'have not gone their separate way' from formative Judaism (148). It is not surprising that two scholars quoted on the jacket of Overman's book understand his position quite differently.

ignores or underplays numerous passages (in most of which the evangelist's own hand is evident) which suggest that the Christian communities to whom Matthew is writing are defining themselves over against Judaism and are being encouraged to accept Gentiles freely.

In the wake of the parting of the ways

The view that Matthew's community still stands within Judaism, even if rather awkwardly, has been contested by a number of scholars. Some are so impressed by the Gentile features of the gospel (at least in its final redaction) and by the ferocity of Matthew's attack on Judaism that the evangelist himself is seen as a Gentile: his community has long since given up any interest in debate or dialogue with 'the synagogue across the street'. This position will be considered below as the fourth way the relationship of Matthew to contemporary Judaism has been understood.

I prefer what is essentially a 'mediating position'. The *intra muros* view just discussed is implausible, as is the claim that Matthew writes as a Gentile for whom the tensions between Christians and Jews were merely a matter of past history. I am convinced that Matthew's communities have parted company with Judaism and that some Gentiles have been accepted. Nearly every pericope of the gospel reflects rivalry between 'church' and 'synagogue'. Matthew's communities are *extra muros*, but they are still responding in various ways to local synagogues and they still hope that even if Israel has been rejected by God, individual Jews will be converted. On this view the gospel can be seen, at least in part, as an apology – a defence of Christianity over against non-Christian Judaism.

What I am referring to as the third way of understanding Matthew's relationship to contemporary Judaism seems to have attracted wide support for the first time in the 1960s.

Three scholars were particularly influential.[1] C.F.D. Moule suggested that the gospel was compiled by a scribe (in the secular, not the rabbinic, sense). He may or may not have been a Jew himself, but he belonged to a Christian group who lived so close to antagonistic Judaism that it needed to be well informed about the credentials of Christianity and about the best way to defend itself against non-Christian attack. Christianity is true Judaism over against the spurious Judaism of the anti-Christian synagogue.[2]

In his lengthy Preface to the revised 1968 edition of his *The School of St Matthew*, K. Stendahl wrote as follows:

Matthew's community now existed in sharp contrast to the Jewish community in town. For in this church things Jewish meant Jewish and not Jewish Christian versus gentile Christian. In such a setting traditions could be preserved and elaborated in a style which in other communities had become suspect or outdated. On the basis of such traditions and in such a milieu Matthew brings his gospel to completion. That he was once a Jew cannot be doubted. That he had had Jewish training in Palestine prior to the War is probable. That he belongs to a Hellenistic community is obvious. That this community includes gentiles is sure. What does this make the gospel?

[1] See also W.G. Kümmel's *Introduction to the New Testament*, E.tr. 2nd ed. 1975. On p.114 he concludes that the church of Matthew sees itself as over against Judaism; the evangelist is a birthright Jew writing for Jewish Christians. For references to other scholars, see G. Künzel, *Gemeindeverständnis*, 215ff. See also L. Cope, *Matthew: a Scribe Trained for the Kingdom of Heaven*, 214ff., who concludes that the gospel was written by a Jewish Christian whose church was already separated from Judaism – though Matthew is less close to full separation than John's gospel.

[2] 'St. Matthew's Gospel: Some Neglected Features', *Studia Evangelica* II, TU 87, Berlin 1964, 91-99; reprinted in his collected essays, *Essays in New Testament Interpretation*, Cambridge 1982, 67-74. See also Moule's widely used *The Birth of the New Testament*, London 1962, 3rd ed. 1981, 124-8.

> A witness to a far smoother transition from Judaism to Christianity than we usually suppose.[1]

These comments are perceptive and, in my judgement, plausible, though I detect much more pain in the parting of the ways between the 'churches' to whom Matthew wrote and local synagogues.[2]

E. Schweizer claimed that the Jewish Christian characteristics of the gospel cannot be overlooked or confined to the traditions used by the evangelist. The Pharisees are undoubtedly Matthew's most important 'conversation partners'. Schweizer accepts that whereas Luke 6. 22 seems to assume that Christians have been excluded from synagogues, the parallel passage in Matt 5. 11 speaks much less specifically of general abuse and persecution. This might be taken as an indication that the community has not yet parted company with Judaism, but passages such as 23. 34 and 10. 23 which refer to persecution from town to town and, indeed, of the 'death and crucifixion' of those disciples sent out by Jesus, confirm that the relationship between church and synagogue is most definitely not *intra muros*.[3]

It is one of the main purposes of this book to give more precision to this general understanding of the relationship of Matthew's gospel to contemporary Judaism.[4] I shall now set out briefly some of the main considerations which, taken cumulatively, support this third view. Chapter 4, and Chapters 6–11 in this book provide further reasons.

(i) In Matthew Jewish religious leaders and groups – and in particular scribes and Pharisees – are consistently placed in a negative light. The invective against the scribes and Pharisees in ch. 23 brings to a climax hostility which runs

---

[1] *The School of St Matthew*, 2nd 1968 ed., xiiif.
[2] See Chapter 6.
[3] *Matthäus und seine Gemeinde*, SBS 71, Stuttgart 1974, 11f. and 36f.
[4] Recent supporters of this third approach include W.A. Meeks, S. Freyne, B. Przybylski, U. Luz, and D.A. Hagner. See the Bibliography for references.

right through the gospel and which is sharper and more sustained than in the other gospels. Whereas Mark refers to the Pharisees as hypocrites only once (7. 6) and Luke not at all, Matthew has twelve such references, six of which are in ch. 23.

The bitterness is unrelieved by any suggestion that some individual scribes or Pharisees might be sympathetic to Jesus or his followers. There is no sign in Matthew of the friendly Pharisees who, according to Luke 7. 36 and 14. 1, invited Jesus to dine with them; nor is there a reference to Pharisees who warned Jesus that Herod wanted to kill him (Luke 13. 31). Mark's sympathetic scribe (12. 28) becomes a hostile Pharisee (Matt 22. 35). So it is no surprise to find that in his important summary statement at the end of the Sermon on the Mount (7. 29), Matthew carefully distances Jesus and the scribes by adding 'their' (αὐτῶν) to the reference to 'the scribes' at Mark 1. 22.

Matt 8. 18-21 is all of a piece. The eager scribe who seeks to follow Jesus merely on his own initiative and without a prior 'call' from Jesus is repudiated, but someone else, who is not a scribe, is portrayed as a disciple and reminded sharply of the radical nature of discipleship.[1] In typical Matthean fashion, the repudiated scribe addresses Jesus as 'teacher' (διδάσκαλε) while the true disciple addresses Jesus as 'Lord' (κύριε).

At 9. 18-26 Matthew revises radically Mark's striking portrait of Jairus whose daughter Jesus heals. Mark refers to Jairus four times as a 'ruler of the synagogue' (5. 22, 35, 36, 38, ἀρχισυνάγωγος).[2] In Matthew he is still portrayed as a man of faith, but he loses his name and becomes merely an anonymous 'official' (9. 18, 23, ἄρχων); there is not even a

---

[1] See J.D. Kingsbury, 'On Following Jesus: the "Eager" Scribe and the "Reluctant" Disciple (Matthew 8. 18-22)', NTS 34 (1988) 45-59. RSV translates ἕτερος in 8. 21 as 'another of the disciples', thereby implying that both men are scribes and are accepted by Jesus as true disciples. NEB and REB correctly translate 'another man, one of his disciples', thereby avoiding any suggestion that he is a scribe.

[2] On Mark 5. 21-4, 35-43 see especially C.D. Marshall, *Faith as a Theme in Mark's Narrative*, Cambridge 1989, 90-100.

hint that he has any connection with a synagogue.[1] Matthew and Luke both include the Q tradition of the healing of the centurion's servant (Matt 8. 5-13 = Luke 7. 1-10), but there is no sign in Matthew of Luke's note that the centurion loves the Jewish nation and has built a synagogue (7. 5).[2]

In Matthew Jewish leaders are always at odds with Jesus and his disciples (and later followers), so a 'ruler of the synagogue' cannot be a 'man of faith', and a scribe cannot be portrayed as a true disciple. The wide gulf between scribes and Pharisees on the one hand, and Jesus and his disciples on the other, reflects the circumstances of the evangelist's day: 'synagogue' and 'church' have parted company.

(ii) Matthew explicitly associates scribes and Pharisees with synagogues (23. 6, 34; cf. also 10. 17). The evangelist's sustained hostility to the former is echoed in his references to synagogues. At Matt 4. 23; 9. 35; 10. 17; 12. 9; 13. 54, all passages where the evangelist's own hand is clear, he uses the phrase 'their synagogue(s)'; at 23. 34 he uses the redactional phrase 'your synagogues'.[3] With these slight changes Matthew

---

[1] Although ἄρχων is used to refer to a synagogue official or a member of the Sanhedrin in several first century writings (including Luke-Acts and John), *contra* BAG, Matthew never uses the word in this way. His only other reference to ἄρχων as a human official is at 20. 25, where ἄρχοντες are pagan officials, a usage well attested elsewhere. NEB incorrectly translates ἄρχων in Matt 9. 18 as 'a president of the synagogue'; the error was spotted by the REB translators, who have 'an official'.

[2] I do not think that Luke 7. 5 is a Q tradition which Matthew has omitted. Luke has probably expanded the Q tradition himself in order to bring out the parallel with Cornelius in Acts 10. Nonetheless, the contrast between the Matthean and Lucan versions of the same incident is striking.

[3] As far as I know, this point was first made by Kilpatrick, *Origins*, 110. However, in claiming that Matthew's usage was not merely distinctive, but unique, he went too far. At Mark 1. 23, 39 and Luke 4. 15 συναγωγή is followed by αὐτῶν. Kilpatrick noted that in all three cases some mss do not include the pronominal genitive and argued that αὐτῶν was not in the original text, but came into the textual tradition as an assimilation to the Matthean idiom. But the textual evidence for the omission of αὐτῶν is weak and confined almost entirely to some versional witnesses. In this case, as in many others, Matthew extends considerably a Marcan phrase; see Chapter 14 below for several examples.

drives a wedge between Jesus and his disciples on the one hand, and the synagogue on the other.

Matthew uses συναγωγή in only three further passages, 6. 2, 5; 23. 6. In each case there is a strong negative connotation: disciples of Jesus are not to follow the example of scribes and Pharisees in the synagogue.[1] These passages strongly suggest that for Matthew (but not for Mark) the 'synagogue' has almost become an alien institution.

(iii) Over against συναγωγή stands the ἐκκλησία founded by Jesus himself and promised divine protection (16. 18). Matthew uses 'church' (ἐκκλησία) three times (16. 18; and twice in 18. 17), but this term is not found in the other three gospels. The church has its own entrance rite, baptism in the triadic name (28. 19). Matthew's reshaping of Mark's account of the last supper (26. 26-30) reflects liturgical usage and thus confirms that the church in Matthew's day has its own distinctive central act of worship.

In a series of striking passages disciples of Jesus (and their later followers) are promised that Jesus will be present with them in their community life in ways analogous to the ways God was understood to be present in temple and synagogue (8. 23-7; 14. 22-33; 18. 20; 28. 20). At 23. 21 Matthew confirms that many Jews continued to regard God's presence (his shekhina) in the temple as a central belief.[2] But Matthew emphasizes that whereas the Jerusalem temple is 'forsaken and desolate' (23. 38), with the coming of Jesus, 'something

---

[1] At 6. 2, 5 'hypocrites' are referred to, but 5. 20 informs the reader that they are none other than 'the scribes and Pharisees'.

[2] See also Psalm 135. 21; 11Q Temple 29. 7-10; m. Sukkah 5. 4. I owe the references to a summary of a paper by Graham Davies, 'The Shekhina in the Second Temple', published in the British Association for Jewish Studies Bulletin (Oct-Dec 1989). In *TDNT* VII, art. συναγωγή, 824, W. Schrage lists a number of rabbinic traditions which emphasize that God's shekhina is present in the synagogue as well as the temple. In their present form these traditions may be no earlier than c. A.D. 300, but since synagogue and temple were considered even in the first century to be equivalent in many respects, it seems probable that God's shekhina was associated with the synagogue.

greater than the temple is here' (12. 6).[1] A. Schlatter is one of the few to appreciate the importance of this bold Matthean Christological claim; he notes that 'God is present in Jesus to a greater extent than in the temple'.[2]

Whereas the reading of torah and instruction in it were central in the synagogue, in the church the commands of Jesus took precedence. Although Matthew insists strongly on the continuing importance of the law (5. 17-19), hearing and doing the authoritative words of Jesus are of paramount importance (7. 24-7),[3] for the words of Jesus are 'commands' for the life of the church (28. 20).

Matthew's communities seem to be developing structures which are quite independent of the synagogue. They exercise, with divine sanction and on the authority of Jesus, the right of inclusion into and of exclusion from the community (16. 19; 18. 19). Some groups within Christian communities are modelled on their Jewish counterparts: there seem to be Christian prophets (10. 41; 23. 34); Christian scribes (13. 52; 23. 34); and Christian wise men and teachers of the law (23. 34). But in contrast to the synagogue, within the life of the church, no individual or group is to be accorded special honours or titles (23. 6 - 12).

The ἐκκλησία founded by Jesus continues to have a firm commitment to torah, but it has accepted Gentiles and developed its own patterns of worship and of community

---

[1] Matthew has modelled 12. 6 on the 'greater than Jonah' and 'greater than Solomon' Q logia he uses at 12. 41 and 42. See above, 82.

[2] *Der Evangelist Matthäus*, 396. Although Schlatter assumes that 12. 6 is an authentic Jesus logion, he would have agreed that it also represents Matthew's view. See also J.A.T. Robinson, *Redating the New Testament*, London 1976, 104.

[3] Similarly, George W.E. Nickelsburg, who notes that Matt 7. 24-7 is a doubly structured allusion to the doubly structured oracle in Isa 28. 'Salvation and damnation are tied to one's reponse to "my words" rather than to the Torah.' 'Revealed Wisdom as a Criterion for Inclusion and Exclusion: from Jewish Sectarianism to Early Christianity', in *"To see Ourselves as Others See Us": Christians, Jews and "Others" in Late Antiquity*, ed. J. Neusner and E.S. Frerichs, Missoula 1985, 86.

life. Its self-understanding is quite distinct from that of the synagogue.

(iv) Further compelling support for the conclusion that in Matthew's day synagogue and church are going their own separate ways is provided by passages which speak about the 'transference' of the kingdom to a new people who will include Gentiles. At 8. 5-13 Matthew links two Q traditions (Luke 7. 1-10 and 13. 28-9) in order to state starkly that 'those born to the kingdom' will be replaced by Gentiles (including the Roman centurion whose faith is commended) who will sit with faithful Israel (Abraham, Isaac, and Jacob) at the banquet in the kingdom of heaven.

At 15. 13 Matthew adds a strongly polemical saying to a Marcan tradition. The Pharisees are no longer considered to be 'a plant of the heavenly Father's planting'. By implication their place will be taken by another people. This becomes explicit at 21. 41 and 43 in Matthew's redaction of Mark's parable of the wicked husbandmen. The Jewish leaders will be rejected by God. The vineyard will be transferred to other tenants – a people who will yield the proper fruit.

(v) At the climax of his story at 28. 15 the evangelist addresses his readers directly and refers explicitly to the relationship between synagogue and church in his own day. He tells them that a rival account of the resurrection of Jesus – his disciples stole his body from the tomb – 'has been widely circulated among Jews to this very day.' This comment brings out into the open what has been hinted at again and again throughout the gospel. Jews who have not accepted Christian claims are set at a distance and referred to as an entity quite distinct from 'the new people'. They have an alternative story which, the evangelist claims, can be shown to be patently absurd.

For Gentiles not in dispute with Judaism?

Supporters of the fourth view argue that since Matthew's community has clearly cut completely all its ties with Judaism, the evangelist is a Gentile Christian whose community is neither attacking nor defending itself against any strand of Judaism in the Jamnian period, A.D. 70–100. Matthew's community was predominantly Jewish at an earlier phase of its development, but by the evangelist's day most members were Gentiles. Discussion with Judaism had become both impossible and quite irrelevant.

This way of understanding the relationship of the Matthean community to Judaism was very much a minority view until a decade or two ago. Since then it has been proposed by a number of scholars, who, although they differ in their approach and emphases, all stress the distance between Matthew's community and Judaism.

Some stress the historical distance. S. van Tilborg, for example, claims that Matthew lived in a world in which Judaism was no longer a serious competitor. 'If one wishes to call the Jews who have refused to be converted hypocrites, evil people, murderers and imposters, there must be a fairly great and satisfactory distance on a historical level.'[1] For R. Walker Israel is 'distant' in a rather different sense: Matthew's interest in Judaism is purely theological, not historical, for Israel is considered to be a phenomenon of salvation history which lies in the past. The attempt to see the gospel as a polemical or apologetic document must be rejected as faulty: the 'apologetic' and 'polemical' features of the gospel are in fact ingredients of its salvation historical perspective.[2]

The first modern protest against the almost universally accepted view that it is the 'Jewishness' of Matthew which must be accounted for in any discussion of its origin and purpose was raised by K.W. Clark. He insisted that the reasons for believing that Matthew was written by a Jewish Christian are 'more traditional than rational'.[3] He claimed that passages such as 8. 12; 12. 21; 21. 39; 28. 16ff., and the parables in 21. 1 – 22. 14 and in chapter 25, all confirm that

---

[1] *The Jewish Leaders in Matthew*, Leiden 1972, 171.
[2] *Die Heilsgeschichte im ersten Evangelium*, FRLANT 91, Göttingen 1967, 145.
[3] 'The Gentile Bias in Matthew', *JBL* 66, 1947, 165-72.

the rejection of Israel is the central theme of the gospel. Matthew's permanent rejection of Israel is so clear and strong that it must be regarded as evidence that his gospel was written by a Gentile, since no Jewish Christian would have been capable of such a view of Israel.

A decade later P. Nepper-Christensen raised a similar protest against prevailing views: he denied that Matthew should be seen as a 'Jewish Christian' gospel.[1] He showed how insecurely based were many of the arguments used to support the traditional view. He did not set out a particular view of the origin and purpose of the gospel,[2] though he did tentatively make a distinction between the tradition which the evangelist received and the evangelist's own emphases. This distinction has been drawn much more sharply by several other scholars, most notably G. Strecker, who deny that the 'Jewishness' of the gospel is a distinctive feature of the final redaction.

Almost simultaneously, and quite independently, G. Strecker and W. Trilling also rejected the assumption, which had been almost axiomatic in Matthean scholarship, that Matthew was written by a Jew who had become a Christian.[3] After considering at some length whether or not the evangelist was a Jewish Christian, Strecker concluded that the Jewish features of the gospel did not confirm that the gospel comes from Jewish Christian circles: the most characteristic assertions of the final redactor revealed his

---

[1] *Das Matthäusevangelium - ein judenchristliches Evangelium?* Aarhus 1958.

[2] His book was criticised for this reason; see, for example, G. Bornkamm, *Tradition*, 51, and G. Strecker, *Der Weg*, 15 n.4, but the force of his challenge to the traditional view was considerable: C.F.D. Moule, *The Birth of the New Testament*, London 1962, 73 conceded that the evangelist may not have been a Jew, and W.D. Davies, *The Setting*, 325, noted that the Jewish Christian character of Matthew had been too readily assumed in modern scholarship,

[3] G. Strecker, *Der Weg*, 15 n.5, notes that Trilling's and Nepper-Christensen's work, which mark a turn in Matthean scholarship, appeared at almost the same time as his 1958-9 thesis on which his book is based.

distance not only from Palestinian Judaism, but from Judaism generally; the non-Jewish elements of his redaction link his gospel with Gentile Christianity.[1] With rather more caution than some of his critics have supposed, Strecker distinguished between an earlier Jewish Christian phase in the life of the Matthean community and the Gentile Christianity which had become dominant in the evangelist's own day.

W. Trilling also suggested that the community had developed from an early Jewish Christian phase to a point where strong Gentile Christian emphases are prominent. As the final redactor, Matthew thinks resolutely as a Gentile Christian and as a universalist.[2] For Trilling, Matthew is poised at a half way point between Jewish Christianity and Gentile Christianity. In the pericope concerning payment of the Temple tax, 17. 24-7, freedom from the mother religion still lies firmly side by side with association with her.[3]

However in some respects Trilling was closer to the third view discussed above. His central proposal that Matthew's community sees itself as 'true Israel' indicates just how important contemporary Israel continues to be for the evangelist. Both the church and 'false' Israel claim to be the Israel of election and promise, and this explains the polemical situation of the gospel. Since only one 'people' can be the true Israel, every such claim must be denied to the other.[4]

---

[1] *Der Weg*, 34.
[2] *Das wahre Israel*, Studien zum Alten und Neuen Testament 10, 2nd ed. Leipzig, 1961; 3rd ed. Munich, 1964, 215; he notes that in various forms this view has been defended by a number of scholars, starting with F.C. Baur and A. Hilgenfeld. The distinction between Jewish and Gentile Christianity is drawn much less sharply than in Strecker's monograph.
[3] *Das wahre Israel*, 224.
[4] *Das wahre Israel*, 95. D.R.A. Hare rejects Trilling's view. He attaches particular importance to Matthew's use of ἔθνος in 21. 43. The kingdom of God is not being transferred from one part of Israel to another – from false Israel to true Israel or from old Israel to new Israel. 'The transfer is from Israel to *another people*, non-Israel. It is this radical discontinuity between Israel and her successor which requires that we regard the rejection of Israel in Matthew as final and complete.' *The Theme of*

The arguments which have been used to support this fourth view are unconvincing. I shall discuss briefly four which have been appealed to frequently, though not all writers have made use of all four arguments.

(i) The view that Matthew was a Gentile disinterested in contemporary Judaism depends heavily on the assumption that a sharp distinction can be drawn between the traditions on which Matthew drew and his own redaction of them. The former are said to reflect an earlier stage in the history of Matthean Christianity, while the latter (which are said to be strongly pro-Gentile and non-Jewish) reflect the circumstances of the evangelist's own day.

In Chapter 2 I emphasized that Matthew incorporates earlier traditions with little or no modification simply because he accepts them and wishes to preserve them. Earlier traditions reflect Matthew's convictions just as much as his redactional modification.[1] This point has now been widely accepted; it calls in question the claim that the final redaction of the gospel is decisive for our appreciation of the evangelist's purposes.

But even if we were to allow that a sharp distinction can be made between earlier traditions and the final redaction of the gospel, this view would founder. For in *redactional* passages we find phraseology and theological motifs which look like the work of someone steeped in Scripture and in contemporary Judaism. Numerous examples are given in Chapters 6 to 11 in this book. While it is just possible to envisage that the evangelist was a learned Gentile with such a long and close relationship with Judaism that he thought and wrote like a Jew, such an author would have been as interested in the relationship of Christianity to Judaism as any Jewish writer.

(ii) Scholars who support the fourth view regularly claim that in redactional passages the evangelist betrays such ignorance of Jewish parties and laws that he could not have been

Jewish Persecution of Christians in the Gospel According to St. Matthew, SNTSMS 6, Cambridge 1967, 153.
[1] See 41 and 52.

a Jew.[1] It is not possible to discuss all the points which have been raised; I shall concentrate on one of the most intractable problems, Matthew's references to the Sadducees.

Matthew uses the phrase 'Pharisees and Sadducees' five times (3. 7; 16. 1, 6, 11, 12); they are not linked together in this way anywhere else in the NT, or in other first century writings. J.P. Meier claims that no Jew could write a sentence such as 16. 12, which speaks of *the* doctrine common to the Pharisees and Sadducees as if they were one entity set over against the teaching of Jesus: 'Matthew must be considered to have been ignorant of the exact doctrine of the Sadducees. . . and this is extremely difficult to square with the hypothesis of a Jewish-Christian redactor'.[2]

Why did the evangelist add references to the Sadducees in just two places in his gospel: 3. 7, where Pharisees and Sadducees go to John for baptism, and 16. 1-12 where there are four references in all?[3] Why are there redactional references in these particular passages and not elsewhere? There are plenty of passages in which Sadducees might well have been linked with the Pharisees as opponents of Jesus. If Matthew knew little or nothing about the Sadducees, why did he bother to introduce them at all? Surely his argument would not have been weakened by their omission?

There are no easy answers to these questions. But the most plausible explanation of Matthew's usage is the simplest: from the perspective of the evangelist the similarity between Pharisees and Sadducees is more important than their differences; they are alike in their opposition to Jesus and his followers. The occasional linking of Pharisees and Sadducees in Matthew is part of a much broader pattern. Throughout the evangelist's story there is a wide gulf between Jesus and his disciples (and later followers) on the one hand, and

---

[1] L. Gaston even describes Matthew's ignorance as 'astonishing': 'The Messiah of Israel as Teacher of the Gentiles', *Interpretation* 29 (1975) 25-40, here 34.

[2] *Law and History*, 19.

[3] Strictly speaking, 16. 1-4 and 5-12 are separate pericopae, but on any reckoning they are very closely related.

various combinations of Jewish groups and leaders on the other. We need not necessarily conclude that since Matthew was unaware of any differences between the two groups, he was a Gentile far removed from contemporary Judaism.[1]

We know comparatively little about the Sadducees either before or immediately after 70. Most of our information comes from opponents of the Sadducees, so perhaps it is not surprising that the evangelist's usage is so puzzling. Similar problems arise with most of the alleged examples of Matthew's ignorance of contemporary Judaism. There are simply too many gaps in our knowledge of Judaism in the period A.D. 70–100 to enable us to pronounce a confident verdict on the extent and accuracy of the evangelist's knowledge of Judaism.

(iii) It is alleged that Matthew's rejection of Israel is so absolute that for Matthew the struggle with Israel is well and truly over. While it is generally accepted that in the evangelist's eyes unbelieving Israel is judged and rejected, supporters of the fourth view deny that Matthew envisages a continuing mission to Israel.

Discussion of this point has focussed on 28. 19. Does the climax of the gospel, μαθητεύσατε πάντα τὰ ἔθνη, 'make disciples of all nations', include Israel or not? If not, then supporters of the fourth way of understanding Matthew's relationship to contemporary Judaism have a strong argument. There has been a lively debate on the meaning of πάντα τὰ ἔθνη. In a joint article, D.R.A. Hare and D.J. Harrington insist that πάντα τὰ ἔθνη in 28. 19 should be translated 'all the Gentiles'; Israel has been rejected finally and completely.[2] In a reply J.P. Meier argues, surely correctly, that in 21. 43, the crucial Matthean redactional addition to

---

1 Here I am in broad agreement with Strecker, who concludes that the references to the Sadducees are part of the evangelist's 'historicizing'; they reflect not the situation within contemporary Judaism, but the theological position of the Matthean community. *Der Weg*, 140. Cf. also J. Le Moyne, *Les Sadducéens*, Paris 1972, 123: 'C'est un assemblage artificiel qui ne représente pas la réalité historique.'

2 ' "Make Disciples of all the Gentiles" (Mt. 28. 19)', *CBQ* 37 (1975) 359-69.

Mark's parable, the ἔθνος to whom the Kingdom will be given includes both Jews and Gentiles. 24. 14 also confirms that πάντα τὰ ἔθνη should be translated 'all nations'. I have myself insisted that 23. 39 does not rule out the possibility that some individual Jews will still become Christians: on the contrary, it expresses the confident hope that at the parousia some will say joyfully, 'Blessed is he who comes in the name of the Lord.'[1] And, finally, since the evangelist intends his references to the disciples and the crowds to be 'transparent' and to refer partly to Christians in his own community, then references to Jewish persecution of Christians in 10. 17 and 23. 34 presuppose a continuing mission to Jews as well as to Gentiles.

(iv) Is Matthew's anti-Jewish polemic so strong that we are forced to conclude that the evangelist himself cannot have been a Jew? The strength of Matthew's anti-Pharisaism was one of the reasons why Clark concluded that Matthew was a Gentile. S. van Tilborg has also claimed that the simplest explanation of the strong anti-Jewish currents in the gospel is that he himself was not a Jew.[2]

I believe that the reverse is more likely to have been the case. As Hare has noted, 'Whereas the Gentile Luke speaks of the synagogue with the detachment natural to one for whom it is a foreign institution, Matthew speaks as one for whom it has only recently become an alien institution.'[3]

Ferocious conflict is often a hallmark of a close 'family-like' relationship. In Chapter 11 I shall argue that 5 Ezra, which may have been written shortly after A.D. 135, has been strongly influenced by Matthew's gospel. This short writing includes strong anti-Jewish polemic, but it also bears the marks of deep Christian anguish over Israel. Not only is Israel completely and finally rejected, but she is to be scattered (1. 33; 2. 7) and to have no posterity (1. 34; 2. 6). In 5 Ezra God is turning to 'a people soon to come' (1. 35, 38), 'another people' (1. 24) who will replace Israel. The anti-Jewish and

---

[1] See Chapter 10, 249-50.
[2] *Jewish Leaders*, 171.
[3] *Jewish Persecution*, 165.

pro-Gentile views are even more pronounced than they are in Matthew, but from its form, its contents, and its phraseology there can be no doubt at all that its author is a Jewish Christian.

Matthew's anti-Jewish polemic, and chapter 23 in particular, is part of the process by which Matthew distances himself and his communities from his Pharisaic rivals: the tensions are real, not a matter of past history. This point will be discussed further in Chapter 6.

I have now considered the four general explanations of Matthew's relationship to Judaism which scholars have proposed. There is little to be said in favour of either the first or the fourth view. The first is undermined by acceptance of Marcan priority. And the fourth view can be sustained only on the basis of an untenable distinction between pre-Matthean 'Jewish' sources and the evangelist's own later 'Gentile' redaction.

A decision between the second and third views is more difficult. Why have scholars differed in their conclusions? D.A. Hagner has correctly noted that there are undoubted tensions within the gospel itself and that the two opposing groups of scholars emphasize different sets of passages, 'to the neglect, if not the exclusion, of data on the other side.'[1]

If, as I have argued, the third view is to be preferred, how are the 'pillar passages' which seem to support the second view to be interpreted? Of the three passages which have been appealed to frequently, Matt 10. 5-6 is the most straight forward. Here Matthew's readers are reminded that Jesus and his original circle of disciples did confine their proclamation of the kingdom 'to the lost sheep of the house of Israel'. Perhaps some Christians in Matthew's day were reluctant to accept a Gentile mission, but the evangelist offers no concessions to their point of view. At the climax of the gospel – the

---

[1] 'The *Sitz im Leben* of the Gospel of Matthew', in *SBL 1985 Seminar Papers*, 249.

key to its understanding[1] – the Risen Lord pronounces with divine authority that his followers are henceforth to make disciples of all nations (28. 19). With the resurrection a new era has dawned.

Matthew does not wait until the end of his gospel to make this crucial point. The mission discourse in ch. 10 itself confirms that the words of Jesus in 10. 5 forbidding a Gentile mission will one day be countermanded. As the discourse unfolds, readers and listeners in the evangelist's day become aware that they themselves are being addressed: they can expect to be brought before (non-Jewish) governors and kings on account of their commitment to Jesus; they will be called to testify before them *and the Gentiles* (10. 18). The same point is repeated even more vigorously at 24. 9-14.

Within the mission discourse itself readers are given a reason for the expansion of the mission to Israel to include Gentiles. On account of the harsh treatment of followers of Jesus by Jewish courts and synagogues, the message of the kingdom will be taken to Gentiles (10. 17-18). Here Matthew anticipates his interpretation of the parable of the wicked husbandmen (21. 33-43). Jewish rejection of Jesus is the reason why 'the vineyard will be handed over to other tenants' (21. 41), and 'the kingdom will be taken away from you and given to a nation that yields the proper fruit'. (21. 43).

Matt 23. 2-3 must also be interpreted in the light of the thrust of the whole discourse which follows. These two verses seem to indicate that the scribes and Pharisees are the true heirs and guardians of the teaching of Moses; while their hypocritical behaviour is to be shunned, their teaching is to be followed.

But as the discourse unfolds, it becomes clear that much of the *teaching* of the scribes and Pharisees is unacceptable (23. 4, 16, 18). Once again readers become aware that the circumstances of their own day are being addressed. Followers of Jesus will be persecuted severely in synagogues by scribes and

---

[1] O. Michel made this important point in 'The Conclusion of Matthew's Gospel', E.tr. in *Matthew*, 35.

Pharisees who will be rejected and judged by God (23. 35-8). From Matthew's perspective, the authority of the scribes and Pharisees is eroded completely by their hypocrisy, their unacceptable teaching, and their hostility to disciples of Jesus. Their teaching is to be followed (23. 3a), but only in so far as they truly expound the Mosaic law. Only by removing 23. 2-3 from the context of the whole discourse is it possible to interpret these verses as a tactical ploy on the part of Matthew to avoid a complete rupture between synagogue and church.

Of the three passages which have been taken by some to confirm that Matthew's communities still retain ties with Judaism, Matt 17. 24-7 is the most puzzling. In order to avoid giving offence, disciples of Jesus are urged to pay a tax for the general support of the temple. The Romans' destruction of the temple in A.D. 70 brought that apparently optional tax to an end. Since Matthew undoubtedly wrote after A.D. 70, payment of the temple tax was no longer an issue for his readers. The tax introduced by the Romans to replace the temple tax,[1] the *fiscus Judaicus*, was compulsory, so that tax is not in view in this passage.

Why did Matthew incorporate this passage into his gospel? It is unlikely that he included an anachronistic tradition simply on the grounds of his faithfulness to the sources at his disposal. Perhaps his intention was to remind his readers that followers of Jesus were once within Israel – numerous other passages show that those days are over. Or perhaps from Matthew's perspective an anachronistic tradition has been included because it can be understood as a 'parable' which urges Christians to adopt as far as possible a conciliatory attitude towards Jews.[2] If so, then the thrust of this passage may be comparable with Matt 24. 20. In chapter 8 I shall argue that Christians are to pray that 'flight on the sabbath' may be avoided so that they will not give further offence to hostile Jewish authorities. At 17. 24-7 and 24. 20 Matthew's readers are urged to avoid unnecessary

---

[1] So Josephus, *Bell.* VII. 218.
[2] So S. Légasse, 'Jésus et l'impôt du Temple (Mt 17, 24-27)' *ScEs* 24 (1972) 361-77. I owe this reference to U. Luz, *Matthäus* II, 536 n.53.

141

provocation of their hostile Jewish neighbours from whom they have parted company.

In all three cases passages which seem to imply that Matthew's communities are conscious of continuing links with contemporary Judaism must be interpreted in the light of the thrust of the whole gospel. When that is done, they do not undermine confidence in the view I am advancing.

Matthew and the birkath ha-minim

If Matthew's gospel was written shortly after a painful separation from Judaism, is it possible to be more specific about its historical setting? For many decades now most Matthean scholars have linked the origin of the gospel with the alleged introduction into the synagogue liturgy in about A.D. 85 of a curse upon Christians, the *birkath ha-minim*. Some scholars have claimed that since the impact of this anti-Christian 'decree' cannot be seen clearly within the gospel, the evangelist must have written prior to its insertion and prior to the parting of the ways between Christians and Jews. Others have claimed that Matthew's sustained anti-Pharisaic polemic and the parting of the ways were the direct result of the introduction of the *birkath ha-minim*.[1]

I believe that the *birkath ha-minim* has been a red herring in Matthean scholarship, just as it has been in discussion about the historical setting of the fourth gospel. Before I give my reasons for this judgement, it will be helpful to summarize our knowledge of the origin of the *birkath ha-minim*. According to a *baraitha* (a saying included in the Talmud which was unrecorded in the Mishnah, but dates from that time) at *Ber.* 28b-29b, a 'benediction of the heretics' (*birkath ha-minim*) was 'ordered' by Samuel the Small at the request of Gamaliel II in Jamnia to be added (as number 12) to the

---

[1] Discussion goes back some time. In his review in *JTS* 48 (1947) 219 of G.D. Kilpatrick's *Origins*, T.W. Manson suggested that the Matthean phenomena may represent an earlier stage of tension which finally breaks out in the *birkath ha-minim*, rather than a sequel to it.

Eighteen Benedictions (*Shemoneh Esreh*). The names mentioned in the immediate context suggest that this was done towards the end of the first century. The wording of the Eighteen Benedictions varies considerably in the Hebrew texts which have survived. In many texts (but not all) *minim* are referred to; in some, *noserim* (Nazarenes = Christians).

Matthean scholars have usually assumed that the 1898 Cairo Geniza form of the additonal benediction is relevant and have often quoted it:

> For apostates let there be no hope, and the kingdom of insolence mayest thou uproot speedily in our days; and let the Nazarenes (*noserim*) and the heretics (*minim*) perish in a moment, let them be blotted out of the book of life and let them not be written with the righteous. Blessed art thou, O Lord, who humblest the insolent.

Several problems have been conveniently overlooked by scholars anxious to make a direct link between the *birkath ha-minim* and the origin of Matthew. (a) We do not know exactly when the additional benediction was added to the *Shemoneh Esreh*. (b) We do not know whether the addition was adopted immediately and universally. Many scholars have assumed, without any evidence, that the addition was promulgated and then adopted automatically by Jews everywhere. Its impact is assumed to have been similar to that of a medieval papal decree on Christians. (c) The original wording is uncertain. Since the shorter simpler version of the text is more likely to be original, the reference to 'Nazarenes' may well be a later secondary addition. (d) The interpretation of *minim* is uncertain. P. Schäfer has claimed that the additional prayer was a plea for liberation from the political oppression of the Romans and for the annihilation of the heretics.[1] R. Kimelman insists that only Jews, whether

---

[1] P. Schäfer, 'Die sogenannte Synode von Jabne', *Judaica* 31 (1975) 54-64 and 116-124; reprinted in P. Schäfer, *Studien zur Geschichte und Theologie des rabbinischen Judentums*, Leiden 1978.

sectarian or Christian, are envisaged.[1] In his thorough discussion W. Horbury argues that Christians, both Jew and Gentile, were cursed in synagogue. 'It was not decisive on its own in the separation of church and synagogue, but it gave solemn liturgical expression to a separation effected in the second half of the first century through the larger group of measures to which it belongs.'[2] This seems to me to be a plausible historical reconstruction, but Horbury does concede that the wording of the benediction was variable, and that no surviving text can be assumed to reproduce a specimen form of the Jamnian prayer.

In short, too many uncertainties surround the *birkath ha-minim* to allow us to link it directly to the origin and purpose of Matthew's gospel. It is, however, possible to be a little more confident about associating Matthew with Jamnian Judaism, named after the academy which, according to several rabbinic traditions, was founded at Yavneh (Jamnia) about A.D. 85 or 90 by Rabbi Johannan ben Zakkai. This academy or council is said to have been responsible for the introduction of the *birkath ha-minim*.

It is clear from recent intensive research into the Jamnian period (led initially by J. Neusner) that it is not possible either to set out with any confidence the agenda, decisions, and dates of the Jamnian academy, or even to say much about the individual leaders involved.[3] However, there is now general agreement that in the decades after 70 far-reaching

---

[1] '*Birkat Ha-Minim* and the Lack of Evidence for an Anti-Christian Prayer in Late Antiquity', in *Jewish and Christian Self-Definition* II, ed. E.P. Sanders, London 1981, 226-44.

[2] 'The Benediction of the *Minim* and Early Jewish-Christian Controversy', *JTS* 33 (1982) 19-61.

[3] J.A. Overman, *Matthew's Gospel and Formative Judaism*, provides a summary and assessment of recent scholarship, 35-71. See in particular Jacob Neusner, 'The Formation of Rabbinic Judaism: Yavneh from A.D. 70 – 100', *ANRW* II. 19.2 (1979) 3-42 (and in numerous other writings). See also G. Stemberger, 'Die sogenannte "Synode von Jabne" und das frühe Christentum', *Kairos* 19 (1977) 14-21; P. Schäfer, 'Die sogenannte Synode von Jabne' (cited on 143); A. Saldarini, *Pharisees, Scribes and Sadducees in Palestinian Society*, Wilmington 1988.

reconstruction and consolidation of Judaism took place which included a more careful drawing of the boundaries of acceptable diversity within Judaism. The separation of Matthean Christianity from Judaism was almost certainly one part of this process.

J. Neusner has won considerable support for his claim that the institutional reconstruction which took place during the Jamnian period was led by Pharisees who were joined by scribes to form what became the rabbinic academy, and, in due course, the rabbinic court.[1] The relevance of this proposal for the student of Matthew is clear once we recall that it is Matthew who associates closely scribes and Pharisees and implies that together they are the leaders of Judaism. There are, however, grounds for caution. We do not know how far the authority of the Jamnian academy extended at any particular point in time. Since we do not know where Matthew was written, or even precisely when, it would be rash to assume without further ado that it was written in the shadow of Jamnia. This seems to me to be a strong probability, but we cannot say more.[2]

---

[1] See J. Neusner, 'The Formation of Rabbinic Judaism'.

[2] In *The Setting of the Sermon on the Mount*, W.D. Davies argued for a much closer link between Matthew and Jamnian Judaism.

Chapter Six

The Gospel of Matthew and Judaism

Matthew's vigorous anti-Jewish polemic is acutely embarrassing to most modern readers of this gospel.[1] The fierce denunciations of the scribes and Pharisees in chapter 23 and the evangelist's apparent concern to stress God's rejection of Israel have been discussed in several recent German and American books and in collections of essays concerned with the general theme of Christian – Jewish relationships.[2] For no apparent reason, this important and sensitive issue has been discussed less frequently in the United Kingdom. I hope to make a small contribution to what I hope will be an ongoing discussion.

In this chapter I shall try to show that Matthew has strengthened still further the anti-Jewish polemic which is found in the sources at his disposal. I shall suggest that this Matthean emphasis is related to the greater prominence the evangelist gives to apocalyptic themes. By taking seriously

[1] The T.W. Manson Memorial Lecture delivered in the University of Manchester on 3 November 1983.

[2] See, for example, G. Baum, *Is the New Testament Anti-Semitic?* Glen Rock, N.J. 1965; S. Sandmel, *Anti-Semitism in the New Testament*, Philadelphia 1979; J. Koenig, *Jews and Christians in Dialogue: New Testament Foundations*, Philadelphia 1979; D.J. Harrington, *God's People in Christ: New Testament Perspectives on the Church and Judaism*, Philadelphia 1980. See also *Antijudaismus im Neuen Testament?* eds. W.P. Eckert, N.P. Levinson and M. Stohr, Munich 1967; F. Mussner, *Tractate on the Jews*, E.tr. London and Philadelphia 1984; H. Conzelmann, *Heiden-Juden-Christen: Auseinandersetzungen in der Literatur der hellenistisch-römischen Zeit*, Tübingen 1981.

these twin Matthean themes, which many modern readers of this gospel prefer to ignore because they find them either puzzling or unacceptable, some fresh light can be shed on the setting from which Matthew's gospel comes.

Our conclusions will necessarily be somewhat tentative, for two reasons. Firstly, the evangelist is closely dependent on his sources. Where we can trace with some confidence modifications he has made to his sources, we usually find that he is not an innovator but an interpreter of the traditions on which he has drawn.[1] This means that it is not always easy to isolate the distinctive contribution which the evangelist himself has made.

My second reason for hesitation is closely related. Over the last four decades redaction critical study has led to important advances in our understanding of Matthew.[2] At first sight this gospel seems well suited to the redaction critical approach. It seems to be possible to trace the evangelist's revision, re-arrangement and re-interpretation of Mark and of Q. But redaction criticism does not always live up to our expectations, for we soon discover that Matthew contains several divergent and even contradictory emphases. We frequently find that it is easy to account for part (or even most) of the evidence, but not all of it.

Theological or historical significance should not be attached to every single change which the evangelist has made to his traditions: sometimes his modifications are purely stylistic. And it is important to note that the evangelist does not intend to tell us about his own community, but to set out both his story of the origins, life and ultimate fate of Jesus of Nazareth and also his convictions about the significance of Jesus.

For these and other reasons which I have discussed in Chapter 2, I am convinced that the redaction critical method needs to be scrutinized carefully. This approach does not

---

[1] See Chapter 14 in this volume.

[2] For a survey of recent Matthean scholarship, see G.N. Stanton, 'Origin and Purpose'.

provide solutions for all the puzzling features of Matthew's gospel.

So how can we proceed? I shall try to complement use of the redaction critical method with an appeal to a range of roughly contemporary Jewish and Christian writings. Only by setting Matthew's gospel firmly in its first century Jewish and Christian context can we hope to avoid the dangers which are inherent in a narrow and wooden use of redaction criticism.

Matthew's anti-Jewish polemic

In recent discussion Matthew's anti-Jewish polemic has been approached in several quite different ways. Some writers have insisted that the seeds of later Christian anti-Semitism can be seen in Matthew, especially in the cry of the people gathered before Pilate, 'His blood be on us and on our children' (Matt 27. 25).[1] Lloyd Gaston claims that since Matthew taught the church to hate Israel, a distinction must be drawn between the acceptable attitude of Jesus towards Judaism on the one hand, and the unacceptable attitude of the evangelist which can no longer be part of the personal canon of many Christians. Gaston appeals, with W.G. Kümmel, to Luther's

---

[1] On Matt 27. 25 see especially K.H. Rengstorf in *Kirche und Synagoge: Handbuch zur Geschichte von Christen und Juden* I, Stuttgart 1968, 33f. Rengstorf notes that the early church fathers did not cite Matt 27. 25 when they referred to the guilt of the Jews for the death of Jesus. Only after the fourth century did they begin to make use of this verse in order to defend Christian oppression of Jews; only at this later period did 'secular' hatred of Jews begin to win a place in the church. Rengstorf suggests that in its Matthean context 27. 25 means that if Pilate can discover nothing which would allow Jesus to be executed, then the accusers of Jesus are ready to take on themselves the full responsibility for his death. On this verse see also J.A. Fitzmyer, 'Anti-Semitism and Matthew 27. 25', *Theological Studies* 26 (1965) 667-671; H. Kosmala, '"His Blood on Us and Our Children" (The Background of Matthew 27. 24-25)', *Annual of the Swedish Theological Institute*, 7 (1970) 94-136; V. Mora, *Le Refus d'Israël. Matthieu 27, 25*, Lectio Divina 125, Paris 1986.

hermeneutical dictum, *urgemus Christum contra scrip-turam.*[1]

Some writers have claimed that Matthew's harsh polemic should be understood (and perhaps partly excused) in the light of the special circumstances in which the gospel was written. On this view, which, as we shall see, has a good deal to commend it, the evangelist wrote immediately after a period of intense hostility between Matthew's Christian community and the synagogue 'across the street' – hostility which had finally led to a parting of the ways.

Other writers have noted, quite correctly, that modern readers of the gospel often fail to notice that the evangelist is at least as fierce in his denunciations of unfaithful Christians as he is in his criticisms of the Jewish leaders. Some have insisted that the harsh words of Jesus recorded in Matthew should be seen as prophetic anguish rather than as anti-Jewish polemic.[2]

Before we consider further the reasons for the ferocity of Matthew's attack on Judaism, we must examine briefly a few important passages. I hope to show just how sustained the evangelist's polemic is, and how frequently he strengthens considerably the polemic already found in the earlier traditions he has used.

(i) At the end of the Beatitudes Matthew includes two Q sayings which refer to persecution and rejection: 'Blessed are you when men revile you and persecute you . . . for so men persecuted the prophets who were before you' (Matt 5. 11-12). Matthew's readers know full well that, according to a well-established interpretation of Israel's history, the prophets always stood with the faithful minority over against the

---

[1] L. Gaston, 'The Messiah of Israel as Teacher of the Gentiles', *Interpretation* 29 (1975) 40.

[2] For Matthean polemic against Christians see, for example, 23. 8 ff.; 22. 11-12; 13. 36-43, 47-50. At 7. 5 and 24. 51 there are references to Christians as 'hypocrites'. See also S. Légasse, 'L' "antijudaïsme" dans l'Evangile selon Matthieu', in *L'Evangile selon Matthieu: Rédaction et Théologie*, ed. M. Didier, Gembloux 1972, 417-28.

majority, unfaithful and rebellious Israel.[1] Similarly in the evangelist's own day: God's favour (μακάριοί ἐστε ὅταν... 5. 11) rests on the faithful minority which is again under attack. In verses 11 and 12 the evangelist reproduces his Q tradition fairly closely, but in the preceding verse we read, 'Blessed are those who are persecuted for righteousness' sake, for theirs is the kingdom of heaven.' This verse is so Matthean in its phraseology and content that it almost certainly comes from the evangelist himself.[2] Matthew has extended a theme found in his source.

Just a few verses later he drops a broad hint as to the identity of the persecutors. In another redactional verse Matthew's readers are contrasted sharply with another group: 'unless your righteousness exceeds that of the scribes and Pharisees, you will never enter the kingdom of heaven' (Matt 5. 20). So, already at the beginning of the Sermon on the Mount, we sense that the evangelist's community is under great pressure from scribes and Pharisees.

(ii) In chapter 6 we find the term 'hypocrites' for the first time. In a passage which Matthew is generally considered to have taken directly from a source, the ways the hypocrites carry out their almsgiving, prayers and fasting are held up as examples to be avoided. In the original tradition the identity of the hypocrites is not disclosed: they are simply people who give alms, pray and fast. But from the context in which the evangelist sets this passage, it is clear that *he* has in mind the scribes and Pharisees to whom he has drawn particular attention at the beginning of the preceding section at 5. 20. So two verses added by the evangelist himself as part of his re-interpretation of his traditions (5. 10 and 5. 20), turn out to have far reaching importance.

---

[1] See O.H. Steck, *Israel und das gewaltsame Geschick der Propheten. Untersuchungen zur Überlieferung des deuteronomischen Geschichtsbildes im Alten Testament, Spätjudentum und Urchristentum*, Neukirchen 1967.

[2] This is now generally accepted. See most recently B. Przybylski, *Righteousness in Matthew and His World of Thought*, Cambridge 1980, 80-7, and R. Guelich, *The Sermon on the Mount: a Foundation for Understanding*, Waco, Texas 1982, 155-61.

(iii) In the Q tradition which relates the healing of the Roman centurion's servant, his faith is said to surpass that found in Israel. Matthew underlines and extends this point by placing here sayings found elsewhere in Q: 'I tell you, many will come from east and west and sit at table with Abraham, Isaac and Jacob in the kingdom of heaven while the sons of the kingdom will be thrown into outer darkness; there men will weep and gnash their teeth' (Matt 8. 11-12). The original setting of these sayings in Q was as part of a call to the half-hearted to repent.[1] Matthew has extended the rejection theme and made it refer to 'the sons of the king-dom', i.e. faithless Israel in general.[2] By setting the sayings in a new context he contrasts the faith of the Gentile centurion with the complete rejection of Israel.

(iv) A similar point is made in 21. 43, a verse which Matthew himself adds at the end of the parable of the wicked husbandmen which he takes over from Mark. 'Therefore I tell you, the kingdom of God will be taken away from you, and given to a nation producing the fruits of it.' This verse is probably the clearest indication in the gospel that the Matthean community saw itself as a separate and quite distinct entity over against Judaism. The Marcan parable had already concluded with the words 'he will give the vineyard to others' (Mark 12. 9). In his additional words Matthew is elucidating his Marcan tradition, but the contrast between the rejection of Israel, the majority, and the acceptance of an ἔθνος, 'nation', which will reproduce the fruits of the king-dom is now drawn much more sharply.

At the end of the Marcan parable Jesus refers to Psalm 118. 22-3: 'The stone which the builders rejected has become the

---

[1] See Luke 13. 28-9. With many others I take the Lucan context to be more likely to represent the original Q version. T.W. Manson's crisp, clear discussion is, as always, worth consulting: *The Sayings of Jesus*, Cambridge 1949, 124-6. See also D. Lührmann, *Die Redaktion der Logienquelle*, Neukirchen 1969, 57f. and, for a different view, E. Schweizer, *The Good News according to Matthew*, E.tr. London 1976, 213.

[2] On 'sons of the kingdom' see W. Trilling, *Das wahre Israel*, 88f.: 'Die Wendung geht wohl mit Sicherheit auf den Evangelisten zurück.'

151

head of the corner. . .' In Mark this is almost certainly an allegorical reference to Jesus himself, but by his additional verse, 'the kingdom of God will be taken away from you and given to an ἔθνος which will produce its fruits' (21. 43), I believe that Matthew sees the new ἔθνος (his own community rather than Jesus) as the stone rejected at first by the Jewish leaders but accepted by God. In the narrative conclusion of verse 45 we read: 'When the chief priests and the Pharisees heard his parables they perceived that he was speaking about them (περὶ αὐτῶν), not just against them (πρὸς αὐτούς) as in Mark 12. 12. The Pharisees are introduced here by Matthew himself: the parable is about them and the chief priests; they are rejected in favour of the ἔθνος whom they themselves have rejected.[1]

(v) The unusual exegesis of the Matthean version of the parable of the wicked husbandmen which has just been offered is supported by the passage which follows immediately in chapter 22. The parable of the King's Marriage Feast is also addressed to the chief priests and the Pharisees. In its Matthean version it seems to have been influenced by the preceding parable: several similar phrases and motifs appear in both parables.[2]

In the similar parable recorded in Luke 14. 16-24 a servant is sent to summon those who have been invited to the great

[1] As far as I know, this exegesis of Matt 21. 41-5 has not been advanced before. Attention is often drawn to the importance of the Matthean addition at 21. 43, but the implications of that addition for the interpretation of 21. 42 seem to have been missed. Trilling, for example, discusses Matthew's interpretation of the parable at length (*Das wahre Israel*, 55-65) and writes: 'Die christologische Ausweitung bei Markus wird von einer "ekklesiologischen" überdeckt. An die Stelle des Bekenntnisses zum erhöhten Christus tritt jenes zur Wirklichkeit des neuen Gottesvolkes.' (58). But he does not discuss 21. 42. A.H. M'Neile's comment on 21. 42, from a totally different perspective, is interesting: 'If the quotation is by Jesus Himself, it is an explanation of v. 41, and leads directly to v. 43: the pious members of the Jewish race oppressed and misused by their religious leaders will be advanced to honour'. (*The Gospel according to St Matthew*, London 1915, 311).

[2] For the details see J. Jeremias, *The Parables of Jesus*, E.tr. rev. ed., London 1963, 69 n. 77.

banquet. In the Matthean version *two* sets of servants are sent to issue the summons. The original version of the parable has clearly been allegorised to a considerable extent. The first set of servants refers to the prophets sent to Israel. The second set of servants is the equivalent of 'the stone rejected by the builders' of 21. 42. They are servants in the new era: Christian prophets and messengers who are seized, treated shamefully, and killed (22. 6). Matthew the evangelist makes the same point at 23. 34, where the rejection of Christian prophets, wise men and scribes sent to Israel leads to her rejection. In the parable the rejection of the second set of (Christian) servants results immediately in judgement: 'the king was angry, and he sent his troops and destroyed those murderers and burned their city' (22. 7). Finally, the Gentiles are summoned to the Marriage Feast.

In these five passages the evangelist re-interprets his sources considerably and sharpens the anti-Jewish polemic. In three cases (5. 10-12; 21. 41-3; 22. 6f.) the polemic is linked to the persecution and rejection of followers of Jesus by opponents. In Matthew 5 and 6 the scribes and Pharisees seem to be identified as the opponents; as I argued earlier, this is implied by the important Matthean addition, 5. 20. At the conclusion of the parable of the wicked husbandmen the chief priests and the Pharisees are identified explicitly by the evangelist as the opponents (21. 45). And at the end of the parable of the King's Marriage Feast which follows at the beginning of chapter 22, the Pharisees in particular are singled out by the evangelist (22. 15). The opponents come into sharper focus as the gospel unfolds.

(vi) It is, of course, the next chapter, 23, with its seven woes addressed to the scribes and Pharisees which contains the evangelist's most sustained anti-Jewish polemic. It is this chapter more than any other part of the gospel which so acutely embarrasses Christians today. As in the passages we have just considered briefly, the evangelist conflates his sources and sharpens and extends considerably their polemic.

The last of the seven woes is the most significant part of the chapter for my present purposes. Here Matthew claims much more explicitly than in the underlying Q tradition that the scribes and Pharisees are the sons of those who murdered the prophets: they, too, are murderers (23. 31). The scribes and Pharisees are then addressed as 'You serpents, you brood of vipers'– the very phrase John the Baptist addresses to the crowds at Luke 3. 7, but to the Pharisees and Sadducees in Matt 3. 7. Then follows the reference to the 'Christian' prophets, wise men and scribes whom Jesus is sending to them, the verse (23. 34) which I have just linked closely with Matthew's allegorisation at 22. 6. Some of these 'new' messengers will be killed and *crucified* just like Jesus himself. Some will be scourged in the synagogues of the Pharisees and scribes and persecuted from town to town. As a result, God's judgement will come upon those who have persecuted and murdered the followers of Jesus (23. 34-6). Harsh words indeed. Here the polemic found in a Q tradition has been intensified by Matthew himself.[1] Here themes prominent earlier in the gospel are summarized and sharpened still further in the evangelist's final collection of the sayings of Jesus.

The function of the anti-Jewish polemic

Why is this anti-Jewish polemic so prominent in Matthew? What is the evangelist's intention? Although his polemic is frequently directed against the scribes and Pharisees, he is not merely concerned with the Jewish leaders. The final verses of chapter 23 make it quite clear that Judaism as a whole is rejected: 'Jerusalem, Jerusalem, killing the prophets and stoning those sent to you. . . Behold, your house is forsaken and desolate' (23. 37-8). The same point is made in two verses to which we have already referred, 21. 43 and 27. 25.[2] So what is the function of this anti-Jewish polemic?

Several answers have been given to this question. Some writers have refined the traditional view – which goes back to the early church – that Matthew is writing *to* the Jews. R.

[1] So also D.R.A. Hare, *Jewish Persecution*, 92.
[2] See P. Richardson, *Israel in the Apostolic Church*, SNTSMS 10, Cambridge 1969, 188-94.

Hummel, for example, sees the polemic as part of a very real dispute between Matthew's Christian community and contemporary Pharisaic Judaism. On Hummel's view, which G. Bornkamm also accepted in his earlier writings, the debate is *intra muros*, for Matthew's community has still not parted company with a very diverse Judaism immediately after A.D. 70.[1]

Other writers have claimed that Matthew's intention is evangelistic and should be likened to the denunciations which were poured out by the Old Testament prophets and which were intended to lead to repentance. Gregory Baum has commented: 'However grave the transgressions of the people and however terrible the punishment in store for them, the message was delivered for the sake of the people's conversion to a God who was always willing to forgive them.'[2] Is Matthew intending to *provoke* the Jewish leaders of his day to accept Christian claims about Jesus? That would seem to be an odd evangelistic strategy, would it not? The Old Testament parallels cited by Baum are significant, but explanations along these general lines tend to overlook the fact that in chapter 23 it is the crowds and disciples who are being addressed and *not* the scribes and Pharisees at all.

A much more plausible, but not completely convincing, explanation has been offered in two recent monographs. Sjef van Tilborg suggests that the leaders of the Jewish people are in the eyes of Matthew, the *antithesis* of the disciples of Jesus. The anti-Pharisaism of Matthew is 'at the service of his own ethics'.[3] In his detailed sudy of chapter 23 David Garland argues that the woes against the scribes and Pharisees have 'a pedagogical function' for Christian scribes. The reproach 'hypocrites' has 'as much significance for Matthew as a negative warning for Christians as it has a deprecatory char-

---

1 R. Hummel, *Auseinandersetzung*, 82-9. G. Bornkamm, 'End Expectation and Church in Matthew', in *Tradition*, 19f. and 39. This essay was originally published in 1956. By 1970 Bornkamm had modified his view; see 'The Authority to"Bind" and "Loose" in the Church in Matthew's Gospel", now reprinted in *Matthew*, London 1983, 88.

2 G. Baum, *Is the NT Anti-Semitic?* 69.

3 S. van Tilborg, *The Jewish Leaders in Matthew*, Leiden 1972, 26 and 98.

acterization of the Jewish leaders.'[1] A similar conclusion is reached by Donald Senior in his monograph on Matthew's Passion narrative: '. . . in many cases the interest of Matthew is not directed toward the Jewish leaders' hostility for its own sake. It serves rather as an effective foil to the majesty and dignity of Jesus. . . Matthew's stress on Jewish responsibility, while an evident characteristic of presentation, is ultimately subordinate to a more fundamental fascination with the majesty of Jesus.'[2]

These views can all be supported by some passages. At 23. 8, 10 the evangelist is clearly contrasting Jesus, the one teacher and the one master, with the scribes and Pharisees who let themselves be called rabbi and master. Garland is right to draw attention to the importance of the audience to whom the woes of chapter 23 are addressed: it is not the scribes and Pharisees themselves, but the crowds and disciples – in other words, the evangelist's own community rather than the synagogue across the street. In some passages, and perhaps most notably in 6. 1-18, the scribes and Pharisees are held up as a negative warning to Christians. But the woes in chapter 23 do not seem to have this function. In the first twelve verses of the chapter the crowds are told not to follow the example of the scribes and Pharisees, but once the sevenfold woes start at 23. 13, this point is not made again in the chapter.

I want to suggest that an alternative explanation of Matthew's intensified anti-Jewish polemic is more plausible. Matthew's community has recently parted company with Judaism after a period of prolonged hostility. Opposition, rejection and persecution from some Jewish quarters is not just a matter of past experience: for the evangelist and his community the threat is still felt strongly and keenly. Matthew is puzzled – indeed pained – by Israel's continued rejection of Jesus and of Christian messengers who have

---

[1] D.E. Garland, *The Intention of Matthew 23*, NovTSup 52, Leiden 1979, 118ff.

[2] D.P. Senior, *The Passion Narrative according to Matthew*, Leuven 1975, 338.

proclaimed Jesus as the fulfilment of Israel's hopes. The polemic is *real* and not simply used in the service of the evangelist's Christology or of his ethics, as recent writers have maintained. The evangelist is, as it were, coming to terms with the trauma of separation from Judaism and with the continuing threat of hostility and persecution. Matthew's anti-Jewish polemic should be seen as part of the self-definition of the Christian minority which is acutely aware of the rejection and hostility of its 'mother', Judaism. Kinniburgh has suggested that for Matthew's church '. . .faced with the problem of the failure of the Jewish mission and the ruin of the Jewish nation, the attribution of such a message of condemnation to Jesus was a source of comfort, even if it were to prove an embarrassment to later generations.'[1]

This is precisely the point I wish to establish. The harsh words directed against the scribes and Pharisees are not to be explained as a setting up of straw men as an example of the reverse of Christian discipleship. The evangelist is not addressing scribes and Pharisees in direct confrontation or debate, but his denunciations are nonetheless polemical. They represent in part anger and frustration at the continuing rejection of Christian claims and at the continued hostility of Jews towards the new community. In part they also represent the Matthean community's self-justification for its position as a somewhat beleaguered minority 'sect' cut off from its roots.

I have now declared my hand. I now wish to give four reasons why this is a plausible explanation of the anti-Jewish polemic in Matthew and of the circumstances from which and for which it was written.

A proposed setting for Matthew's gospel

The first pillar which supports my suggestions about the setting of this gospel is my insistence that Matthew's community still felt seriously threatened by Jewish opposition at

---

[1] E. Kinniburgh, 'Hard Sayings - III', *Theology* 66 (1963) 416. I owe this reference to D.E. Garland, *Intention*, 89.

the time the evangelist wrote. This has been denied by several scholars on both theological and historical grounds. Some have claimed that in Matthew's view Israel is utterly and finally rejected: the evangelist and his community are no longer concerned in any way with a mission to Israel. Even though the evangelist stresses that the mission of Jesus was confined to Israel, that era is over. The Matthean community is engaged solely with a mission to Gentiles.[1] Israel and her hostility are both a matter of *past* history.

I am convinced, however, that this view is ruled out by the cumulative force of several considerations. When Matthew refers to Christian disciples in his own day who are sent out to πάντα τὰ ἔθνη (28. 19), he means 'all nations', including individuals within Israel.[2] The key passage is 24. 9, 'You will be hated by all nations (πάντα τὰ ἔθνη) for my name's sake'. In this verse 'by all nations' has been added to the Marcan logion by the evangelist himself, but it cannot refer to non-Jewish nations, the Gentiles, and exclude hatred by Jews. At 10. 17f. Matthew has redacted his Marcan traditions to make it quite clear that disciples of Jesus sent out as missionaries are to expect hatred and mistreatment by both Jews and Gentiles.

In Matthew 10 the evangelist sets out his account of the sending out of the disciples by the historical Jesus, but it is clear that at the same time he is portraying Christian disciples in his own day who have been sent out 'to make disciples of all nations' (28. 19). The evangelist has a 'dual perspective'. It is significant that no attempt is made to hide the fact that the first mission was to Israel.

In Matthew's allegorical expansion of the parable of the King's Marriage Feast (22. 4f.), to which we have already referred, the second set of (Christian) servants is sent to the

---

[1] See especially R. Walker, *Die Heilsgeschichte im ersten Evangelium*, Göttingen 1967.

[2] See also J.P. Meier, 'Nations or Gentiles in Matthew 28. 19?', *CBQ* 39 (1977) 94-102. For a different view, see D.R.A. Hare and D.J. Harrington, ' "Make Disciples of all the Gentiles" (Mt. 28. 19)', *CBQ* 37 (1975) 359-69.

same invited guests (i.e. Israel) as the first set of servants (the Old Testament prophets). The Matthean version of this parable clearly implies a Christian mission to Israel even though its complete failure (which leads to judgement) is underlined.

At 23. 36 God's judgement is announced on those who 'kill and crucify. . . scourge. . . and persecute' Christian prophets, wise men and scribes. Here the evangelist surely has in mind present (or future) judgement on Israel: it is not a matter which is over and done with. At 23. 39 that judgement is referred to again: 'You will not see me again until you say, "Blessed is he who comes in the name of the Lord"'. Although the interpretation of this verse is much disputed, I take it (and the immediate context) to imply that there is hope that Israel may possibly yet be saved, even if this seems unlikely.[1]

In Matthew's view, then, the rejection by Israel of its Messiah brings God's judgement, but this does not exclude a mission by the Church to Israel; the failure of that mission underlines Israel's guilt.[2]

It is also possible, I think, to refute the claim that Jewish persecution of Christians is past history by the time the evangelist writes. This view has been set out by D.R.A. Hare in his fascinating monograph, *The Theme of Jewish Persecution of Christians in the Gospel according to Matthew*, Cambridge 1967. He believes that Jewish persecution of Christian missionaries belongs essentially to the past. He builds his case primarily on the lack of evidence for such a persecution in the period between A.D. 70 and the Bar Kokhba revolt in A.D. 132 – 135.

But Hare fails to do justice to John 16. 2: 'They will put you out of the synagogues; indeed the hour is coming when whoever kills you will think that he makes an act of worship

---

[1] So also D. Allison, 'Matt. 23. 39 = Luke 13. 35b as a Conditional Prophecy', *JSNT* 18 (1983) 75-84.

[2] See also U. Luz, 'The Disciples in the Gospel according to Matthew', E.tr. *Matthew*, 101, and see especially his note 25.

equivalent to the offering of a sacrifice.'[1] While it is true that this threat of lynching may never have been carried out, at about the same time as Matthew's gospel was written the Johannine community was still keenly aware of the very real threat of violent persecution.

Hare rejects too hastily the evidence of I Clement. In a number of passages Clement refers to ζῆλος, envy. At times he has in mind factious people within the church, but, as Geoffrey Lampe has argued, in some passages it refers to the attitude of Jewish opponents of Christianity; this ζῆλος leads literally to death.[2] While Lampe has probably exaggerated his claim that in the late first and early second century the church was faced with a powerful counter-attack from the side of Judaism, some of his evidence from later New Testament writings and from I Clement and Justin Martyr confirms that Jewish hostility could well have posed a very real threat to Matthew's community. More than that we cannot say. But there is little doubt that Matthew *perceived* that his community was living in the shadow of Jewish opposition and rejection.

The second pillar which supports my suggestion that Matthew's community was a rather beleaguered 'sect' is that there is evidence within the gospel which suggests that the evangelist and his readers were very much at odds, not only with contemporary Judaism but also with the *Gentile* world.

In the Sermon on the Mount there are three derogatory references to the Gentiles, 5. 47; 6. 7 and 6. 32. The second reference has probably been added by the evangelist himself; the other two have been taken over from Q. And, as we have seen, in the mission discourse in chapter 10 the disciples are told much more explicitly than in Mark 13 to expect hostility from Gentiles as well as Jews (10. 18, 22).

---

[1] Here I quote the exegesis of B. Lindars, 'The Persecution of Christians in John 15. 18–16. 4a', in *Suffering and Martyrdom in the New Testament*, ed. W. Horbury and B. McNeil, Cambridge 1981, 65 f.

[2] G.W.H. Lampe, ' "Grievous Wolves" (Acts 20. 29)', in *Christ and Spirit in the New Testament* (FS C.F.D. Moule) eds. B. Lindars and S.S. Smalley, Cambridge 1973, 253-68, especially 263ff.

In Matthew's fourth discourse, the Marcan tradition which gives a warning not to cause one of the little ones to stumble is set in an eschatological context by an additional logion inserted by the evangelist: 'Woe *to the world* for temptations to sin. For it is necessary that temptations come, but woe to the man by whom the temptation comes' (18. 7). This apocalyptic saying has been taken from Q in order to introduce a woe on the entire world as a part of the prophecy of the eschatological terrors which are expected soon. Here Matthew has heightened an apocalyptic theme – as he does elsewhere – and he indicates that his community is alienated from a threatening world. Later in the same discourse, at 18. 17, there is a further derogatory reference to Gentiles; as at 5. 46f. they are linked with tax collectors in a general reference to society outside the Matthean community, a society with which the community has little to do.

At 24. 9 there is another reference to the hostility Matthew's community may expect from Gentiles at the end time; the specific reference to Gentiles has been added to the Marcan tradition by the evangelist himself. Finally, we may refer to two further sayings of a very different character which are relevant at this point. In words which have been carefully shaped by the evangelist himself, Matthean followers of Jesus are called to be 'the salt of the earth' and 'the light of the world' (5. 13 and 14). These words suggest that the Matthean community is a minority group set over against the world at large, and yet it is certainly not cut off from society in general.

The evangelist's firm commitment to a mission to the Gentiles is well known. But there is a string of other references to Gentiles and to the world in general which is often overlooked. In many of them Matthew's own hand can be discerned. They suggest that the Matthean community, just like the Pauline and Johannine community, had an ambivalent attitude to society at large: it was committed to the task of evangelism 'to all nations', but it saw itself as a group quite distinct from the 'alien' world at large.

The third pillar in my reconstruction of the setting of the gospel is the increased use the evangelist makes of apocalyptic themes. In chapters 24 and 25 Matthew extends very considerably Mark's eschatological discourse in chapter 13. Some of the material is taken from Q, some is tradition to which Matthew alone had access, and some comes from his own hand. An example of the latter which is particularly important for our present purposes is 24. 10-12: 'You will be hated by all nations for my name's sake. And many will fall away and betray one another, and hate one another. And many false prophets will arise and lead many astray. And because wickedness is multiplied, most men's love will grow cold.' There are a number of traces of Matthean vocabulary and themes in these verses; they are in part a pastiche of phrases used elsewhere in this chapter.[1] External oppression and internal dissension, themes which one would not normally expect to find linked together, are here set side by sidᵉ in the context of calls for vigilance: the parousia is both 'unexpected' and 'near', and judgement is at hand. These themes are prominent throughout chapters 24 and 25.

Why is there increased prominence given to apocalyptic themes in this gospel? What is the *function* of these traditions? Several writers have recently stressed that historical and sociological factors are at work whenever apocalyptic language becomes prominent. In periods of historical crisis and trauma and in periods of a marked sense of alienation from the outside world, Jewish and early Christian writers turned to apocalyptic. P.D. Hanson correctly notes that apocalyptic 'generated a symbolic universe opposed to that of the dominant society'.[2] Wayne Meeks has suggested that

---

[1] For details see J. Lambrecht, 'The Parousia Discourse: Composition and Content in Mt. XXIV-XXV' in *Matthieu*, 320f. See also E. Schweizer, 'Matthew's Church', E.tr. in *Matthew*, 146.

[2] P.D. Hanson, art. 'Apocalypticism', *Interpreter's Dictionary of the Bible*, Supplementary Volume, Nashville 1976, 30ff. See also G.W. Nickelsburg, 'Social Aspects of Palestinian Jewish Apocalypticism', in *Apocalypticism in the Mediterranean World and the Near East*, ed. D. Hellholm, Tübingen 1983, 645.

apocalyptic language is used to reinforce attitudes of group solidarity.[1]

These explanations of the function of apocalyptic are most illuminating. As far as I know, the apocalyptic traditions in Matthew's gospel have not yet been considered from this point of view. But it is not at all difficult to see that these perceptive observations on the social circumstances in which apocalyptic flourishes are readily applicable to Matthew. The thoroughly Matthean passage just cited, 24. 10-12, gives clear evidence of the community's sense of alienation from the outside world and the evangelist's concern to reinforce group solidarity.

There is probably no better illustration of the evangelist's interest in apocalyptic than the apocalyptic vision in 25. 31-46. This passage also confirms the importance of the explanation of the function of apocalyptic in Matthew which I have just sketched out. The final pericope of the lengthy eschatological discourse which Matthew has shaped so carefully is a vision of all the nations gathered for judgement by the Son of Man. The nations are separated as a shepherd separates the sheep from the goats; they are judged on the basis of what they have done for 'one of the least of these my brethren'. Although I cannot defend my interpretation of this passage now,[2] I am convinced that as it stands in Matthew's gospel the phrase 'the least of these my brethren' refers not to men in general, but to members of Matthew's community some of whom have been sent as missionaries 'to all nations'.

The Matthean community is committed to evangelism among all nations, but rejection, opposition and persecution are being experienced. Quite naturally the Matthean Christians have asked, 'Why does God allow his enemies to play havoc with the new people who do bear the proper

[1] See W.A. Meeks, ' "Since then you would need to go out of the World": Group Boundaries in Pauline Christianity', in *Critical History and Biblical Faith: New Testament Perspectives*, ed. T.J. Ryan, Villanova, Pa. 1979, 4-29; also his 'Social Functions of Apocalyptic Language in Pauline Christianity' in *Apocalypticism*, ed. D. Hellholm, 687-705, and his *The First Urban Christians*, New Haven 1983, 171-80.

[2] For a full discussion, see Chapter 9.

fruit?' The answer is that at the end all men will certainly be judged, rewarded and punished on the basis of their acceptance or rejection of followers of Jesus. This apocalyptic passage functions in exactly the same way as many other Christian and Jewish apocalyptic writings. It is a final note of consolation and encouragement to a community acutely aware of the hostility of the Jewish and Gentile world at large.

This very theme is prominent in two Jewish apocalypses written at about the same time as Matthew's gospel, about A.D. 90. Following the triumph of the Romans in A.D. 70 there was bound to be bewilderment and confusion and this is reflected in 4 Ezra and 2 Baruch. Let me refer to just two passages. In 4 Ezra 7. 37, in a final judgement scene we read as follows:

> Then the Most High will say to the excited nations:
> Consider and know those whom you denied
> Or those whom you have not served
> Or whose faithfulness you have spurned.
> Look on this side, then on that:
> Here are rest and delight
> There fire and torments.

Suddenly at the last judgement nations are confronted with God's people whom they have denied and failed to serve and they are judged on that basis.[1] The close parallel with the interpretation of Matt 25. 31-46 which I have just given is, I hope, obvious.

In 2 Baruch 72 all the nations are summoned before the Messiah for judgement. Nations which have not opposed Israel will be spared, but those who have ruled over her will be given up to the sword. The nations are judged on the basis of their attitude to Israel.

---

[1] I have quoted the translation by J.H. Myers in his commentary in the Anchor Bible, *I and II Esdras*, Garden City, N.Y. 1974. Myers translates the Syriac text, not the Latin text which lies behind the translations in the RSV and NEB Apocrypha.

The final discourse in chapters 24 and 25 may not be the most attractive part of Matthew's gospel for modern readers, but these chapters reflect, perhaps more clearly than any other part of the gospel, the setting from which it comes. The apocalyptic themes are the response to the trauma of the parting of the ways from Judaism, to the perceived hostility of both Jewish and Gentile society at large and to serious internal dissension within the community. I am suggesting that the heightened anti-Jewish polemic and the greater prominence given to apocalyptic are both related to the particular circumstances of Matthew's community. If this is so, then it is no coincidence that Matthew 23, with its bitter denunciations of the scribes and Pharisees in the sevenfold woes, is juxtaposed with the extended apocalyptic traditions in chapters 24 and 25.

In discussions of the structure of Matthew's gospel and the five discourses, scholars often do not quite know what to do with chapter 23, since it does not seem to fit naturally with chapters 24 and 25. If my suggestions are sound, then chapter 23 belongs with 24 and 25: polemic and apocalyptic are both the responses of a minority community very much at odds with the world at large.

The fourth pillar which supports my suggestions about the setting of Matthew is the simple observation that the themes in Matthew to which I am appealing are found in other early Christian writings. Elsewhere prominence is given to the persecution and hostility experienced by Christian community from both the Jewish and the Gentile world. Elsewhere apocalyptic seems to be the response to rejection, hostility and the consequent feeling of alienation. Elsewhere we can find some classic examples of communities which some anthropologists now call 'millenarian sects'.[1] In using that term they are not drawing attention to heretical or unorthodox views but rather to the ways in which minority

[1] See, for example, B.R. Wilson, *Magic and the Millennium: a Sociological Study of Religious Movements of Protest among Tribal and Third-World Peoples*, London 1973, and K. Burridge, *New Heaven, New Earth: a Study of Millenarian Activities*, Oxford 1971.

165

religious groups which are deeply alienated from the macrosociety turn to eschatological and apocalyptic themes in order to reinforce attitudes of group solidarity.

Let me give four examples. In I Thessalonians, as in Matthew, we find a community which is acutely aware of the hostility of Jews. In both writings anti-Jewish polemic and apocalyptic themes are prominent. In *The First Urban Christians* Wayne Meeks has noted that in I Thessalonians the threat to the community is turned into a reinforcement of the believers' solidarity with one another. 'Apocalyptic sets the context of the paraenesis i.e. the reminders and encouragement of the ways in which Christians are expected to behave.'[1] In I Thessalonians, as in Matthew, there is a strong emphasis on internal discipline. I do not believe that Matthew and I Thessalonians are directly related. This makes the similarities (in spite of obvious chronological and geographical differences) all the more striking.

The Thessalonian and Matthean communities are both, as it were, beleaguered 'sects'. Yet both Paul and Matthew are supremely confident of their convictions. Both are concerned to proclaim the Christian message to society at large in spite of their alienation from the Jewish and Gentile world which surrounded them.

My second example is the fourth gospel. Although most apocalyptic themes are conspicuous by their virtual absence, anti-Jewish polemic is even more bitter than it is in Matthew. Most scholars now accept that the fourth gospel was written shortly after a most painful parting from Judaism. Like the Matthean community, Johannine Christians see themselves as alienated both from Judaism and from the world in general: they are under attack and are misunderstood, but they live confidently as 'branches abiding in the vine' (John 15. 4f.) Like the Matthean community, Johannine Christians are a 'sect' which has in large measure

---

[1] W.A. Meeks, *The First Urban Christians*, 174ff.

defined itself by the trauma of its recent rupture from Judaism.[1]

My third and fourth examples are from the Matthean corner of the map of early Christianity, the Didache and the two Christian chapters added to 4 Ezra which are usually known as 5 Ezra. The Didache seems to have been written a decade or so after Matthew, and 5 Ezra immediately after the disastrous Bar Kokhba revolt of A.D. 132–135. In both writings we find anti-Jewish polemic, perceived hostility and persecution from Jews, and also apocalyptic fervour.[2] These two communities are strongly Jewish yet acutely aware of alienation from Judaism. In both writings paraenesis is set in an apocalyptic framework. The Didache and 5 Ezra are almost certainly both dependent on Matthew's gospel, but the more significant links are at a deeper level.

Together with Matthew these early Christian writings all bear the marks either of a very strained relationship with Judaism (I Thessalonians) or of a painful parting from Judaism (the other four writings). They represent different strands of early Christianity, but all five reflect the experiences of minority Christian groups who felt threatened by and alienated from Jewish and Gentile society. It is against this setting that their anti-Jewish polemic is to be understood, even if it cannot be condoned.

Before I close, let me try to meet two obvious objections to my explanation of the anti-Jewish polemic in Matthew and my suggestions about the setting of the gospel. First, how does this understanding of Matthew square with evidence set out in all the standard textbooks which shows that the evangelist was a learned teacher, perhaps even a converted scribe? I do not believe that my suggestions are incompatible with traditional explanations of the origin of the gospel. We need look no further than Qumran for a parallel: there we find a minority group which has cut itself off from mainstream

---

[1] See especially W.A. Meeks, 'The Stranger from Heaven in Johannine Sectarianism', *JBL* 91 (1972) 44-72.

[2] Didache 1. 3 and 5 Ezra 2. 47. On the Didache, see K.H. Rengstorf, *Kirche und Synagoge* I, 56. On 5 Ezra, see Chapter 11 in this volume.

religious life, a group which indulges in fierce polemics against unfaithful Israel and which lives on apocalyptic fervour, a group much concerned with internal discipline. Alongside these features of the Qumran community which are broadly similar to the features of Matthew's gospel to which I have tried to draw attention, there is also, as in Matthew, a keen interest in and 'scholarly' approach to the re-interpretation of Scripture for the new circumstances in which the community believed itself to be living.

If my suggestions are correct, a second objector might well ask, 'Why did the evangelist not address the needs of his community directly in an epistle like I Thessalonians rather than in a gospel?' Or, to put the same point in a different way, surely Matthew is primarily concerned to set out the story of Jesus? Is not Christology the single most important theological emphasis of his gospel? I accept the force of this objection. Indeed I believe that the traditions of Mark's gospel and of Q were an even greater influence on the evangelist than any of the circumstances to which I have drawn attention. What I have tried to do is to account for a few of the strands which make up the skein. I readily concede that the evangelist is primarily concerned with the story of Jesus and with his convictions about the significance of Jesus. And yet, since he interprets that story in the light of the needs of his own community, it is possible to try to understand the concerns and the fears of that community. Whether my suggestions are plausible or not is for others to judge.

There is an important corollary to the view I have set out. Matthew does far more than simply react polemically to the perceived hostility of the synagogue across the street. He sets out his account of Jesus partly in the light of specific Jewish accusations and criticisms and partly in the light of possible Jewish objections to Christian claims. In short, in Matthew's skein there are apologetic as well as polemical and apocalyptic strands. I cannot now discuss Matthew's apologetic, but I hope I have shown that for much of early Christianity, and for Matthew in particular, the relationship between Christianity and Judaism was the central problem for Christian theology.

Chapter Seven

Christology and the Parting of the Ways

In the preceding chapters of this book I have argued that Matthew has written his gospel to a cluster of Christian communities which have recently parted company painfully with Judaism. Many of the gospel's most distinctive features are related to the 'parting of the ways': the strengthening of anti-Jewish polemic; the greater prominence given to apocalyptic themes; the evangelist's claim that the church is the true heir and interpreter of Scripture; the care with which a Gentile mission is defended. Matthew's call for a 'greater righteousness' and concern over internal dissent, as well as his warnings to his readers to be prepared for the parousia promote group cohesion; this cohesion is necessitated both by the perceived threat from Judaism and by the new communities' need for self-definition and legitimation.

Are Matthew's rich and varied Christological themes related in any way to this social setting? At first sight, in sharp contrast to John's gospel, Matthew's Christology seems to have little to do with 'the parting of the ways'. In Matthew, as in John, there is a strong emphasis on Jesus as the Son (of God); in both gospels Jesus repeatedly refers to God as his Father.

In John 5–10 the claim that Jesus is the Son of God and the relationship of the Son to the Father are at the heart of the disputes between Jesus and the Jewish leaders, disputes which are usually taken to reflect a community at odds with the local synagogue. In Matthew, however, matters seem to be different. The claim that Jesus is the Son of God is one of

169

the most important and impressive features of Matthew's Christology, but it is rarely opposed by the Jewish leaders.[1] With the exception of Matt 11. 27 (Q), there is hardly any discussion of the precise relationship between Jesus and the Father. Most of the Christological claims which are made by Jesus himself, by his disciples, and by would-be disciples, go unchallenged by the Pharisees and the other religious leaders who are so prominent in Matthew's story.

First appearances, however, are often deceptive. In this chapter I want to argue that closer inspection of a number of passages indicates that hostile accusations levelled against Jesus are being carefully countered: we are in touch with the claims and counter-claims of Jews and Christians in the evangelist's day. Matthew was well aware that his rivals saw Jesus as a magician and a deceiver of Israel. And as we shall see, in four redactional passages acknowledgement of Jesus as the 'Son of David' by participants in Matthew's story provokes hostility from the Jewish leaders. Since no other major Christological theme in Matthew provokes such sustained opposition from the Jewish leaders, our suspicions are roused: are the 'Son of David' passages intended by the evangelist to be a response to some of his critics? Although the Christological disputes are neither as intense nor as sustained as they are in John's gospel, they are an important feature of Matthew.

Most of Matthew's Christological emphases should be seen primarily as an extension (which is sometimes considerable) of themes which were already prominent in the sources on which the evangelist drew. However since some of those themes are set by Matthew himself in the context of disputes with Jewish leaders, they are related to the conflicts and

---

[1] Matt 27. 39-44 is an interesting exception. On Matthew's Son of God Christology, see, for example, J.D. Kingsbury, *Matthew: Structure, Christology, Kingdom*, 42-83. Kingsbury has shown that 'Son of God' is the most prominent Christological title in Matthew, but his further claim that other Christological themes are subsumed under this title is not convincing. See also D. Verseput's important article, 'The Role and Meaning of the "Son of God" Title in Matthew's Gospel', *NTS* 33 (1987) 532-56.

apologetic of the evangelist's own day. The text of the gospel itself points clearly in this direction: Matthew claims that the allegation that the disciples stole the body of Jesus from the tomb 'has been spread among Jews to this day' (28. 15), and takes pains to refute the charge.

Jesus is a magician and a deceiver

In Matthew two hostile comments from the opponents of Jesus are of particular interest.[1] The first is the threefold accusation that the exorcisms of Jesus have been carried out 'by the prince of demons': 9. 34; 10. 25; 12. 24, 27. As we shall see, the first and the last of these are responses to acknowledgement of Jesus as 'Son of David'. In the second hostile comment Jesus is referred to as 'that deceiver' (ἐκεῖνος ὁ πλάνος) and his life is summed up as 'deception' (πλάνη, 27. 63-4).

These two criticisms are closely related to the double accusation against Jesus which is found in a wide range of early Christian and Jewish writings: Jesus is a magician and a deceiver. In Chapter 10 I shall show that the accusation that Jesus was a deceiver was a stock jibe which is found in some Jewish traditions (which are admittedly difficult to date) and in a remarkably wide range of early Christian writings.[2] In many of these writings (most notably Justin *Dialogue* 69,

---

[1] Most of the other critical questions and comments on the lips of opponents fall into one or more of the following categories: they are neutral (e.g. 12. 38, 'Teacher, we wish to see a sign from you'); they concern the law rather than the person of Jesus (e.g. 15. 2); they are taken from the evangelist's sources without emphasis or development (e.g. 9. 3, 'This man is blaspheming'; 9. 11 'Why does your teacher eat with tax collectors and sinners'; 9. 14, 'Why do your disciples not fast?').

There are of course several passages in Matthew which may well be a response to hostile allegations: e.g. 1. 18-25; 5. 17-20.

[2] In the original publication of Chapter 10 in *NTS* 31 (1985) 377-92, I referred to Matt 27. 63, but I was then unaware of the possible relevance of the threefold accusation in Matthew that Jesus was in league with the prince of demons.

171

b.Sanh 43a and *b.Sanh* 107) it is linked with a second critical comment: Jesus is a magician (μάγος).

It is not at all far-fetched to associate the sharp criticisms of Jesus as exorcist which are so prominent in Matthew with the charge that Jesus was a magician or sorcerer. Exorcism is unquestionably the best attested form of magic among the Jews before Bar Kokhba.[1] In Acts 19. 11-20 Luke almost equates exorcism and magic. According to Josephus, Solomon 'composed incantations by which illnesses are relieved, and left behind forms of exorcisms with which those possessed by demons drive them out, never to return.' He then recalls that he himself witnessed an exorcism carried out with magical rites and incantations by a fellow Jew called Eleazer in the presence of Vespasian (*Ant.* VIII. 45-9). Justin Martyr refers to Jewish exorcists, who, like the heathen, use fumigations and magic knots (*Dialogue* 85. 3).

Jewish and pagan opponents of Christianity in the late first century and in the second century readily claimed that the exorcisms (and miracles) of Jesus (and of his later followers) were the result of magical powers. One of the central planks in the attack made on Jesus by Celsus's Jew is that the healings and exorcisms of sorcerers are the result of possession by an evil demon (Origen *Contra Celsum* I. 68); 'the actions of Jesus were those of one hated by God and of a wicked sorcerer' (I. 71). The pagan philosopher Celsus agrees with the Jew whom he quotes: 'it was by magic that Jesus was able to do the miracles which he appeared to have done' (Origen *Contra Celsum* I. 6). While it is true that not all exorcisms involved magical practices (and vice versa),[2] critics

---

[1] So P.S. Alexander, 'Incantations and Books of Magic', in E. Schürer, *The History of the Jewish People in the Age of Jesus Christ* III.1, eds. G. Vermes, F. Millar, and M. Goodman, Edinburgh 1986, §32.VII, 342-79, here 342.

[2] H.C. Kee, *Medicine, Miracle and Magic in New Testament Times* Cambridge 1986, 114, criticizes J.M. Hull's assumption that in the Hellenistic period all exorcisms were magical. Kee notes that belief in angels and demons was operative in Judaism (especially apocalypticism) and in early Christianity in contexts where magic was not present or not a significant factor.

of Jesus (and of his later followers) naturally wrote off his exorcisms as the deeds of a magician or sorcerer.

Matthew seems to have known that his readers might well be confronted by their Jewish rivals with this stock criticism of Jesus. Since this is, I think, a fresh suggestion as far as Matthew's gospel is concerned, we must now look at the evidence on which it is based.

1. 'He exorcizes by the prince of demons'

The first two of Matthew's three references to this accusation, 9. 34 and 10. 25, come from the hand of the evangelist himself. The third, 12. 24, 27, is taken from Mark 3. 22 and from Q (=Luke 11. 19), but as we shall see, Matthew has redacted his traditions considerably at this point. Whereas Mark includes this jibe against Jesus once (3. 22), and Luke twice (in the same passage, 11. 15, 18), it is found no less than four times (in three different passages) in Matthew. So there are strong grounds for concluding that the evangelist had a special interest in this criticism of Jesus.

(a) Matthew 9. 34

Matthew's first reference to the charge that Jesus performed his exorcisms by the prince of demons comes at the climax of the cycle of miracle stories in chapters 8 and 9. It is followed by the second of Matthew's important summary accounts of the teaching, preaching and healing ministry of Jesus (4. 23 and 9. 35). Immediately before this summary, which marks a major structural division in the gospel, the evangelist includes the first versions of two stories he will repeat later (cf. 9. 27-31 and 20. 29-34; 9. 32-4 and 12. 22-3). Commentators usually note that both pericopae are included here in order to prepare for the list of miracles recorded in 11. 5, but most fail to observe the important role 9. 34 plays in Matthew's overall presentation of the story of Jesus.

The reaction of the crowds to the healing of the two blind men and the exorcism of the demon from the dumb man is almost ecstatic: 'Never was anything like this seen in Israel' (9. 33). It is balanced antithetically in good Matthean fashion by the sharp comment of the Pharisees: 'He casts out demons by the prince of demons' (9. 34). Here, as also in the 'second edition' of this tradition (12. 24), the evangelist changes 'the scribes who came down from Jerusalem' (Mark 3. 22) to 'the Pharisees'. As in two other pericopae in this cycle of miracle stories, Matthew has singled out redactionally the Pharisees as the arch opponents of Jesus.[1] The hostile reaction of the Pharisees to Jesus in 9. 34 comes as the first climax in Matthew's careful presentation of the developing conflict between Jesus and the Pharisees.[2] Not until 12. 14 is the reader informed of the Pharisees' conspiracy to destroy Jesus.[3] 9. 32-4 functions as a literary foreshadowing of the conflict which will dominate chapter 12.[4]

Many recent writers have simply accepted without discussion the decision of the editors of the 26th edition of the Nestle-Aland text to include Matt. 9. 34. But the absence of the whole verse in a handful of manuscripts is striking and should not pass without comment.[5] Although 9. 34 is omitted in the New English Bible (1970)[6] and in the Revised

---

[1] Compare Matt. 9. 11 and 9. 14 with Mark 2. 16 and 2. 18.

[2] See J.D. Kingsbury, 'The Developing Conflict between Jesus and the Jewish Leaders in Matthew's Gospel: A Literary-Critical Study', *CBQ* 49 (1987) 57-83.

[3] In Mark matters are different. The first reference to a plot against the life of Jesus comes much earlier in the story at 3. 6 where the Pharisees are joined by 'the Herodians'.

[4] See B.J. Malina and J.H. Neyrey, *Calling Jesus Names*, 59.

[5] U. Luz is an exception. In his commentary (II, 1990, 62 n.2) he includes this brief comment: 'Er ist nicht nur gut bezeugt, sondern auch kompositionell als Fortsetzung von 9, 1b-17 und als Vorbereitung auf 10, 25 unentbehrlich.' Similarly, B.M. Metzger (*A Textual Commentary of the Greek New Testament*, London & New York 1971) suggests that 9. 34 seems to be needed to prepare the reader for 10. 25. This line of argument is plausible, but it can be reversed: an early scribe may have felt that 10. 25 was so enigmatic that an explanation at an appropriate earlier point in the gospel was necessary. Neither Luz nor Metzger attempts to account for the omission of the verse in some witnesses.

[6] The first edition of the New English Bible (1961) contains a curious error. 9. 33b and 34 are translated as follows: 'Filled with amazement the onlookers said, "Nothing like this has ever been seen in Israel. He casts out demons by the prince of devils"'. Both the positive and the negative assessments of Jesus are placed on the lips of the crowds! This

English Bible (1989), I am convinced that the cumulative arguments for its inclusion as the first part of a carefully constructed threefold criticism of Jesus (and corresponding set of responses) are strong.

(i) According to the apparatus of the Nestle-Aland text, with the exception of Codex Bezae, two Old Latin manuscripts (a and k), the Sinaitic Syriac palimpsest, and Hilary of Poitiers, the verse is found in all the ancient witnesses to the text.[1] (ii) The NEB and the REB seem to have omitted it on the basis of a misguided preference for the shorter reading and a lingering commitment (here, and in other passages) to Westcott and Hort's theory of 'western non-interpolations'. However several textual critics have recently argued that the *lectio brevior potior* rule of thumb is misleading.[2] (iii) The wording of 9. 34 differs from the parallel passages within Matthew (10. 25 and 12. 24, 27) and from Mark 3. 22, the only parallel passage in Mark. Hence 9. 34 is unlikely to have originated as an addition by a 'harmonising' scribe. (iv) If 9. 34 is accepted as part of the original text, why is it omitted in some witnesses? In this case it is not difficult to account for later abbreviation of the text. A few scribes were reluctant to allow the Pharisees to have the last word about Jesus at the climax of this section of the gospel; they preferred to conclude the pericope (and the preceding cycle of miracle traditions) with the positive response

translation is not supported by a single manuscript and seems to be an error which mysteriously escaped detection until the second edition of the NEB was published in 1970. Prior to the Passion narrative the crowds in Matthew never respond negatively to Jesus.

[1] Rather surprisingly, the Huck-Greeven *Synopse*, Tübingen 1981, fails to note the absence of 9. 34 in some witnesses, though the Huck-Lietzmann *Synopse* which it replaces had noted the absence of the whole verse in D sy⁵ Hil.

[2] See, for example, P.M. Head, 'Observations on Early Papyri of the Synoptic Gospels, especially on the "Scribal Habits"', *Biblica* 71 (1990) 240-7. Head refers to a thesis by J.M. Royse (which I have not seen) which shows that six important papyri (45, 46, 66, 72, 75) all demonstrate a tendency to shorten the text. See also J.K. Elliott, 'Why the International Greek New Testament Project is Necessary', *Restoration Quarterly* 30 (1988) 203.

of the crowds: 'Never was anything like this seen in Israel' (9. 33b). Surely it is most unlikely that a later scribe would have added a hostile criticism of Jesus on the lips of the Pharisees as the climax of the cycle of miracle traditions in chapters 8 and 9.

Taken cumulatively, then, there are good reasons for accepting 9. 34 as part of the original text; the longer reading is more difficult than the shorter reading and should be retained.

(b) Matthew 10. 25

The next reference to this jibe against Jesus is part of the 'missionary discourse' in chapter 10. In 10. 25 Jesus states that his opponents have called him Βεεζεβούλ. This enigmatic accusation is not explained in the immediate context. Presumably Matthew's readers knew who Βεεζεβούλ was, since Matthew does not explain that he was 'the ruler of the demons' until 12. 24. In 10. 25 Jesus warns his disciples to expect the same reaction to their own preaching and healing ministry as he himself has received: εἰ τὸν οἰκοδεσπότην Βεεζεβοὺλ ἐπεκάλεσαν, πόσῳ μᾶλλον τοὺς οἰκιακοὺς αὐτοῦ. This sentence rounds off a set of carefully structured statements in which Matthew has expanded considerably a Q logion (cf. 10. 24-5 and Luke 6. 40). The context leaves the reader in no doubt that Jesus is referring to himself as ὁ διδάσκαλος, ὁ κύριος, and ὁ οἰκοδεσπότης. Disciples of Jesus form a household of which he is the master.[1]

For our present purposes two points are of special interest. First, even though Christological titles are not used, the whole passage contains a rich Christology which stems from the evangelist himself. And secondly, the accusation that Jesus is *himself* Βεεζεβούλ is an intensification, in a highly compressed logion, of the charge in 9. 34 and 12. 24 that he is

---

[1] Both R.H. Gundry (commentary ad loc.) and M.H. Crosby, *House of Disciples*, 66-7, claim that there is a play on words in 10.25: Βεεζεβούλ = 'master of the house'. Even if this is the correct interpretation of rather complicated linguistic evidence, Matthew has failed to unravel the word play for his readers, few of whom are likely to have known Hebrew or Aramaic.

in league with the prince of demons. The jibe in 10. 25 points back to 9. 34; the disciples are warned that the bitter abuse hurled at Jesus will also be thrown at them. Since the sayings in the second part of Matthew 10 refer so clearly to the post-Easter period,[1] 10. 25 implies that the persecution of Christians in the evangelist's own day will include this form of abuse (cf. 10. 16-23 and also 5. 11). In other words, the accusation that Jesus and his followers are in league with the prince of demons is not a matter of past history; for Matthew and his readers it is a present experience.

(c) Matthew 12. 24, 27

The third reference to this hostile assessment of Jesus is in two verses in the Beelzebul controversy, 12. 22-30. The first, v. 24, is taken from Mark 3. 22; the second, v. 27 from Q (cf. Luke 11. 19). As in 9. 34, Matthew makes two important redactional changes: Mark's 'scribes who came down from Jerusalem' become 'the Pharisees', and their reaction is contrasted with the favourable comments of the crowds: 'Perhaps this is the Son of David' (12. 23).[2]

Only in this passage is there a reply to the threefold accusation that the exorcisms of Jesus are the result of collusion with the prince of demons. Matthew insists that it is not ἐν Βεεζεβούλ that Jesus casts out demons, but ἐν πνεύματι θεοῦ (12. 28). This exact antithesis is the result of Matthean redaction of the Q logion (Luke 11. 20) which referred to the finger of God.[3]

Matthew includes further references to the Spirit of God immediately before and immediately after this pericope. In the preceding verses the evangelist has claimed that God's promise given through Isaiah the prophet (Isa 42 .1) has been fulfilled in Jesus: God has placed his Spirit upon his servant Jesus (12. 17-21); the healing ministry of Jesus is the result of

---

[1] See U. Luz, 'Disciples', in *Matthew*, 98-128, especially 100.

[2] See the further discussion of this verse below, 181-2.

[3] If 'Spirit of God' was the original wording of the Q logion, Luke's special interest in the Spirit would have discouraged him from making a change to 'finger of God'.

the gift of the Spirit (cf. vv. 15b and 18c). Immediately after the Beelzebul pericope Matthew combines Mark 3. 10 and the Q saying behind Luke 11. 10. The end result in 12. 31-2 is a most solemn double warning that blasphemy against the Spirit will never be forgiven. The διὰ τοῦτο λέγω ὑμῖν of v. 31 leaves no room for doubt: in Matthew's view the Pharisees' claim that Jesus is in league with the prince of demons is blasphemy against the Spirit of God.

The anti-Pharisaic polemic is sustained in the pericopae which follow. The Pharisees are 'a brood of vipers' (12. 34; cf. 3. 7 and 23. 33); they are 'evil' (12. 34f.). The polemic continues in 12. 38-45, where Matthew has reversed the order of Q traditions in order to sharpen his counter-accusation. The scribes and Pharisees are part of an adulterous and evil generation which seeks a sign (12. 38-9), a generation which is possessed by seven evil spirits (12. 43-5). The latter point, which is the climax of the sustained polemic which becomes ever more intense throughout chapter 12, is made by the evangelist's own addition to the Q parable (cf. Luke 11. 24-6): 'So shall it be also with this evil generation.' The Pharisees and the scribes are demon possessed, not Jesus.

In Matthew, then, there is a threefold accusation that the exorcisms of Jesus have been carried out by dint of collusion with Beelzebul, the prince of demons (9. 34; 10. 25; 12. 24, 27). But there is also a threefold insistence that Jesus acts ἐν πνεύματι θεοῦ (12. 18, 28, 31-2). Why are the charge and the response so prominent in passages in which the evangelist's own hand is evident? The most obvious reason is that the significance of Jesus is still being bitterly contested in Matthew's own day. This conclusion is strongly implied by 10. 25b: disciples (i.e. readers of the gospel) who belong to the 'household' whose master has been so savagely maligned in the past, must expect that 'all kinds of evil will be spoken against them falsely on account of their commitment to Jesus' (cf. ἕνεκεν ἐμοῦ, 5. 11).

2. 'That deceiver'
The final words attributed to the Jewish leaders in Matthew include a second important critical judgement on Jesus. In 27.

63-4 he is referred to as 'that deceiver' (ἐκεῖνος ὁ πλάνος) and his life is summed up as 'deception' (πλάνη). Once again the Pharisees are singled out as the arch-opponents. They have been conspicuously absent from Matthew's story line since the end of chapter 23, but in 27. 62-6 they join the chief priests (whose presence is demanded by the preceding narratives) in petitioning Pilate. The whole pericope is thoroughly Matthean, so here we have further evidence of the evangelist's own special interest in a hostile assessment of Jesus.[1]

This time Matthew does not reply directly to the polemic. He takes great pains to convince the reader that the resurrection of Jesus from the tomb in which he was buried was not the 'final deception', but he simply lets the Jewish leaders' critical comments stand. Presumably he is convinced that readers of his gospel will readily agree that the claim of the Jewish leaders that Jesus is a 'deceiver' is monstrous; perhaps the closing verses of the gospel (28. 18-20) were intended to prove the point. Matthew stresses that the chief priests and Pharisees are without excuse: they themselves 'remember' that Jesus had told them that he would rise from the dead (v. 63). In a final poignant note the evangelist notes that the tale of the bribing of the soldiers who had guarded the tomb of Jesus 'has been spread among Jews to this day' (28. 15). This comment underlines once again the yawning gulf between the Christian communities to whom the evangelist is writing and local synagogues.

Matthew, then, was well aware of the double accusation regularly levelled against Jesus by Jewish opponents: he was a magician and a deceiver. The evangelist does not respond directly to the second taunt, but the first is taken very seriously indeed. As we have seen, in Matthew 12 the evangelist himself insists that the Pharisees' assessment of Jesus is wrong-headed: Jesus does not act ἐν Βεεζεβούλ, but ἐν πνεύματι θεοῦ. The threefold accusation that Jesus is demon-possessed is matched by the threefold reference to the Spirit

---

[1] For details of Matthean vocabulary and style in this pericope, see R.H. Gundry's commentary *ad loc.*

of God. The Pharisees' accusations against Jesus are hurled back at them: *they* are possessed by evil spirits, not Jesus.

Matthew's emphasis on the Spirit's relationship to Jesus is a neglected aspect of his Christology. This is one of the first notes he sounds in his presentation of the story and significance of Jesus. In 1. 18-25, where once again his own hand is clearly evident in the vocabulary and style, he stresses twice that Jesus was conceived 'of the Holy Spirit'. As has often been noted, Matthew's insistence on the role of the Spirit in the conception of Jesus may be (in part) a response to Jewish claims that Jesus was born as the result of an illegitimate union.

Hostility to Jesus the Son of David

There is a further set of passages in Matthew which seem to be related to disputes with Jewish opponents in the evangelist's day concerning the significance of Jesus. Matthew expands Mark's three references to the title 'Son of David' to nine: 1. 1; 9. 27; 12. 23; 15. 22; 20. 30, 31 (= Mark 10. 47, 48); 21. 9, 15; 22. 42 (=Mark 12. 35), where the title Son of David is implied. Why does Matthew open his gospel with a reference to Jesus as 'Son of David' and then proceed to add five further references in contexts which are broadly Marcan (9. 27; 12. 23; 15. 22; 21. 9, 15)? As several writers have noted, Matthew connects the 'Son of David' title with the healing ministry of Jesus,[1] but that observation hardly accounts for the evangelist's strong emphasis on this particular Christological theme.

---

[1] So, for example, C. Burger, *Jesus als Davidssohn*, Göttingen 1970, 72-106; J.M. Gibbs, 'Purpose and Pattern in Matthew's Use of the Title "Son of David"', *NTS* 10 (1963-4) 446-464; J.D. Kingsbury, 'The Title "Son of David" in Matthew's Gospel', *JBL* 95 (1976) 591-602; D.C. Duling, 'The Therapeutic Son of David: An Element in Matthew's Christological Apologetic', *NTS* 24 (1978) 392-409; U. Luz, 'Eine thetische Skizze der matthäischen Christologie' in *Anfänge der Christologie* (FS F. Hahn) eds. C. Breytenbach and H. Paulsen, Göttingen 1991, 223-6.

While four of the six redactional passages are connected with the healing ministry of Jesus, most scholars have over-looked the fact that another motif is equally prominent in the 'Son of David' passages which come from the evangelist's own hand. In four such passages acknowledgement of Jesus as the 'Son of David' by participants in Matthew's story provokes hostility from the Jewish leaders.[1] These four passages come at critical points in the evangelist's presenta-tion of one of his major themes: the conflict between Jesus and the Jewish leaders.[2] From these general observations we may conclude that Matthew insists vigorously that Jesus is the Son of David, even though he is aware that some of his readers will soon learn that this claim is unacceptable to their Jewish rivals.

Before I suggest a more specific setting for these disputes, we must consider the four redactional passages in which the claim that Jesus is Son of David is disputed.

(a) Herod the king was troubled (2. 3)
Narrative critics have reminded us of the crucial importance of the openings of writings. Matthew's gospel is no exception. 'Son of David' is the very first Christological title used by the evangelist in his opening line which functions as a heading (1. 1). The genealogy sets out carefully the Davidic origin of Jesus. At the end of its first section the reader is reminded that David was king over Israel (1. 6).

In the account of the birth of Jesus Joseph is addressed by an angel of the Lord as 'son of David' (1. 20) and great pains are taken to show how Jesus was adopted into the kingly line of David, even though Joseph was not his physical father. The first reaction to the birth of Jesus, king of the Jews, is

---

[1] A notable exception is D. Verseput, 'The Role and Meaning of the "Son of God" Title in Matthew's Gospel', *NTS* 33 (1987) 533-7. Verseput does not discuss the reasons for this link.

[2] See J.D. Kingsbury, 'The Developing Conflict between Jesus and the Jewish Leaders in Matthew's Gospel', *CBQ* 49 (1987) 57-73. Kingsbury fails to note that confession of Jesus as 'Son of David' provokes hostility from the Jewish leaders.

positive: the magi (who are clearly Gentiles) search out the place of his birth in order to worship him.

But their arrival in Jerusalem causes consternation. At the news of the birth of the Davidic king, who is explicitly identified in the narrative as the Messiah (2. 4), Herod the king is terrified (ἐταράχθη) and *all* Jerusalem (πᾶσα - a good Matthean word) with him (2. 3). An even stronger verb is added by Matthew to Mark's narrative to describe the reaction caused by the 'triumphal' entry of Jesus into Jerusalem: all Jerusalem is deeply stirred (ἐσείσθη πᾶσα ἡ πόλις) (21. 10). This is only one of a number of themes from chapters 1 and 2 which recur later in Matthew's story.

At this point Matthew associates the chief priests and the scribes with Herod: as the story develops they take over his role as the arch-opponents of Jesus. Before the plot against Jesus unfolds, a strongly ironical note is introduced: the Jewish religious leaders are well aware of the Scriptural prophecy concerning the birth of the promised king of Israel (2. 5-6). The same ironical note recurs at the very end of Matthew's story: the Pharisees know that Jesus had predicted that he would rise again from the dead; they are able to quote the words of 'that impostor' to Pilate (27. 63).[1]

The implacable hostility of Herod (and, by implication) of the Jewish religious leaders is contrasted sharply with the determination of the magi to find the Davidic Messiah and to worship him. Later in the gospel various individuals will seek out Jesus with equal determination (and in some cases faith) and worship him.

Why are Herod and the religious leaders so hostile to the birth of the promised Messiah? The obvious answer is surely the correct one: they perceive the Davidic King to be a threat. Matthew hints (but does not explain fully) that their understanding of Messiahship is faulty. Their hostility is certainly ridiculed: Jesus is but a child! In chapter 2 the evangelist does not refer to Jesus as 'king of the Jews' beyond 2. 2, but he uses the phrase 'the child and his mother' five times. Later in the gospel Matthew's portrait of Jesus as the harmless and

---

[1] Cf. John 5. 39.

humble Davidic Messiah becomes one of its most distinctive features.

(b) 'Have mercy on us, Son of David. . . .Lord' (9. 27-8)

Matthew rounds off his presentation of Jesus as 'Messiah of Deed' in chapters 8 and 9 with two pericopae in which his own hand is evident. The penultimate pericope in this section of the gospel (9. 27-31) is a careful rewriting of the Marcan account of the healing of two blind men (Mark 10. 46-52). (This same Marcan passage is used a second time at Matt 20. 29-34). The two blind men cry out to Jesus, 'Have mercy on us, Son of David' and later address Jesus as 'Lord' (κύριε) (9. 27-8). These Matthean phrases express the believing response of the blind men.

The final pericope in this chapter is also the first part of a reduplication of another Marcan tradition (Mark 3. 22 = Matt. 9. 32-4 and 12. 22-4). This time Matthew has incorporated some Q material (Luke 11. 14). The two incidents are carefully linked together by Matthew: the dumb demoniac approaches Jesus as the two men who have received their sight are going their way (9. 32). So the contrasting responses of the crowds and of the Pharisees are in effect responses to both incidents.

Once this is observed, it is clear that the hostile comment of the Pharisees in 9. 34, 'He casts out demons by the prince of demons', is a reaction to the confession of Jesus as 'Son of David' in 9. 27. Their critical accusation occurs as the climax of an important section in the gospel. This is the final pericope in the cycle of traditions in chapters 8 and 9; it is followed immediately by the evangelist's summary of the teaching, preaching and healing ministry of Jesus and his introduction to the mission of the disciples (9. 35-8).

(c) The crowds said, 'Perhaps this is the Son of David' (12. 23)

A similar pattern is found in Matthew's second account of the healing of the dumb demoniac. The crowds respond hesitantly, but positively: μήτι οὗτός ἐστιν ὁ υἱὸς Δαυίδ, which we may translate as 'Perhaps this is the Son of David'. Since the crowd's reaction is contrasted with the negative reaction of the Pharisees in the verse which follows, μήτι can hardly have its more usual sense as an introduction to a question which expects a negative response, i.e. 'Surely this can't be the Son of David'?[1] Once again reference to Jesus as 'Son of David' draws an exceedingly hostile response from the Pharisees: 'It is only by Beelzebul, the prince of demons, that this man casts out demons.'

(d) 'Hosanna to the Son of David' (21. 9, 15)
By introducing a direct reference to Jesus as 'Son of David' Matthew makes a major change to Mark's account of the acclamation of the crowds as Jesus enters Jerusalem (21. 9). Immediately after his account of the cleansing of the temple, Matthew notes that Jesus healed the blind and the lame, and that children in the temple repeated the acclamation of the crowds at the 'triumphal' entry (21. 9, 15). Once again reference to Jesus as 'Son of David' draws an angry response from Jewish religious leaders (here, the chief priests and the scribes): 'they were indignant' (21. 14-15).

This clash is followed immediately by the cursing of the fig tree (21. 18-22), the challenge from the same opponents, 'Who gave you this authority?' (21. 23-27), and the important trilogy of polemical and very 'Matthean' parables (21. 28 – 22. 14). At this point in the gospel the gulf between Jesus and the Jewish religious leaders becomes steadily wider. The double confession of Jesus as 'Son of David' by the crowds at the 'triumphal entry' and by the children in the temple sparks off the bitter disputes between Jesus and his opponents which follow.

We have now noted four redactional passages in which acknowledgement of Jesus as 'Son of David' is vigorously opposed by the Jewish religious leaders. This is the very first conflict in the gospel (2. 1-6); two passages are found at important turning points in the evangelist's story (9. 34; 21. 9, 15); the fourth passage (12. 23) is an integral part of the

---

[1] Other examples of μήτι with a hesitant or positive sense are noted in Blass-Debrunner-Funk's *Grammar*, §427 (2). See especially John 4. 29 and 7. 26.

important set of claims and counter-claims in chapter 12 which we discussed above.

Why does the evangelist stress so strongly that Jesus is the Son of David? Why is acknowledgement of Jesus as 'Son of David' so vigorously opposed by the Jewish religious leaders? And why does Matthew set out so carefully this fourfold pattern of positive response by some and rejection by the Jewish leaders?

Once again we are in contact with claims and counter-claims being made at the time Matthew wrote. The evangelist is well aware that his communities will face fierce opposition to their claims that Jesus was indeed the Davidic Messiah. Matthew insists that this claim is part of the very essence of Christian convictions about the significance of Jesus. But at the same time in several redactional passages he sets out a portrait of the Davidic Messiah which differs from many current expectations. The one born 'king of the Jews' is the child Jesus, the Davidic Messiah (2. 2-6); in accordance with prophecy Jesus heals every disease and infirmity (8. 17); Jesus is the one who is 'meek and lowly in heart' (11. 29), the chosen Servant of God (12. 17-21), 'the humble king' (21. 5). All these passages bear the stamp of the evangelist himself. They convey a quite distinctive portrait of Jesus.[1] What lies behind it?

An early form of the 'two parousias' schema

I now wish to build on the above observations concerning Matthew's portrait of the Davidic Messiahship of Jesus. I hope to show that it is part of the early form of the 'two parousias' schema which is found in Matthew, a Christological schema which became a prominent feature of later Christian disputes with Jewish opponents.[2]

---

[1] See the discussion of these passages by G. Barth in *Tradition*, 125-31.

[2] H. Conzelmann (*The Theology of Luke*, E.tr. London 1961, 17 n.1) noted that it is quite justifiable to speak of 'two advents' in Luke, even though

In the middle of the third century Origen noted that critics of Christianity who based their case on the interpretation of Scripture 'failed to notice that the prophecies speak of two advents of Christ. In the first he is subject to human passions and deeper humiliation. . . . in the second he is coming in glory and in divinity alone, without any human passions bound up with his divine nature.' (*Contra Celsum* I. 56) The schema of two contrasting advents is found nearly a century earlier in Justin, who insists that some of the words spoken by the prophets refer 'to the first coming of Christ, in which he has been proclaimed as about to appear both without form and mortal, but others have been spoken with reference to his second coming, when he will be present in glory and upon the clouds. . . .' (*Dialogue* 14. 8; cf. 40. 4; 49. 2-7; 52. 1; 110. 1-5) Similarly, and perhaps from about the same time as Justin, the *Anabathmoi Iakobou II* source of the Pseudo-Clementines: 'He (Moses) therefore intimated that he (Christ) should come, humble indeed in his first coming, but glorious in his second. . . .' (*Recognitions* I. 49).[1]

This schema became both popular and widespread in the later Christian tradition. For our present purposes it is important to note that it seems to have arisen as a response to Jewish claims that the 'unsuccessful' life of Jesus did not correspond at all to the prophecies of Scripture concerning the coming triumphant Messiah. Origen quotes the objection raised by Celsus's Jew (c. 177-180): 'The prophets say that the one who will come will be a great prince, lord of the whole earth and of all nations and armies, but they did not proclaim a pestilent fellow like him (Jesus).' (*Contra Celsum* II. 29) But Origin treats the criticism with disdain by appealing to the 'two advents' schema he had expounded earlier.

---

the actual terminology is not found. However he did not relate this observation to later Christian apologetic.

[1] I owe this reference to O. Skarsaune, *The Proof from Prophecy*, Leiden 1987, 285. Several writers have accepted G. Strecker's identification of the source behind the Pseudo-Clementines as *Anabathmoi Iakobou II*. See his *Das Judenchristentum in den Pseudo-Clementinen*, TU 70, Berlin 1958.

Justin's Jewish opponent Trypho also raised the same objection: '. . . passages of Scripture compel us to await One who is great and glorious, and takes over the everlasting kingdom from the Ancient of Days as Son of Man. But this your so-called Christ is without honour and glory.' (*Dialogue* 32. 1; cf. 39. 7; 89. 1-2; 90. 1; 110. 1-5) Justin, like Origen, insists that the Scriptures had prophesied two contrasting advents of Christ.

As far as I know, explicit evidence for the Jewish objection that the life of the Christian Messiah did not fulfil scriptural prophecies, and for the Christian response in terms of the 'two advents' schema appears for the first time in the middle of the second century. But the roots of this dispute may well be much deeper. Early in the post-Easter period Christians began to claim that their convictions about Jesus were 'in accordance with the Scriptures'. It would not have been difficult for opponents to refute such claims on the basis of Scripture. In particular, in Jewish circles where there were lively expectations concerning the triumphant Davidic Messiah, it would have been natural to insist that Christian claims concerning the Messiah did not correspond to Scripture.[1] And a Christian counter-claim in terms of the 'two advents' of the Messiah, both foretold in Scripture, may also have been formulated long before Justin's day.

An early form of the 'two advents' schema as a Christian response to Jewish objections is found, I suggest, in Matthew. This proposal is based on a set of cumulative arguments. (i) As noted above, Matthew repeatedly reminds his readers that in his earthly life Jesus was the Son of David. In this emphasis (as in so many others) Matthew developed a theme found in earlier Christian traditions. Matthew seems to concede that such a claim flew in the face of some Jewish expectations concerning the Davidic Messiah,[2] for in four

---

[1] Luke refers repeatedly to Paul's disputes over Scripture with Jews, but tells us little about the issues: Acts 17. 2; 18. 4; 19. 8; 28. 23-8.

[2] Jewish messianic expectations were very varied, but there is no doubt that in some circles there were lively hopes for a future triumphant Davidic Messiah. See *Judaisms and their Messiahs at the Turn of the*

redactional passages acknowledgement of Jesus as 'Son of David' is vigorously opposed by the Jewish religious leaders.

(ii) In Matthew's day, as in Justin's, Christians and Jews could agree that certain passages in the prophets referred to the *future* coming of the Messiah, but agreement concerning the 'first coming' was another matter. The burden of proof clearly lay with Christians, for they were making the novel claims. In these circumstances it is no surprise to find that nine out of Matthew's ten formula quotations claim that the 'coming', teaching and actions of Jesus are in fulfilment of Scripture.[1]

(iii) In a series of redactional passages Matthew emphasizes more strongly than the other evangelists the humility of the earthly life of Jesus the Son of David, the glory of his future coming as Son of Man and judge, and the contrast between the two 'comings'. The main features of Matthew's distinctive portrait of Jesus as the humble servant have been sketched above (p.185). Matthew's extension of the apocalyptic themes found in his sources is well-known. He repeatedly emphasizes redactionally the future glorious coming of Jesus as Son of Man;[2] he is the only evangelist to use the word παρουσία of the future coming (24. 3, 27, 37, 39).

Although Matthew does not refer to the life of Jesus as his παρουσία, he does contrast sharply the humble life of the Davidic Messiah with his future coming in glory in ways which are reminiscent of the later 'two parousias' schema. The Jesus who must go to Jerusalem and suffer many things (16. 21-3) is contrasted much more sharply than in Mark with the Son of Man who will come in the glory of his Father and then reward each person for what he has done (16. 27-8). The 'humble king' who enters Jerusalem (21. 5) will come in glory, sit on his throne, and as king he will judge the nations

---

Christian Era, eds. J. Neusner, W.S. Green, E.S. Frerichs, Cambridge 1987, and also E. Schürer, *The History of the Jewish People in the Age of Jesus Christ* II, eds. G. Vermes, F. Millar and M. Black, Edinburgh 1979, §29 'Messianism', 488-549.

[1] See Chapter 15; B. Lindars, *Jesus Son of Man*, London 1983, 115-83.

[2] See 161-5 and 222.

(25. 31-46). At the hearing before the sanhedrin Jesus is asked by the high priest, 'Are you the Christ, the Son of God?' The reply of Jesus is either evasive or hesitant. By adding to Mark 14. 62 a strongly adversative πλήν and ἀπ᾽ ἄρτι, Matthew contrasts the present role of Jesus with his future role as Son of Man and judge (27. 64).

Matthew's redactional juxtaposition of the present humility of Jesus and his future coming in glory is not related to the incarnational pattern found in other New Testament writings in which the one who was with God humbled himself among men (even to death) and was exalted by God (e.g. Phil 2. 6-11; 2 Cor 8. 9). Nor is it related to the pattern of reversal found in Acts: in raising Jesus God reversed the actions of those who put Jesus to death (e.g. Acts 2. 23-4; 3. 13-15). Matthew simply sets the two contrasting 'comings' side by side, just as Justin and Origen were to do much later.

The development of the 'two parousias' schema in the second and third centuries may have been partly influenced by Matthew's gospel, but there are no signs of direct literary dependence. In Matthew, Justin, the so-called *Anabathmoi Iakobou II* source behind the Pseudo-Clementines, and in Origen, the 'two advents' schema is a response to the sharp criticisms of Jewish opponents who insisted that Christian claims about the Davidic Messiahship of Jesus were not in accordance with the prophets.

What is the relationship of Matthew's Christology to the 'parting of the ways'? Most of Matthew's major Christological emphases are a development or modification of themes which were already prominent in the sources on which the evangelist drew, and hence not directly related to the 'parting of the ways'. Some of Matthew's Christological themes are clearly related *indirectly* to the parting, but they have not been discussed in this chapter. For example, Matthew's strong insistence in redactional passages on the presence of Jesus with his people (1. 23; 8. 23-7; 14. 22-33; 18. 20; 28. 20) and his claim that 'something greater than the temple is here' (12. 6) is undoubtedly set out as a counterpoise to Jewish views about God's presence.

In this chapter I have concentrated on themes and passages which may be related more directly to disputes between Christians and Jews, and hence to the 'parting of the ways'. At the very end of his gospel Matthew refers explicitly to the rival explanations of the empty tomb held by Christians and Jews in his own day (28. 1-15). This passage strongly suggests that other passages earlier in Matthew's gospel may also reflect rival assessments of the significance of Jesus.

I have argued that two accusations levelled against Jesus, that he was a magician and a deceiver, are related to stock anti-Christian polemic. It is no coincidence that these hostile accusations of Jewish leaders occur in Matthean passages which are clearly redactional: they almost certainly reflect the claims and counter-claims of Christians and Jews in the evangelist's day – though the roots of the polemic may be even deeper.

Matthew's repeated insistence that in his earthly life Jesus was Son of David may well have been a response to known Jewish objections. The four redactional references to the hostility evoked among the opponents of Jesus by this assessment of Jesus strongly suggests that this was the case.

In the final part of this chapter I have taken a further step. In Matthew we have an early form (perhaps the earliest) of the 'two parousias' schema which was one of the ways Christians countered Jewish claims that the life of Jesus did not correspond to the prophecies concerning the future coming of the Messiah.

Matthew contrasts the humility and meekness of the life of Jesus the Son of David with the glory of his future coming as Son of Man and judge. This Christological pattern reflects (in part) the self-understanding of the communities for whom Matthew wrote his gospel: Christology and ecclesiology are inter-related. Matthew's Christian readers are encouraged to live by the conviction that the Risen and Exalted Lord is with them (28. 20); they are urged to be ready for the parousia of the Son of Man. But since their Lord who was sent by God (10. 40; 21. 37) is also the humble servant of God who was confronted at every turn by his opponents, they themselves must reflect that role. Their message and ministry are the same as those of Jesus himself (10. 7-8). They are 'the little ones' (10. 42; 18. 6, 10, 14; 25. 40) who must face fierce opposition (5. 10-12; 10. 11-42; 23. 34), but their cause will be vindicated at the future coming of the Son of Man himself (25. 31-46).

Matthew's Christology is not as rich as the fourth evangelist's, and in many ways it is very different. But there are some striking similarities. Both evangelists are keenly aware of Jewish objections to Christian claims about Jesus. The Christology of both gospels has been shaped (in part) by the experiences and self-understanding of minority 'sectarian' communities at odds with their Jewish neighbours.

Chapter Eight

'Pray that your Flight may not be in Winter or on a Sabbath': Matthew 24. 20

Why does Matthew add two phrases to Mark 13. 18: 'your flight' (ἡ φυγὴ ὑμῶν) and 'nor on a Sabbath' (μηδὲ σαββάτῳ)? In his eschatological discourse Mark encourages those who are in Judaea to flee to the mountains when they see 'the desolating sacrilege set up where it ought not to be' (Mark 13. 14). In v. 18 Mark is still referring to this flight when he writes: 'pray that it may not come in winter' (προσεύχεσθε δὲ ἵνα μὴ γένηται χειμῶνος). Throughout this pericope Matthew follows Mark closely (Matt 24. 15-22 = Mark 13. 14-20), so these two additional phrases are striking. What is their significance? Many commentators and writers on Matthew 24 have slipped past this Matthean addition without even noting it, let alone discussing it. No doubt they have decided that there are plenty of more pressing issues to consider in this chapter.[1]

On the other hand, some scholars have used these additional phrases to support far-reaching conclusions about the author, readers, and date of Matthew's gospel. Many writers have claimed that since Matt 24. 20 strongly emphasizes the importance of keeping the Sabbath, this confirms that the evangelist is a 'conservative' Jewish

---

[1] Two perceptive discussions of Matt 24–25 have recently been published, neither of which refers to Matthew's additions in 24. 20. See J. Dupont, *Les trois apocalypses synoptiques*, Paris 1985, 49-97, and F. Hahn, 'Die eschatologische Rede Matthäus 24 und 25' in *Studien zum Matthäusevangelium* (FS W. Pesch) ed. L. Schenke, Stuttgart 1988, 107-26.

Christian. Scholars who claim that Matthew is a Gentile Christian who is writing for a predominantly Gentile community whose Jewish roots are past history have had to find an explanation for this difficult verse.[1] One recent commentator has insisted that Matt 24. 20 indicates that the gospel was written in A.D. 65–67, (i.e. well before the destruction of Jerusalem) on the grounds that the command to pray against having to flee on the Sabbath would have been irrelevant later.[2]

Matt 24. 20 has been interpreted in at least six quite different ways. I shall discuss the main explanations briefly before setting out what I consider to be the correct interpretation. I hope to show that the most plausible resolution of this exegetical puzzle is based on an acceptance of redaction criticism as the basic tool for serious study of Matthew. But I also hope to show that redaction critical studies are more compelling when they are complemented by sociological and literary critical insights.

(1) In his important commentary E. Klostermann (1927) rejected the view of B. Weiss (1898) and A. Loisy (1907) that at this point Matthew had retained the original form of the tradition which was found in an abbreviated form in Mark. Klostermann quoted with approval Wellhausen's opinion (1904) that Matt 24. 20 belongs with the other Judaizing passages in Matthew's gospel: 'Christians keep the Sabbath strictly, just as they also still sacrifice (5. 23) and pay the Temple tax (17. 27)'.[3] Several recent writers continue to maintain that Matt 24. 20 confirms that Matthew's community kept the Sabbath strictly.[4] As we shall see below,

---

[1] See Chapter 5, 131-9.

[2] R.H. Gundry, *Matthew*, 607-8.

[3] W.C. Allen had reached a similar conclusion in his ICC commentary in 1912: 24. 20 was 'clear proof of the Jewish predilections of the Evangelist'. Allen linked 24. 20 with 5. 18; 10. 6, 23; 19. 9; 23. 3, 23. He also suggested that the saying with this addition was probably familiar to Matthew from his Palestinian sources; 'it may even have stood in the Logia'.

[4] See, for example, R. Hummel, *Auseinandersetzung*, 41, and D. Patte, *Matthew*, 351. D.R.A. Hare, *Jewish Persecution*, 6, notes that the addi-

consideration of Matt 12. 1-14 makes it difficult to defend this view.

(2) In his commentary which was first published in 1930, A. Schlatter claimed that Matthew was the first gospel to be written, even though by then Marcan priority had become the dominant view. Nonetheless Schlatter's views on Matt 24. 20 (as on many other passages in Matthew) are perceptive. He believed that this verse reflected the fears of Palestinian followers of Jesus who had parted company completely with the Temple and with Jewish piety, and who did not keep the Sabbath. For them flight on the Sabbath was especially dangerous, for every fleeing person would be recognized immediately.[1] E. Hirsch also claimed that this verse reflected fear of the Jewish authorities: 'a Christian congregation fleeing on the Sabbath would have been as recognisable in Palestine as a spotted dog'.[2] Although it is most unlikely that Matthew's gospel originated in Palestine, we shall see that there is a good deal to be said for this view.

(3) With the development of redaction critical study of Matthew in the decades following World War II, it became clear that the modifications made by the evangelist to his sources could not all be labelled 'Judaizing'. Redaction critics who claimed that the final redaction of Matthew was undertaken by a Gentile were naturally baffled by Matt 24. 20: the extra phrase μηδὲ σαββάτῳ suggested Jewish rather than Gentile concerns. G. Strecker, for example, insisted that Jewish elements in Matthew were the result of community tradition and were not to be taken as characteristic of the evangelist; he claimed that 24. 20 may reflect the original form of the Jewish apocalyptic tradition.[3] But since most of

tion of μηδὲ σαββάτῳ in Matt 24. 20 indicates that 'the Sabbath continued to be an important institution'.

[1] I have used the 6th edition (1963) of Schlattter's commentary. See also his comments on Matt 12. 1-14.

[2] E. Hirsch, *Die Frühgeschichte des Evangeliums* II, 1941, 313. I owe this reference to G. Barth in G. Bornkamm, G. Barth and H.J. Held, *Tradition*, 92.

[3] G. Strecker, *Der Weg*, 18; see also 30. W. Trilling also had difficulty ascribing μηδὲ σαββάτῳ to the evangelist; the phrase 'displays most

the differences between Matt 24. 1-36 and Mark 13. 1-32 can be ascribed with little difficulty to the evangelist Matthew, an appeal to 'community tradition' is hardly necessary. It looks like special pleading when redactional changes which do not fit a particular understanding of Matthew's distinctive viewpoint are set aside as earlier tradition.

(4) In his influential study, 'Matthew's Understanding of the Law', which was first published in 1960, Gerhard Barth reopened discussion of this verse on the basis of a brief discussion of Jewish attitudes to the Sabbath at the time the evangelist wrote.[1] Barth noted that already in the time of the Maccabeans the older standpoint that it was better to allow oneself to be killed on the Sabbath than to desecrate it by fighting had been given up; he referred to I Macc. 2. 32ff. and Josephus, *Ant.* 12. 274 ff. He then cited several further passages from Josephus and concluded that escape on the Sabbath occurred frequently in the Jewish wars and was not regarded as scandalous.

In the light of this evidence Barth turned to Matt 24. 20.[2] This verse, he claimed, does not suggest that Matthew considered flight on the Sabbath a serious sin, because that would mean that 'on the whole Sabbath question he adopted a stricter view than that known by the rest of Judaism' (92). Against this, Matt 12. 1-14 shows that Matthew's community observed the Sabbath, 'but not so strictly as the Rabbinate'. Barth concluded that the evangelist makes the addition in 24. 20 so that the evangelist's community 'will not give offence'.

---

clearly the limited perspective of Judea and Jewish thought and betrays the influence of a strange hand'. *The Gospel according to St Matthew for Spiritual Reading*, E.tr. London 1969, 435. W. Rordorf, *Sunday*, E.tr. London 1968, 68 and 130, suggested that the addition μηδὲ σαββάτῳ (or even the whole verse?) derives from a late Jewish (Maccabean?) milieu, or perhaps from late Jewish apocalyptic circles, or from nationalist and zealot circles. Rordorf's curious comments illustrate the difficulties which arise when one attempts to explain the additions in Matt 24. 20 without ascribing them to the evangelist Matthew.

[1] See G. Bornkamm, G. Barth and H.J. Held, *Tradition*, 91-2.
[2] Barth also refers to the rabbinic evidence set out in Billerbeck's *Kommentar* I, 953.

In other words, for the sake of good relationships with the Jewish authorities, Matthew's community was prepared to keep the Sabbath more strictly than was necessary according to its own convictions.

A solution along these lines has been accepted by several writers,[1] but it is far from convincing. If, as Barth claimed, in the latter decades of the first century flight on the Sabbath was generally acceptable whenever Jews were seriously threatened by enemies, why would Matthew's community have given offence by fleeing on the Sabbath? Even if Matthew's community observed the Sabbath less strictly than its Jewish opponents, on Barth's view both Matthew and his opponents would have accepted that *in extremis* flight on the Sabbath was in order. So the Matthean addition can hardly reflect a desire to maintain reasonable relationships with Jewish leaders.

(5) E. Lohse claimed that Matt 24. 20 offers an example of the keeping of the Sabbath by a Jewish Christian congregation which still remained within Judaism.[2] He also noted that since flight on the Sabbath was considered to be legitimate when there was danger to life, we must look for an alternative explanation of the verse.[3] So he claimed that desecration of the Sabbath in face of the terrors of the end-times could lead only to an escalation of the catastrophe. At first sight this seems to be an attractive solution of what is a fascinating but puzzling *crux interpretum*. Unfortunately Lohse offers no evidence from contemporary Jewish writings to confirm that such a view was current when Matthew wrote.[4] One might of course argue that Matt 24. 20 itself provides evidence for the existence of an apocalyptic motif not attested elsewhere. But does the evangelist imply that the

---

[1] See, for example, E. Schweizer in his commentary (1973; E.tr. 1976), *ad loc.*

[2] E. Lohse, art. σάββατον in *TDNT* VI, E.tr. Grand Rapids 1971, 29.

[3] *TDNT* VI, 30 and see also 14 lines 24ff.

[4] In his note at this point Lohse rejects the conjecture of K. Holl (1914) that behind Matt 24. 20 lies the idea of the Day of Saturn as an unlucky day.

flight about which he is anxious will be caused by end-time terrors? As we shall see below, neither the immediate context in Matthew 24, nor the evangelist's earlier references to the flight of disciples supports this explanation.

(6) A very different solution has recently been proposed. Matthew's addition μηδὲ σαββάτῳ is taken to be an anachronism, merely a 'historicizing addition'.[1] Does Matthew add this phrase in order to point out to his readers that earlier disciples of Jesus did once keep the Sabbath very strictly? Why would he want to do this?

For several reasons this is an unlikely explanation. (i) At some point no later than the early decades of the second century most readers of Matthew's gospel had abandoned Sabbath observance. No doubt many of them read this verse as confirmation that an earlier generation of Christians had kept the Sabbath strictly and had therefore been anxious about flight on a Sabbath; they were well aware that Matt 24. 20 was no longer directly applicable in their own day.[2] But is the evangelist himself likely to have *added* this phrase in order to make this point? (ii) If the evangelist is adding an anachronistic historicizing phrase, then he is sharply differentiating earlier disciples of Jesus (who kept the Sabbath strictly) from followers of Jesus in his own day who (presumably) have abandoned it. But in the preceding verses (and earlier in the gospel) the evangelist uses the disciples as models for Christians in his own day.[3] (iii) The evangelist is unlikely to have made such a 'historicizing' addition to a sentence which, from its context, he intended to refer to the future rather than to the past, for in this verse disciples are

---

[1] See R. Walker, *Heilsgeschichte*, 86: 'μηδὲ σαββάτῳ ist schon für Matthäus (wie für die heutigen 'Heidenkirchen') ein Anachronismus und kann gerade so also irrelevant im Text stehen bleiben'. Similarly, J. Lambrecht, 'The Parousia Discourse: Composition and Content in Mt. XXIV-XXV', in *Matthieu*, 322.

[2] There is no serious disruption in the textual tradition of 24. 20, so the verse does not seem to have been problematic for Matthew's later readers.

[3] See U. Luz, 'Disciples', in *Matthew*, 98-128.

urged to pray that (at some point in the future) their flight might not be on a Sabbath.

'Your flight'

In all these varied explanations of Matt 24. 20, Matthew's addition of the phrase μηδὲ σαββάτῳ is the focus of attention. Matthew's first addition to Mark 13. 18, however, is regularly overlooked. I hope to show that by considering carefully Matthew's addition of ἡ φυγὴ ὑμῶν it is possible to clarify his intention in 24. 20.

Although there is no explicit subject for the verb γένηται in Mark 13. 18, the reader infers readily from the context that it is the flight of 'those in Judaea' which should not happen in winter – a flight which is sparked off by the setting up of the 'desolating sacrilege' (v. 14). In Mark 13 it is clear that the same flight and the same participants are referred to in verses 14 and 18: those involved in the flight in winter (v. 18) are clearly οἱ ἐν τῇ Ἰουδαίᾳ (v.14). Those who may be forced to flee are not necessarily the four disciples to whom Jesus addresses these words, Peter, James, John, and Andrew (13. 3 - 5).

In this pericope Matthew appears to be following Mark closely, but he modifies Mark considerably with a series of redactional changes, just as he frequently does throughout his gospel. At the beginning of the eschatological discourse (Matt 24. 3-4), Jesus addresses disciples *in general*, not four named disciples as in Mark.[1] Long before reaching Matthew 24, the careful reader has become aware that when Jesus addresses his disciples in this gospel, he is often speaking not only to his followers in Galilee or Judaea, but also to Christians in the evangelist's own day.[2]

By his addition of the phrase ἡ φυγὴ ὑμῶν in 24. 20, Matthew indicates to the reader that those who are to pray

---

[1] In Mark 13. 1 *one* disciple asks Jesus about the temple and Jesus replies to him; in Matt 24. 1-2 the individual is replaced by 'the disciples'.

[2] For discussion of this important Matthean phenomenon, see U. Luz, 'Disciples', in *Matthew*, 98-128.

198

that their flight will not be in winter or on a Sabbath are not necessarily confined to οἱ ἐν τῇ Ἰουδαίᾳ who are urged in v. 16 to flee. The ὑμῶν is crucial: it must refer to those to whom the discourse is addressed, i.e. to disciples in general. While some disciples *may* be in Judaea, the context strongly implies that they are not in that locality.

Twice in the immediately preceding verses (24. 9-14) Matthew's redactional changes to Mark strongly imply a geographical setting beyond Judaea and suggest a reason for the flight referred to in v. 20. Disciples will be delivered up εἰς θλῖψιν and killed; they will be hated not simply ὑπὸ πάντων (as in Mark 13. 13), but ὑπὸ πάντων τῶν ἐθνῶν (24. 9b). In v. 14 Matthew retains Mark's reference to the preaching of the gospel εἰς πάντα τὰ ἔθνη (Mark 13. 10), but underlines its importance by adding ἐν ὅλῃ τῇ οἰκουμένῃ. The link between the disciples' proclamation of 'this gospel of the kingdom' to all nations and their rejection ὑπὸ πάντων τῶν ἐθνῶν is clearly implied in 24. 9, 14. The same point is made in the second Matthean discourse where the reader is told clearly in Matt 10. 18 and 22 that disciples sent by Jesus to proclaim the coming kingdom will be rejected by Jewish and Gentile leaders alike. These generalized references in chapters 10 and 24 to the setting in which proclamation is to take place and in which rejection is to be expected suggest that the evangelist's readers are not necessarily in Judaea.

A further redactional change made by Matthew confirms this. In Matthew 23 the evangelist has used Mark 12. 37b-40 as the framework for the construction of his bitter attack on the scribes and Pharisees. But the pericope which follows immediately in Mark, the account of the widow's mite (12. 41-4), is one of the very few Marcan passages which Matthew omits. The omission enables the evangelist to make a much more direct link between the reference in 23. 34, 37 to the rejection of the disciples by Jewish leaders and the reference in 24. 9 to the hatred and persecution they must expect at the hands of 'all nations'. In both passages disciples are warned that some will be put to death. And in both passages, I suggest, the evangelist indicates that persecution of disciples in his own day will lead to their flight.

This is clearly stated in Matt 23. 34. At the climax of his polemic against the Jewish leaders, Matthew reshapes and extends a Q tradition (cf. Luke 11. 49). Prophets, wise men, and scribes are being sent by Jesus to the Jewish leaders. 'Some you will kill and crucify; some you will scourge in your synagogues; some you will persecute from town to town (διώξετε ἀπὸ πόλεως εἰς πόλιν).' An identical warning to disciples is given in 10. 23: ὅταν δὲ διώκωσιν ὑμᾶς ἐν τῇ πόλει ταύτῃ, φεύγετε εἰς τὴν ἑτέραν.[1]

Given the strong link between persecution of disciples and their flight which is forged in Matt 10. 23 and 23. 34, there can be little doubt that the addition made by Matthew in 24. 20, ἡ φυγὴ ὑμῶν, refers to the flight of disciples in the face of fierce opposition. In Mark 13 there is a close link between 'those in Judaea' who may have to flee (v. 14), and the prayer that 'it' may not happen in winter (v. 18), but there is no necessary link with the four named disciples to whom the discourse is addressed. In Matthew matters are very different. 'Those in Judaea' (24. 16) are *not* necessarily those who are to pray that their flight may not be in winter or on a Sabbath (24. 20). Those who are urged to pray, however, *are* to be identified with the disciples to whom the whole discourse is addressed – the implied readers of the gospel.[2]

---

[1] For recent discussion of this verse with reference to earlier literature, see V. Hampel, '"Ihr werdet mit den Städten Israels nicht zu Ende kommen". Eine exegetische Studie über Matthäus 10, 23', *TZ* 45 (1989) 1-31. Although Hampel does discuss briefly the meaning of the verse as it stands in Matthew's gospel, his primary interest is in the logion as a saying of Jesus. Hampel defends the unity of the two parts of the logion. In view of the close parallel between Matt 10. 23a and 23. 34, and in view of the fact that 'from city to city' is a Matthean redactional addition in the latter verse, I think it is likely that the evangelist himself is responsible for Matt 10. 23a.

[2] If this interpretation is correct, Matt 24. 20 is not related in any way to the traditions recorded by Eusebius and Epiphanius about a flight of Christians to Pella at the time of the Jewish war against Rome. We need not consider here whether Matt 24. 16 or Mark 13. 14 is related to those traditions. Two contrasting studies have recently been published. J. Verheyden, *De vlucht van den Christenen naar Pella. Onderzoek van het getuigenis van Eusebius en Epiphanius,* Brussels 1988, argues that

At this point we turn briefly to some literary critical considerations. The theme of flight from Jewish persecutors is stated at the very outset of Matthew's story in chapter 2; it is brought to a climax in 24. 20. In chapter 2 drama and irony are as prominent as in any other part of the gospel. At the outset of his story the evangelist introduces a strongly ironical note: the Jewish religious leaders and learned teachers do know about the Scriptural prophecy of the birth of the Messiah, but (unlike Herod) they make no attempt to worship Jesus, even with mixed motives. As the story unfolds, they take over the role of Herod and their opposition to Jesus becomes steadily more marked.[1] Herod's attempt to destroy Jesus is thwarted by the flight into Egypt; the wise men are also forced to flee.

Later in the story disciples (and the implied reader) are given a broad hint that they may have to follow the example of Jesus and of the wise men and flee for their very lives from persecution. In this respect, as in many others in this gospel, Jesus is a model for disciples. But the flight of Jesus in the face of opposition is not a point which the evangelist develops later in his gospel. R.H. Gundry's claim that even outside chapter 2 'Jesus exemplifies his command to flee persecution' is not convincing.[2] Gundry suggests that the evangelist uses the verb ἀναχωρέω to develop this theme. While the verb is undeniably important in chapter 2 (it is used in vv. 12, 13, 14, 22), it is by no means certain that in the three further passages in which Matthew uses the verb redactionally to refer to Jesus (Matt 4. 12; 14. 13; 15. 21), with-

---

Epiphanius depends on Eusebius; the tradition appears for the first time in Eusebius, who introduces it in order to solve the problem of the fate of the Jerusalem Christians during the Jewish war. C. Koester, 'The Origin and the Significance of the Flight to Pella Tradition', *CBQ* 51 (1989) 90-106, defends the traditional view that Epiphanius is not dependent on Eusebius. He leaves open the possibility that Luke 21. 20-2 refers to a flight to Pella; the Marcan and Matthean traditions are not considered.

[1] For a similar view, see J.D. Kingsbury, 'The Developing Conflict between Jesus and the Jewish Leaders in Matthew's Gospel: A Literary - Critical Study', *CBQ* 49 (1987) 57-73, especially 65.

[2] *Matthew*, 59.

drawal *in the face of opposition* is in mind.[1] This is undoubtedly the case in Matt 12. 15, but in this verse Matthew
takes over Mark's ἀναχωρέω and underlines a point already
clear in Mark.

There is a further reason why I am not convinced that
beyond chapter 2 Matthew presents Jesus as an example of
flight from persecution. In a recent perceptive discussion of
Matthew's literary methods A.T. Lincoln has shown that in
the gospel as a whole the implied reader's situation is similar
to that of the disciples, not that of Jesus. The implied readers'
'identification with characters in the story is more with the
disciples, whose portrayal includes development and
uncertainty, than with Jesus, who is in many ways more
static and fulfils his narrative role or implied task in a fairly
straightforward and unambiguous fashion.'[2]

The implied reader of Matthew 2 is encouraged to identify
with the wise men who come to worship Jesus, but end up by
'fleeing' from the machinations of Herod. As R.H. Gundry
notes, in Matt 2. 12 the 'flight' of the wise men 'offers an
example for persecuted Christians to follow'.[3] As Matthew's
story unfolds, the disciples take over the role of the wise men
and the reader identifies readily with them.

Already in chapter 10 there is a clear link between the
rejection of disciples by Jewish and Gentile authorities and
the approach of the end-times (Matt 10. 15, 17-18, 22-23).
Flight from persecution is set in an eschatological context
(Matt 10. 23)! The same link is made in Matt 23. 34-9.

In chapter 24 there is an explicit link between the end-
times, persecution of disciples, wars and natural disasters,
and apostasy within the community: πάντα δὲ ταῦτα ἀρχὴ
ὠδίνων (Matt 24. 8).[4] Matt 24. 15-20 belong to the same

---

[1] See W. Schenk, *Die Sprache des Matthäus*, Göttingen 1987, 28.

[2] A.T. Lincoln, 'Matthew - a Story for Teachers?', in *The Bible in Three Dimensions*, eds. D.J.A. Clines, S.E. Fowl, S.E. Porter, Sheffield 1990.

[3] *Matthew*, 32.

[4] πάντα is added redactionally by Matthew. I am assuming, with many exegetes, that there is no chronological distinction between Matt 24. 4-8 and 9-15. I take τότε at the beginning of 24. 9 to mean 'at the time referred to in the previous sentences' rather than 'next'.

setting.[1] The flight referred to in Matt 24. 20, we may conclude, is not specific. With the additional phrase ἡ φυγὴ ὑμῶν, disciples, who include readers or listeners in the evangelist's day, are addressed directly. They are warned once again that they may have to flee from persecution. In Matt 10. 17-18, and 22 persecution from both Gentiles and Jews is referred to. In Matt 24. 20 the reference to Sabbath suggests that, as in Matt 23. 34, persecution from Jewish religious leaders is in mind.

'On a Sabbath'

Why does the evangelist suggest that followers of Jesus pray lest their flight from persecution should take place on a Sabbath? The reference to flight in winter which immediately precedes μηδὲ σαββάτῳ suggests that increased hardships would be involved. But why? In the light of our discussion above of the various interpretations of Matt 24. 20, there are only two possible explanations. Perhaps disciples who perceive that they are in danger of persecution keep the Sabbath so strictly that they would not attempt to escape and would therefore be in increased danger. Or perhaps their dilemma is quite different: since they do not keep the Sabbath strictly, they would not hesitate to escape on the Sabbath; however, they know that in so doing they would antagonize still further some of their persecutors.

Did Matthew's community keep the Sabbath strictly? With the exception of Matt 28. 1, the only references to Sabbath in Matthew are in Matt 12. 1-14.[2] In his redaction of the two Marcan pericopae (Mark 2. 23-8 and 3. 1-6) and his inclusion of extra material in Matt 12. 5-7 and 12. 11 (for part or all of

---

[1] Matt 24. 21 seems to mark a new phase: θλῖψις μεγάλη is contrasted with the θλῖψις of 24. 9. Although Matthew's eschatological time-scale is not as clear as many exegetes have supposed, all agree that 24. 29 is a turning point.

[2] Matthew omits Mark's two positive references to the Sabbath: Mark 1. 21 and 6. 2.

which the evangelist himself is responsible) Matthew develops a much more subtle line of argument than Mark does. But G. Barth's claim that Matthew's community *observed the Sabbath* (a view which several more recent writers have acccepted) is much too confident.

In Matt 12. 5 Scripture is said to confirm that temple duties take precedence over Sabbath commandments. This is followed by the astonishing declaration that Jesus himself is greater than the temple (Matt 12. 6).[1] So at the climax of the pericope it comes as no surprise to the reader to be told (even more pointedly than in Mark) that Jesus as Son of man is lord of the Sabbath (Matt 12. 8). The pericope which follows provides a graphic illustration. It reaches its climax with a pronouncement which so enrages the Pharisees that they plot to destroy Jesus: ἔξεστιν τοῖς σάββασιν καλῶς ποιεῖν (Matt 12. 12).

Do these two pericopae indicate that Matthew's community still retains the Sabbath? If, as I have argued in Chapter 5, Matthew's community has cut its ties completely with Judaism, Matt 12. 1-14 could well have been taken to legitimate abandonment of the Sabbath. Although he has exaggerated his case by minimizing the importance of theological factors, S. Bacchiocchi has shown that in many parts of early Christianity Sunday observance was closely related to the parting of the ways from Judaism.[2] Adoption of Sunday observance was often part of the process of Christian self-definition over against the 'mother' religion, Judaism.

Was this the case in Matthew's day? This must be left as an open question since I do not think we have clear-cut evidence from the gospel itself which enables us either to confirm or to deny this possibility. However we do know that within one or two generations a 'Matthean' community was worshipping on 'the Lord's Day' rather than the Sabbath. The *Didache* is undoubtedly dependent on Matthew, and is both

---

[1] The reading μεῖζων found in some MSS is clearly inferior; it makes explicit the reference to Jesus which is implied by the neuter μεῖζον.

[2] S. Bacchiocchi, *From Sabbath to Sunday: a Historical Investigation into the Rise of Sunday Observance in Early Christianity*, Rome 1977.

Jewish and Matthean in its ethos.[1] The community is urged to 'come together, break bread and hold Eucharist' κατὰ κυριακὴν δὲ κυρίου (14. 1).[2] In one other respect the community from which the *Didache* comes was defining itself over against Judaism: it did not fast on 'Mondays and Thursdays' (the usual Jewish days for fasting) but on 'Wednesdays and Fridays' (8. 1).

While we do not know the way in which Matthew's community kept the Sabbath (if at all), in the light of Matt 12. 1-14 it is impossible to accept that it kept the Sabbath strictly and was therefore reluctant to flee on a Sabbath. So we are left with the alternative mentioned above. Since the Matthean community did not keep the Sabbath strictly, it would not have hesitated to escape on a Sabbath; however, it knows that in so doing it would antagonize still further some of its persecutors.

As we noted above, G. Barth discusses the evidence for Jewish attitudes to flight on a Sabbath in time of war. He concludes that flight on a Sabbath would not have been considered to be scandalous.[3] However Martin Hengel's more thorough examination of the evidence indicates that opinion on this issue changed from time to time and that at the time of the Jewish war opinion was divided.[4] The Shammaites and the zealots did permit armed attacks, although in other respects they kept the Sabbath rigorously. But their views were not shared universally, and there was a strong body of opinion which continued to emphasize the importance of

---

[1] For a good recent discussion, see O. Knoch, 'Kenntnis und Verwendung des Matthäus-Evangeliums bei den apostolischen Vätern' in *Studien zum Matthäusevangelium* (FS W. Pesch) ed. L. Schenke, Stuttgart 1988, 157-78.

[2] I have cited the Loeb text and translation, *The Apostolic Fathers*, ed. K. Lake, London 1912).

[3] *Tradition*, 92.

[4] See M. Hengel's excursus (with a full discussion of the relevant sources and the secondary literature) 'The Observance of the Sabbath and the Holy War', in *The Zealots*, E.tr. Edinburgh 1989, 287-90.

keeping the Sabbath strictly in all circumstances.[1] The comments of Josephus himself are not consistent.[2]

So it is seems likely that in the immediate aftermath of the Jewish war the Matthean community feared (rightly or wrongly) that since flight on a Sabbath would provoke further hostility from some Jewish leaders, it was to be avoided if at all possible. Sociological studies have shown that it is common for a minority group which has parted company with its parent body to exaggerate the threat posed by its rival. This may well have happened in Matthew's community. In the 80s and 90s of the first century there were any number of geographical locations in which the local Jewish synagogues outnumbered Christian communities. So our interpretation of Matt 24. 20 does not presuppose a Palestinian setting for the gospel. Unlike most of the explanations noted above, it allows Mark's χειμῶνος and Matthew's addition μηδὲ σαββάτῳ to be taken as parallel statements: flight at either time would be perilous.

---

[1] See especially CD 10 and 11; IQM 8f.; Jubilees 50. 12f.
[2] M. Hengel (as cited above) notes the difference between Bell. 2, 392ff. and Vita 159 = Bell. 2, 634.

Chapter Nine

Once More: Matthew 25. 31 – 46

With the exception of the Sermon on the Mount, no passage in Matthew's gospel has attracted more attention from exegetes, theologians, and preachers, than the final pericope of the fifth and final discourse. The interpretation of Matt 25. 31-46 has been keenly disputed since at least the third century.[1] It is salutary to modern scholars to find that in spite of the more sophisticated techniques of analysis available to them, and their much greater knowledge of first century Judaism, they are sometimes no nearer to solutions of notoriously difficult exegetical problems than interpreters were hundreds of years ago. In recent decades general acceptance of redaction criticism has not brought agreement on the interpretation of this passage any closer.

There are two main interpretations of this pericope, each with several variations. In the twentieth century variations have proliferated. According to Sherman Gray's recent com-

---

[1] The history of interpretation has recently been fully documented by Sherman W. Gray, *The Least of My Brothers: Matthew 25. 31-46: A History of Interpretation*, SBLDS 114, Atlanta 1989. Gray's study is impressively wide-ranging. In his survey of modern interpretation of this passage, however, he pays insufficient attention to the *methods* adopted by different scholars. I have included as an appended note to this chapter some early interpretations of Matt 25. 31-46 which Gray has missed.

For the history of interpretation, see also W. Brandt, 'Die geringsten Brüder. Aus dem Gespräch der Kirche mit Mt 25, 31-46', *Jahrbuch der theologischen Schule Bethel* 8 (1937) 1-8; J. Friedrich, *Gott im Bruder. Eine methodenkritische Untersuchung von Redaktion, Überlieferung und Traditionen in Mt 25, 31-46*, Stuttgart 1977, 181-9.

prehensive survey, as many as thirty two 'variously nuanced positions' have been advanced.[1]

Many exegetes insist that Matthew's apocalyptic revelation discourse should be seen as a dramatic and powerful insistence that in the final judgement men and women of all nations will be separated like sheep and goats on the basis of their concern and care for the poor and needy. Acceptance of those in need is acceptance of Jesus himself. On this first major line of interpretation (the 'universalist' interpretation) the pericope is read as a continuation of the strong exhortations of the preceding sections of Matthew's fifth discourse, but now non-Christians as well as members of Matthew's communities are in view.

An important variation insists that in Matthew's eyes the Gentile nations will have been evangelised before the final judgement, so it is *Christians* (and not humankind in general) who are to be judged on the basis of their attitude to those in need. A further variation limits 'the needy' to the needy within the church.

On the second main interpretation the non-Christian nations (among whom Israel may or may not be included) will be judged on the basis of their acceptance or rejection of Christians (or a particular group within Christian communities, such as missionaries or apostles). 'The least of these my brothers' (25. 40, 45) are not the poor and needy of the world, but Christians who form a minority within society at large. If this 'particularist' interpretation is adopted, the pericope has the same general purpose as many apocalyptic writings: to offer consolation and encouragement to minority communities who are hard-pressed by the dominant society which surrounds them and which is perceived to be threatening. More specifically, the pericope functions as an answer to the question, 'Why are the enemies of the gospel allowed to trample over the followers of Jesus?' Or, 'Why do the nations triumph?' The evangelist's answer to his readers is that God will ultimately bring the nations to judgement. To their great surprise, those who have shown active caring

---

[1] *The Least of My Brothers*, 255-7.

concern for Christians will receive their reward, for in accepting the messengers and representatives of Jesus the Son of man, they will have accepted Jesus himself.

The nub of the exegetical dispute can be put quite simply. Is this pericope concerned with the attitude of the world in general to the needy (the 'universalist' interpretation), or is it, rather, the world's attitude to the church which is in view (the 'particularist' interpretation)? A decision depends very largely on answers given to two questions: Who are πάντα τὰ ἔθνη, 'all the nations', gathered at the throne of the Son of man for judgement (verses 31 and 32)? Who are τούτων τῶν ἀδελφῶν μου οἱ ἐλάχιστοι, 'the least of these my brothers', (verses 40 and 45), for whom deeds of mercy have been done?

This passage has been keenly discussed with very different results for over 1700 years partly because it contains apocalyptic, parabolic, and poetic language,[1] language which by its very nature is evocative and elusive, rather than didactic. Interpretation has been disputed vigorously for the further reason that it raises four major theological questions. (i) Does this passage teach that judgement will be on the basis of good works rather than faith in Christ? Needless to say, this issue was prominent in sixteenth century discussion, but it has rarely been off the agenda. (ii) Is this passage primarily about care of the needy and marginalised in society? If so, then its frequent use by modern preachers to jolt the social conscience of affluent and complacent Christians is justified. (iii) Does this passage associate Jesus the Son of man *with* the poor? If so, it suggests not so much a 'natural theology' as a 'natural Christology': Jesus is not merely the man for others, he *is the other man*. V.P. Furnish, for example, notes that in this passage we have ample New Testament warrant for Luther's continuing insistence that Christ himself may be met in the neighbour.[2] In his discussion of this passage, C.E.B. Cranfield has written movingly about the Real Presence of the Risen Christ in the poor as comparable with

---

[1] The passage is neither an apocalypse, nor a parable, nor a poem, but an apocalyptic discourse. I shall discuss its genre further below.

[2] *The Love Command in the New Testament*, Nashville 1972, 81.

the presence of Christ in Scripture and sacrament.[1] (iv) Is it possible to distinguish between the evangelist Matthew's interpretation of this passage and an earlier very different interpretation, perhaps one which goes back to Jesus himself? Some have claimed that the original form of the passage was a strong exhortation to all men to show concern for the poor. Matthew, however, has restricted the scope of the pericope by changing the poor and marginalised into Christians who are at odds with the dominant society. And the reverse position has also been argued: Jesus had in mind his immediate circle of disciples, but Matthew widened the scope of his teaching. If it is possible to make a sharp distinction between an earlier and a later form of the tradition, which form should be given priority as 'Scripture' for the life of the church today, and on what basis? Major hermeneutical issues are at stake.

This passage clearly raises a set of fascinating and important theological questions. Hence it is no surprise to discover that down through the centuries interpreters have read the passage in the light of their particular doctrinal concerns; their initial theological questions and pre-suppositions have strongly influenced their exegesis.[2]

For the interpreter who is primarily interested in the ways the first recipients of Matthew were intended to understand the text, further questions arise. Matt 25. 31-46 forms the climax of Matthew's presentation of the teaching of Jesus in his five grand discourses. What does this passage tell us about the evangelist's overall concerns in his gospel? What does it tell us about the social setting of the first recipients?

If the pericope refers to judgement of the nations at the parousia on the basis of their treatment of followers of Jesus, the 'particularist' interpretation, then it is related to a quite specific social setting. These verses are intended to console anxious Christians who perceive themselves to be threatened both by the local Jewish leadership and by Gentile society at

---

[1] 'Diakonia. Matthew 25, 31-46', *London Quarterly and Holborn Review* 186 (1961) 275-81.

[2] Sherman Gray brings out this point effectively in his survey, *The Least of my Brothers*.

large. In short, on the 'particularist' interpretation this passage reflects the social setting of Matthew's gospel which is envisaged in this book.

In this chapter I shall concentrate on what I take to be the central exegetical issues in this passage, but readers will be relieved to learn that I shall not attempt to assess the thirty two ways it has been interpreted in recent scholarship. I hope to offer some fresh observations in support of the 'particularist' interpretation. I shall stress the importance of the redactional apocalyptic motifs in this passage, and I shall relate what I take to be its central theme to a prominent concern of several apocalyptic writers who wrote at about the same time as Matthew.

Since theological presuppositions and differences over method have been so prominent in discussion of these verses, I must set out the main principles with which I am working. I accept without hesitation that many strands of both the Old and New Testaments exhort God's people to show active concern for the marginalised in society and I believe strongly that the church today is constrained to take this bias to the poor with the utmost seriousness. In short, on theological grounds I am predisposed to read Matt 25. 31-46 as a solemn exhortation to the church (and indeed, to all men and women) to give priority to the hungry, thirsty, and needy of the world. As an exegete, however, I must consider the possibility that the evangelist's intentions and the ways the first recipients are likely to have understood this passage may have been very different. If so, I shall not abandon my own convictions, for they are supported by plenty of other Biblical passages.

My approach is primarily redaction critical; it is complemented by some literary critical and sociological observations. Since Matthew's redactional hand can be discerned in several key phrases in this passage, it is possible to relate them to other passages in the gospel where his distinctive emphases can be detected. This is a basic tenet of redaction criticism. With most redaction critics I am assuming that Matthew interprets the traditions at his disposal in a reasonably consistent way. The evangelist is not an anthologist who

211

has juxtaposed earlier traditions in a random way: if that were the case, there would not be any point in trying to relate one part of his gospel to another.

Who is gathered for judgement?

Two exegetes, Victor Furnish and Ulrich Wilckens, have argued independently that the judgement spoken of in 25. 32 is judgement *of the church*.[1] They both note that Matthew emphasizes that the 'gospel of the kingdom' will be preached throughout the whole world as a testimony to all nations before the end comes (24. 14). 'All the nations', writes Furnish, 'are the evangelised nations, the world-wide "kingdom" out of which the unrighteous will be separated (13. 41).' (p. 82f.) Wilckens makes a similar point: Matt 25. 31-46 should be taken as comparable with the parable of the tares and its interpretation in chapter 13.

But does Matthew envisage that the nations to whom the gospel of the kingdom has been proclaimed have become 'the kingdom'? Is Matthew that optimistic? The evangelist does not indicate that missionary endeavour will be successful. On the contrary, he takes pains to stress that there will be intense opposition, and not only at the hands of the Jews. Note Matthew's twofold use of Mark 13. 13: 'You will be hated by all for my name's sake'. The evangelist has transfered this logion to a new context, the sending out of the disciples, where there are clear hints of the opposition disciples may expect from Gentiles in the post-Easter period (10. 22; cf. 10. 17-18). In 24. 9 he uses the same logion a second time, now in its original Marcan eschatological context, but with a significant addition: 'You will be hated by all *nations*'. The evangelist envisages that Christians will receive the same rough treatment at the hands of the nations that God's people have always received from hostile opponents. This

[1] V.P. Furnish, *The Love Command in the New Testament*, 79-84. U. Wilckens, 'Gottes geringste Brüder – zu Mt. 25, 31-46' in *Jesus und Paulus* (FS W.G. Kümmel) eds. E.E. Ellis and E. Grässer, Göttingen 1975, 363 -83.

theme is prominent elsewhere: 5. 10-11; 23. 29-37; cf. also 10. 17-18 and 10. 23 and 25b.

Along with other exegetes, Ulrich Wilckens notes that judgement of *the church* is prominent in Matthew and emphasizes strongly that from 24. 32 onwards, Matthew's fifth discourse contains repeated warnings to the disciples not to allow the coming judgement to take them unawares. In view of the chronological construction of the discourse, a scene of judgement (of the church) is expected.[1]

However, this important point can be countered by three related observations. (a) In common with writers of the Jewish apocalypses, Matthew is not as concerned with logical consistency as are some of his modern interpreters. (b) Since a judgement of Christians is implied at several points in the pericopae which precede 25. 31-46, it is possible that a rather different judgement is in view in the final pericope. (c) Unlike the preceding four pericopae, 25. 31-46 is not a parable, but an apocalyptic discourse. The new genre suggests a break in the flow of the argument.

At this point it is worth noting that if, as I have suggested, Matthew *implies* in his final discourse that there will be two judgements, then he is in good company. In several intertestamental and early Christian writings there are two or even three judgement scenes which involve different groups. In the Testament of Benjamin 10. 8-9, for example, we read: 'Then, too, all men will rise, some to glory and some to disgrace. And the Lord will judge Israel first for the wickedness done to him; for when he appeared as God in the flesh, as a deliverer, they did not believe him. And then he will judge all the Gentiles, everyone of them who did not believe him when he appeared on earth.'[2] Luke 21. 20-8, 4 Ezra 13. 33-50, and I Enoch 90 and 91 provide further examples.

Wilckens believes that the οἱ ἐκλεκτοί, 'the elect', of 24. 31 who will be gathered by the Son of man's angels at his coming, are to be identified with those on the right hand of

---

[1] 'Gottes geringste Brüder', 367.

[2] Although in its present form this passage is clearly Christian, it may well be an expansion of an earlier Jewish tradition.

the Son of man in 25. 32. I also accept that Matt 24. 30f. (where Matthew has heavily redacted Marcan material) is to be related closely to 25. 31ff. But surely 24. 30, with its reference to 'all the tribes of the earth', confirms that in 25. 31 the evangelist has in mind all non-Christian peoples. 'All the tribes of the earth' who mourn at the appearance of the sign of the Son of man can hardly refer to the *evangelised nations*. So there are difficulties in taking πάντα τὰ ἔθνη as all Christian people, or all the evangelised nations. Matthew's redactional emphases in 24. 30f. do not support this interpretation.

Most damaging of all to this interpretation, however, is the fact that in Matthew τὰ ἔθνη is never used to refer to Christians, or even to Christians and non-Christians together. It is always used to refer to Gentiles, over against Christians or Jews.[1] In 24. 9 and 14, and in 25. 32 πάντα τὰ ἔθνη must refer to all non-Christians. As in 28. 18-20 (and in many other passages in his gospel), in the final pericope in his fifth discourse Matthew develops themes he has emphasized earlier, but he tranposes them into a new key.

Who are 'the least of these my brothers'?

In the closing logion of the 'missionary' discourse in chapter 10, Matthew uses the phrase ἕνα τῶν μικρῶν τούτων, 'one of these little ones' in a context which makes it quite clear that οἱ μικροί are disciples of Jesus. Matthew is indebted to Mark 9. 37-41 at this point, but he has dropped all reference to children.

Near the beginning of the fourth discourse in chapter 18 Matthew returns to the same Marcan pasage (18. 6 = Mark 9. 42), and once again it is clear that οἱ μικροί are disciples. And just a few verses later in 18. 10 and 14 (Matthew's version of

---

[1] So too, for example, W. Schenk, *Die Sprache des Matthäus*, Göttingen 1987, 217; E. Brandenburger, *Das Recht des Weltenrichters. Untersuchungen zu Mt 25, 31-46*, SBS 99, Stuttgart 1980, 102-19; J. Friedrich, *Gott im Bruder*, 254.

the parable of the lost sheep) there are two further redactional uses of the phrase. So there can be little doubt that for Matthew οἱ μικροί is a quite specific term for disciples.[1]

The phrase ἑνὶ τούτων τῶν ἐλαχίστων in 25. 40, 45 is very similar to the phrase in 10. 42, ἕνα τῶν μικρῶν τούτων, so we can be all but certain that it refers to disciples.[2] Why is the superlative used in ch. 25? It can be argued that the superlative here has almost the same sense as the positive. In the NT 'true' superlatives are very rare; superlatives with an elative sense ('very') are much more common.[3] The REB catches the nuance of the elative superlative here: 'one of these, however insignificant'. The difference between 'the little ones' (10. 42) and 'the insignificant ones' (25. 40, 45) is not great.[4] Hence it is not surprising that at 10. 42 some scribes altered οἱ μικροί to οἱ ἐλάχιστοι, and that at 25. 40 and 45 some scribes made the opposite change. In both cases 10. 42 and 25. 40, 45 have been brought into close correspondence with one another quite deliberately[5]

The phrase τῶν ἀδελφῶν μου which is found in 25. 40 (but not in v. 45) strengthens still further the conclusion that in our pericope the nations are to be judged on the basis of their

---

[1] See Chapter 11 for a discussion of οἱ μικροί in 5 Ezra and in the Nag Hammadi *Apocalypse of Peter*. Both writings seem to represent a continuation of Matthean Christianity in the second century.

[2] D. Marguerat, *Le Jugement dans l'Évangile de Matthieu*, Geneva 1981, 481-520, defends the 'universalist' interpretation vigorously. He accepts that in Matthew οἱ μικροί refers to Christians, but insists, without adequate arguments, that in 25. 40, 45 'les ἐλάχιστοι sont qualifiés, simplement, par un état de *pauvreté objective*' (509).

[3] See BDB §6, 33 and C.F.D. Moule, *An Idiom Book of New Testament Greek*, Cambridge 1953, 97-8.

[4] It is just possible that the superlative has been chosen to identify one particular group among the disciples. But if that was Matthew's intention, I think he would have been more specific about the group he had in mind.

[5] See the appended note at the end of this chapter for details of the textual variants.

acceptance or rejection of Christian disciples.[1] Matthew uses οἱ ἀδελφοί 18 times to refer to fellow members of the Christian family; no fewer than 12 of the 18 are redactional.[2] As in many other cases, Matthew has taken a word found in his sources and used it himself so frequently that it becomes part of his distinctive vocabulary.

Matthew's use of both οἱ ἐλάχιστοι and οἱ ἀδελφοί as terms for Christian disciples is firmly established. Nonetheless some scholars have resisted this conclusion. Some deny that in Matthew οἱ μικροί and οἱ ἀδελφοί have a special sense, but their arguments fail to carry conviction.[3] Ulrich Wilckens accepts that the pre-Matthean version of this pericope referred to disciples / missionaries, but claims that Matthew broadened the tradition so that it referred to all needy men.[4] Matthew, however, is much more likely to have used οἱ μικροί and οἱ ἀδελφοί in the same ways he has used them in similar contexts in his discourses in chapters 10 and 18. A much more plausible theory is advanced (with differences in details) by J. Friedrich, D.R. Catchpole, and Schuyler Brown, who reverse Wilckens's hypothesis.[5] In their view it is Matthew's redactional additions which have *limited* the original sense of the discourse, which may go back to Jesus himself.

---

[1] The omission of τῶν ἀδελφῶν μου in v. 45 is simply a slight abbreviation. Matthew often avoids an exact repetition of a phrase. The omission of the phrase in some mss at v. 40 (the first hand of B, 1424, ff[1] and ff[2]) and early church fathers (Clement of Alexandria; Eusebius, and Gregory of Nyssa) is not significant. The latter may have been quoting from memory; the former may have harmonised v. 40 with v. 45.

[2] For the details, see W. Schenk, *Die Sprache des Matthäus*, 14.

[3] See, for example, W.G. Kümmel, *Promise and Fulfilment*, E.tr. London 1957, 92-4. D. Marguerat, *Le Jugement*, 511, claims that 'the poor' *become* 'brothers' by a decree.

[4] 'Gottes geringste Brüder', in *Jesus und Paulus*, 363-83.

[5] J. Friedrich, *Gott im Bruder*; D.R. Catchpole, 'The Poor on Earth and the Son of Man in Heaven: a Re-appraisal of Mt xxv. 31-46', *BJRL* 61 (1979) 355-97; S. Brown, 'Faith, the Poor and the Gentiles: a Tradition-Historical Reflection on Matthew 25: 31-46', *Toronto Journal of Theology* 6/2 (1990) 171-81. See also J.M. Court, 'Right and Left: the Implications for Matthew 25. 31-46', *NTS* 31 (1985) 229-33.

There is a further consideration which strongly supports the interpretation I am defending. Perhaps the most startling aspect of this passage is the identification of the Son of man – King with 'the least of these my brothers'. Several scholars have noted that it is difficult to find Jewish traditions which *identify* God with the poor and needy. Difficult, but not impossible. D.R. Catchpole quotes *m. Tannaim* xv. 9 in which God says to Israel, 'My children, when you gave food to the poor, I counted it as though you had given it to me.'[1] However, there are no passages in Matthew, or in early Christian writings generally, which *identify* Jesus with the poor.[2]

It is, of course, just possible that Matthew did take a bold and unprecedented step. But from what we know of the evangelist's methods elsewhere, it is much more likely that in the final pericope of his final discourse he would develop points made elsewhere in his gospel rather than set out a wholly new idea.

On the other hand, if we take 'the least of these my brothers' to be a reference to followers of Jesus, then the identification of Jesus with them is not unexpected. The claim at the very opening of the gospel that the birth of Jesus means that God is with his people (1. 23) is matched by the closing promise of the Exalted Christ to be *with* his disciples to the end of the age (28. 20). The closing logia of the missionary discourse, 10. 40-2, foreshadow the closing pericope of the final discourse.[3] In verse 40 Jesus identifies himself closely with his disciples: 'he who receives you, receives me.' Verse 42 is an extension of this theme: acceptance of 'one of these little ones' by giving a cup of cold water because he is a disciple is acceptance of Jesus himself.

In short, whereas early Christian writings do not identify Jesus with the poor and needy, the close identification of

---

[1] 'The Poor on Earth', 391.

[2] So too U. Wilckens: the thought that the Son of Man identifies himself with the poor is 'ausserordentlich und ohne Parallele.' 'Gottes geringste Brüder', 376

[3] D. Marguerat, *Le Jugement*, 485, notes that Matt 10. 40-2 is a 'hermeneutical canon' for the 'particularist' interpretation of 25. 31-46.

Jesus with his disciples is a thoroughly Matthean theme which is also found elsewhere.[1]

Who are the needy?

The phrases in Matt 25. 31-46 which have been considered so far indicate that the non-Christian nations are to be judged by the Son of man on the basis of actions they have done (or not done) to followers of Jesus. At first sight the list of six groups of needy people (which is given four times in the pericope) fits awkwardly with this interpretation. It seems to be much more plausible to take it as a list of groups of needy people to whom men and women of goodwill (whether Christians or not) might be expected to show mercy. So we must consider the function of the list.

Of several similar lists in the Old Testament, Isa 58. 6-7 is undoubtedly the closest to Matt 25. 31-46. There we also have a sixfold list, though the first two, or even three items, seem to refer to the same group: 'loose the fetters of injustice', 'untie the knots of the yoke', 'set free the oppressed', 'share food with the hungry', 'take the homeless poor into your house', 'clothe the naked'. From the context it is clear that this is a list of the ways God's people are expected to have acted towards society at large. That might suggest that the list in Matt 25 should be construed similarly. However the differences suggest that Matthew is not dependent on this list and that the evangelist's list may have had a different function.

Intertestamental, rabbinic and early Christian writings, and even the Egyptian Book of the Dead and Persian sources have all been cited as offering possible parallels to Mattthew's list.[2] In each case it is a question of some similarities, but also of differences which seem to rule out dependence one way or the other. These partial parallels, however, do bring to light

---

[1] See also I Cor 8. 12; Acts 9. 4-5; 22. 8; 26. 15; Ignatius, *Eph* 6. 1; Didache 11. 4; Justin, *I Apol* 16. 9-10; 63. 5.

[2] See J. Friedrich, *Gott im Bruder*, 164-72.

several striking omissions from Matthew's list if it is taken as a general list of the needy in society.

The list in Matt 25 does not refer to widows and orphans, to those who mourn, to the physically disabled, or to burial of the dead. The absence of 'widows and orphans' is particularly unexpected, for in numerous Old Testament passages and in several Christian writings concern for them is prominent (e.g. Psalm 146. 9; Polycarp 6; Ignatius, *Smyrn* 6; Justin *I Apol* 67). In James 1. 27 'religion that is pure and undefiled before God and the Father' is defined as 'visiting orphans and widows in their affliction'.

The long list of the needy in 5 Ezra 2. 20-3, an early Christian writing which has been strongly influenced by Matthew,[1] confirms that Matthew's list is truncated if it is taken as a conventional list of the needy: 'Guard the rights of the widow, secure justice for the fatherless, give to the needy, defend the orphan, clothe the naked, care for the injured and the weak, do not ridicule a lame man, protect the maimed, and let the blind man have a vision of my splendour. Protect the old and the young within your walls; when you find any who are dead, commit them to the grave and mark it.'

It is possible to take the six groups referred to in Matt 25 as a general list of the needy in society. But in comparison with other such lists in Biblical, early Jewish, and early Christian writings, there are so many omissions that it is worth considering alternative explanations.

Is the list congruent with the interpretation of 'all the nations' and 'the least of these my brothers' set out above? If my interpretation of these two key phrases is correct, non-Christian nations are to be judged on the basis of what they have done (or not done) to followers of Jesus. They should have welcomed the 'brothers of the Son of man, however insignificant', for in so doing they would have welcomed the Son of man himself.

On the 'particularist' interpretation the list must be taken as a list of the ways in which the nations might have shown their acceptance of the followers of Jesus. Is this plausible?

[1] See Chapter 11.

Matt 10. 11-15 and 40-2 undoubtedly point in this direction. In the latter passage, those who welcome and provide hospitality to disciples of Jesus welcome him (δέχομαι); 'whoever gives a cup of cold water to one of these little ones because he is a disciple' will be rewarded. Didache chs. 12–13 are also relevant: acceptance of Christian prophets (in this case by the Christian community, not society at large) consists (in part) in provision of shelter, food, drink, and clothing.

The implication of these passages is that failure to provide followers of Jesus with the basic necessities of life would be a mark of rejection, for it would lead quickly to intolerable hardships. There are a number references in New Testament writings to the hardships which Christians endured at the hands of society at large which are not dissimilar to the list in Matt 25: I Cor 4. 11-13; II Cor 6. 4-5; 11. 25-7[1]; 3 John 5-7.; cf. also *Acts of Thomas* 145.

The only item in the list which fits rather awkwardly with the 'particularist' interpretation is the reference to visiting prisoners.[2] Christians are encouraged to visit prisoners in Heb 10. 34 and 13. 3 (cf. Ignatius *Smyrn* 6.2), but it is difficult to envisage non-Christian Gentiles *visiting* Christians imprisoned for their faith.[3] However, we need to bear in mind that in antiquity prisoners (even under house arrest) would be liable to starve unless someone took food and water to them. So 'visiting prisoners' (or not visiting them) may refer to responsible (or irresponsible) treatment of them by the nations. As we shall see in a moment, Joel 3. 3 provides an interesting parallel to the interpretation I am defending: the nations will be brought to judgement for their improper treatment of prisoners taken from among God's people.

---

[1] J. Friedrich, *Gott im Bruder*, 169, notes that this passage is so close to the list in Matt 25 that Paul's knowledge of the tradition cannot be excluded.

[2] There are no references in the Old Testament to 'visiting prisoners', though there are references to 'setting prisoners free': e.g. Psa 146. 7; Isa 42. 7; 58. 6.

[3] E. Schweizer presses this point against the interpretation I am defending. See 'Matthäus 21–25', *Orientierung an Jesus: zur Theologie der Synoptiker* (FS J. Schmid), ed. P. Hoffmann, Freiburg 1973, 371 n.14.

The list of six items in Matt 25. 31-46 does not settle the interpretation of this passage as a whole. The list is congruent with the 'particularist' interpretation demanded by the key phrases 'all the nations' and 'these my brothers, however insignificant', for it can be taken as a series of ways in which the Gentile nations mark their acceptance or rejection of disciples of Jesus.

However, in spite of the striking omissions noted above, the list can be explained readily as a list of 'deeds of mercy' which are expected to be to be to be shown to all men and women in need. The list is undoubtedly the strongest bastion of the 'universalist' interpretation.

Since the list can be used to support both the 'universalist' and the 'particularist' interpretations, it is possible that it formed the core of a pre-Matthean 'universalist' tradition (which may go back to Jesus). By making several redactional additions to the original form of the passage (but not necessarily to the list itself) Matthew altered its thrust radically. Whereas it was originally an exhortation to all to show loving concern for all men and women in need, it became an assurance to Matthew's anxious readers that the nations would ultimately be judged on the basis of their treatment of Christians.[1]

An apocalyptic discourse

Whatever its original form may have been, in its present form Matt 25. 31-46 is an apocalyptic discourse. Several redactional phrases and motifs in this passage, its antithetical structure, and (as I shall argue) its central thrust are all strongly reminiscent of passages in apocalyptic writings such as 4 Ezra, I Enoch, 2 Baruch, and the Apocalypse of Abraham.[2]

---

[1] For references to traditio-historical explanations along these lines, see above, 217.

[2] See, for example, the detailed discussion of phrases in J. Friedrich, *Gott im Bruder*, 111-73. Friedrich does not discuss the *shared central theme* which I shall stress.

Some have even claimed that Matthew is dependent on passages in I Enoch.[1] In Matt 25. 31-46 the evangelist undoubtedly strengthens and extends apocalyptic themes found in his sources, as he does elsewhere, particularly in 13. 36-43, 49-50; 16. 27-8; 19. 28; and in earlier pericopae in the fifth discourse, where Mark 13, Q and 'M' traditions are reshaped under the influence of apocalyptic motifs.

Supporters of the 'universalist' interpretation have insisted that since there is no structural or syntactical break in Matthew's fifth discourse at 25. 31, this passage, like the preceding parables, must be interpreted as an exhortation to faithfulness and vigilance; in particular, the evangelists' readers are urged to persevere in showing loving concern for those in dire need.[2] However, even on this interpretation there is a break in the thrust of the discourse as a whole, for it is no longer solely Christians who are being addressed, but men and women in general.

Unlike the preceding pericopae, Matt 25. 31-46 is not a parable. Its genre as an apocalyptic discourse prepares the reader or listener for a change of direction in the argument of the discourse as a whole.[3] Since apocalyptic writings usually function as a consolation to groups of God's people who perceive themselves to be under threat or alienated from the society in which they live, this is likely to be the central thrust of Matt 25. 31-46. I now wish to show that this is indeed the case.

---

[1] J. Theisohn, *Der auserwählte Richter. Untersuchungen zum traditions-geschichtlichen Ort der Menschensohngestalt der Bilderreden des Äthiopischen Henoch*, SUNT 12, Göttingen 1975, argues that the influence of the Similitudes of Enoch (chs. 37-71) can be found in Matt 13. 37-43; 19. 28; and 25. 31; Theisohn's view is accepted by D. Marguerat, *Le Jugement*, 489. See also D.W. Suter, *Tradition and Composition in the Parables of Enoch*, SBLDS 45, Ann Arbor 1978, 25-8, who cautiously claims that Matthew knew both the the parables of Enoch (chs. 37-71) and the judgement scene in the apocalypse of the animals (90. 20-7).

[2] See, for example, D. Marguerat, *Le Jugement*, 497.

[3] For a good discussion of the structure of the discourse, see J. Lambrecht, 'The Parousia Discourse: Composition and Content in Mt. xxix - xxv', in *Matthieu*, 309-42.

Although I do not think that *literary dependence* between Matthew and any apocalyptic writings can be established beyond reasonable doubt, the central theme of 25. 31-46 is also found in several apocalyptic writings. Matthew's gospel, 4 Ezra, 2 Baruch, and at least two sections of I Enoch come from a broadly similar social setting. Their similar 'symbolic worlds' function as consolation to hard-pressed groups of God's people.

In these apocalyptic writings the prophetic declaration that God will judge the nations 'on the last day' is a response to the complaint of God's people, or their representative: 'Why do the nations prosper at our expense?' The response functions as an encouragement to persevere even in the face of severe oppression and persecution meted out by the nations who trample over God's chosen people. They are assured that in the final judgement the apparently triumphant nations will be brought to book and God's faithful people will be rewarded. At present gross injustice may seem to be rampant, but in the final judgement roles will be reversed and the minority group will prevail.

The 'crimes' of the nations are usually summed up in very general terms as 'wickedness' or 'lawlessness'. In several passages, however, their treatment of God's people is mentioned explicitly as the criterion on which they will be rewarded or punished.

Supporters of the 'universalist' interpretation of 25. 31-46 usually overlook the genre of this passage and ignore its apocalyptic motifs and themes. This is not surprising, for apocalyptic writings do not provide any support for that line of interpretation. The 'particularist' interpretation, however, is closely related to a theme found in apocalyptic writings.

The relationship between Matthew 25 and apocalyptic writings which were also written towards the end of the first century strengthens considerably the interpretation of Matthew's final judgement scene which I am defending. Since it has been overlooked by scholars who share my interpretation of Matt 25. 31-46, I shall discuss briefly the key passages.

The roots of this apocalyptic motif are deep. The *locus classicus* is Joel 3. 1-3 (LXX 4. 1-3):

When that time comes, on that day
when I reverse the fortunes of Judah and Jerusalem,
I shall gather all the nations together
(συνάξω πάντα τὰ ἔθνη, cf. Matt 25. 31)
and lead them down to the valley of Jehoshaphat.
There I shall bring them to judgement
on behalf of Israel, my own people,
whom they have scattered among the nations;
they have shared out my people by lot,
bartering a boy for a whore
and selling a girl for a drink of wine. [REB]

Although it is not clear which exile or dispersion the prophet is referring to, Israel is reassured that the nations' harsh oppression will not be overlooked. The final three lines are of special interest; they refer to the nations' gross mistreatment of *prisoners*, the very theme which, as we saw, seems to fit awkwardly into the list of 'deeds of mercy' in Matt 25. 35-39 and 42-44.

In the wake of the trauma of A.D. 70 apocalyptic writers announced that on the last day God would judge the nations on the basis of their treatment of his people. In the opening verses of 4 Ezra, Ezra contrasts 'the desolation of Zion' with 'the wealth of those who live in Babylon' (3. 2). His complaint to the Most High is soon more specific. He wishes to inquire 'about those things which we daily experience: why has Israel been given over to the Gentiles as a reproach' (4. 23; see also, e.g., 5. 23-30; 6. 57-9)? Ezra is repeatedly assured that the nations will not escape God's judgement; they will be punished for their ungodliness and wickedness (e.g. 12. 31-3; 13. 37). There is a clear implication that their 'wickedness' includes their mistreatment of God's chosen people.

This theme becomes explicit in a judgement scene in 7. 37-8. Suddenly at the last judgement the nations are confronted with God's people whom they have denied and failed to serve and they are judged on that basis:[1]

> Then the Most High will say to the excited nations:
> Consider and know those whom you denied
> Or those whom you have not served
> Or whose faithfulness you have spurned.
> Look on this side, then on that:
> Here are rest and delight
> There fire and torments.

2 Baruch (the Syriac Apocalypse of Baruch) was also written towards the end of the first century to console a minority group in distress; it is so closely related to 4 Ezra that some scholars have claimed that there is literary dependence.[2] In chapter 72 the vision of the 'bright waters' is explained:

> After the signs have appeared, which you were told about before, when the nations are in confusion, and the time of my Messiah is come, he will call the nations together, and some of them he will spare, and some of them he will destroy. This is what will happen to the nations spared by him. Every nation that has not exploited (lit. 'known') Israel and has not trampled the race of Jacob underfoot will

---

[1] I have quoted the translation by J.H. Myers in his commentary in the Anchor Bible, *I and II Esdras*, Garden City, N.Y. 1974. Myers translates the Syriac text, not the Latin text which lies behind the translations in the RSV, NEB, and REB Apocrypha. The Latin reads, 'Videte et intellegite quem negastis vel cui non servistis . . .' The Armenian is similar; see *The Armenian Version of IV Ezra*, edited and translated by M.E. Stone, Missoula 1978. The Syriac, however, has the more difficult reading and is to be preferred. Whereas the Latin and Armenian texts reflect the common view in apocalyptic writings that the nations are judged on the basis of their denial of God, in the Syriac it is the treatment of God's people which is at stake.

[2] For a recent discussion of the dating of 2 Baruch and of its relationship to 4 Ezra, see Gwendolyn B. Sayler, *Have the Promises Failed? A Literary Analysis of 2 Baruch*, SBLDS 72, Chico Calif. 1984, 103-10 and 123-34.

be spared. And this will be because some out of all the nations will become subject to your people. But all those who have had dominion over you, or have exploited (lit. 'known') you, will be given over to the sword. And when he has brought low everything that is in the world, and has sat down in peace for ever on the throne of his kingdom, then shall joy be revealed ... (72. 2 – 73. 1)[1]

There are several similarities to Matt 25. Judgement of the nations takes place 'after the signs have appeared' (cf. Matt 24. 3, 15, 24, 30; 25. 31). Judgement is delegated by God to his Messiah / Son of man who has a glorious throne or a throne 'of his kingdom'. In both strongly antithetical passages, final judgement is on the basis of the nations' treatment of God's people. Both passages are intended to reassure an anxious minority group which perceives itself to be God's people.[2]

Similar motifs and themes are found in two originally quite separate sections of I Enoch. In ch. 62, part of the 'book of parables' which was probably written about the same time as Matthew, 'the kings and the mighty and the exalted, and those who dwell upon the earth' are told:

(62. 3) And on that day all the kings and the mighty and the exalted, and those who possess the earth, will stand up; and they will see and recognize how he (the Son of Man) sits on the throne of his glory. . . (62. 9) and they will set their hope upon that Son of Man and will entreat him, and will petition for mercy from him. (62. 10) But that Lord of Spirits will then so press them that they will hasten to go out before him . . . (62. 11) And the angels of

---

[1] I have quoted from L.H. Brockington's revision of R.H. Charles's translation, *The Apocryphal Old Testament*, ed. H.F.D. Sparks, Oxford 1984, 884.

[2] Gwendolyn Sayler, *Have the Promises Failed?*, compares 2 Baruch with five 'related writings': Pseudo-Philo, 4 Ezra, the Apocalypse of Abraham, the Paraleipomena of Jeremiah, and Matthew. Her comments on Matthew are very brief and include only one puzzling sentence (145-6) on Matt 25. 31-46, where, she claims, there is an 'indissoluble connection between Torah and the return of Jesus as judge'.

punishment will take them, that they may repay them for the wrong which they did to his children *and his chosen ones*. (62. 12) *And they will become a spectacle to the righteous* and to his chosen ones; they will rejoice over them . . .[1]

Once again judgement is on the basis of the nations' treatment of 'God's children and his chosen ones', a point missed by writers who are bemused by the question of literary dependence between I Enoch 62 and Matthew 25. 31-46.

The same theme is found, albeit in a different form, in I Enoch 103-4, in the epistle of Enoch which may have been written about 100 B.C., some two centuries before the passage just quoted. In 103. 9 the 'righteous and holy' complain bitterly and at length (to the Great One) and are given a solemn assurance that their plight has not been forgotten:[2]

(103. 9) In the days of our affliction we toiled laboriously and saw every affliction and met many evils; we were spent and became few, and our spirit small. (103. 10) We were destroyed, and there was no one who helped us with words or deeds; we were powerless and found nothing. . . (103. 12) Those who hated us and those who goaded us were masters of us. . . (103. 14) We complained about them to the rulers in our distress and cried out against those who devoured us, but they took no notice of our cry and did not wish to listen to our voice. (103. 15) And they helped those who plundered us and devoured us and those who made us few, and they concealed their wrongdoing . . . (104.1) I swear to you, you righteous, that in heaven the angels remember you for good before the

---

[1] M.A. Knibb's translation in *The Ethiopic Book of Enoch. A New Edition in the Light of the Aramaic Dead Sea Fragments*, II, Oxford 1978. The phrases in italics in 62. 11 and 12 are omitted in some Ethiopic mss, but the point I am making is not affected.

[2] I have paraphrased the Greek of the Chester Beatty papyrus. The Ethiopic is awkward; see M.A. Knibb's note, *The Ethiopic Book of Enoch*, 241. In the quotation which follows, I have cited M.A. Knibb's translation.

glory of the Great One . . . (104. 2) Be hopeful! For you were formerly put to shame through evils and afflictions, but now you will shine like the lights of heaven and will be seen, and the gate of heaven will be opened to you.[1] . . . (104. 3) And persevere in your cry for judgement, and it will appear to you, for (justice) will be exacted from the rulers for all your distress, and from all those who helped those who plundered you. (104. 4) Be hopeful, and do not abandon your hope, for you will have great joy like the angels of heaven.

In this passage the righteous see themselves as a very hard-pressed minority. Their self-understanding is typical of many groups for whom apocalyptic writings were intended to act as a consolation in deep anxiety and distress: 'we became few'; 'we were powerless'. The role of the rulers (of the nations – the immediate context makes this clear) is particularly striking. Although they have not persecuted the righteous *directly*, they are nonetheless held to be culpable for their failure to restrain those who were treating the righteous harshly. Similarly in Matt 25. 31-46: the nations' treatment of 'the little ones' is not direct, open persecution; it is indirect, and 'concealed' (cf. I Enoch 103. 15) from the world at large.

Jewish and Christian writers turned to apocalyptic in periods of historical crisis and trauma. Apocalyptic regularly functions as consolation for groups which perceive themselves to be under duresse. Apocalyptic language is also often used to reinforce attitudes of group solidarity amongst minority groups at odds with society at large; clear lines are drawn between 'insiders' and 'outsiders'. This is the social setting of the passages from 4 Ezra, 2 Baruch, and I Enoch quoted above. It is also the social setting of the book of Revelation, which announces judgement and doom for the powerful and complacent, and in so doing provides hope of ultimate vindication for the powerless and oppressed people of God.

[1] Cf. Matt 13. 43 (MtR).

Matt 25. 31-46 comes from a similar social setting and was intended to function similarly for the first recipients of the gospel.

In these verses the evangelist returns to some of the themes of the opening pericopae of the fifth discourse. In the time before the end, the 'gospel of the kingdom' is to be preached throughout the whole world as a testimony to all nations (24. 14). Matthew's readers and listeners are warned that followers of Jesus will be put to death and hated *by all nations* for his sake (24. 9). The time before the end will be marked by political and social upheaval (24. 6-8). Christians will be divided; the love of many will grow cold (24. 10). Since these verses at the beginning of the fifth discourse have been redacted by Matthew himself, they reflect directly his concerns. In this setting Matt 25. 31-46 is a final consolation to the recipients of the gospel. God's enemies will not have the last word, for they will be judged on the basis of their treatment of the brothers of the Son of man, however insignificant.

These verses have also been foreshadowed in other passages earlier in the gospel, nearly all of which are redactional. Judgement at the parousia is associated with the Son of man (16. 27; 19. 28; 24. 30). Provision of hospitality is a mark of acceptance of disciples of Jesus; failure to do so is a mark of rejection (10. 11-14; 40-2). Acceptance of disciples of Jesus is acceptance of Jesus himself (10. 40). Those who reject disciples will be judged and punished (10. 15). Rejection is to be expected from an οἰκία (household, 10. 13-14), from political and religious authorities (10. 17-18), and also from a whole πόλις (town, 10. 15). The town which rejects followers of Jesus will be punished on the day of judgement (10. 15) – here we are not far from Matt 25. 32, where an even larger entity, the nations, will be judged on the basis of their treatment of followers of Jesus. Persecution of followers of Jesus has been referred to in 5. 10-12; 10. 16-25; 23. 34-5; in two redactional passages persecution at the hands of the nations is mentioned specifically (10. 17-18; 24. 9b).

J.D. Kingsbury has shown that in a number of places in the five discourses Jesus 'speaks past' the immediate 'story-

229

audience' and addresses directly the situation of the implied reader.[1] The final pericope of the fifth discourse is the last opportunity for the evangelist to do this. So we may reasonably expect this pericope to be related particularly closely to the social setting to which the gospel as a whole points. And given Matthew's fondness for repetition with variation, it is no surprise to find that many themes of the discourses are repeated and elaborated here. Just as the grand finale to the gospel as a whole in 28. 18-20 is in a sense an anti-climax since so many of its themes have been anticipated earlier,[2] so too with 25. 31-46. This passage is a dramatic statement in apocalyptic garb of many of the evangelist's most distinctive concerns.

Appended note on the history of interpretation

In his history of the interpretation of Matt 25. 31-46, Sherman Gray includes a careful discussion of some the earliest allusions and references to this passage. There are three further passages which are of some interest and importance:

(i) Although Gray includes a discussion of textual variants (pp. 5-6), he fails to note the significant variants in 25. 40 and 45. In two sixth century uncials, Σ and 067, τῶν μικρῶν is inserted, thus making an explicit link between this passage and Matthew's use of οἱ μικροί at 10. 42; 18. 6, 10, and 14. A similar link is made in 25. 45 in minuscule 700 and possibly in the Sahidic, where μικρῶν replaces ἐλαχίστων. These variants are noted in the Huck - Greeven *Synopse der drei ersten Evangelien*, Tübingen 1981, but not in the apparatus to the 26th edition of Nestle-Aland. The latter does, however,

---

[1] *Matthew as Story*, 2nd ed. 1988, 107-11.

[2] J. Lange, *Das Erscheinen des Auferstandenen im Evangelium nach Matthäus*, Forschung zur Bibel 11, Würzburg 1974, claims (with some overstatement, but many perceptive insights) that 28. 18-20 is a 'new edition' of Matt 11. 27 = Luke 10. 22 which recalls many themes prominent elsewhere in the gospel.

note that at 10. 42, D and the Old Latin and Vulgate replace μικρῶν with ἐλαχίστων; and 1424 and a few other minuscules add ἐλαχίστων alongside μικρῶν. All these variants bring 10. 42 and 25. 40, 45 into close correspondence with one another quite deliberately. They are clearly of importance for the history of interpretation, for they confirm that in several circles in the early church 25. 40 and 45 were taken to be references to disciples.

(ii) In 5 Ezra 2. 20-23, which is closely dependent on Matthew's gospel and which may date from about A.D. 140, Matthew's list of the needy seems to have been extended considerably.[1] Paradise is promised after the general resurrection to those within the Christian community who have cared for those in need.

(iii) In II Enoch 5. 9-18 (= Slavonic Enoch), which was known to Origen, there is an important parallel to Matt 25. 31-46. In the standard edition of the text, A. Vaillant, *Le Livre des Secrets d'Hénoch: text slave et traduction française*, Paris 1952, p. xi, the editor concludes (I think correctly, though this is disputed) that II Enoch is an imitation of a Jewish apocalypse by a Christian who knows Matt 25. Enoch is shown Paradise, a place 'prepared for the righteous, who will endure hardships in this life, and mortify themselves . . . and execute true justice, to give bread to the hungry, and to cover the naked with a garment, and to lift up anyone who has fallen, and to help those who have been wronged, who live their lives in the Lord's presence and serve him alone. For them is this place prepared as their eternal inheritance.'[2] A description of the place prepared for the wicked who have done evil deeds follows; many of the evil deeds are the exact reverse of the deeds of the just, as in Matt 25. Here we seem to have a curious combination of two lines of interpretation of Matt 25: the just care for the needy and they themselves suffer hardships.

---

[1] On 5 Ezra, see Chapter 11 below.

[2] I have quoted A. Pennington's translation of Vaillant's rendering of the Slavonic, *The Apocryphal Old Testament*, ed. H.F.D. Sparks, Oxford 1984, 331.

Chapter Ten

Aspects of Early Christian – Jewish Polemic and Apologetic

Writing about A.D. 177 Celsus claimed that Christians and Jews quarrel with one another very foolishly. 'Their wrangle with one another about Christ is no different from that called in the proverb a fight about the shadow of an ass.'[1] Celsus continues: 'There is nothing worthy of attention in the dispute of Jews and Christians with one another.'

Celsus is writing here, of course, with his tongue in his cheek: he himself does show considerable interest in the issues at stake between Christians and Jews, as does Origen in his reply to Celsus. One of the contentions of this chapter is that in the 100 years between the Fall of Jerusalem and Celsus's perceptive criticisms of Christianity, Christians and Jews were not squabbling needlessly; their vigorous polemic and apologetic is of considerable interest to students both of early Christianity and of early Judaism.

In this period (and certainly for a long while afterwards) few more difficult problems faced Christians than the necessity to spell out the extent of continuity and the extent of discontinuity with contemporary Judaism. This theologi-

---

[1] Origen, *Contra Celsum* III, 1 ed. H. Chadwick, Cambridge 1953. See also *Contre Celse* Vol. II, ed. M. Borret, Paris 1976. For the proverbial expression Borret cites Plato, *Phaedo* 260c and Suidas (lexicon) II, 15 sub ὄνου σκία. This proverbial expression should not be confused with the well-known anti-Semitic jibe that Jews worship the ass and that this is why there was an ass's head in their Temple. See J.N. Sevenster, *The Roots of Anti-Semitism in the Ancient World*, Leiden 1975, 8-11.

cal task had to be accomplished in the face of opposition (and occasionally overt hostility) from Judaism. If early Christianity was almost constantly engaged in defining itself over against contemporary Judaism, Judaism could not and did not ignore the new 'godless and lawless αἵρεσις', to use Justin's phrase to which we shall return.

I am not alone in stressing that debate and argument between Christians and Jews continued right through the early centuries of the Christian era, admittedly with varying levels of intensity in different localities and in different periods.[1] But many New Testament scholars over-emphasize the importance of the events of A.D. 70 in early Christian-Jewish relationships. Many assume too readily that following a so-called 'parting of the ways' about A.D. 85 the former rivals soon had very little to do with one another.[2] Long after

[1] See especially M. Simon's now classic study, *Verus Israel: Étude sur les Relations entre Chrétiens et Juifs dans l'Empire Romain (135-425)*, Paris 2nd ed. 1964. In his postscript Simon claims that in the 15 years since the publication of the first edition (1948) his central thesis has not been refuted: 'le judaïsme, très loin encore d'avoir achevé son repli, a été pour le christianisme, tout au long de la période envisagée, un concurrent réel, actif, souvent efficace.' 477. See also the opening chapter of R. Wilken's fine study, *Judaism and the Early Christian Mind: a Study of Cyril of Alexandria's Exegesis*, New Haven and London 1971.

[2] This view is especially associated with A. Harnack; see further below. Harnack's position has recently been defended by D. Rokeah, *Jews, Pagans and Christians in Conflict*, Jerusalem and Leiden 1982. Rokeah argues that with the partial exception of Justin, A.D. 135 marks a turning point in relations between Christians and Jews. Before 135 Christians and Jews were engaged in 'polemic', which Rokeah defines as a campaign or conflict having the aim of changing an opponents' view or his religion; after that date there was only a 'dispute' – 'an interchange of words aiming at clarification of various matters.' (9) This distinction is artificial. M. Simon and R.L. Wilken (as noted above) show clearly that between the second and fifth centuries Christians and Jews were engaged in rather more than 'clarification'. Justin's *Dialogue* is seen by Rokeah as 'the last Christian treatise which, like the Synoptic Gospels, attempted to persuade the Jews to put an end to their stubbornness and to admit the divinity of Jesus'. (66) Rokeah believes that after 135 the Jews were 'middlemen' – almost 'neutral' in the pagan-Christian conflict. (78, 83)

Christian communities felt themselves to be quite distinct from Judaism, the direct and indirect criticisms of the synagogue 'across the street' continued to engage the attention of Christians.

In this chapter just a few related aspects of early Christian-Jewish polemic and apologetic will be discussed with reference to particular passages. In both the first two main sections I shall take Justin Martyr's *Dialogue with Trypho* chapter 108 as my starting point. I hope to show that some parts of this fascinating chapter are closely related to passages in the *Testament of Levi* and also to passages in several New Testament and other early Christian writings.

Before turning to particular passages I must set out briefly my main assumptions about Justin's *Dialogue* and the *Testaments*. Although Justin's Trypho can almost certainly not be identified as Rabbi Tarphon,[1] it is now clear that on the whole Justin has a good knowledge of contemporary Judaism.[2] It is probably impossible to assess to what extent Justin reproduces an actual debate which took place shortly after A.D. 135. That may not be a very important question. The issues Trypho raises are clearly *felt* by Justin to be of importance: many of them are found in other early Christian writings, and some can be related to Jewish evidence.

In short, the *Dialogue* contains a considerable amount of invaluable information about the issues at stake between Christians and Jews in the middle of the second century. Justin takes Trypho's objections seriously. In the *Dialogue* a conventional Hellenistic genre is adopted in order to refute Jewish criticisms and objections and to expound the

---

[1] See N. Hyldahl, 'Tryphon and Tarpho', *ST* 10 (1956) 77-88.

[2] See the detailed and learned study by Oskar Skarsaune, *The Proof From Prophecy: a Study in Justin Martyr's Proof-Text Tradition: Text-Type, Provenance, Theological Profile*, Leiden 1987. See also P. Sigal, 'An Inquiry into Aspects of Judaism in Justin's Dialgue with Trypho', *Abr-Nahrain* 18 (1978-9) 74-100; T. Stylianopoulos, *Justin Martyr and the Mosaic Law*, Missoula 1975; L.W. Barnard, 'The Old Testament and Judaism in the Writings of Justin Martyr', *VC* 14 (1960) 395-406; A.B. Hulen, 'Dialogues with the Jews as Sources for the Early Jewish Argument against Christianity', *JBL* 51 (1932) 58-71.

Christian case.[1] There is little reason to doubt that Justin expected that his *Dialogue* would assist his fellow Christians in their attempts to convert Jews. Although Justin is not explicit about the location of the debate he records, Eusebius, perhaps on the basis of a well-established tradition, reports that it took place in Ephesus.[2] Certainty is not possible, but it is worth noting that Ephesus is not far from Sardis. And from Sardis, as A.T. Kraabel has shown, we now have clear evidence of the strength and vigour of Judaism in the latter half of the second century.[3]

These assumptions are not shared universally. Two very different conclusions have been reached. On the one hand Harnack believed that by Justin's day genuine discussion and debate between Christians and Jews was virtually over and that Justin's dialogue with Trypho was in truth the mono-logue of a victor. 'Nicht der Gegner selbst spricht mehr; Justin lässt sich sprechen.'[4] On the other hand some scholars have insisted that the polemical character of the *Dialogue* is so very strong that it cannot have been addressed to Jews; rather, it was intended to be an exposition of Christian philosophy for pagans.[5] As we proceed we shall see why both these ways of approaching the *Dialogue* are less plausible than the view sketched above.

---

[1] See M. Hoffmann, *Der Dialog bei den christlichen Schriftstellern der ersten vier Jahrhunderte*, Berlin 1966; B.R. Voss, *Der Dialog in der frühchristlichen Literatur*, Münich 1979.

[2] Eusebius, *H.E.* IV, xviii, 6.

[3] A.T. Kraabel, 'The Diaspora Synagogues: Archaeological and Epigraphic Evidence since Sukenik', *ANRW* II, 19, 1 (1979) 477-510. See now Paul R. Trebilco, *Jewish Communities in Asia Minor*, Cambridge 1991.

[4] A. Harnack, *Judentum und Judenchristentum in Justins Dialog mit Tryphon*, Leipzig 1930. Harnack contrasts Justin with Matthew, Paul and the fourth evangelist; the latter all reflect a vigorous struggle in everyday life, but in Justin this appears to be over.

[5] E.R. Goodenough, *The Theology of Justin Martyr*, Jena 1923; N. Hyldahl, *Philosophie und Christentum: eine Interpretation der Einleitung zum Dialog Justins*, Copenhagen 1966. On this approach, see T. Stylianopoulos, *Justin*, 34.

The *Testaments of the Twelve Patriarchs* raise very different issues. They have clearly had a long and complicated history as *Jewish* writings. But as they now exist in the best critically reconstructed text they can and should be read as Christian writings.[1] Christian 'interpolation' is an inappropriate term, for that suggests words or phrases which can be readily removed in order to expose the original Jewish document.[2] Christian 'redaction' is a more appropriate term, for Jewish traditions have been taken over, abbreviated and expanded by Christians, and in the process completely reinterpreted.

The dating of the main Christian redaction is difficult. J. Jervell's arguments for a date before the end of the first century are not persuasive, but a good case can be made out for the second half of the second century, perhaps shortly after Justin wrote the *Dialogue*.[3] At the end of his paper to

[1] Here I agree with M. de Jonge who has accepted for some time that the Testaments have had a long history as Jewish writings prior to Christian redaction. See, for example, 'The Testaments of the Twelve Patriarchs and the NT', *Studia Evangelica* (TU 73, 1959) 550, and his 1969 article (from *NovT* 4) reprinted in *Studies on the Testaments of the Twelve Patriarchs*, ed. M. de Jonge, Leiden 1975, 196. See also his recent articles, 'The Testaments of the Twelve Patriarchs: Central Problems and Essential Viewpoints', *ANRW* II, 20,1, Berlin and New York 1987, 359-420 and 'The Pre-Mosaic Servants of God in the Testaments of the Twelve Patriarchs and in the Writings of Justin and Irenaeus', *VC* 39 (1985) 157-170; the latter is now reprinted in M. de Jonge, *Jewish Eschatology, Early Christian Christology and the Testaments of the Twelve Patriarchs*, Leiden 1991.

[2] The 'interpolation' theory is defended in H.C. Kee's introduction and translation of the Testaments in ed. J.H. Charlesworth, *The Old Testament Pseudepigrapha* I, Garden City and London 1983, 775-828. See also J. Jervell, 'Ein Interpolator interpretiert. Zu der christlichen Bearbeitung der Testamente der zwölf Patriarchen' in *Studien zu den zwölf Patriarchen*, ed. W. Eltester, Berlin 1969, 30-61.

[3] J. Jervell, 'Ein Interpolator' 54f. suggests that the Christian interpolations were added towards the end of the first century. He makes four observations: (i) the motif of the church as the new Israel is not yet found; (ii) the interpolations are Jewish-Christian, but not yet of the later heretical type; (iii) salvation of the Jews is a major concern, but that theme all but disappeared from later Christian writings; (iv) the Christology is early and Jewish-Christian. These comments presuppose

the 1979 S.N.T.S. meeting in Durham Professor de Jonge urged that we should now try to find the inner logic of the views in the *Testaments* on Jesus, Israel and the nations.[1] I hope to take a small step in that direction.

Jewish polemic and Christian responses

Justin's *Dialogue* 108 contains an important short account of the content of Jewish anti-Christian propaganda.[2] At 108. 2 Justin refers back to 17. 1 where there is a very similar reference to Jewish leaders being sent everywhere to counter Christian claims. In chapter 17 the content of their proclamation is much briefer, but the same phrase, αἵρεσις ἄθεος is used to refer to Christianity. Some of the phraseology of the alleged anti-Christian propaganda comes from Justin himself, some of it possibly from Matt 28. 13, 15, but there are good reasons for supposing that Justin may here be drawing on Jewish allegations. (i) Justin is not simply setting up an artificial list of Jewish claims in order to refute them one by one, for this does not happen immediately after either chapter 17 or chapter 108. Some of the allegations are dealt with elsewhere in the *Dialogue* but some are not. Curiously the charge that the disciples stole the body of Jesus from the tomb is not refuted. (ii) The reference to Christianity as a αἵρεσις is striking and unique in Justin: he uses the term elsewhere to refer to factions *within* Judaism (62. 3; 80. 4) and *within* Christianity (35. 3; 51. 2), but not to Christianity *per*

a rather wooden view of the development of early Christianity. As we shall see below, the close links with Justin suggest a Christian redaction in the latter half of the second century. Additional support for this dating has recently been provided by O. Skarsaune, *Proof from Prophecy*, and by M. de Jonge, 'Pre-Mosaic Servants', both noted above.

[1] 'The Main Issues in the Study of the Testaments of the Twelve Patriarchs', *NTS* 26 (1979-80) 508-524.

[2] J.C.T. Otto's Greek text is used (Jena 1877), but for the sake of convenience the usual verse numbers are used, rather than the line numbers of Otto's text. Where an English translation is quoted, the edition by A. Lukyn Williams (London 1930) has been used.

se.[1] (iii) The reference to Christianity as a godless and lawless αἵρεσις raised by Jesus does not come from the gospels, nor does the reference to the *disciples* as deceivers. So there are some grounds for suggesting that Justin may here be drawing on (as well as filling out himself) Jewish allegations, or, possibly, an earlier Christian source. Certainly this chapter sets out what Justin *felt* to be the heart of Jewish arguments against Christianity. It also gives details of the anti-Christian moves to which Justin refers several times: Jews have chosen and sent out messengers and instigated others to join in opposition to Christians; they have cursed Jesus and those who believe on him. These passages are often taken to be references to the *birkath ha-minim* introduced into the synagogue liturgy about A.D. 85.[2]

The reference to Jesus as τις πλάνος is particularly striking, for, as we shall see, this term is found widely in early Christian writings and very similar terms are also used in *b. Sanh* 43a and the closely related but possibly independent *b. Sanh* 107b. The allegation in *TLevi* 16. 3 that those who plotted to kill Jesus categorised him as πλάνος is one of several similarities between *Levi* 10 and 16 and *Dialogue* 108.

At Matt 27. 63 the same allegation that Jesus is ὁ πλάνος is made to Pilate by the chief priests and the Pharisees. In this verse (and also at Matt 21. 45) the Pharisees are introduced into the narrative redactionally by the evangelist, a clear example of Matthew's sharpening of polemic against the Pharisees.[3] This verse forms part of the evangelist's elaborate attempt to refute what he takes to be Jewish counter-propaganda that the disciples stole the body of Jesus.

---

[1] In order to establish this point I have checked the references listed under αἵρεσις by E.J. Goodspeed, *Index Apologeticus sive Clavis Iustini Martyris Operum*, Leipzig 1912.

[2] See W. Horbury, 'The Benediction of the *Minim* and Early Jewish-Christian Controversy', *JTS* 33 (1982) 19-61, esp. 20 n.2 for earlier literature; J.L. Martyn, *History and Theology in the Fourth Gospel*, Nashville 2nd ed. 1979, 54-55, n.69.

[3] See above, 148-57.

There is a further important parallel in John 7.[1] In this chapter we seem to be able to overhear the disputes between the Johannine community and the local synagogue in the evangelist's own day. Three times there is a division among the people (7. 12, 25ff., 40) on account of Jesus. For our present purposes there are four points of particular interest. (i) There is a two-fold accusation that Jesus leads the people astray – the verb πλανάω is used in verses 12 and 47. (ii) The allegation is related closely to attempts to arrest Jesus: in other words the context of the allegation is very similar to that in *Dialogue* 108, *TLevi* 16 and Matt 27, in all of which the πλάνος allegation is linked to the trial or the crucifixion of Jesus. (iii) The evangelists Matthew and John both specifically single out the Pharisees as the arch-opponents of Jesus. This is one of several points of agreement between Matthew and John. (iv) In *TLevi* 16, in *Dialogue* 108 and in John 7 the πλάνος accusation occurs in the context of discussion about who keeps the law: is it Jesus (and his followers) or is it his opponents? We shall return to this point in a moment.

In Luke 23 there are three similar accusations against Jesus. This time the Pharisees are not singled out, and neither πλάνος nor πλανάω is used, but the allegation is essentially the same: Jesus leads the people astray. In verse 2 the verb is διαστρέφω, in verse 5 ἀνασείω and in verse 14 ἀποστρέφω. These clauses are certainly not taken from Matthew or from John; in all probability, as G. Schneider has recently shown, they come from Luke's redaction of Marcan traditions rather than from pre-Lucan material.[2]

It is worth noting at this point that in the New Testament these similar allegations against Jesus are found in passages where the hands of the evangelists Matthew, Luke and John can almost certainly be traced. This suggests that this Jewish line of polemic may have first arisen in the decade or so after

---

[1] See J.L. Martyn, *History and Theology in the Fourth Gospel*, 73-81 for a stimulating discussion.

[2] G. Schneider, 'The Political Charge against Jesus', in *Jesus and the Politics of his Day*, eds. E. Bammel and C.F.D. Moule, Cambridge 1984, 403-414.

A.D. 70. It has recently been argued by A. Strobel that this accusation was in fact central in the Sanhedrin trial.[1] On any showing the evidence for such a hypothesis is at best indirect and contrasts sharply with the explicit evidence for such an allegation from about A.D. 85 .

There is a further example of the πλάνος allegation in the *Acts of Thomas*, a third century writing which very probably uses second century traditions. In chapter 48, in one of the many liturgical passages with which the narratives are interspersed, Thomas prays, 'Jesus Christ, who wast called a deceiver (πλάνος) and dost deliver thine own from deception. . .' While this passage may possibly have been taken from Matt 27. 63f., there are grounds for suggesting independence. The immediate context contains allusions to several New Testament writings, but not to Matthew. And, more important still, there are two further passages in the *Acts of Thomas* which suggest that the πλάνος allegation in chapter 48 should be seen as another example, independent of Matthew's gospel, of the Jewish claim that Jesus was ὁ πλάνος.

In a strongly polemical passage in chapter 96 Charisius rounds on his wife Mygdonia: 'I have heard that that *magician and deceiver* (ὁ μάγος ἐκεῖνος καὶ πλάνος) teaches that a man should not live with his own wife. . .' He said to her again, '. . . be not led astray by deceitful and vain words nor by the works of magic.' The phrase 'magician and deceiver', is, as we shall see, very similar to rabbinic allegations against Jesus. The same phrase is used in chapter 102, and again (though in separate sentences) in chs. 106-7.[2]

---

[1] So A. Strobel, *Die Stunde der Wahrheit*, Tübingen 1980. See also the important discussion by D.R. Catchpole, *The Trial of Jesus*, Leiden 1971, 1-71. Catchpole allows (see 9) that it is just possible that Jesus was condemned on the basis of a charge derived from Deut 13. 6-11; in conversation about this point Professor Catchpole has told me that he now considers this highly unlikely.

[2] The English translation is taken from E. Hennecke, *New Testament Apocrypha* II, ed. R. Wilson, London 1965. The Greek text is from *Acta Apostolorum Apocrypha* II/2 ed. M. Bonnet, Hildesheim 1903, repr. 1959. The reference in chapter 48 to Jesus as ὁ πλάνος is noted, but

These passages in the *Acts of Thomas* are very different from the examples of this allegation which have been referred to above. Here there is hardly a trace of Christian – Jewish polemic or apologetic and with the exception of chapter 48, these accusations are made against the apostle Thomas, not Jesus. But there is no doubt at all that Thomas is an *alter ego* of Jesus.[1] The use of the very phrase μάγος καὶ πλάνος which is found so widely in early Christian and Jewish writings can hardly be a coincidence. In the *Acts of Thomas* a 'stock' Jewish criticism of Jesus has survived in a very different setting.

In the even later *Acts of Philip* precisely the same criticism is heaped upon Philip – this time by 'the Jews' (chapter 69 of the Greek version).[2] Once again a disciple is an *alter ego* of Jesus. In the very different Syriac version, which is generally held to be a revision of the Greek, the Jews of Carthage summon a Jew who has become a Christian and say: 'Do not renounce Moses and believe in the Messiah, because the Messiah was *an impostor*, and his disciples go about with *sorcery*.'[3] Isa 6. 9-10 is then quoted as a reproach, followed by a cluster of examples of Israel's rejection of God's messengers – very much along the lines of Acts 7, but with different examples.

Why has a 'stock' phrase survived for so long in very different early Christian writings? While it is possible that some of these passages are dependent on earlier examples of this allegation, the fact that the same criticism of Jesus and/or

without discussion, by J.L. Martyn, *History and Theology in the Fourth Gospel*, 79 n.110, and by A. Strobel, *Die Stunde der Wahrheit*, 90, but they do not refer to chs. 96 or 106-7. A.F.J. Klijn, *The Acts of Thomas*, Leiden 1962, 271, includes a note on the 'sorcerer' accusation which is made against Thomas in numerous passages, but does not comment on the πλάνος accusation or on the combination of μάγος and πλάνος noted above.

[1] See, for example, chapters 2, 11 and 45.
[2] For the Greek text of the *Acts of Philip*, see M. Bonnet's edition noted above.
[3] For a translation of the Syriac version, see W. Wright, *Apocryphal Acts of the Apostles* II, 1871, 69-82.

his followers recurs in a number of writings over a long period of time is striking. Christians clearly *felt* (rightly or wrongly) that this was a standard criticism levelled at them.

The same accusation is almost certainly also found in rabbinic traditions, notably *b.Sanh* 43a, *b.Sanh* 107b and several related traditions which are based on Deut 13.[1] In that chapter the one who gives a 'sign or wonder' and entices the people to serve other gods, and teaches rebellion against the Lord is to be put to death. Enticement to worship another god is also mentioned explicitly in *m.Sanh* 7. 10, referred to by J.L. Martyn as 'the classic passage which defines the offense of "leading Israel astray"'.[2] Although it is probable that the central offence of Deut 13, enticement to serve other gods, was used in the first and second centuries to counter Christian claims about Jesus, exploration of this Christological theme cannot be attempted here.[3]

There is, however, another aspect of the rabbinic accusations which is relevant. The charge of 'beguiling' and 'leading astray' in *b.Sanh* 43a and *b.Sanh* 107b (where only the latter term is used) is linked to 'practising magic', just as it is in Justin *Dialogue* 69, where Jesus is called μάγος καὶ λαο-πλάνος and in the *Acts of Thomas* and in the *Acts of Philip*.[4]

---

[1] For a fuller discussion than is possible here, see D.R. Catchpole, *The Trial of Jesus*, 1-71; J.L. Martyn, *History and Theology in the Fourth Gospel*, 73-81; W. Horbury, *JTS* 33 (1982) 19-61; J. Maier, *Jesus von Nazareth in der talmudischen Überlieferung*, Darmstadt 1978.

[2] See J.L. Martyn, *History and Theology in the Fourth Gospel*, 78-9 n.108 and n.110.

[3] See especially A.F. Segal, *Two Powers in Heaven: Early Rabbinic Reports about Christianity and Gnosticism*, Leiden 1977. Segal, however, discusses the πλάνος material only briefly, at 97 n.128.

[4] On the μάγος charge, see especially G. Poupon, 'L'accusation de magie dans les Actes apocryphes' in *Les Actes Apocryphes des Apôtres: Christianisme et Monde Païen*, eds. F. Bovon et al., Geneva 1981, 71-94. Poupon does not discuss the combination of μάγος καὶ πλάνος referred to above.

The criticism that Jesus is simply a magician is not found explicitly in the New Testament passages referred to above. As J.L. Martyn, *History and Theology in the Fourth Gospel*, notes in passing on p. 77, one possible exception is John 8. 48.

This close correspondence between the *double* accusation against Jesus (and/or his followers) found in rabbinic traditions, in Justin, and in the apocryphal Acts is surely significant: in each case the terms occur in the same order, an order which reverses the order of Deuteronomy where the 'sorcery' theme does not become prominent until Deut 18. 9-14.[1]

If, as seems highly probable, the charge that Jesus led Israel astray (which was often linked to the further charge of 'sorcery') was pressed vigorously by Jewish opponents of early Christianity, how did Christians respond? One Christian response seems to have run like this: it is not Jesus who has led Israel astray but the Jewish leaders. Precisely this point is made in *TLevi* 10. 2 with the verb πλανάω: Levi declares that his descendants will lead Israel astray, for *they* will act against Christ the Saviour of the world. The same response, but in much more general terms, is found in many passages in Justin and of course in the New Testament.

A second Christian response was to raise the issue of who was keeping and who was rejecting the law. In Deut 13 the discussion about the one who leads Israel astray is linked closely to an exhortation to keep the commandments of the Lord (13. 4f., 18). The clear implication is that those who follow the one leading Israel astray are abandoning the law. So it is not surprising to find in several early Christian writings that the allegation about 'leading Israel astray' is connected with accusation and counter-accusation about who keeps and who rejects the law. There is a fascinating and important relationship, which goes back ultimately to Deut 13, between two of the major lines of Jewish polemic: Jesus is a deceiver and Christianity is a lawless sect.

---

[1] J. Maier, *Jesus von Nazareth in der talmudischen Überlieferung*, has claimed that *b.Sanh* 43a did not originally refer to Jesus: that identification was made only in post-Talmudic redaction. W. Horbury, however, has argued strongly that the sentences 'on Passover Eve they hanged Jesus' and 'Jesus the Nazarene. . . practised sorcery and deceived and led astray Israel' may be older than their immediate context: *JTS* 33 (1982) 19-61 (57).

I shall now explore briefly this second accusation, starting again with *Dialogue* 108. In verse 2 Christianity is referred to as a αἵρεσίς τις ἄθεος καὶ ἄνομος. A few lines later Justin tells us that Trypho has accused both Jesus and his followers of teaching ἄθεα καὶ ἄνομα καὶ ἀνόσια. In the earlier reference to anti-Christian propaganda at 17. 1, Christianity is said to be a αἵρεσις ἄνομος. What is meant by these charges?

Right at the beginning of the *Dialogue* the very first accusation that Trypho presses against Justin is that he has forsaken God and placed his hope on a man and has abandoned the law – specifically circumcision, the Sabbath, the feasts, and God's new moons (8. 3). The same charges are repeated in chapter 10 and it becomes clear that Christianity is judged to be ἄθεος because it is ἄνομος: these are twin charges. Justin is very sensitive to these allegations and spends a good part of the *Dialogue* dealing with them.

The Jewish claim that Christianity has abandoned the law is not found explicitly in the *Testaments*, but it may well lie behind the charge from the Christian side that those who have rejected Jesus are the ones who have acted lawlessly – *TLevi* 10. 3 and *TBenj* 3. 8. Here ἄνομος might be taken simply as a conventional term meaning little more than 'wicked', but *TLevi* 16. 2 suggests that this is not so. Those who reject Jesus as ὁ πλάνος are referred to in unusual and striking words: τὸν νόμον ἀφανίσετε καὶ λόγους προφητῶν ἐξουθενώσετε. In the *Testaments*, with their repeated pleas to keep the law, this is a very strong statement. It is, I suggest, Christian polemic against Judaism, in response to the charge that Christians have abandoned the law.

A similar Jewish accusation may lie behind Marcion's addition at Luke 23. 2. He allows the Jewish opponents of Jesus to claim to Pilate that Jesus destroyed (καταλύω) the law and the prophets.[1] We might be tempted to conclude that in his version of Luke Marcion has simply taken over part of Matt 5. 17 for his own purposes. Marcion certainly understood Matt 5. 17 as an affirmation of the law and the prophets, for in his *Antithesen* he claimed that this verse

---

[1] Earlier editions of Aland's *Synopsis* read incorrectly ναόν for νόμον.

was an addition made by Judaizers. But the Jewish accusation in Marcion's version of Luke 23. 2 may not come from Matt 5. 17, for two reasons. First, Marcion does not use any phrases from Matthew in his version of Luke. And secondly, the same addition, apparently quite independently of Marcion, is found in a number of Old Latin manuscripts. Marcion's addition at Luke 23. 2, which is placed on the lips of Jewish accusers, may well reflect the same charge pressed by Trypho: Christianity has abandoned the law and the prophets.[1]

But what about Matt 5. 17 itself? Although many exegetes have claimed that the evangelist is refuting the view of antinomians that Jesus has destroyed the law and the prophets, G. Strecker has shown how unlikely this view is.[2] Is it not at least possible that Matthew is aware that Jewish opponents claim that Christians have abandoned the law and lowered ethical standards? The evangelist's strong emphasis on a δικαιοσύνη which exceeds that of the scribes and the Pharisees (5. 20) suggests that he may, in part, be setting out a Christian defence against Jewish allegations. This explanation has been advanced by C.F.D. Moule, who has revived an older view which has been unfairly neglected by Matthean specialists.[3]

In several early Christian writings, then, there is strong evidence that one of the most persistent Jewish objections against Christianity was that Christians neglected or abandoned the law. Christians were extremely sensitive to this criticism. Indeed this charge placed them in an awkward dilemma, for most Christians could not claim that they kept the *whole* law.

In this connection the *Testaments* are particularly interesting. The Christian community which re-interpreted these

---

[1] Perhaps it is just possible that the longer reading at Luke 23. 2 is original; it may have been abbreviated at a very early stage as a result of Christian sensitivity to this very accusation from Jewish opponents.

[2] See G. Strecker, *Der Weg der Gerechtigkeit*, Göttingen 3rd ed., 1971, 276. See also 47-9 above.

[3] C.F.D. Moule, 'St Matthew's Gospel: Some Neglected Features', now reprinted in his *Essays in New Testament Interpretation*, Cambridge 1982, 69.

Jewish traditions retained their very strong emphasis on keeping the whole law, in spite of its own acceptance of Gentiles. And yet it is hard to find specific references to individual Pentateuchal commandments and very easy to find parallels with Hellenistic ethics. In *TLevi* 16. 3 Jesus is spoken of as the one who *renews* the law by the power of the Most High. The verb used, ἀνακαινοποιέω might be taken simply as a re-affirmation of the law or it might mean that Jesus brings a new perspective on the law; the verb is just about as ambiguous as πληρόω in Matt 5. 17!

The *Testaments* seem to come from a community acutely aware of possible or actual allegations from Jews that it sits lightly to the requirements of the law. So it doggedly affirms that the law must be kept and it is very happy to retain a strong emphasis on Hellenistic ethics.[1] But it is not at all clear whether the community kept the Sabbath or observed purity regulations.

Justin is less of an enigma. He is stung by the criticism that Christians cite the Old Testament and yet do not keep the law. Trypho rounds on him: 'You say you worship God, and think yourself superior to other people, but you separate from them in no respect, and do not make your life different from the heathen. . .' (10. 3) Justin claims that the law was a temporary expedient because of the stubbornness of the Jews: he even has the audacity to claim that it is *Christians* who truly understand the intention of the Old Testament, for Trypho does not understand its sense: shades of John 5. 39![2] I do not need to show that early Christian writers are pre-occupied with the *sense* in which the Old Testament law is still relevant for Christians. My point is that this was done *partly* as a response to sustained Jewish objections that Christians had abandoned or neglected the law.

---

[1] See H.C. Kee in *The Old Testament Pseudepigrapha* I, ed. J.H. Charlesworth, 779-80.

[2] For a fuller discussion than is possible here, see T. Stylianopoulos, *Justin Martyr and the Mosaic Law*, Missoula 1975.

Christian polemic and apologetic:
Sin – Exile (Punishment) – Return (S-E-R)

I turn now from Jewish polemic and Christian responses to *Christian* anti-Jewish polemic. De Jonge's work on the Sin-Exile-Return pattern found in nearly all of the *Testaments of the Twelve Patriarchs* has been widely acclaimed.[1] A vigorous denunciation of the sins of the descendants of the patriarchs is followed by an equally vigorous declaration of their punishment by God. This punishment frequently includes exile and in some cases the destruction of the Temple. But there is then an equally strong affirmation of an eventual return. As far back as 1960 de Jonge noted that the S-E-R passages were adapted to Christian needs in a variety of ways and conceded that since some of them contained no sign at all of Christian adaptation, 'there was at least *one Jewish stage* in the composition of these passages. . .'[2]

A Biblical and specifically Deuteronomic pattern which was used in inner-Jewish polemic has been adapted and extended by Christians in debate and dispute with non-Christian Jews. *TLevi* 10 and 16 are two important examples of the S-E-R pattern. Both chapters juxtapose strong polemic against those who have acted against Jesus and a fervent expectation of an eventual return.

Attention has already been drawn above to important parallels between the *Testament of Levi* and *Dialogue* 108. I now want to suggest that this chapter of the *Dialogue* contains a further example of the S-E-R pattern. Justin roundly condemns the leaders of the Jews for their anti-Christian actions (Sin) and asserts that the capture of Jerusalem and the ravaging of the land is a punishment from

---

[1] See, for example, J. Jervell, 'Ein Interpolator interpretiert', 30-61; J. Becker, *Untersuchungen zur Entstehungsgeschichte der Testamente der zwölf Patriarchen*, Leiden 1970; A. Hultgård, *L'Eschatologie des Testaments des Douze Patriarches*, I, Uppsala 1977, 82 n.1.

[2] The emphasis is my own since many still misunderstand de Jonge's position.

God (Exile). But finally and quite unexpectedly Justin expresses the hope that his Jewish opponents will repent and find mercy from a compassionate God (Return).[1]

The final expression at the end of chapter 108 of hope of an eventual return *spoils* Justin's carefully worked out argument which contrasts the the Ninevites in Jonah's day with Israel at the time of Jesus. The Ninevites repented and their city was not destroyed; likewise the Gentiles repented and accepted 'the word' proclaimed by the apostles. But even destruction of Jerusalem did not lead to Israel's repentance: instead it led on to vigorous hostility to Christians. The whole context demands that Justin should end on a note of strong *contrast* between unrepentant Israel and the repentant Ninevites (Gentiles), but instead the last sentence of chapter 108 spells out, awkwardly to our way of thinking, hope for and expectation of the repentance of Israel. This is not Justin's mere after-thought, but his use of a well-established Biblical S-E-R pattern, and, possibly, of source material.

It is true that in the *Testaments* the 'return' of Israel is often eschatological and often initiated by God, unlike *Dialogue* 108. But this is not always so: in fact in the *Testaments* the 'return' motif is expressed in very different ways. Perhaps *Judah* 23. 5 is the closest parallel to the *Dialogue*: here the return motif is set out in a way strongly reminiscent of chapter 108. 'When you return to the Lord, penitent and living according to all his commandments, the Lord will visit you in mercy.'

In the final verses of Matt 23, and also in the underlying Q tradition, there is a further example of the theological S-E-R pattern which is so prominent in the *Testaments* and which is also found in *Dialogue* 108. The long catalogue of woes against the scribes and Pharisees culminates in expression of

---

[1] O. Skarsaune, *The Proof from Prophecy: a Study in Justin Martyr's Proof-Text Tradition*, Leiden 1987, has also observed (independently) that the S-E-R pattern of the Testaments is found in Justin; on 281 he refers to *I Apol* 52. He does not refer to *Dialogue* 108 in this connection. On 281 n.85 he lists phrases which Justin and the Testaments share, but he does not suggest literary dependence. On 288-9 he seems to confuse the S-E-R pattern with the 'killing of God's messengers' theme.

judgement in verse 38 on those who kill, crucify or persecute the prophets, wise men and scribes sent by Jesus: 'Behold your house is forsaken and desolate.' Then follows the puzzling verse 39. 'For I tell you, you will not see me again until you say, "Blessed is he who comes in the name of the Lord." '

Exegetes have differed considerably in their interpretation of these words. Some have felt that given the nature of the polemic in the preceding verses, Matt 23. 39 must continue the judgement theme. Calvin, for example, comments, 'He (Jesus) will not come to them (the Jews) until they cry out in fear – too late – at the sight of his majesty, "truly he is the Son of God." '[1]

The difficulty with this interpretation is that Ps 118. 26 which is cited in Matt 23. 39 is surely an expression of joyful praise rather than of fear or mourning. In his account of the entry of Jesus into Jerusalem Matthew has already used Ps 118. 25-6 in a positive sense (21. 9). Does the evangelist now use it at the end of chapter 23 in quite the opposite sense?[2]

Not surprisingly, some exegetes have taken Matt 23. 39 to mean that when Messiah comes, Jerusalem will know salvation. But the expression of a declaration of salvation immediately after such a strong declaration of judgement does seem odd.[3] As D.C. Allison has written recently, 'One naturally expects a harsher note to conclude the preceding lines. So if Matt 23. 39 = Luke 13. 35b is simply a promise of salvation, then one is almost compelled to treat it as a

---

[1] I owe this reference to D.C. Allison, 'Matt 23: 39 = Luke 13: 35b as a Conditional Prophecy', *JSNT* 18 (1983) 75. Allison cites a number of exegetes who adopt a similar interpretation.

[2] In Luke the lament over Jerusalem (13. 34-5) is separated from the 'woes on the scribes and Pharisees' at 11. 37-54, and the lament precedes the citation of Ps 118. 26 in 19. 38. So the exegetical problem does not arise in quite the same way as it does in Matthew.

[3] See D.P. Senior, *The Passion Narrative according to Matthew*, Leuven 1975, 207: 'Even if the pericope had a positive meaning, in Mt this traditional *Heilsruf* is now associated with an unconditional recognition of judgement.'

secondary – infelicitous – addition.' And, with reference to the Q tradition, this is how Bultmann explains the dilemma.[1]

But apparently harsh juxtaposition of a declaration of judgement and a declaration of a 'return' and salvation is *the* characteristic feature of the S-E-R pattern in the *Testaments*, and, as I have suggested, in *Dialogue* 108. The juxtaposition of judgement and salvation may seem awkward to us, but it is a thoroughly Biblical and well-established Jewish pattern: it goes back ultimately to Deuteronomy, where blessing sometimes follows curse.[2]

So Matt 23. 39 is not an infelicitous secondary addition of a note of salvation, nor is it to be interpreted unnaturally as an expression of judgement. It is, rather, a further example of the S-E-R pattern found repeatedly in the *Testaments* and also in *Dialogue* 108. Matthew, perhaps following the compiler of Q, has used the S-E-R pattern in the context of anti-Jewish polemic.

It is, of course, the 'return' motif which seems so harsh to us immediately after judgement. We expect the pattern of polemic to run as it does in Acts 7. 51-2: 'As your fathers rejected God's messengers, the prophets, so have you rejected Jesus (and his followers).' This very different pattern, which is also Deuteronomic, is found in Matt 5. 11; 23. 31-4; I Thess 2. 15, and in many places in Justin and elsewhere.[3]

What is the *function* of this apparently odd S-E-R pattern? In Matthew, in the *Testaments* and in Justin this Biblical pattern has been taken over and developed by Christians as Christian apologetic vis à vis Judaism. For several reasons it was a most useful line of apologetic. (i) It allowed Christians

---

[1] R. Bultmann, *The History of the Synoptic Tradition*, rev. ed. Oxford 1968, 115.

[2] See M. de Jonge in 'The Testaments of the Twelve Patriarchs: Central Problems and Essential Viewpoints', *ANRW* II, 20,1, Berlin and New York 1987, 359-420, with reference to the work of K. Baltzer, *Das Bundesformular*, Neukirchen-Vluyn 1960. See especially Deut 4. 25-31; 28. 45-68 and 30. 1-10.

[3] O.H. Steck, *Israel und das gewaltsame Geschick der Propheten*, Neukirchen-Vluyn 1967. See also O. Skarsaune, *The Proof From Prophecy*, 288-95.

to use anti-Jewish polemic to distance themselves from Judaism and yet at the same time to claim continuity in God's purposes. Israel's sin has always been (and is even now) followed by punishment (and/or exile) and then by eventual return to God. (ii) Israel's refusal to accept Jesus as Messiah deeply troubled many early Christians – the S-E-R pattern, however, provided a ready-made answer: Israel's refusal is the result of 'sin'.

(iii) The pattern provides a pro-Christian interpretation of history. Exile, destruction of the Temple, and overthrow of the nation are all to be seen as God's judgement on unrepentant Israel. On the Christian interpretation of history, Israel should have withered away after A.D. 70 and 135, but recovery and vigorous renewal followed these catastrophes. In these circumstances unmitigated expressions of condemnation and judgement, which we do find in some early Christian writings, sounded hollow. The S-E-R pattern allowed Christians to keep alive hopes for an eventual conversion of at least some within Israel.

(iv) In the decades after A.D. 70 Christians became more self-confident and began to see themselves as a quite distinct entity over against Judaism on the one hand and 'the world' on the other. As this happened, the underlining of hope for at least the partial conversion of the rival religious group may perhaps be seen as part of Christian legitimation. And, on the other hand, the strong polemic which is an integral part of the S-E-R pattern may be seen as part of Christian self-definition.[1]

These comments on the probable function of the S-E-R pattern within Christian polemic and apologetic bring me to my final observations. As is well known, Justin works out thoroughly and impressively his understanding of Christians

---

[1] In his stimulating article, 'The Christian additions to the Apocryphal Writings', in *Jewish and Christian Self-Definition* II, eds. E.P. Sanders et al., London 1981, 27-55, J.H. Charlesworth also suggests that the polemical passages in the Christian 'interpolations' in the Testaments 'help us to understand the scribe's (and probably his community's) search for self-definition'.(40)

as a 'third race', 'the true spiritual nation of Israel' (*Dialogue* 11. 5), over against both Judaism and the world at large.[1] The beginnings of this process may be seen in the *Testaments* and in Matthew.

It is true that in the *Testaments* the formal terminology for the Christian community – especially ἐκκλησία – is absent. But the Christian polemic against those who have opposed Jesus and the strong commitment to πάντα τὰ ἔθνη suggest that the community which redacted Jewish *Testament* traditions felt itself to be a religious entity distinct from Judaism. In his stimulating essay on the Christian purpose of the *Testaments*, J. Jervell points to the future salvation of Israel as the most distinctive theological theme. This is certainly present, but equally prominent are the repeated references to acceptance of the Gentiles. These references frequently occur in the most explicitly Christian sections of the *Testaments*, right alongside strong condemnation of those who have opposed Jesus. [2]

Juxtaposed with this strong affirmation of acceptance of the Gentiles we do find some curious anti-Gentile statements, especially in exhortations not to take Gentiles as wives, and not to behave like the Gentiles.[3] This might be understood as 'careless' retention of an anti-Gentile stratum of Jewish *Testament* traditions. But perhaps it can more plausibly be seen as part of the community's ambivalence towards the Gentiles: it is committed to acceptance of them, but it also distinguished itself from them.

I have suggested that there is a similar ambivalence towards the Gentiles in Matthew's gospel.[4] In Matthew and in the *Testaments* we see the first steps towards the Christian self-understanding found in Justin, where Christians see

---

[1] See especially G.P. Richardson, *Israel in the Apostolic Church*, Cambridge 1969.

[2] For details see M. de Jonge, 'The Testaments of the Twelve Patriarchs', *ANRW* II, 20.

[3] See J. Jervell, 'Ein Interpolator interpretiert' in *Studien zu den zwölf Patriarchen*, ed. W. Eltester, Berlin 1969, 46 n.58.

[4] See above, 160-1.

themselves as an entity over against both Judaism and the Gentile world.[1]

Similar specific Jewish anti-Christian allegations and similar specific Christian anti-Jewish polemic can be traced in several early Christian writings and, admittedly less confidently, in some rabbinic traditions. Christians were especially sensitive to the Jewish accusation that Jesus was a deceiver who had led Israel astray and the related charge that he (or his followers) had abandoned the law, for this polemic drew (to Christian embarrassment) on Biblical themes, especially Deuteronomy 13. Christian responses were varied, but there was a strong insistence that it was in fact the Jewish leaders who had led Israel astray and it was Jews, not Christians, who were misunderstanding the Scriptures.

It has often been argued or implied that following an alleged 'parting of the ways' about A.D. 85, early Christianity and early Judaism were not interested in one another. Matthew, the *Testaments* and Justin (and indeed other early Christian writings) suggest that this was not the case. Christians continued to be sensitive to Jewish allegations long after they felt themselves to be a quite distinct religious entity.

Polemic against Judaism (and especially against Jewish leaders held to be responsible for the death of Jesus) is most fierce when Christians are still disputing with Jews and are most conscious of considerable continuity with Judaism, as, for example, in Matthew and the *Testaments*. That is not as surprising as it sounds at first: left wing political parties often engage in furious warfare with one another rather than mount an effective attack on entrenched right wing positions.

In the *Testaments* the S-E-R pattern is used as part of the Christian apologetic mounted by a community distinct from but still defining itself over against Judaism. That there

---

[1] E.F. Osborn makes the interesting suggestion (but without detailed discussion) that Justin's work 'may be best understood as the continuation of the apologetic of the first evangelist.' *Justin Martyr*, Tübingen 1973, 109.

should also be examples of the same pattern in *Dialogue* 108 and in Matthew 23 suggests that other early Christians used this schema to hold together – perhaps rather awkwardly to modern ways of thinking – strong condemnation of Jewish leaders and hope for their future salvation.[1]

If these suggestions are plausible, there are implications for the origin and purpose of these early Christian writings. We need not conclude that Justin is so polemical that he cannot be engaged in genuine dialogue, nor need we conclude that his expressions of hope for the conversion of Trypho are simply an artificial device dictated by the dialogue form. The S-E-R pattern in chapter 108 is an important form of early Christian apologetic vis à vis Judaism. Justin is engaged in a genuine dispute and New Testament scholars will do well to read him carefully.

The *Sitz im Leben* of the *Testaments* in their present Christian form is much more problematic. But if we observe carefully the polemic against the disobedient, lawless descendants of the patriarchs who reject Jesus and his followers and note carefully the frequency with which πάντα τὰ ἔθνη occurs in distinctively Christian sections, we can perhaps see a Christian community defining itself over against Judaism yet expressing continuity with patriarchal traditions.

If my interpretation of Matt 23. 39 is plausible, we may need to rethink the relationship of Matthew's gospel to Judaism. The evangelist's strong condemnation of Jewish leaders and his emphasis on God's judgement on Judaism need not carry as a corollary abandonment of any hope for salvation for at least some Jews.[2] The S-E-R pattern suggests that fierce polemic and expressions of judgement can be juxtaposed with hope for eventual conversion.

---

[1] In the discussions which followed this paper at the 1984 Basel SNTS meeting and also at a Senior Seminar at the University of Sheffield in February 1985, it was suggested that Rom 11 offers another example of the S-E-R pattern. While there are some broad similarities, it seems to me that Paul's argument is moving along rather different lines.

[2] See above 137-8. For the opposite view, see, for example, D.P. Senior, *The Passion Narrative according to Matthew*, Leuven 1975, 208.

Finally, a brief postscript. While I was preparing this study I had a quite minor illness. Several Christian New Testament scholars wrote to me and said that they were praying to God for my healing and recovery. I was deeply moved when a distinguished Jewish scholar who is keenly interested in early Christian writings wrote using *precisely* the same phraseology. I was reminded, of course, of the closing lines of Justin's *Dialogue*, where Justin and Trypho pray for one another. Christians and Jews do share convictions about God and the world and we can and do pray in similar terms. But there are, of course, ways in which Christian prayer is distinctive – and that is our continuing dilemma.

Today neither Christians nor Jews would wish to continue the polemic found in Justin's *Dialogue*, the *Testaments*, or in Matthew's or John's gospels. But we should not allow the vigorous polemic used by both sides to distract us from careful investigation of the underlying issues at stake between Jews and Christians in the first and second centuries. Many of them are still on our agenda today.

Chapter Eleven

5 Ezra and Matthean Christianity
in the Second Century

Second century Christianity is like a giant jigsaw puzzle, so many pieces of which are missing that not even the outlines of parts of the picture are clear.[1] The discovery of a new piece always arouses keen interest and intense study. But some pieces have been available for a long time and have still not received the scholarly attention they deserve. One such piece is 5 Ezra, the Christian document which is now usually printed as the first two chapters of 4 Ezra.[2] 5 Ezra is in a rather tattered condition; it has survived in only a few Latin manuscripts which date from the ninth century and later and which vary so much that it is a formidable task to reconstruct a critical Latin text, let alone a probable Greek original.[3] In

---

[1] An earlier draft of this chapter was read at a senior seminar on Apocalyptic held at King's College, London. I am grateful to members of the seminar, especially Professor M. Knibb and Dr. R. Murray, for a number of helpful comments.

[2] The standard edition is R.L. Bensly, *The Fourth Book of Ezra*, Cambridge 1895. Many editors, commentators and writers on 4 Ezra have ignored the first two chapters. Two exceptions are W.O.E. Oesterley, *II Esdras*, London 1933, and J.M. Myers, *I and II Esdras* (The Anchor Bible) New York 1974. 5 Ezra is included in E. Hennecke, *New Testament Apocrypha*, ed. W. Schneemelcher, E.tr. London 1965, II, 689-95.

[3] J. Daniélou argues that 5 Ezra was originally written in Latin as there are no citations in Greek or Oriental languages; but this is an argument based on silence. See 'Le Ve Esdras et le Judéo-Christianisme Latin au Second Siècle' in *Ex Orbe Religionum I: Studia Geo Widengren Oblata* =

addition, it is so difficult to interpret some phrases that it is not easy to bring it into contiguity with appropriate parts of second century Christianity. But none the less it is surprising that 5 Ezra has been almost completely overlooked in most of the standard literature in which some use of its evidence might have been made.[1]

The present discussion hopes to show that 5 Ezra provides further evidence of the use of Matthew's gospel by second century writers. This comes as no surprise, for the far-reaching influence of Matthew on the early church is now well established.[2] A further contention, which is advanced rather more tentatively, is potentially of much greater significance: 5 Ezra, together with the recently published Nag Hammadi *Apocalypse of Peter*[3] confirm not only that Matthew's gospel was used widely, but also that some of the distinctive features of Matthean Christianity continued well into the second century in Judaeo-Christian[4] and gnostic circles.

Studies in the History of Religions, 21 (Supplements to *Numen*) Leiden 1972, 162-71.

[1] J. Daniélou did not refer to 5 Ezra in his *Théologie du Judéo-Christianisme*, Paris 1958. One partial exception is the lengthy footnote included by O.H. Steck, *Israel und das gewaltsame Geschick der Propheten*, Neukirchen-Vluyn 1967, 230, n. 6.
The present article was first published in 1977; since then there has been renewed interest in 5 Ezra. See 277 n.1 for the recent literature.

[2] See especially E. Massaux, *Influence de l'Évangile de saint Matthieu sur la littérature chrétienne avant saint Irénée*, Louvain and Gembloux 1950. Massaux does not refer to 5 Ezra.

[3] See *The Facsimile Edition of the Nag Hammadi Codices: Codex VII*, Leiden 1972, p.70, 13-84, 14. A literal German translation and a brief discussion have been published by A. Werner and the Berliner Arbeitskreis für koptisch-gnostische Schriften: 'Die Apocalypse des Petrus', *ThLZ* 99 (1974) cols. 575-84. This document should not be confused with the well-known *Apocalypse of Peter* listed among the disputed writings by the Muratorian Canon.

[4] This term is chosen deliberately. R. Murray's distinction is useful: 'Jewish Christianity' should be used for the sociological phenomenon of Jews who were Christians; 'Judaeo-Christianity' for J. Daniélou's ideological sense. See R. Murray, 'Defining Judaeo-Christianity', *HJ* 15 (1974) 303 ff. and the references given there. In addition, see M. Simon,

The setting of 5 Ezra

It is now a widely accepted convention to refer to the first two chapters of 4 Ezra as 5 Ezra, even though their position in the manuscripts varies, as does the enumeration of the Esdras-Ezra material in Greek and Latin manuscripts and in printed editions of the Bible.[1] As these two chapters are found in the Latin manuscripts of 4 Ezra, but not in any of the other versions, there is general agreement that they constitute an originally independent document: how and when they were first linked with 4 Ezra remains unclear. It has been suggested that 5 Ezra is a Jewish apocalypse (or part of one) which has been subjected to Christian interpolation.[2] This is an unlikely hypothesis. While it is not difficult to remove explicitly Christian verses, the remaining passages do not 'hang together' as a viable document. The 'Jewish' sections and the alleged 'Christian' interpolations dovetail together so neatly that 5 Ezra has undoubtedly been written by a Christian who is deeply indebted to the Old Testament and to later apocalyptic traditions.

The French (S A) and the Spanish manuscripts (CM (N V L)) of these two chapters differ so very much more than they do in 4 Ezra 3 – 14 that they may be regarded as different recensions. R. L. Bensly based his edition of the text of the first two chapters of 4 Ezra on the French manuscripts; the text of C (with the variants of M listed) is printed as an appendix. M. R. James provided a lengthy introduction to Bensly's edition and argued that the readings of the Spanish recension should

---

'Réflexions sur le Judéo-Christianisme' in *Christianity, Judaism and other Greco-Roman Cults: Studies for Morton Smith at Sixty*, ed. J. Neusner, Leiden 1975, Part II, 53-76, and A.F.J. Klijn, 'The Study of Jewish Christianity', *NTS* 20 (1974) 419-31.

[1] For the details, see M.R. James's introduction to R.H. Bensly's edition, xiiff., and J.M. Myers, *I and II Esdras*, 1 and 108ff.

[2] See P. Riessler, *Altjüdisches Schriftum ausserhalb der Bibel*, Augsburg 1928, 1285; also O.H. Steck, *Israel und das gewaltsame Geschick der Propheten*, Neukirchen-Vluyn 1967, 230 n.6, and references listed there.

not be neglected.[1] His further argument that on the whole
the Spanish manuscripts have preserved an older form of
the Latin version than the French is less convincing: neither
recension should be given priority.

In view of the textual difficulties, it is necessary to be
extremely cautious in suggesting parallels, allusions, or
literary dependence on other documents. From a comparison
of the two recensions it becomes clear that in the course of
transmission one or other has frequently been influenced by
the wording of a Biblical passage.[2]

When was 5 Ezra written? Attempts have been made to
trace allusions and quotations from 5 Ezra in later Christian
writings, but it would be precarious to date 5 Ezra on the basis
of external evidence which is itself extremely difficult to
assess and date.[3] J. Daniélou has collected a number of interesting parallels to words and phrases from 5 Ezra in Jewish
apocalyptic and second century writings. He claims that they
enable us to date 5 Ezra at the end of the second century. The
alleged parallels are not all entirely convincing. They do
make a second century date more plausible, but they are not

---

[1] In view of this, it is surprising that the RSV and NEB translations
(which are printed as the first two chapters of 4 Ezra) have followed
Bensly's text which is based solely on the French manuscripts and have
paid little or no attention to the Spanish recension. H. Duensing's
translation in Hennecke, *New Testament Apocrypha*, is based on an
eclectic text. J. Daniélou, 'Le Vᵉ Esdras et le Judéo-Christianisme', 162,
claims that the variations in the two recensions are comparatively
unimportant, but this is a serious error of judgement.

[2] For examples, see M.R. James's introduction to Bensly's edition, xlivff.

[3] *Contra* M. Labourt, 'Le cinquième livre d'Esdras', *RB* 17 (1909) 412 ff.,
and D. de Bruyne, 'Fragments d'une Apokalypse perdue', *Revue
Bénédictine*, 32 (1921) 97 ff.: they claim that 5 Ezra is a fifth or sixth-
century writing. For a discussion and rejection of their case, which is
based largely on the absence of 5 Ezra from the *Decretum Gelasianum*,
see A. Oepke, 'Ein bisher unbeachtetes Zitat aus dem fünften Buche
Esra', *ZNW* 42 (1949) 158-72. Oepke accepts (without giving reasons) a
second century date: he notes that 5 Ezra 1. 24 is quoted in *De alterca-
tione Ecclesiae et Synagogae*, which is found in editions of Augustine's
writings, but which was probably written c. A.D. 1000. Other possible
quotations are assembled by M.R. James in Bensly's edition, xxxviii ff.,
and by H. Duensing in E. Hennecke, *New Testament Apocrypha* II, 690.

themselves conclusive and need to be supported by other considerations.[1]

In the discussion which follows some points are more significant than others, but taken together, they form a strong cumulative case for a date in the middle of the second century, perhaps shortly after the Bar Kokhba rebellion.[2] The first four points will be discussed and defended in more detail below.

1. The author of 5 Ezra has been deeply influenced by Matthew's gospel: this takes us beyond the end of the first century. The author is probably not acquainted with any other part of the New Testament: in a document of this kind, which draws heavily on Biblical traditions, a writer at the end of the second century or later might have been expected to show dependence on several other New Testament writings.

2. The replacement of Israel by the 'coming people' is the main theme of 5 Ezra. The intensity with which Christian-Jewish relationships are expressed points to a second century date. As M. Simon has shown, contact between Christians and Jews continued long after Justin's time.[3] However, in various ways most later Christian apologetic and polemic stressed the differences between the church and the synagogue, whereas 5 Ezra takes pains to stress that the 'coming people' inherit, apparently without modification, all the privileges of Israel.

3. Christian prophets seem to be an accepted part of the community from which 5 Ezra stems. From the late second century onwards Christian prophecy is no longer the norm, but is an unexpected phenomenon.

4. 5 Ezra seems to be related to, but is almost certainly earlier than, the gnostic *Apocalypse of Peter*. While there are

---

[1] 'Le Ve Esdras et le Judéo-Christianisme', 162-71.

[2] See the excellent examination of the rebellion, which takes account of recent discoveries, in E. Schürer, *The History of the Jewish People in the Age of Jesus Christ*, I, ed. G. Vermes and F. Millar, Edinburgh 1973, 534 - 57.

[3] *Verus Israel*, 2nd ed., Paris 1964. See also A. Lukyn Williams, *Adversus Judaeos*, Cambridge 1935.

a few phrases in 5 Ezra which may have a gnostic background or which lend themselves readily to gnostic interpretation,[1] it has been deeply influenced by Judaeo-Christian rather than gnostic traditions. The *Apocalypse of Peter* confirms that some Judaeo-Christian circles were dominated by various forms of gnosticism in the second half of the second century. The publication of all the Nag Hammadi material is stimulating further work in this difficult area, and new light may eventually be shed on the origin and date of Judaeo-Christian documents such as 5 Ezra.

5. The apocalyptic form of 5 Ezra supports a date about the middle of the second century. In Christian apocalyptic writings before this date (including 5 Ezra and the final chapter of the Didache), imminent expectation of the end is dominant, whereas in later writings interest moves to the Anti-Christ and related themes, and to detailed descriptions of Heaven and Hell.[2]

6. The separation of the church from Israel is felt so keenly in 5 Ezra that it may well have been a recent event. The striking metaphor of a mother and her sons is used several times: 'Mater, quae eos generauit dicit illis: ite, filii quia ego uidua sum et derelicta. . . ' (2. 2) – the last clause recurs at 2. 4. At 2. 5 f. even stronger words are used in the Lord's address to Ezra: 'Ego autem te, pater, testem inuoco super matrem filiorum, quia noluerunt testamentum meum seruare, Vt des eis confusionem et matrem eorum in direptionem, ne generatio eorum fiat. Dispergantur in gentes, nomina eorum deleantur a terra. . . '[3]

Who is the mother? As in Old Testament passages such as Isa 49. 19 ff. and 54. 1, Jerusalem is thought of as the mother of

---

[1] Note, for example, e.g., the references to 'rest' in 5 Ezra 2. 24 and 34; see P. Vielhauer, ' Ἀνάπαυσις, zum gnostischen Hintergrund des Thomas-Evangeliums', *Apophoreta*, ed. W. Eltester, Berlin 1964, 281 - 99.

[2] So P. Vielhauer in E. Hennecke, *NT Apocrypha*, II, 600, and W. Schneemelcher, ibid., 751.

[3] In both quotations the French recension has been used. At 2. 2 the Spanish is difficult to construe and seems to be corrupt: at 2. 5 f. it does not differ significantly.

Israel.[1] A few verses later the Lord announces that following the disobedience and rejection of Israel, the 'kingdom of Jerusalem' which was once offered to Israel is to be given to the Christian community (2. 10). The metaphor of a mother and her sons is repeated at 2. 15; 2. 17 and 2. 31, but now it refers to the church and to Christians. This metaphor, which dominates the second half of 5 Ezra, is used to stress not only the finality of the separation of the church from Israel, but also that Christians have the same mother, Jerusalem, which Israel had.

Biblical metaphorical language is used to describe the complete rejection of Israel. But the description of 'mother' Jerusalem who has lost her sons is so vivid that one might well ask whether it has been precipitated by a historical event. Identification of references to historical events in apocalyptic writings is always a hazardous exercise. However, the failure of the Bar Kokhba rebellion and the establishment of Jerusalem as a thoroughly Hellenized city (*Aelia Capitolina*), which meant that all hopes of restoring Israel as a nation were finally dashed, would be very appropriate.

Is the trauma of this period reflected in 5 Ezra? Jerusalem the mother of Israel is widowed and deserted, her children scattered, and she is told that no offspring may come after them: these phrases refer to the actions of God and Israel; but at 2. 6 *direptionem* can hardly refer to either. Who has ravaged Jerusalem? This word fits awkwardly into the extended metaphor of Jerusalem as mother both of Israel and the church. The 'coming people' have the same mother, Jerusalem, as Israel – and yet Israel's mother is ravaged! For a moment the author seems to slip from the metaphorical to the historical plane and to be alluding to the destruction of the nation or of the physical city of Jerusalem by Hadrian. The events of 132–5 must have brought the question, 'Why?' to the lips of Christian groups with close ties with Judaism, just as the events of 70 led to the deep anguish portrayed so powerfully in 4 Ezra. 5 Ezra, then, may offer, from a Christian

---

[1] Gal 4. 26; Rev 17. 5; and 4 Ezra 10. 38 ff. provide interesting parallels, but there is no need to posit literary dependence.

perspective, a reason for the cataclysmic events of 132–5. Israel's disobedience has led to her rejection; Christians are now the sons, but they share with the rejected sons the same mother, Jerusalem.

A further theme in 5 Ezra may also point to the Bar Kokhba rebellion. The 'coming people' have experienced hardship and persecution (2. 23 ff.). In the final verses Ezra receives a vision of a large crowd receiving crowns and palms from the Son of God, whose name they have confessed so valiantly (2. 42 ff.). Ezra is then told to go and convey this vision to 'the people'. The community is being encouraged in the face of persecution. The origin of the persecution is not clear,[1] but harsh opposition from Jews is not ruled out. Justin Martyr informs us that Christians suffered severely at the hands of Jews during the Bar Kokhba revolt.[2] There is no reason to doubt this. The messianic claims of Bar Kokhba himself involved deep suspicion, to say the least, falling on those who confessed Jesus as Messiah or Son of God, for they were traitors to the Jewish cause.

5 Ezra, then, seems to stem from a community for whom the Bar Kokhba rebellion was a recent painful memory. The case for a date in the middle of the second century rests not only on the passages which were interpreted above as references to the Bar Kokhba rebellion, but on a strong cumulative argument. The problems which surround the origin and textual tradition of 5 Ezra should not be exaggerated; they are not significantly more complex than in the case of many other second century writings; and they should not deter us from considering carefully the significant evidence for the development of a second century Christianity which 5 Ezra provides.

---

[1] At 2. 28 there is a reference to the pagan nations who will envy (*zelabunt*) the Christian people, but this hardly suggests vigorous persecution and martyrdom. In addition, the jealousy of the nations seems to be preceded by the hardships with which Christians are faced.

[2] 1 *Apol.* 33. 6; cf. also Eusebius, *Chron. ad ann. Abrah.* 2149, which is quoted in E. Schürer, *History of the Jewish People* I, 545, n.141.

5 Ezra and Matthew's gospel

5 Ezra is largely taken up with a vigorous exposition of a theme which is also prominent in Matthew's gospel – God has rejected Israel and is turning to a 'people soon to come' (1. 35, 38). The opening verses are cast in the form of a prophetic complaint against Israel. They rehearse, from Old Testament passages, the disobedience, complaints, and forgetfulness of Israel. In the Old Testament individuals are rejected; Israel is punished for her sins and threatened with destruction, but she is never totally and finally rejected as God's people, as in 5 Ezra.

Suddenly and unexpectedly the first hint that Israel is to be replaced as God's people comes at 1. 24 'Quid tibi faciam, Iacob? Noluisti me obaudire, Iuda (S A; C M read *noluit obaudire me Iuda*). Transferam me ad gentem alteram (C M; S A read *ad alias gentes*), et dabo illi nomen meum et custodientes custodient legitima mea.'

This is an allusion to Matt 21. 43, a particularly important verse in Matthew's construction of chapters 21–25, the final narratives and discourses before the Passion drama unfolds: ἀρθήσεται ἀφ' ὑμῶν ἡ βασιλεία τοῦ θεοῦ καὶ δοθήσεται ἔθνει ποιοῦντι τοὺς καρποὺς αὐτῆς.[1] Ezra seems to have been influenced deeply by this verse and by the two preceding parables (21. 28-43) and the parable which follows (22. 1-14), all of which deal with God's rejection of Israel (or, rather, its leaders) and his acceptance of others.

The allusion to 21. 43 is less clear in the reading of the Spanish recension (*ad alias gentes*), which is followed by the RSV and NEB translations.[2] But the singular is more likely to

---

[1] Taken in isolation 2. 24 might be seen as a parallel rather than as an allusion to Matt 21. 43. But the numerous references to Matt 21–25 which will be noted below leave little doubt that 21. 43 is alluded to here. In addition, 'the kingdom of Jerusalem' (2. 10) which will be taken from 'the people' and given to 'the coming people' is probably dependent on ἡ βασιλεία τοῦ θεοῦ in Matt 21. 43.

[2] This important variant is not included in M. R. James's discussion of the variant readings of the 5 Ezra manuscripts in Bensly's edition, xciv ff.

be original for the following reasons: (i) The plural represents the usual New Testament and early Christian usage: replacement of the singular by the plural would be a natural 'correction'; and the reverse is less easy to explain. (ii) At 2. 34, where the context indicates that Christians are being addressed, S A read *uobis dico, gentes. . .* (or *gentibus*), whereas C M read simply *uobis dico. Gentes* is surely a later explanatory expansion in S A and the plural is also likely to have been introduced in this recension at 1. 24. (iii) At 2. 7 and 2. 28 *gentes* is used for Gentile (non-Christian) nations. The reading of C M at 1. 24, *ad gentem alteram*, is part of a careful three-fold distinction between God's people Israel (*populus*), the coming 'Christian' people (who are referred to as *gens altera* at 1. 24 but simply as *populus* whenever the context rules out confusion with Israel), and the non-Christian *gentes*. The introduction in S A of *gentes* at 1. 24 and at 2. 34 to refer to Christians blurs this distinction and reflects a later period when the *gentes* and Christendom could be equated.[1]

In 5 Ezra, then, Christians are beginning to see themselves as a *tertium genus*, over against Israel and the Gentiles.[2] As in some passages in Matthew, especially 21. 43; 25. 31 ff.; and 28. 19, there are hints rather than a carefully worked out doctrine of Christians as a *tertium genus*.

But 5 Ezra is much more concerned with the relationship of the 'coming people' to Israel: Christians are a *secundum genus* rather than a *tertium genus*. The first reference to the 'other people' is followed dramatically by a three-fold rejection of Israel (1. 25 f.)[3]:

Quoniam me dereliquistis, et ego uos derelinquam:
petentibus uobis a me misericordiam, non miserebor
    uestri.

---

[1] A. Oepke, 'Ein bisher unbeachtetes Zitat aus dem fünften Buche Esra', *ZNW* 42 (1949) 159 f., also accepts the singular as the original reading, but does not note the allusion to Matt 21. 43.

[2] Cf. P. Richardson, *Israel in the Apostolic Church*, Cambridge 1969, 22 ff. and 204.

[3] S A are quoted: in the Spanish recension the first sentences are combined, but the point made above is not affected.

Quando inuocabitis me, ego non exaudiam uos. . .

The carefully worked out chiastic form of each of the three logia confirms that 5 Ezra is no hastily composed anti-Jewish polemic, for it bears the marks of deep Christian prophetic anguish over Israel. Not only is Israel completely and finally rejected, but she is to be scattered (1. 33; 2. 7) and to have no posterity (1. 34; 2. 6).

The high point in the catalogue of charges laid against Israel is her rejection and killing of God's servants the prophets (1. 32 and cf. 1. 26): 'Ego misi pueros meos prophetas ad uos, quos acceptos interfecistis et laniastis corpora illorum: quorum sanguinem exquiram, dicit dominus.'[1] This verse might well be seen as a paraphrase of Matt 23. 29-39 and 21. 33 ff. (*Laniastis* is probably a corruption of *lapidastis*: if so, dependence on Matt 23. 37 is even clearer.)[2]

Rejection is complete: 'domus uestra deserta est' (1. 33 and cf. also 2. 1 ff.) reflects use of Matt 23. 38 (ἰδοὺ ἀφίεται ὑμῖν ὁ οἶκος ὑμῶν ἔρημος),[3] especially as Matt 23. 37 has been used three verses earlier. There Israel is given a final reminder of God's faithfulness: 'Ita uos collegi ut gallina pullos suos sub alas suas',[4] is a reference to Matt 23. 37 (Ιερουσαλημ Ιερουσαλημ. . . ποσάκις ἠθέλησα ἐπισυναγαγεῖν τὰ τέκνα σου,

---

1 C M read *corpora apostolorum*, which is accepted as the original reading by M.R. James in his introduction to Bensly's edition, 1f. But a reference to persecution of Christian apostles cannot be original, as 5 Ezra wishes to stress that whereas the servants sent by God to Israel were rejected, the servants sent to 'the coming people' will be protected, 2. 23ff. (on this passage see further below). The reference to 'apostles' probably comes from Luke 11. 49, but 5 Ezra is deeply indebted to Matthew (who does, not have apostles at 23. 34, the parallel passage) rather than to Luke.

2 So M.R. James in his introduction to Bensly's edition, li, n. 1.

3 ἔρημος is not found in some manuscripts; 5 Ezra seems to be dependent on the longer reading.

4 So C M. The French recension (S A) reads *filios*, which may reflect τὰ τέκνα in the preceding clause in Matt 23. 37. The point being made here is not affected.

ὅν τρόπον ὄρνις ἐπισυνάγει τὰ νοσσία αὐτῆς ὑπο τὰς πτέρυγας, καὶ οὐκ ἠθελήσατε).[1]

At this point in 5 Ezra the expected reference to Israel's rejection of Jesus, who, like the prophets, was sent to God's people Israel, is studiously avoided. Why? Perhaps there was reluctance to concede to opponents that Jesus might be seen as another prophet, though Matt 21. 37f. uses 'son' and 'heir' in order to separate Jesus from the prophets, and Acts 7. 52 uses 'the righteous one' for the same reason. More probably the rejection of Jesus was so well established that it hardly needed to be stressed in a context where the contrast between God's people Israel and the 'people to come' is the central theme. 5 Ezra is not a polemical writing which is intended to be used against Jewish opponents. It is an apologetic document which explains why a final separation from Israel has recently occurred and it intends to give hope and comfort to a Christian group facing persecution.

The rejection of Israel is expressed so vigorously that discontinuity of the 'new' people from Israel would seem to follow as a corollary. However, although the 'newness' theme is found frequently in Christian writings from the first half of the second century and in Justin, it is completely absent from 5 Ezra.[2] The 'people who will come' will be given God's name and the statutes (1. 24), the patriarchs (1. 39), the prophetic writings (1. 36, 39 and 2. 18), the splendour of God's presence (2. 11), and the 'kingdom of Jerusalem' (2. 10). Israel and the 'coming people' are *both* referred to repeatedly as *populus*, and they share the same mother, but Christians are

---

[1] In some cases the Latin manuscripts vary so much that it is difficult to decide whether an allusion is closer to the Matthean or to the Lucan form of a Q passage. But in 5 Ezra 1. 28 ff. there are allusions to the so-called Wisdom logion (Matt 23. 34ff.), and to the 'Jerusalem' logion (Matt 23. 37 ff.). These logia are found in Luke in different contexts (11. 49 ff. and 13. 34 ff.).

[2] Cf. P. Richardson, *Israel in the Apostolic Church*, Cambridge 1969, 27. R. Murray, *Symbols of Church and Kingdom*, Cambridge 1974, 41 ff., shows that the doctrine that the chosen people of God have been replaced by a new people, 'the nation from the nations', is particularly important in the fourth century Syriac Fathers.

not called a *new* people, as in the *Epistle of Barnabas* 5. 7 and in the *Apology of Aristides* 16. 4.

This can hardly be a coincidence. There is a complete rupture between the church and Israel, but there is also continuity. The church is neither the new Israel nor the true Israel, nor the new people of God, but simply 'the people'. There is no hint that 'the people' interpret the Scriptures in a different way from Israel. Nor is there even a suggestion that Christian convictions are already anticipated in the Old Testament.[1] There is no criticism of sacrifices *per se*, no suggestion that they were temporary and are now superceded; 5 Ezra differs markedly from *Barnabas* 2. 4-10, for example. Israel is told that her sacrifices, feasts, new moons, and circumcisions are to be rejected, not because they were inadequate or unnecessary, but because she has been disobedient and unfaithful (1. 31).[2]

5 Ezra is at the opposite end of the theological spectrum from Marcion. The 'coming people' will do all that Israel should have done: they will carry out completely the law of the Lord (2. 40),[3] and they will obey the prophets (1. 36). They are no mere 'afterthought' as God's people, consequent upon the rejection of the Jews, for they were called *ab initio* (2. 41): the mother of Israel is their mother too.

Continuity between the two peoples is underlined by a firm insistence that the Old Testament prophetic writings are being transferred to the 'people soon to come'. In 5 Ezra there is a special interest in the prophets. Its form and style are modelled closely on the prophets. In some manuscripts Ezra is called a prophet.[4] Israel was given the commandments

---

[1] For example, one might have expected an insistence that Abraham was promised that nations would spring from him.

[2] C reads 'sabbata et circumcisiones non mandabi uobis'. This is much more closely in line with standard Christian apologetic and is a later modification of the more difficult reading. Cf. Justin, *Dial.* 10.1 ff.

[3] The French recension reads 'qui legem domini compleuerunt'. *Suppleberunt* in C M is a later corruption in line with the traditional Christian position.

[4] In his introduction to Bensly's edition, xliv ff., M.R. James notes that 'prophet', which is found in some manuscripts at 1. 1 is an unusual

through God's servants the prophets,[1] but she did not listen to them and she abandoned God's counsels (2. 1). Her rejection is linked closely to her treatment and persecution of the prophets (2. 32). This is a well established theme in Matthew and in many other writings from this period,[2] but 5 Ezra goes a step further: the 'coming people' have not seen the prophets, yet they will obey them (2. 36); and they will be given the three patriarchs and the twelve prophets.[3] They are promised that God's servants Isaiah and Jeremiah will be sent to help them (2. 18). Why are these prophets singled out in this way?

J. Jeremias refers to this passage in support of his view that while later Jewish literature does not speak of any eschatological mission of Jeremiah, his expected return may be inferred from Matt 16. 14, on which 5 Ezra 2. 18 depends.[4] But why should 5 Ezra mention Isaiah with Jeremiah? A much simpler solution is to be preferred. They are singled out in 5 Ezra because they are so prominent in Matthew. Isaiah is referred to much more frequently than in the other gospels; and Jeremiah is mentioned three times in Matthew, but nowhere else in the New Testament.[5] In any case 5 Ezra does not intend to promise an eschatological return of Isaiah and

designation for Ezra which may be original. On the other hand, 4 Ezra 12. 42 refers to Ezra as 'one of the prophets', and 'prophet' would be a natural ascription by a later scribe in view of the prophetic *form* of 5 Ezra.

[1] This phrase probably depends on Ezra 9. 10 f., though Matt 11. 13 also links the law very closely with the prophets.

[2] See O.H. Steck, *Israel und das gewaltsame Geschick der Propheten*, Neukirchen-Vluyn 1967, *passim*, and D.R.A. Hare, *Jewish Persecution*, 61f. and 137ff.

[3] See M.R. James's discussion of the variants in his introduction to Bensly's edition, lii ff.

[4] Art. Ἰερεμίας in *TDNT* III, 218 ff.; see E. Schweizer, *The Good News according to Matthew*, E.tr. London 1976, 339 f., for the same view.

[5] The most likely reason is that suggested by H.F.D. Sparks, *JTS*, N.S.1 (1950) 155 f.: Matthew is accustomed to a canon of the 'latter prophets' in which Jeremiah stood first, as that mentioned in *j Baba Bathra* 146 (baraitha).

Jeremiah; the prophetic writings, like the law, are being transferred from Israel to the 'coming people'.

Discontinuity could hardly be sharper, for Israel is totally and finally rejected. Continuity could hardly be stronger, for there is not even a hint that as the prophets and the law pass from Israel to the 'coming people' they are to be modified in any way. How is this apparent paradox to be explained?

There would seem to be only two possible explanations. 5 Ezra might be seen as an unsophisticated apocalyptic document in which the hermeneutical problems posed by the transfer of the law and the prophets to the church were by-passed. But apocalyptic writings are not the literary deposits of naïve visionaries: they usually bear the marks of considerable theological reflection. 5 Ezra is no exception.

It is much more plausible to see the community from which 5 Ezra stems as struggling to define itself over against a Judaism which could not be ignored. Israel's privileges are to be transferred to the church without remainder and without modification. This suggests a community primarily concerned to establish its continuity with Israel in spite of a recent final rupture for which a thorough explanation has had to be found.

5 Ezra is out of step with Matthew at this point. In Matthew λαός is used only of Israel. The evangelist might well have used λαός instead of ἔθνος at 21. 43 to refer to the Christian community as the replacement of Israel. But, unlike the author of 5 Ezra, he deliberately refrained from doing so. The Christological interpretation of the Old Testament which is deeply embedded in Matthew's gospel seems to have escaped the author of 5 Ezra. But many parts of Matthew, especially 5. 17-19, could have been interpreted readily as underlining the continuing significance of the law and the prophets for the church.

The parable of the wicked husbandmen in Matt 21. 33-43 could also be taken to stress continuity. 5 Ezra has used the important logion at 21. 43 (which was attached to the Marcan parable by the evangelist himself) and seems to have been influenced by the parable. It insists that the tenants of God's vineyard, Israel, rejected God's servants the prophets and were in turn rejected by God. The vineyard is to be let out to other tenants who will give him the fruits in their seasons (21. 41). This verse, which is also an addition by the evangelist, could be seen as an indication of continuity: in spite of the replacement of the original tenants by other tenants, the vineyard remains unchanged. In Matt 21. 43 the kingdom of God which is transferred from Israel to the church is the 'link of continuity.' In 5 Ezra 2. 10 ff. the link is the 'kingdom of Jerusalem', 'mother Jerusalem' which passes from one people to the other.

There is a further theme which is prominent in both 5 Ezra and Matthew. Both repeatedly warn the 'other people' to be vigilant, for the end is at hand. Once again 5 Ezra reveals dependence on Matthew: 'Expectate pastorem uestrum . . . quoniam in proximo est ille, qui in finem saeculi adueniet' (2. 34 S A) is almost certainly dependent on Matt 25. 32 ff. 5 Ezra 2. 20ff.; 2. 35, 41 also indicate use of this Matthean pericope.[1] But there is a significant difference in emphasis. Whereas in Matthew the Christian community is warned to be vigilant, since not even they are immune from punishment and rejection, this theme is absent in 5 Ezra. Here the imminent end brings consolation and hope to a community facing persecution; for Matthew's community, on the other hand, persecution probably belongs to the past.[2]

The author of 5 Ezra is steeped not only in the Old Testament, but also in Matthew's gospel.[3] It is not just a question of verbal parallels, allusions, or even of literary dependence: the two chapters of 5 Ezra are largely taken up with themes with which Matthew himself is very much concerned. It can hardly be a coincidence that 5 Ezra makes more use of Matt 21–25 than any other part of the gospel, for

[1] The author of 5 Ezra and many other interpreters of Matt 25. 31-46 have misunderstood Matthew's original intention. See Chapter 9 above.

[2] This is the conclusion reached by D.R.A. Hare, *Jewish Persecution*, 126 ff., but the evidence probably does not allow a confident conclusion.

[3] Most of the more important examples of 5 Ezra's use of Matthew's gospel have been discussed above, but there are a number of other probable allusions. See the references listed by W.O.E. Oesterley and J.M. Myers in their commentaries.

it is in these chapters that the evangelist is particularly concerned with the relationship of the church to Israel. Their explanations of the reasons for the final separation of the church from Israel differ,[1] but both insist that Israel has been replaced by 'another people'. Both writers claim that in spite of the radical discontinuity the rupture has brought, there is continuity between the two peoples. For Matthew this continuity is grounded in the person of Jesus who is the fulfilment of the Old Testament: for 5 Ezra continuity lies in the privileges of Israel, the law and the prophets, which are transferred to the 'coming people'.

Matthew's gospel comes from a community which has held a prolonged discussion and polemical debate with Judaism. The final separation of the church and the synagogue has been precipitated partly by the events of A.D. 70. Matthew cannot mask the rupture which has taken place, but in his redaction of his sources he takes pains to stress the continuity of the church and Israel. If the preceding discussion is valid, 5 Ezra reflects the aftermath of A.D. 135 which was even more traumatic than A.D. 70, both for Israel and for Christian communities still in close contact with her. Thus it is no surprise to find that since the break between the two peoples is felt even more keenly in 5 Ezra than in Matthew, continuity is emphasized even more carefully.

The Nag Hammadi Apocalypse of Peter

Although 5 Ezra is a very short document, half of which is taken up with a mosaic of numerous Old Testament passages, it has drawn to a quite remarkable extent not only on the text of Matthew's gospel, but also on themes which are prominent in Matthew. 5 Ezra is probably directly dependent on no other part of the New Testament.[2] In its preoccupation

---

[1] For example, Matthew, but not 5 Ezra, attaches particular blame to the leaders of Israel. 5 Ezra does not mention Israel's rejection of Jesus.

[2] While it is not difficult to assemble a list of New Testament parallels to words and phrases in 5 Ezra, parallels do not necessarily imply

with the relationship of the church to Israel, 5 Ezra is as 'Matthean' as any other second century writing. The Nag Hammadi *Apocalypse of Peter* has also used Matthew's gospel extensively and in some ways is thoroughly Matthean.[1] Both the *Apocalypse of Peter* and 5 Ezra seem to represent a continuation into the second century of Matthean Christianity. There is insufficient evidence to establish this suggestion as a firm conclusion; but it is put forward tentatively in the hope that it will stimulate further study.

E. Schweizer has recently claimed that the Matthean church was 'the body of these little ones who are ready to follow Jesus', a group with an ascetic charismatic character, that found its continuation in the church of Syria, finally merging into the monastic movement of the Catholic church.[2] This bold hypothesis received unexpected support from the Nag Hammadi *Apocalypse of Peter*. There is no doubt that this community saw itself as a group of 'these little ones' (the phrase recurs several times in a relatively short document). 'The little ones' joined issue with those 'who let themselves be called bishop, and also deacons, as if they had received authority from God, who recline at table after the law of the places of honour.'[3] Schweizer believes that the *Apocalypse of Peter* offers the first direct evidence of 'an ascetic Judaeo-Christian group of "these little ones" with no bishops or deacons, still experiencing heavenly visions and prophetic auditions.'[4]

---

literary dependence. In the final verses there are a number of motifs for which there are parallels in Revelation, but many of them are also found with closer verbal correspondence in Hermas. In their commentaries both W.O.E. Oesterley and J.M. Myers note a number of parallels but do not discuss the extent of 5 Ezra's dependence on the New Testament.

[1] So also A. Werner, *ThLZ* 99 (1974), cols. 575 ff.

[2] E. Schweizer, 'Observance of the Law and Charismatic Activity in Matthew', *NTS* 16 (1970) 229; see also E. Schweizer, *Matthew*, 182 ff.

[3] E. Schweizer, 'The "Matthean" Church', *NTS* 20 (1974) 216; there is a similar brief note in *ZNW* 65 (1974) 139. Schweizer refers to Matt 23. 6-10 and 18. 10.

[4] *NTS* 20, 216.

5 Ezra offers further support for this conclusion, for it too stems from a Judaeo-Christian community which sees itself as 'the little ones' and in which Christian prophecy continues. In the final verse, which is very similar to the conclusion of the *Apocalypse of Peter*, Ezra is instructed by the angel of God to go and convey to the Christian community his prophetic vision (2. 48): he is also commanded to take the *words* of the Lord to them (2. 10). Ezra is portrayed as a prophet who speaks against Israel very much in the manner of Old Testament prophets (2. 4, 8, 12, 15, etc.). Whereas Israel rejected the Old Testament prophets (and Ezra himself, 2. 33), the clear implication is that the 'coming people' will not only obey the Old Testament prophets but will accept the prophetic words and visions given by God through Ezra. At 2. 26 there is probably an explicit reference to Christian prophets: 'Seruos quos tibi dedi, nemo ex eis interiet, ego enim eos requiram de numero tuo.'[1]

Who are the servants who have been given to the community? The only candidates seem to be Christian prophets. In three earlier passages Old Testament prophets are referred to as God's servants (1. 32; 2. 1; 2. 18).[2] In the passage just quoted there is a carefully worked out contrast with Israel's treatment of the prophets which is referred to at 1. 32 as follows: 'Ego misi pueros meos prophetas ad uos, quos acceptos interfecistis et laniastis corpora illorum: quorum sanguinem exquiram, dicit dominus.'[3] Israel's prophets were repeatedly disobeyed and persecuted, but prophets among 'the coming people' will be obeyed and especially protected, though there is no suggestion that they

---

[1] The French recension has been quoted: the Spanish manuscripts do not differ significantly.

[2] In all three passages Old Testament prophets are referred to as *pueros*: at 2. 26 *seruos* is used. This variation may have arisen because of the ambiguity of the underlying Greek παῖς. Or *seruos* may have been chosen in order to indicate that the prophets sent to the Christian community are not identical with the Old Testament prophets.

[3] This is the reading of the French recension. In the Spanish there is a reference to *animas* with *sanguinem* and to the mutilation of the bodies of the apostles: both are later insertions.

will escape the opposition which God's servants the prophets always attract. The word *prophetas*, then, probably stood originally at 2. 26; if so, a later scribe has not understood the reference to Christian prophets and has generalized it.[1]

5 Ezra is a pseudonymous apocalyptic prophecy. Its form is no mere literary convention; but it reflects the continuing activity of Christian prophets.[2] In this respect 5 Ezra, like the *Apocalypse of Peter*, is Matthean. Matthew's warning against the activity of false prophets in 7. 18-23 presupposes the activity of true prophets, an activity which is confirmed by 5. 12; 10. 41; 23. 34.

In early Christian writings prophecy and apocalyptic are linked closely together[3] : the Johannine apocalypse refers to itself as a prophecy. Hence it is no coincidence that Matthew, 5 Ezra, and the *Apocalypse of Peter* all have apocalyptic passages and imply that prophetic activity continues.[4]

5 Ezra also seems to share the self-designation of the Matthean community, 'the little ones', which is prominent in the *Apocalypse of Peter*.[5] At 1. 37 the Lord speaks the following words through Ezra: 'Testor populi uenientis gratiam, cuius paruuli exultant cum laetitia, me non uidentes oculis carnalibus, sed spiritu credent quae dixi.'[6] Elsewhere *filii* is used several times to refer both to Israel and to the Christian community and might have been used here. *Paruuli* cannot refer to small children in this verse, though it is used in this sense at 1. 28. The context strongly suggests the

---

[1] The Spanish recension represents a further step in this direction. It drops *seruos* and reads *Quia quos tibi dedi . . .* An original *quos* is unlikely to have been changed to the much more specific and unexpected *seruos*.

[2] At 1. 37 there may possibly be a reference to charismatic enthusiasm in the community of the 'coming people': cuius paruuli exultant cum laetitia, me non uidentes oculis carnalibus, sed spiritu credent quae dixi.

[3] So W. Schneemelcher in E. Hennecke, *NT Apocrypha* II, 684.

[4] In chapter 24 Matthew repeatedly adds apocalyptic motifs to his sources. For a discussion of apocalyptic motifs in 5 Ezra, see J. Daniélou, 'Le Vᵉ Esdras et le Judéo-Christianisme'.

[5] On οἱ μικροί in Matthew, see E. Schweizer, *NTS* 16, 222 f.

[6] In the Spanish recension *paruuli* are replaced by *apostoli*, a correction of a word which made little sense to a later scribe.

paruuli is equivalent to the Matthean οἱ μικροί and that, as in Matthew, it is a self-designation of the community.

A prophetic saying attributed by Epiphanius to Montanus uses οἱ μικροί in a similar sense: λέγει τί λέγεις τὸν ὑπὲρ ἄνθρωπον σῳζόμενον; λάμπει γὰρ (φησίν) ὁ δίκαιος ὑπὲρ τὸν ἥλιον ἑκατονταπλασίονα, οἱ δὲ μικροὶ ἐν ὑμῖν σῳζόμενοι λάμψουσιν ἑκατονταπλασίονα, ὑπὲρ τὴν σελήνην.[1] This saying is an adaptation of Matt 13. 43. In all probability Montanus was also deeply influenced by Matthew's gospel. Would that more early Montanist traditions were available!

There is a further important self-designation in the *Apocalypse of Peter* which may also be shared with Matthew and 5 Ezra. Towards the end Peter (to whom the visions and words are given throughout) is commanded to pass on what he has seen to the *allogenes* who do not come from this aeon.[2] The Greek word *allogenes* stands in the Coptic text. Why is this phrase used as a self-designation? Does it reflect the community's Judaeo-Christian background and the fact that it stands over against Judaism? There is polemic directed against Judaism (p. 72. 4 ff.), and there is certainly evidence of Judaeo-Christian traditions. As in 5 Ezra, there is an acute awareness that Israel has been replaced as the chosen people by 'another people'. The importance of the phrase *ad gentem alteram* in 5 Ezra 1. 24 was noted above, as was its dependence on Matt 21. 43. The Matthean community saw itself as the ἔθνος which replaced rejected Israel, though the evangelist was reluctant to use λαός of Christians. There is some evidence, then, which suggests that a second Matthean self-designation survived in Judaeo-Christian circles which were influenced by Matthean Christianity.

In 5 Ezra and in the *Apocalypse of Peter* Matthean traditions are prominent. In all three documents there is evidence of continuing prophetic activity and there is polemic with

---

[1] *Panarion*, XLVIII. x. 3 (*GCS* text).
[2] p. 83. 15ff. A. Werner, *ThLZ* 99 (1974) col. 577, notes that the same word is used three times in Epiphanius' account of the Archontici, but probably not as a self-designation.

Judaism, but also a deep sense of continuity in spite of the parting of the ways. But perhaps the probability that all three communities shared two self-designations is even more important. All three saw themselves as 'the little ones' and defined themselves over against Judaism as a different ἔθνος (Matthew), as *altera gens* (5 Ezra), and as *allogenes* (*Apocalypse of Peter*).

In this discussion some confident conclusions about the origin and purpose of 5 Ezra have been drawn. Several further suggestions have been made rather more tentatively in the final paragraphs. If they are plausible, they indicate that some of the distinctive features of Matthean Christianity survived well into the second century. Various attempts have been made, with some success, to trace the 'afterlife' of Pauline, Johannine, and Lucan Christianity. There may now be sufficient evidence available to enable an attempt to be made to assemble some of the Matthean pieces of the second century jigsaw puzzle. 5 Ezra, the *Apocalypse of Peter*, and perhaps Montanus, may prove to be at least as significant for the Matthean corner as James and the *Didache*.[1]

---

[1] Since this chapter was first published (*JTS* 28, 1977) the following important literature has appeared: A.F.J. Klijn, ed., *Der lateinische Text der Apokalypse des Esra*, TU 131, Berlin 1983; R.A. Kraft, 'Greek Transmission of Jewish Scriptures: a Methodological Probe,' in *Paganisme, Judaïsme, Christianisme: Mélanges offerts à Marcel Simon*, Paris 1978, 207-26; R.A. Kraft, '"Ezra" Materials in Judaism and Christianity', *ANRW* II.19.1 (1979) 119-36; R.A. Kraft, 'Towards Assessing the Latin Text of "5 Ezra": the "Christian" Connection', *HTR* 79 (1986) 158-69; Theodore A. Bergren, 'The "People Coming from the East" in 5 Ezra 1: 38', *JBL* 108 (1989) 675-83; Theodore A. Bergren, *Fifth Ezra: The Text, Origin, and Early History*, Atlanta 1990.
On the use of Matthew's gospel in the second century, see now the revised edition of E. Massaux, *Influence de l'Évangile de St. Matthieu sur la littérature chrétienne avant St. Irénée*, Louvain 1950; BETL 75, Leuven 1986. The revised edition includes a Bibliography for 1950-1985 prepared by B. Dehandschutter. See also W.-D. Köhler, *Die Rezeption des Matthäusevangeliums in der Zeit vor Irenäus*, Tübingen 1987.

Conclusions to Part II

Matthew has strengthened considerably polemic against the Jewish leaders which was already present in the sources on which he drew. He does this both by modifying earlier traditions and by adding phrases and occasionally whole sentences, and also by setting them in new contexts. The evangelist's much sharper anti-Jewish polemic is an assured result of redaction critical studies. Numerous examples have been given in the preceding chapters. That Matthew's more strongly worded polemical traditions reflect a 'parting of the ways' can be affirmed with confidence.

Sociological and literary observations point in precisely the same direction and usefully complement redaction critical conclusions. Many of the distinctive (i.e. redactional) features of this gospel can be paralleled in writings which come from minority groups which have parted company painfully with parent bodies. In Chapters 4 and 6 a number of Jewish and early Christian writings provided useful comparisons with Matthew from sociological perspectives.

The evangelist has used several literary strategies in order both to press his case against the Jewish leaders and to convince his readers and listeners that as a 'new people' they are expected to carry out diligently the will of their Father in heaven. Matthew's most obvious literary device is repetition of his main points. But he also uses more subtle strategies. J.D. Kingsbury has shown clearly that Matthew's story sets out with considerable literary skill the 'developing conflict' between Jesus and the religious leaders.[1] In Chapter 3 I

---

[1] 'The Developing Conflict between Jesus and the Jewish Leaders in Matthew's Gospel: a Literary-Critical Study' *CBQ* 49 (1987) 57-73.

suggested that the evangelist has used the rhetorical strategy of 'comparison' in order to show that Jesus is greater than Moses, John the Baptist, the temple, Jonah, and Solomon.

A further literary device may be noted briefly. In several important and impressive ways the infancy narratives foreshadow the main themes of the evangelist's story. In antiquity foreshadowing was widely used in biographies, in novels, in histories, and in drama.

The hostility of the Jewish puppet king Herod to the child Jesus foreshadows the implacable hostility of the Jewish leaders to Jesus and his followers. The chief priests and scribes are shown to be thoroughly conversant with the prophecies of Scripture concerning the birth of the Messiah. But as the whole story unfolds the heavy irony becomes apparent: in spite of being steeped in Scripture, they reject Jesus who has fulfilled its promises. Herod's attempt to kill Jesus is thwarted by God who, by revelatory dreams, preserves the life of the child and his mother so that Scripture might be fulfilled. Since the first recipients of Matthew's gospel are likely to have known in outline the story of Jesus before they first heard this gospel read aloud, they would have appreciated readily the skill with which the story (and its outcome) is foreshadowed in the infancy narratives.

In addition to the redaction critical, sociological and literary considerations to which I have appealed regularly in the preceding chapters, a further approach has been used in Chapters 10 and 11, and more briefly in several other chapters in Part II. Matthew's gospel has been set alongside other early Christian writings which reflect the parting of the ways between Christians and Jews. In recent decades much New Testament scholarship has become highly specialised and narrow in its focus; the broader approach I have used has not been prominent. Of course there are dangers. Writings which frequently baffle the interpreter and whose social setting is only partly known will not help us greatly in the elucidation of equally enigmatic writings. But there are potential gains, as I hope I have shown. The issues at stake between Christians and Jews when Matthew wrote were grappled with in other parts of early Christianity, both before and soon after the evangelist wrote. The more we know about the map of the parting of the ways between Christians and Jews, the more likely we are to be able to set Matthew's gospel in its appropriate first century context.

On the basis of these various methods and approaches, a number of conclusions have been drawn in Part II. I shall now summarize the more important results; I shall list them according to the degree of confidence which can be attached to them.

(i) The evangelist Matthew was a learned Jew who wrote for Jews who had accepted some Gentiles into their Christian communities. In numerous redactional passages there are phrases and theological motifs which are the work of someone steeped in Scripture and in contemporary Judaism. The ferocity of the evangelist's anti-Jewish polemic strongly suggests a family quarrel.

(ii) The communities for which Matthew wrote have recently parted company painfully with local synagogues. 'Church' and 'synagogue' are at odds with one another. This is confirmed not only by the evangelist's insistence that Gentiles must be accepted, but also by the ways Jesus and his followers are distanced from the Jewish leaders. Matthew's increased use of apocalpytic motifs, his strong call for a 'greater righteousness', and his insistence on 'high community boundaries' are all related to this social setting.

(iii) The evangelist responds both directly and indirectly to to the criticisms of Jewish opponents of the 'new people'. Matthew counters their rival explanation of the empty tomb, and in his account of the birth of Jesus he *may* perhaps be aware of polemical jibes that Jesus was born illegitimately. The evangelist is aware of the claim that Jesus is a magician and a deceiver: he responds vigorously to the former and assumes that his whole story is a response to the latter. He knows that the Davidic Messiahship of Jesus is a contentious issue and sets out a carefully considered response. He is sensitive to the allegation that Christians have abandoned the law, though his defence of its continuing importance is sometimes somewhat imprecise.

(iv) There is no evidence from within the gospel itself that Jewish leaders at Jamnia (or anywhere else) initiated the separation of church and synagogue by adding the *birkath ha-minim* to the synagogue liturgy. From evidence outside the gospel it is just possible that the *birkath ha-minim* was a factor in the 'parting', but if so, it was no more than one factor among many.

(v) While the social setting of Matthew's gospel can be reconstructed with some confidence, it is much more difficult to set out the *history* of the relationships of Matthean Christians with Judaism. The sketch which follows is at least plausible. At first Jews who had become Christians within the communities with which the evangelist was associated maintained their Jewish loyalties and most aspects of their Jewish identity. However, gradual acceptance of some Gentiles led to intolerable tensions between Christian and non-Christian Jews. Matthew wrote his gospel partly in order to strengthen his readers' resolve to continue to accept Gentiles. The parting of the ways was gradual. It was not precipitated by any one historical event, nor was a formal decision taken by either group. It was the eventual result of mutual incomprehension and suspicion. Matthew envisages that his communities may continue to face hostility and persecution, but there is no way of knowing with certainty whether this was a real and sustained threat, or merely the perception of the minority group. Perhaps the evangelist and his fellow-Christians moved from Palestine to Syria partly as the result of Jewish hostility.

A reconstruction on these lines must inevitably draw heavily on the disciplined imagination of the historian. One's overall map of the parting of the ways between Christians and Jews in the latter half of the first century and in the early decades of the second will be as important as the text of the gospel itself. Matthew's gospel contains no more than a few hints which can be clarified to a limited extent by careful separation of earlier tradition and later redaction.

Part Three

Studies in Matthew

I tell you,
unless your righteousness is far better
than that of the scribes and Pharisees,
you can never enter
the kingdom of heaven.

Matthew 5. 20

Chapter Twelve

Interpreting the Sermon on the Mount

No other short section of the Bible has been more prominent in theological discussion and in the general life of the church than the Sermon on the Mount. Even in our modern secular societies the Sermon's influence continues. Though they may have given the matter little careful thought, many men and women who have little or no contact with the church believe that the Sermon contains clear ethical teaching for all people of goodwill.

The Sermon is well known to Christians today, but few appreciate the richness of these sayings of Jesus. Their radical promises and demands have often been blunted either through familiarity or as a result of a precipitate quest for immediate relevance. Interpretation of this influential and apparently simple passage is far from easy, but the scholar, preacher, or lay person who perseveres will be amply rewarded, for the Sermon sets out powerfully both the gift and demand of the Gospel.

There are two versions of the Sermon: the Sermon on the Mount (Matt 5. 3 – 7. 27) which contains 106 verses, and the Sermon on the Plain (Luke 6. 20b–49) which contains 29 verses. The term 'the Sermon on the Mount' goes back to the title which Augustine gave to his important commentary on Matt 5–7, *De Sermone Domini in Monte*, which was probably written between 392 and 396. In spite of Augustine's enormous influence on many later Christian writers, Matt 5–7 was not generally referred to as 'the Sermon on the Mount' until the sixteenth century. The term 'Sermon on the Plain' is modern; it is used primarily to distinguish Luke's much shorter Sermon from Matthew's.

The two Sermons may be interpreted either as integral parts of Matthew's and Luke's gospels, or as collections of sayings of the historical Jesus. In the former case scholars who accept Marcan priority and some form of the Q hypothesis conclude that Matthew has composed chapters 5–7 as the first of his five carefully constructed discourses. Matthew's Sermon is a considerably expanded version of the Q 'sermon' on which Luke drew with few changes in the Sermon on the Plain, Luke 6. 20-49. By his arrangement and, in some cases, adaptation of earlier traditions, Matthew has sought to meet the needs of Christians in his own day. Matthew's first discourse contains many of his own distinctive emphases. Luke's Sermon is also related to his overall purposes, though much less clearly.

If the sayings of Jesus in Matt 5–7 or Luke 6. 20-49 are used to reconstruct the teaching of the historical Jesus, it is important to recognize that they have been modified by the evangelists and also at earlier stages in the transmission of the gospel traditions. They can be appreciated fully only when they are interpreted alongside related sayings from other parts of the gospels. Although Matthew's Sermon on the Mount is often assumed to be a summary of the ethical teaching of Jesus, this is mistaken: there are important ethical sayings of Jesus which are not included in Matthew's Sermon, and not all the traditions in these chapters are ethical.

The Sermon in Q and in Luke

The term 'Sermon on the Plain' comes from Luke's introduction to his version of the Sermon. Following his account of two sabbath controversies (6. 1-11) Luke notes that Jesus went out into the hills to pray and continued in prayer to God all night. When day came he called his disciples and came down with them and stood *on a level place* (6. 12, 17). In the presence of a large crowd Jesus addressed his disciples with the words of the Sermon (6. 20b-49). Although Luke's Sermon is much closer to the earlier version in Q than to Matthew's, the Sermon on the Plain has attracted less attention down through the centuries than the Sermon on the Mount.

Almost the whole of Luke's Sermon is also found in Matt 5–7. Where the two gospels overlap in content, there is often close agreement in the wording of the traditions. A number of verses, however, are similar in content but differ in wording. The most plausible explanation of this phenomenon is that Matthew and Luke drew on different versions of the Q Sermon, which are often abbreviated as Q^{Mt} and Q^{Lk}.

The chart below, which is based on Luke's order, shows that in spite of their great disparity in size, the two versions agree strikingly in the order of the traditions.

	Luke 6	*Matt 5–7*
Introduction	20a	5. 1-2
Beatitudes	20b-23	5. 3-12
Woes	24-26	
Love of enemy	27-36	5. 38-47
Golden Rule	31	7. 12
Judge not	37-38	7. 1-2
The blind guide	39	
Teacher and disciple	40	
Speck and log	41-42	7. 3-5
The tree and its fruit	43-45	7. 16-20
Lord, Lord	46	7. 21
House on the rock	47-49	7. 24-7

Matthew differs from Luke's order at only one significant point: the Golden Rule does not appear, as we might have expected, at 5. 38-47, as part of the 'love your enemy' traditions, but as the climax of Matthew's Sermon in 7. 12. With only three major exceptions, the whole of the Sermon on the Plain is found in Matt 5–7: Matthew does not have woes to counter-balance the Beatitudes, as Luke does; the saying about the blind guide appears at Matt 15. 14, and the saying on the relationship of a disciple to his teacher is found in Matt 10. 24.

This close agreement in order and in content has led most scholars to conclude that Q contained an earlier form of the Sermon. Luke has retained the order of the traditions in Q. Although Luke has modified some Q traditions, and has perhaps omitted a few verses from Q and added a few others which were not part of Q, his version of the Sermon is usually considered to be very close to the original version in Q.

An alternative explanation has been defended by a small number of scholars. They argue that for his own purposes Luke drastically abbreviated Matthew's sermon and included many of the omitted traditions at other points in his gospel. Luke is thus seen as the first interpreter of Matthew's Sermon. Opponents of this view claim, surely correctly, that if Luke did use Matthew, he acted in a quite arbitrary way. He has included only just over a quarter of Matt 5–7; he has failed to include numerous sayings at any point in his gospel (5. 17, 19-20, 21-4, 27-8, 33-9a, 43; 6. 1-8, 16-18; 7. 6, 15); he has placed the remainder in six different places with little regard for Matthew's order. Although attempts have been made to explain why Luke might have revised Matthew's Sermon so radically, they have not been persuasive. At least in this case, the Q hypothesis offers a much simpler and more plausible explanation of the evidence.

In most reconstructions of Q, the traditions behind Luke 6. 20b-49 form the initial collection of the sayings of Jesus: these verses were already an 'inaugural sermon' in Q, preceded only by John's preaching of the Coming One (Luke 3. 7-9, 16-17) and the temptation traditions (Luke 4. 1-13). The opening beatitudes in Q pronounce God's blessing on those in dire need: the poor, those who hunger, sorrow, and suffer persecution (Luke 6. 20b-23). These sayings declare that the coming of God's kingdom brings about radical transformation: they proclaim good news.

Matthew has followed Q's lead and used the beatitudes as the opening section of his Sermon. Luke places the Sermon on the Plain at a later point in his gospel, but he may nonetheless have been strongly influenced by the position of the beatitudes as the opening of an 'inaugural sermon' in Q.

If, as is likely, the Q beatitudes are to be understood as the fulfilment of Isa 61. 1-3, it is significant that this very passage is quoted in Luke's dramatic and programmatic account of the opening of the ministry of Jesus in the synagogue at Nazareth (Luke 4. 16-30). Quite independently, both Matthew and Luke may have been influenced by Q's insistence that the significance of Jesus is to be seen in terms of Isa 61. 1-3, a claim which goes back to Jesus himself.

Luke has not reshaped the Q Sermon in the way that Matthew has, but two emphases are clear and important. In four places Luke has added 'now' to the traditions: to the beatitude and corresponding woe on hunger (6. 21a and 25a), and to the beatitude and woe on mourning and laughing (6. 21c and 25c). These additions reveal the evangelist's concern for Christian life here and now. A similar emphasis is found in numerous passages in Luke. For example, Luke 9. 23 stresses that taking up one's cross and following Jesus is to be carried out *daily* (cf. Mark 8. 34).

In Luke, but not in Matthew, there are four woes which correspond precisely to his four beatitudes (cf. Luke 6. 20-1 and 24-6). Most scholars accept that Luke has added the woes to the Q Sermon, either from independent tradition, or on his own initiative. In this way Luke underlines the contrast between, on the one hand, people who are in desperate circumstances (the poor, the hungry, those who mourn, and those who are persecuted) and, on the other hand, people who are self satisfied and complacent. This a favourite theme of Luke's: in numerous passages he attacks complacency and stresses the particular concern of Jesus for the poor, for those in need, and for those on the margins of society.

History of interpretation

A brief survey of the history of interpretation of the Sermon confirms just how influential these chapters have been and how many major theological issues they raise.

The first commentary on the Sermon was probably written by Origen in the middle of the third century, but only a short

289

fragment of it has survived. The two most important expositions of the Sermon in the early church were written by Chrysostom and Augustine at the end of the fourth century, both of whom insisted that the Sermon was the perfect pattern for the life of all Christians. In his homilies on the Sermon Chrysostom attacked the heretical views of Gnostics and Manicheans. He rejected their view that the body is evil and only the mind and spirit are good; he insisted that 5. 29 teaches that it is the 'evil mind' which is accursed, not bodily organs such as the eye and hand. Chrysostom also refuted 'those heretics who say that the old covenant is of the devil'; the sayings of Jesus do not repeal the old law, they 'draw out and fill up its commands.'

Augustine also grappled with the relationship of the Sermon to the law of Moses. The Manichean Faustus had claimed that 5. 17 was a saying neither of Jesus nor of Matthew: someone else had written it under Matthew's name! In his *Reply to Faustus* Augustine stressed the continuity of the 'old law' and the 'new' more strongly than was usually the case in the early church. In his own exposition of the Sermon, however, the more common line of interpretation is prominent. Augustine drew attention to the sharp discontinuity between the 'old law' and the 'new' by distinguishing between the 'lesser precepts given by God through his holy prophets and servants to a people who still needed to be bound by fear' (i.e. to Israel before the coming of Christ) and 'the greater precepts given through his Son to a people now ready to be freed by love.'

Augustine is not the only interpreter who interpreted 5. 17-48 in different ways either in different contexts or at different points in his life. Augustine may have been inconsistent, but the issue is still with us today. To what extent and in what ways is the ethical teaching of the Old Testament still important today? How 'new' is the teaching of Jesus and does it have priority over Scripture, i.e. the Old Testament? Do we retain the parts of Scripture to which Jesus refers, and ignore or reject the rest?

In the thirteenth century, Thomas Aquinas also stressed the discontinuity between the old law ('the law of bondage') and the new law ('the law of liberty') but without conceding that the latter contradicted or abrogated the former. In his interpretation of the Sermon he used the analogy of the tree (the new law) which is in a sense contained in the seed. Aquinas also introduced a distinction which was to become very influential in Catholic thought. In addition to the *commandments* of the new law which are necessary in order to gain salvation, there are also optional *counsels* which 'render the gaining of eternal bliss more assured and expeditious'. The latter are intended for those who strive for perfection; they are based on poverty, chastity and obedience and are therefore primarily for those who join the religious life. This distinction is hardly hinted at in interpretation of the Sermon in the early church, though it may be implied by the harsh saying of Jesus concerning the renunciation of marriage: 'let those accept it who can' (Matt 19. 11-12).

Luther, Zwingli and Calvin wrote extensively on the Sermon. They all insisted that Matt 5–7 represents the true interpretation of the law of Moses which had been obscured in Judaism. On the whole they emphasized the continuity between the 'law of Christ' and the 'law of Moses' more than their Catholic opponents. They rejected the use made of the Sermon by radical Anabaptist groups who claimed that the ethical teaching of Christ was a clear development beyond the law of Moses, parts of which have been abrogated. Anabaptists claimed that the Sermon should be interpreted literally and that Christians should therefore never use violence (5. 39), never swear oaths (5. 34), and never hold office as a judge or ruler (7. 1). Their literal interpretation of the Sermon led them to opt out of secular government completely.

In a series of sermons on Matt 5–7 (and in other writings) Luther developed his well-known doctrine of the two realms, the secular and the spiritual. The Christian lives in both spheres. In the spiritual sphere (i.e. within the life of the church) the Christian must obey all the commands of the Sermon; in the secular sphere, natural law or 'common sense' must prevail. For example, in his remarks on Matt 5. 38-42 (the use of violence and compulsion), Luther claimed that most interpreters failed to distinguish properly between the kingdom of Christ and the kingdom of the world. In these verses 'Christ is not tampering with the responsibility and authority of the government, but he is teaching individual Christians how to live personally, apart from their official position and authority. . . A Christian should not (use violence to) resist evil; but within the limits of his office, a secular person should oppose firmly every evil.' For Luther a 'secular person' included Christians participating in the secular realm.

Luther also discussed the Sermon in terms of 'law' and 'gospel'. In some of his writings he emphasized that the Sermon is the 'law of Christ' that makes people aware of the gospel of God's grace through Christ: 'we are not able properly to fulfil one tittle out of our own strength. . . . but must always crawl to Christ.' But in other passages Luther stated that the Sermon is not just the accusing law that points to sin: it is also 'gospel'. This is especially true of the beatitudes (5. 3-12). Christ 'does not press, but in a friendly way entices and speaks: "Blessed are the poor."'

By referring in different passages in his writings to the Sermon both as 'law' and as 'gospel', Luther confused some of his later followers. Many Lutheran theologians have stressed that the Sermon is the law that awakens knowledge of sin. But some (notably J. Jeremias [1961]) have claimed that the demands of Jesus in the Sermon are preceded by 'gospel', that is, by his proclamation of the kingdom and by his encouragement to his disciples to share his own sense of sonship.

In his comments on Matt 5. 21 Calvin noted that 'we must not imagine Christ to be a new legislator, who adds anything to the eternal righteousness of his Father. We must listen to him as a faithful expounder . . . ' Calvin partially anticipated eighteenth and nineteenth century discussion of the sources of the Sermon in his recognition that Matt 5–7 is 'a brief summary of the doctrine of Christ. . . collected out of his many and various discourses'.

1. *Twentieth century interpretation*

All the various approaches just sketched can be found in modern discussion of the Sermon. Twentieth century scholarship, however, has added two new issues: the extent to which the Sermon reflects the views of Jesus (or of Matthew) concerning the end-times (eschatology), and the extent to which Matthew the evangelist has shaped the traditions he has incorporated into chapters 5–7.

In 1892 Johannes Weiss published a short but influential discussion of Jesus' proclamation of the kingdom of God; he claimed that Jesus expected that the kingdom would shortly be ushered in through a cataclysmic divine intervention. In 1901 Albert Schweitzer developed this approach even more vigorously. Both writers believed that the ethical teaching of Jesus was intended as a preparation for the short period before the end ('interim ethics'); the sayings of Jesus were not intended to be used by later generations, as most readers of the Sermon down through the centuries had simply assumed. Thus most of the issues with which earlier interpreters of the Sermon had grappled were declared to be irrelevant. Weiss and Schweitzer raised in an acute form the relationship between the ethical teaching of Jesus and his proclamation of the coming kingdom. Discussion of this issue has to range far beyond Matt 5–7 and consider all the relevant sayings of Jesus.

B.W. Bacon (1902) was one of the first writers in English to attempt to reconstruct the earliest attainable form of the Sermon. He concluded that in its original form Jesus spoke as a prophetic interpreter of a new law; Jesus did not lay down rules, but opened up principles. These conclusions were hardly novel, but in his isolation of the 'intrusive additions' of Matthew Bacon paved the way for later redaction critical studies. Bacon claimed that Matthew has supplied 'neo-legalistic touches' in verses such as 5. 16 ('good works'); 5. 18-19; 5. 32 (the 'exception' to 'no divorce'); 7. 12b. The original Sermon of Jesus is not legislative (as Matthew seems to have regarded it) but prophetic.

Since 1945 interpretation of the Sermon and of Matthew's gospel as a whole has been dominated by redaction criticism.

This approach explores the ways in which the evangelist has reshaped the traditions at his disposal in the light of the needs of his first readers. Redaction criticism has confirmed that Matthew is more than a compiler. Matthew's five discourses have been composed in the same way: in all five the evangelist has rearranged and reinterpreted the sayings on which he drew. He often elucidates earlier traditions with extra phrases or even (on occasion) with whole verses which he himself has composed. The following may be noted as possible examples: 5. 10, 13a, 14a, 16, 20; 6. 10b and c, 13b; 7. 12c, 19, 20, 21. In many places in the Sermon Matthew's own distinctive vocabulary and emphases are evident. For example, the five important references to 'righteousness' (5. 6, 10, 20; 6. 1, 33) are all redactional additions made by the evangelist himself.

In recent decades numerous studies of the Sermon and several detailed commentaries have been published. In nearly every case the Sermon has been isolated from the rest of Matthew's gospel and treated as a separate entity simply for convenience; there has been no suggestion that Matt 5–7 has a quite distinctive origin or purpose which set it apart from the rest of Matthew's gospel, and also from Mark and Luke.

There are, however, two important exceptions. In his influential study of the Sermon (1964) W.D. Davies suggests that 'one fruitful way of dealing with the Sermon on the Mount is to regard it as the Christian answer to Jamnia. Using terms very loosely, the Sermon is a kind of Christian, mishnaic counter-part to the formulation taking place there.' (p. 315) Davies sets out at length a cumulative case which rests on a large number of observations; he himself recognizes that some of his points are stronger than others. Davies appeals both to the Sermon and to other parts of Matthew's gospel. Some of the latter passages are undoubtedly significant. For example, Davies is able to show that the evangelist's community was at odds with contemporary Judaism. But the evidence from the Sermon itself is not compelling. None of the *direct* links proposed between the Sermon and the reconstruction taking place within Judaism during the Jamnian period is entirely satisfactory. It is the whole of Matthew's gospel, not the Sermon in isolation, which can plausibly be related (though only indirectly) to the Jamnian period. Although Davies suggests that 'there was an outside stimulus for the Evangelist to shape the Sermon' (p. 315), he does not claim that Matt 5–7 contains theological emphases which are quite distinct from the rest of the gospel. Davies seems to accept that the Sermon and the rest of Matthew come from the same social setting, though he does not discuss this point.

More recently a much bolder explanation of the origin and purpose of the Sermon on the Mount has been proposed by H.D. Betz (1985). Betz claims that the Sermon and the rest of Matthew contain different theologies: they do not come from the same *Sitz im Leben*. The Sermon is a pre-Matthean tradition which has been incorporated without modification by the evangelist and reinterpreted only minimally. In its literary genre it is an epitome, a summary of the theology of Jesus. In Betz's view the Sermon stems from a conservative Jewish Christian and anti-Pauline community which is still part of diverse first century Judaism.

Betz's hypothesis, however, is implausible. There is a full discussion of it in Chapter 13 of this book. Here we may note that the links with the epitomes of the Graeco-Roman rhetorical tradition are not strong, and the claim that the theological perspective of the Sermon is said to be at odds with Matthew's own theology is difficult to defend. Betz overlooks the extent to which in chapters 5–7 the evangelist Matthew has shaped and re-interpreted the traditions at his disposal in ways which are completely consistent with the methods and themes developed elsewhere in his gospel.

The latter point is one of the pillars of redaction critical study of the Sermon. From a quite different angle narrative critics (led by J.D. Kingsbury) have recently underlined the ways in which the Sermon is part and parcel of the evangelist's overall presentation of the story of Jesus. Not surprisingly, however, the Sermon (and the other Matthean discourses) have not proved to be very fertile ground for *narrative* critical study.

2 *Five questions for current interpretation*

The above survey of the history of interpretation confirms that careful study of these chapters involves a large number of issues, some of which are theological, some ethical, some historical, and some exegetical. For convenience they may be divided into five sets of overlapping questions, some of which are discussed further in later sections of this chapter.

(i) Does Matthew's Jesus simply interpret or clarify the law of Moses? Or does he present radically new teaching? Is Jesus portrayed as the 'new Moses' who 'goes up on the mountain' (Matt 5. 1) in order to present on a 'new Mt. Sinai' a 'new law' for a 'new people'?

(ii) What is the relationship between Matt 5–7 and Paul's gospel of grace? Is the Sermon (as 'law') intended to make the reader or listener aware of his need of 'grace'? Or does the Sermon *presuppose* God's forgiveness and acceptance of the sinner?

(iii) To whom is the Sermon addressed? To men and women in general, or to those committed to the way of Jesus? The text itself is ambiguous at this point. The introduction and conclusion (5. 1 and 7. 28) imply that the Sermon was addressed to the crowds, but 5. 2 notes that 'when the disciples had gathered around him Jesus began to address them'. While many parts of the Sermon seem to set out an 'ethic of Christian discipleship', the final verses of the whole gospel imply that the teaching of Jesus is to be part of the message taken to 'all nations' (28. 18-20).

(iv) Are all parts of the Sermon to be interpreted literally, as some have claimed? Or do some sayings (such as 5. 22, 39, 43) contain hyperbole? Does the Sermon set out a *code* of ethics, or principles or attitudes appropriate for 'members of the kingdom'? These questions arise whether the intention of Matthew or of Jesus is in view.

(v) To what extent are individual sayings dominated by the expectation (either of Jesus or of Matthew) of the approach of the end-times (i.e. eschatology)? For example, does Jesus commend a casual attitude to food and clothing in 6. 25ff. because of the approach of the end-times, or simply because this is the right attitude regardless of when the end-times come?

Is every petition of the Lord's Prayer (6. 9-13) to be interpreted eschatologically? If so, when we pray, 'Give us this day our daily bread' we are not asking for the basic necessities of everyday life, but requesting a partial anticipation now of the 'feast of heaven' – the 'bread of heaven'. Does the petition 'lead us not into temptation' concern the time of testing expected in the end-times, or everyday temptations?

The modern interpreter will quickly find that interpretation of individual sayings or groups of sayings will be determined by the answers given to all five sets of questions. These questions have been discussed for nearly two thousand years, though some have been more prominent than others in different periods of church history.

The structure of the Sermon

In recent years several proposals concerning the structure of the Sermon have been made. The overall structure of the Sermon is clear. The beatitudes (Matt 5. 3-12) are an introduction to the Sermon as a whole; the similarly structured 'salt' and 'light' sayings in 5. 13-16 form the second part of the introduction. The central section of the Sermon extends from 5. 17 to 7. 12; it opens and closes with references to the law and the prophets, 5. 17-20 and 7. 12. The Sermon is rounded off by an epilogue, 7. 13-27, in which, as we shall see, there is considerable coherence.

It is not difficult to set out the structure of the first half of the Sermon, from Matt 5. 3 to 6. 18. Following the general introduction in 5. 1-16, the important sayings on the continuing significance of the law and the prophets in 5. 17-20 are clarified and expounded, as it were, by the six antitheses in 5. 21-47. 5. 48 is probably intended to round off all the antitheses. 6. 1 introduces three paragraphs on almsgiving, prayer, and fasting (6. 2-18), all of which have exactly the same structure; the Lord's prayer and two related sayings (6. 9-15) partly 'spoil' the very impressive symmetry of this part of the Sermon.

But what about the structure of the second half of the Sermon? Matt 6. 19 to 7. 11 has long puzzled interpreters. This part of the Sermon seems to be a 'rag-bag' of sayings, only some of which are loosely related to others. G. Bornkamm has offered a novel solution: the second half of the Sermon is a 'commentary' on the Lord's Prayer. He notes that 6. 19-24 expounds the first three petitions, 6. 9-10; 6. 25-34 then works out the implications of the bread petition, 6. 11; 7. 1-5 is an exposition of the forgiveness petition, and 7. 6 takes up the theme of 6. 13. Bornkamm's ingenious explanation has not convinced other scholars, but he has shown just how strongly the whole section from 6. 5 to 7. 11 is dominated by the theme of prayer.

U. Luz claims that Matthew's Sermon has been built symmetrically around its centre-piece, the Lord's Prayer, 6. 7-15. The first section, 5. 3-16, corresponds to the last section, 7. 13-27; the second section, 5. 17-20, corresponds to 7. 12; 5. 21-48 corresponds to 6. 19 - 7. 11 (these two passages are identical in length); and 6. 1-6 corresponds to 6. 16-18. Although the theory is not completely convincing (for example, the correspondence between 5. 21-48 and 6. 19 – 7. 11 is forced), there is little doubt that Matthew does intend 5. 17-20 to introduce the central section of the sermon, and 7. 12 to conclude it.

Key sections

1. *The Prologue: the Beatitudes: Matthew 5. 3-12*
In Matthew there are nine Beatitudes, only four of which are found in Luke. The word μακάριος at the beginning of all the Beatitudes has long teased translators. μακάριος echoes LXX usage, where it expresses the happiness which is the result of God-given salvation. The English phrase 'Happy are those who . . .' hardly catches this rich meaning. 'Blessed' is perhaps preferable, but in everyday speech 'blessed' now means 'cursed' more often than not. 'God's gift of salvation is

given to those who. . .' is accurate, but clumsy, especially if repeated nine times!

Matthew and Luke have taken over the four Beatitudes found in Q which referred to the poor, the hungry, those who weep and those who are persecuted. Matthew has added (in part from earlier oral traditions) five further Beatitudes which are found in his gospel alone: the blessings on the meek (5. 5), the merciful, the pure in heart, the peacemakers and a second saying concerning persecution (5. 7-10). These additional Beatitudes and the changes made by Matthew to the Q sayings confirm that he is particularly concerned with ethical conduct. In Luke those in desperate need – those who are literally poor, hungry, weeping, and persecuted (6. 20-23) – are promised that their position will be reversed by God. In Matthew the dominant theme is very different. Those addressed, i.e. the disciples and also the followers of Jesus in the evangelist's own day, are promised that their positive qualities, i.e. their meekness, mercy, purity of heart, and abilities as peacemakers, will be rewarded by God.

This general observation may be illustrated by the two references to righteousness which Matthew adds to Q Beatitudes. The saying at Luke 6. 21 which corresponds to Matthew's fourth Beatitude (5. 6) refers to those who are literally hungry: in their rather desperate state they will be blessed by God and their hunger satisfied. In Luke (but not in Matthew) there is a corresponding 'woe' on the rich (6. 24). In Matthew, however, God's blessing is promised to a rather different group: to those who 'hunger and thirst *after righteousness*' (5. 6), that is, to disciples who are 'hungry' to do God's will.

In 5. 10 those who are 'persecuted for righteousness' sake' are promised that the kingdom of heaven is theirs. This saying (like 5. 20) contains so many of Matthew's favourite words that the evangelist may have created it himself. As in several other similar cases, Matthew develops themes already present in the sources he is using. The second half of 5. 10, 'for theirs is the kingdom of heaven', echoes 5. 3 (Q); the first half of 5. 10 underlines the importance of the Q Beatitude which follows in 5. 11, where disciples are encouraged in the face of persecution. Whereas Luke explains that the fierce opposition being experienced is 'on account of the Son of Man' (6. 22), in 5. 10 Matthew gives a different explanation: followers of Jesus are being pilloried on account of their righteous conduct. A few verses later a more positive note is struck: 'Let your light so shine before men, that they may see your good works and give glory to your Father in heaven' (5. 16). Here 'good works' seems to be synonymous with the 'righteousness', or 'righteous conduct' stressed so strongly in Matthew's Beatitudes.

2. *The law and the prophets: Matthew 5. 17-20*
Matt 5. 17 is often taken as the preface to the central section of the Sermon which runs from 5. 17 to 7. 12. But what is meant by, 'Think not that I have come to abolish the law and the prophets; I have not come to abolish them but to fulfil them' (5. 17)? In the evangelist's day some Jewish opponents may well have claimed that followers of Jesus had abandoned the law completely; in 5. 17 words of Jesus may have been shaped as a response: Jesus did *not*, as some were claiming, come to destroy the law and the prophets.

But what is meant by 'fulfilling' them? From Matthew's perspective, does Jesus set forth the real intention of the law? Or does he confirm or establish the law? The latter suggestion is often supported by linguistic arguments based either on the force of the Aramaic word which Jesus may have used, or by an appeal to 5. 18 and 19. These two verses seem to underline the continuing importance of the law: 'not a letter, not a dot will disappear from the law' (5. 18b [REB]).

However, this strong emphasis on the law may be modified in the last phrase of 5. 18, 'until all things come to pass'. 'The law remains valid only *until all things come to pass* in Jesus' coming and ministry.' (R.A. Guelich, *Sermon*, 148) If this is the correct interpretation of 5. 18, the warning in 5. 19 not to relax 'one of the least of these commandments' may refer to the sayings of Jesus, rather than (as in the more usual interpretation) the law. If, however, 5. 19 does refer to strict and complete retention of the law (without a hint of modification), then this verse must been seen as a very 'conservative' saying which is somewhat out of character with 5. 17, 18, and 20, and with Matthew's emphases elsewhere. In 5. 20 disciples of Jesus are urged to carry out the will of God in their ethical conduct to an even greater degree than the scribes and Pharisees.

3. The Antitheses: Matthew 5. 21-48

In 5. 21-48 six paragraphs of sayings of Jesus all have the same structure: 'You have heard that it was said (by God) to the men of old (i.e. in Scripture). . . but I say to you. . .' . The full formula just quoted introduces the first and fourth paragraphs and thus divides the six into two groups of three; in the other paragraphs the formula is abbreviated. Although three of the six paragraphs have partial parallels in Luke and belonged originally to Q (5. 21-22, 27-28, 33-37), Matthew himself has added the other three groups of sayings which he has drawn from oral tradition.

The phrase, 'but I say to you', occurs in all six passages and *seems* to set sayings of Jesus in opposition to Scripture; hence 5. 21-48 is usually referred to as the 'antitheses'. Matthew is responsible for the striking 'antithetical' structure of all six passages. But as is frequently the case elsewhere, the evangelist develops considerably an earlier tradition: the 'antithetical' structure is already found in embryonic form in Luke 6. 27a (Q), 'but I say to you who hear. . .'.

The term 'antitheses' is something of a misnomer, for it can hardly be claimed that in all six paragraphs the teaching of Jesus is intended to be in direct contrast to, or opposition to, (i.e. is 'antithetical' to) the law of Moses. Matthew has ruled out that possibility in 5. 17 by stressing that Jesus has not come to destroy the law and the prophets. In addition, the six uses of the passive verb 'it was said' almost certainly imply 'it was said *by God* in Scripture'; Jesus could hardly ᵫe understood to be contradicting what God had said. Although it has sometimes been claimed that in at least some of these passages Jesus is contrasting his own teaching with Jewish interpretations of the law current in his own day, rather than the law itself, this explanation is unconvincing. 5. 17-20, which is clearly intended to be an introduction to the an-

301

titheses, prepares the reader for discussion of the relationship of the teaching of Jesus to the law, and not merely for learned scribal discussion about the *intepretation* of the law.

So what is the primary thrust of the antitheses? Is there a consistent theme, or do these six paragraphs point in two (or more) directions? Many scholars have claimed that in some cases Jesus seems to strengthen the teaching of the law (5. 22, 28, 34); in others, he seems to overturn the teaching of Moses (5. 39, 44 and perhaps 32). Given that 5. 21-48 is no mere anthology of sayings of Jesus, but has been very carefully constructed by the evangelist himself, we should expect a consistent pattern unless the text forces us to conclude otherwise.

On the one hand, the antithetical pattern implies that Jesus is not simply confirming the teaching of the law which is quoted. On the other hand, as we have seen, Matthew does not set out sayings of Jesus as a contradiction of God-given Scripture. So how are the antitheses to be understood? Davies and Allison (I, 509f.) correctly suggest that their primary function is twofold: 'to show through six concrete examples, (i) what sort of attitude and behaviour Jesus requires and (ii) how his demands surpass those of the Torah without contradicting the Torah. . . The letter of the law does not give life. All things lawful may not be helpful. One may refrain from murder and still hate, refrain from committing adultery and still lust in the heart, and it is possible to follow the OT's provisions with regard to divorce and oaths and yet be found in sin. . . . Purely legal norms, such as those cited in Matt 5. 21, 27, 31, 33, 38, and 43, can never convey how life is to be lived by those who are genuinely poor in spirit, pure in heart, and full of mercy (5. 3, 7, 8).'

Matt 5. 20 and 48, which act as a 'frame' for the six antitheses in 5. 21-47, confirm that this is the evangelist's intention. (5. 48, like 7. 12, opens with οὖν, 'so', 'therefore'; both verses are intended to act as a summary and conclusion to the preceding block.) 5. 20 insists that the righteousness which followers of Jesus are carry out must exceed that of the scribes and Pharisees; that righteousness is not to be construed as obedience to legislation, but as perfect conformity to God's will (5. 48).

The same fundamental point is illustrated further with three carefully constructed examples in Matt 6. 1-18. In each case the same pattern recurs: 'when you give alms (pray, fast), do not do it as the hypocrites do, but when you give alms (fast, pray), do it in secret, and your Father who sees in secret will reward you. The 'greater righteousness' of 5. 20 is once again purity of motive, rather than mere outward observance.

4. *The Golden Rule: Matthew 7. 12*
'Whatever you wish that men would do to you, do so to them' has been known as the Golden Rule since the eighteenth century. There are numerous parallels to this saying in Graeco-Roman, oriental, and Jewish writings. There is a particularly close rabbinic tradition in *b.Sabb.* 31a: 'What is hateful to you, do not do to your fellow creatures.' Although a negative formulation along these lines is much more common than the positive formulation of Matt 7. 12, the latter is found in some Jewish writings (*Ep Arist* 207; *T Naph* 1; *2 Enoch* 61. 1); hence it is a mistake to claim that the positive form of the Golden Rule is distinctively Christian.

Matt 7. 12 opens with οὖν, 'so', 'therefore'. This word has often been ignored by translators (e.g. NIV; REB). If οὖν is translated, the saying is often placed (as in the RSV) as the conclusion of the preceding block of sayings on 'asking, seeking, finding' (7. 8-11). This is equally mistaken, for 7. 12 does not round off these sayings. Matthew intends οὖν to indicate to the reader that 7. 12 is a summary of and a conclusion to *all* the material in the central section of the Sermon which starts at 5. 17. The evangelist has removed the Golden Rule from the conclusion of the 'Love your enemies' sayings in Luke (and Q) 6. 27-30, and given it an even more important role. This is confirmed by the dramatic words, 'for this is the law and the prophets' which Matthew adds to the Golden Rule. This additional phrase recalls 5. 17 in which the coming of Jesus is the fulfilment of the law and the prophets.

Matthew makes the same point in the explanatory addition which he makes to Mark 12. 28-34, the teaching of Jesus on the two greatest commandments, 'love God, and love your neighbour as yourself'. In Matt 22. 40 the evangelist adds, 'On these two commandments depend all the law and the prophets'. Hence for Matthew the Golden Rule and the 'love commandments' express the very essence of Scripture. These sayings of Jesus (and his whole coming) are a lens through which his followers now read the law and the prophets.

5. *The Epilogue: Two ways: Matthew 7. 13-27*
The epilogue of the Sermon contains a series of contrasts. It opens with the contrast between the gate and the way which lead to destruction and the gate and the way which lead to life (Matt 7. 13-14). A similar contrast between 'two ways' is found in Deut 11. 26; 30. 15; Jer. 21. 8, and in numerous Jewish and early Christian writings.

Matthew continues the general theme in the warnings about false prophets. 'Good fruit' and 'evil fruit' are contrasted (7. 15-20), as are those who do the will of the Father and those who do not (7. 21-3). In both cases there is a clear warning about a 'way that leads to destruction'.

Both Matthew and Luke conclude their Sermons, as did Q, with the parable of the two houses. The general point of the parable is the same in both versions: a sharp contrast is drawn between those who hear and obey the words of Jesus and those who do not. U. Luz notes that the books of Leviticus (ch. 26) and Deuteronomy (30. 15-20), and also several later Jewish writings, end similarly: two alternatives are placed squarely before the reader. Whereas similar Jewish traditions focus on study and practice of the law, hearing and obeying the words of Jesus are central here. Matthew uses eschatological parables as the climax of two of his other discourses, 18. 23-35 and 25. 31-46; in both 'two ways' are once again contrasted.

The wording of the parables in Matthew and in Luke differs considerably. The evangelists have probably drawn on different versions of the Q parable. Luke's version emphasizes the care taken to dig deeply in order to place the foundations of the house on rock; a river which bursts its banks is unable to dislodge it.

Matthew's version is much more carefully structured and rhythmical. The threefold description of the storm is memorable: the rain came down, the floods rose, and the winds beat upon that house . . . (vv. 25 and 27). Matthew adds (or perhaps retains from Q) two references to the last judgement (vv. 24 and 26) which are not present in Luke. The words of Jesus are referred to in a rather general way in Luke (6. 47), but by adding 'these' to 'my words' twice over (5. 24 and 26), Matthew refers specifically to the words of Jesus in the Sermon on the Mount (cf. 28. 20a).

For Matthew, the Sermon is but one part of his attempt to set out the significance of the story and teaching of Jesus for the life of his own communities. The Sermon is the largest and most impressive of his five discourses, but it must not be separated from the rest of the gospel.

Some of the themes Matthew emphasizes in the first of his five discourses are also prominent elsewhere in the gospel. For example, in 5. 20, one of the key verses which Matthew himself has almost certainly composed, disciples are told that their ethical conduct must exceed that of the scribes and Pharisees; in 5. 48, a related verse, they are told to be perfect or whole-hearted. In 6. 1-18 their conduct is contrasted starkly with that of the 'hypocrites' (6. 2, 5, 16) whom the reader naturally assumes to be none other than the scribes and Pharisees of 5. 20.

These same points are developed in chapter 23. The crowds and disciples are urged not to follow the example of the scribes and Pharisees (23. 2-3) who are then referred to explicitly as 'hypocrites' six times. There is even some verbal correspondence between 6. 1, 5 and 16 on the one hand, and 23. 5 and 28 on the other. Both in chapters 5 and 6 of the Sermon, and in chapter 23 the evangelist uses the scribes and Pharisees as a foil: disciples of Jesus are called to 'superior' ethical conduct.

In the verses which immediately precede the Sermon, Matthew provides the interpreter with an important theological clue. Jesus announces the 'good news of the kingdom' (4. 17, 23) and calls Peter, Andrew, James and John into radical discipleship which involves renunciation of their occupation and of their family ties (4. 18-22). As in the Sermon which follows, and as in Matthew's gospel as a whole, grace and demand are linked inextricably. The Jesus of Matthew's Sermon is the Son of God (3. 17, the baptism of Jesus, and 4. 1-11, the temptations) through whom God is acting for humankind: it is his demanding teaching which is to be central in the life of the community and in its discipling of the nations (28. 20).

In the past the Sermon has often been removed from its present setting in Matthew and treated as a convenient summary of the teaching of Jesus. By reading the Sermon as part of Matthew's gospel we are able to see how the evangelist intended his first readers to approach these chapters. But this important principle of interpretation does not resolve all the difficulties. Many verses in the Sermon still puzzle us. Can any man claim to have avoided committing adultery 'in his heart' by not looking on a woman with a lustful eye (Matt 5. 28)? What are the pearls which are not to be thrown to the pigs (Matt 7. 6)? Difficult parts of the Bible often provoke us to think about issues we might otherwise have avoided.

It is a mistake to suppose that we cannot understand the Sermon without the assistance of an expert. We do not need to be musicians to be profoundly moved by a piece of music; nor do we need to be art historians in order to appreciate a work of art. At the very heart of the Sermon we find one of the most radical and demanding of the sayings of Jesus, a saying which sums up the ethos of the Sermon as a whole and is as relevant today as it was in the first century. 'You have learned (from Scripture), "Love your neighbour, hate your enemy." But what I tell you is this: Love your enemies and pray for your persecutors." (Matt 5. 43-4).'

Chapter Thirteen

The Origin and Purpose of the Sermon on the Mount

The Sermon on the Mount has often been studied and expounded in isolation from the rest of Matthew's gospel. This practice, which can be traced right back to Augustine and Chrysostom, was popular in the sixteenth century. In modern times numerous studies of the Sermon and several detailed commentaries have been published.[1] But in nearly every case the Sermon has been treated as a separate entity simply for convenience; there has been no suggestion that these chapters have a quite distinctive origin or purpose which sets them apart from the rest of Matthew's gospel and from Mark and Luke.

There are, however, two notable exceptions. In his widely acclaimed book, *The Setting of the Sermon on the Mount*, Cambridge 1964, W.D. Davies suggests that 'one fruitful way of dealing with the Sermon on the Mount is to regard it as the Christian answer to Jamnia. Using terms very loosely, the Sermon is a kind of Christian, mishnaic counter-part to the formulation taking place there.' (315)

This hypothesis has often been referred to, but rarely examined in detail. As support, W.D. Davies sets out at length a cumulative case which rests on a large number of observations; he himself recognizes that some of his points

---

[1] For the history of the interpretation of the Sermon, see W.S. Kissinger, *The Sermon on the Mount: a History of Interpretation and Bibliography*, Metuchen 1975; U. Berner, *Die Bergpredigt: Rezeption und Auslegung im 20 Jahrhundert*, Göttingen 1979. For recent literature on the Sermon on the Mount, see the Bibliography on pp. 397-9.

are stronger than others. Davies appeals both to the Sermon and to other parts of Matthew's gospel. Some of the latter passages are undoubtedly significant. For example, Davies is able to show that the evangelist's community was at odds with contemporary Judaism. The evidence from the Sermon itself, however, is not compelling. None of the direct links proposed between the Sermon and the reconstruction taking place within Judaism during the Jamnian period is entirely satisfactory.[1] It is the whole of Matthew, not the Sermon in isolation, which can plausibly be related (though only indirectly) to the Jamnian period. Although Davies suggests that 'there was an outside stimulus for the Evangelist to shape the Sermon' (p. 315), he does not claim that Matt 5–7

---

[1] Davies suggests two possible links between the Sermon and Jamnia. (i) Matthew presents the teaching of Jesus 'in a roughly parallel triadic way' to Johannan ben Zakkai's re-interpretation at the time of Jamnia of the 'three traditional pillars' attributed to Simeon the Just in *Aboth* 1. 2. In a discussion with the Emperor Vespasian, Johannan asks permission to go to Jamnia 'in order to teach his disciples, establish a prayer house and perform all the commandments.' (*Aboth de Rabbi Nathan*, quoted by Davies on p. 306 from J. Goldin's edition). Davies claims that Matthew 'confronts the synagogue with a triadic formulation which would not be alien to it'. (307) Matt 5. 17-48 sets forth the Torah of Jesus; 6. 1-18 the true '*bwdh* or worship; and in 6. 19 – 7. 12 we have what corresponds to 'performance of all the commandments.'
But why are the opening and closing sections of the Sermon not part of Matthew's triadic formulation? In addition, Johannan's alleged re-interpretation of the three pillars cannot be linked with any confidence to the Jamnian period. The dialogue in *Aboth de Rabbi Nathan* between Johannan and Vespasian looks like a much later idealising both of Jamnia and of Rabbi Johannan ben Zakkai. Josephus (*BJ* VII. 216f.) tells us that following Masada Vespasian held on to Jewish land as his own private property, leasing it out. Hence it is hardly likely that Vespasian would have said to Johannan (as in *Aboth de Rabbi Nathan*) 'Tell me, what may I give thee?' To which Johannan replied, 'I ask naught of thee, save Jamnia. . .'
(ii) Davies suggests that Matthew's re-interpretation of the Lord's Prayer may have been carried out as a counterpart to the main prayer of the synagogue, the *Shemoneh Esreh*, which was being formulated anew at Jamnia (310). This seems unlikely. Matthew's expansions of the original shorter version (as in Luke 11. 2-4) can all be explained quite simply as Matthean explanatory or interpretative additions.

contains theological emphases which are quite distinct from the rest of the gospel. Davies seems to accept that the Sermon and the rest of Matthew come from the same *Sitz im Leben*, though he does not discuss this point.

In a set of essays published between 1975 and 1984 H.D. Betz has proposed a much bolder explanation of the origin and purpose of the Sermon on the Mount. Betz claims that the Sermon and the rest of Matthew contain different theologies, and that they do not come from the same *Sitz im Leben*. These essays have now been published in one volume, *Essays on the Sermon on the Mount*, Philadelphia 1985; some have been translated from German into English for the first time. The reader is promised that further support for the author's novel proposals will appear in his forthcoming commentary on the Sermon in the *Hermeneia* series. But since Betz hopes that his essays will stimulate discussion before his commentary appears, it seems appropriate to consider his hypothesis now. Betz's views raise in an acute form an issue which has nearly always been prominent in modern discussion of the Sermon, the relationship between 'tradition' and 'interpretation', the theme of the volume in honour of E. Earle Ellis in which this chapter was first published.

In the first part of this chapter I shall discuss Betz's hypothesis that the whole of the Sermon is to be seen as pre-Matthean tradition which has been incorporated without modification by the evangelist and so (presumably) re-interpreted only minimally. I shall then set out some of the reasons why I am convinced that in the Sermon the evangelist Matthew has shaped and re-interpreted the traditions at his disposal in ways which are completely consistent with the methods and themes developed elsewhere in his gospel. It is a great delight to offer this small piece in honour of Earle Ellis, whose scholarship and friendship I have valued for many years, and whose writings on the relationship between tradition and interpretation in Luke have influenced considerably my own understanding and appreciation of the achievement of the synoptic evangelists.

A pre-Matthean epitome?

On Betz's hypothesis, which either challenges or ignores almost all other current scholarly work on the Sermon, Matt 5–7 is a pre-Matthean source composed by a redactor of sayings of Jesus in the mid-50s. It derives from a Jewish Christian community which had a strained relationship with its mother faith, Judaism, but which was still very much part of the diverse Judaism of the period. The source has been transmitted intact.

Betz believes that Matt 5–7 contains a theology that is independent of the rest of Matthew's gospel and different at characteristic points. There is a corollary of some theological importance: the Christian community from which the Sermon stems is distinct but not entirely separate from Judaism, but it has only a minimal Christology and no doctrine of the Cross and Resurrection. Although Betz has not yet set out in full his reasons for accepting that the Sermon contains a different theology from Matthew's gospel, his case seems to rest primarily on three pillars: hostility in the Sermon to the Gentile mission – those who do support it are 'wolves in sheep's clothing' (Matt 7. 15, p. 21); a distinctive eschatology in 7. 21-23; and a minimal Christology. We shall return to these points below.

Perhaps the most intriguing part of Betz's theory is the claim that the literary genre of Matt 5–7 is that of an epitome which presents the theology of Jesus in a systematic fashion. In its form as an epitome the Sermon is 'a kind of systematic theology' (p. 39). In the opening essay of the collection Betz explores the epitome genre in some detail and suggests that the Sermon is related in literary form to Epictetus's *Encheiridion*, a philosphical epitome which dates from the middle of the second century. Since this is clearly too late to be of relevance for consideration of the genre of the Sermon, Betz appeals primarily to what he claims is 'the greatest and most famous example of the epitome in antiquity', and the specific prototype of the *Encheiridion*, Epicurus's *Kyriai Doxai* (p. 11). Betz freely acknowledges that Epicurus himself does not use the term epitome (p. 11).

Few New Testament scholars have done more than Betz to draw attention to the importance of literary genre, but I am not persuaded that Matt 5–7 is analogous in form to the epitomes of the Graeco-Roman rhetorical tradition. In order to elucidate the genre of the Sermon, Betz appeals to the *Kyriai Doxai* which includes forty sententiae or groupings of sententiae taken from the larger works of Epicurus. But there are substantial differences in form between the *Kyriai Doxai* and Matt 5–7. (a) Whereas the *Kyriai Doxai* is a synopsis of the whole of Epicurus's philosophical system, the Sermon includes only part of the teaching of Jesus – the ethical teaching. (b) There are a number of verses in the Sermon, especially in the Antitheses, 5. 21-48, which hardly qualify for inclusion in a concise synopsis on the basis of their 'primary importance'; they seem to have been included in their present context as illustrations (e.g. 5. 39b-42), or as the result either of a catchword connection or of broadly similar content. (c) Whereas the *Kyriai Doxai* probably contains no literary structure at all, the Sermon on the Mount has been carefully composed. Sayings of Jesus have been grouped acccrding to both form and content; in several parts of the Sermon there is a clear structure.[1]

In my view, Betz's claim that the genre of the Sermon is analogous with the philosophical epitome is much less plausible than his proposal that Galatians is an apologetic letter in the Graeco-Roman rhetorical tradition. This hypothesis concerning the genre of Galatians is still the subject of keen scholarly discussion and is likely to stimulate further research for some time to come.[2]

A further strand of Betz's theory is equally intriguing. The Sermon is seen as a pre-Matthean epitome which is critical of the Gentile Christianity known above all from the letters of

[1] On the structure of the Sermon, see R. Riesner, 'Der Aufbau der Reden im Matthäus-Evangelium,' *ThB* 9 (1978) 172- 82; G. Bornkamm, 'Der Aufbau der Bergpredigt', *NTS* 24, (1977-78) 419-432; U. Luz, *Matthäus* I, 185-87.

[2] See, for example, D.E. Aune's review of H.D. Betz, *Galatians. A Commentary on Paul's Letter to the Churches in Galatia*, Philadelphia 1979, in *RSR* 7 (1981) 310-28; G. Kennedy, *New Testament Interpretation Through Rhetorical Criticism*, Chapel Hill 1984, 144-52.

Paul and the gospels. In particular, Matt 5. 17 and 7. 15-23 are
said to contain anti-Pauline polemic. Tucked away in a footnote is the suggestion that in turning away from the Pauline
gospel the Galatians may have been responding to warnings
such as those in Matt 7. 15-23 (p. 156 n. 124). Betz revives the
theory originally proposed by J. Weiss that Matt 5. 19 refers to
Paul. The 'insignificant person' (ἐλάχιστος) who 'relaxes one
of the least of the commandments of the Torah' is none
other than Paul, 'the least of the apostles' (ὁ ἐλάχιστος τῶν
ἀποστόλων) (1 Cor 15. 9).

How strong is this claim that the Sermon contains anti-
Pauline polemic'? Betz believes that Matt 5. 17 is directed
against Pauline law-free Gentile Christians (p. 20). But surely
the phrase μὴ νομίσητε is to be interpreted as a rejection of a
theoretical possibility. The identical phrase recurs in 10. 34
where it is a redactional addition from the hand of the
evangelist. 'Do not think that I have come to bring peace on
earth. . .' In this verse, who is assumed to be thinking along
these lines? Surely there is no specific group which is being
opposed. Hence it is unlikely that 5. 17 is directly polemical.

The suggestion that Matt 5. 19 refers to Paul and that 7. 24
with its reference to 'building on a rock' alludes to Peter will
seem plausible only if there are other strong grounds for
accepting anti-Pauline polemic in the Sermon. The references to 'false prophets' in 7. 15 and to those who say 'Lord,
Lord' and do not do the will of the Father, 7. 21-23, have often
been linked with Pauline groups or at least with antinomians
in general; in these verses there might seem at first sight to
be grounds for accepting Betz's proposal.

But in 7. 15-20 the 'false prophets' are not described in very
precise terms. Even if they are to be linked (as they often are,
but not by Betz) with the false prophets of the end-time at 24.
11, the comments are very general indeed. As G. Strecker has
noted, similar indefinite warnings against false prophecy of
the end-time are found in other early Christian writings.[1]

Matt 7. 21-23 seems to be more specific. Here the Sermon
refers to 'many' who appeal to their charismata, to prophecy

[1] G. Strecker, *Der Weg*, 276.

and to working of miracles. But these verses are not attacking Pauline Christians of any kind. Pauline Christians might have been expected to appeal to πίστις (or even conceivably to γνῶσις) as the basis of their libertinism. Scholars have jumped too quickly from the reference to ἀνομία at 7. 23 to the view that antinomians are being attacked in this passage; ἀνομία is to be taken as a general reference to disobedience to 'the will of the Father'. As David Hill has insisted, the condemned charismatics are neither heretics nor antinomians.[1]

In addition to these exegetical observations, there is a more general reason why Betz's theory that Matt 5–7 derives from a Jewish Christian anti-Pauline community in the mid-50s is implausible. He accepts that the community from which the Sermon comes is suffering persecution from 'official' Judaism and notes that 5. 11-12 indicates that the community is prepared to take the consequences of the teaching of Jesus, even if it means their lives (p. 21). But why, on this view, would so-called official Judaism want to persecute vigorously the community from which the Sermon on the Mount has come?

Betz suggests that its understanding of Torah would have seemed to Paul to involve little more than an abridgement of the law (p. 35). Its soteriology 'is none other than that of the Jewish Torah'. (p. 92) Its ethical teaching is at home in the context of Jewish piety and theology (p. 123). Christology is largely lacking in the Sermon. It does not include any universalist teaching. 'That Jesus was awaited as eschatological defender and intercessor for his followers fits well in the context of contemporary Judaism.' (p. 92) In short, according to the author, the community of the Sermon has not differentiated itself sharply from Judaism, but it is opposed to Pauline Christianity. Admittedly in several essays in the collection Betz does draw attention to teaching in the Matt 5–7 which is 'striking' in terms of contemporary Judaism.[2] But I still find myself bound to ask, 'What was so

---

[1] D. Hill, 'False Prophets and Charismatics: Structure and Interpretation in Matthew 7. 15-23', *Biblica* 57 (1976) 340.

[2] See, for example, Betz, *Essays*, 21, 34-35, 68-69, 123.

313

deeply offensive about this conservative Jewish Christian anti-Pauline community that it attracted persecution?'

A community strongly antagonistic to Paul would seem to me – at least in the mid-50s – to be sufficiently close to Judaism to be unconcerned even about threats of persecution. But since the community of the Sermon on the Mount clearly had experienced persecution (5. 10-12), the corollary would seem to be that it cannot have been as anti-Pauline as Betz supposes.

On the widely accepted view of the origin of Matt 5–7 (which I share) these difficulties do not arise. Matt 5. 10 comes from the hand of the evangelist. This verse strengthens and extends the references in Q to persecution which are used in 5. 11-12, and it reflects the later persecution experienced by Matthew's community which had differentiated itself from Judaism.[1] Matthew's gospel as a whole is neither anti-Pauline, nor has it been strongly influenced by Paul's writings;[2] it is simply un-Pauline.

We have already seen that part of Betz's case depends closely on what is virtually an axiom for his hypothesis, the claim that Matt 5–7 is a pre-Matthean source which the evangelist has incorporated into his gospel. How could this claim be either verified or falsified? Two tests might be applied. First, if the vocabulary, phrases, syntax and literary form of parts and of the whole of the Sermon differ considerably from the rest of Matthew's gospel, then there would be a good case for accepting that the Sermon is an independent pre-Matthean source. And secondly, if the teaching of the Sermon and the setting it presupposes both differ from the rest of the gospel, then we may well suspect that the evangelist has integrated intact a source which derives from a very different *Sitz im Leben*. I shall now discuss these two possibilities briefly.

A detailed comparison of the vocabulary and style of the Sermon on the Mount and the rest of the gospel would be a considerable undertaking. Betz does not in fact appeal to any

---

[1] See further 124-31.
[2] *Pace* M.D. Goulder, *Midrash and Lection*, 53-70.

arguments along these lines. It would not be difficult to compile a list of Matthean words and phrases which are not found in Matt 5–7, but such a list would be of little significance. The absence from the Sermon of what are usually taken to be 'Mattheanisms' may well have more to do with the content of these three chapters than with the presence of a pre-Matthean source. On the other hand, if a number of distinctively Matthean words and phrases from the rest of the gospel are also prominent in the Sermon, then the theory that a source has been integrated intact as chapters 5–7 would seem to be called in question.

At least the following fall into that category. (i) ἀνομία: this word is found four times in Matthew, once in the Sermon at 7.23; probably all four are redactional. ἀνομία is not found in Mark or Luke. (ii) βασιλεία τῶν οὐρανῶν: this phrase is found thirty three times in Matthew, in many cases redactionally; it is used seven times in the Sermon, probably all of which are redactional. The phrase is not found in Mark or Luke. (iii) δικαιοσύνη is used seven times in Matthew, probably all seven are redactional; five occur in the Sermon. δικαιοσύνη is not found in Mark; it is used only once in Luke. (iv) διώκω is found six times in Matthew, four of which are in the Sermon – and all four are redactional, as also in Matt 10. 23; this verb is not found in Mark, and there are only three examples in Luke. (v) θέλημα is used six times in Matthew, twice (redactionally) in the Sermon; of the other four examples, two or three are redactional. θέλημα is used once in Mark, four times in Luke. (vi) νόμος καὶ προφῆται: this phrase is used four times in Matthew, three of which are redactional; it is used twice redactionally in the Sermon. (vii) πατὴρ (+ σου, ἡμῶν or ὑμῶν) with either ἐν (τοῖς) οὐρανοῖς or ὁ οὐράνιος. The phrase is found twenty nine times in Matthew, twelve of which are in the Sermon; many of the twenty nine are redactional. There are only two examples in Mark and four in Luke. (viii) πορνεία is used in Matt 5. 32 and 19. 9; both are redactional as the so-called 'exception' in the context of teaching on divorce. The word is used in a very different context at Matt 15. 19 = Mark 7. 21, but is not found elsewhere in Mark or Luke. (9) τέλειος is used in Matt 5. 48

and 19. 21, both of which are redactional; it is not found in Mark or Luke.

Most of these examples are striking; some reflect Matthean theological themes which are found in the Sermon and also in the rest of the gospel. So has Betz's case collapsed? It is certainly teetering, but perhaps it has not yet fallen, since it is just conceivable that these words and phrases occurred in the pre-Matthean source and were then developed by the evangelist himself in other parts of his gospel.

This possibility has to be conceded since the evangelist does frequently take a word or phrase which is found just occasionally in one of his sources (especially Mark) and use it very much more often himself. Two important examples are worth noting. (i) The phrase συναγωγαὶ αὐτῶν occurs redactionally five times (Matt 4. 23; 9. 35; 10. 17; 12. 9; 13. 54) and is often taken as an indication that the evangelist's community is no longer part of Judaism. But the phrase does also occur at Mark 1. 23 and 39 and at Luke 4. 15. Matthew seems to have developed considerably a phrase found already in Mark.[1] (ii) Matthew's tenfold use of a 'fulfilment formula' to introduce quotations from the prophets as theological comments on his story is well known as one of the most distinctive features of his gospel. But the evangelist's 'formula' is a development and extension of Mark 14. 49c, ἀλλ᾽ ἵνα πληρωθῶσιν αἱ γραφαί, as his redaction of this clause at 26. 54, 56 confirms.[2]

Are there clear differences in teaching between the Sermon and the rest of the gospel? Betz claims that there are (p. 18); he sets out two observations briefly, a third more fully.

(a) Unlike the rest of the gospel, the Sermon is opposed to Gentile Christianity because these chapters are anti-Pauline (p. x and p. 90). But as we have seen, there are insufficient grounds for concluding that Paul or Pauline Christians are attacked in these chapters.

---

[1] G.D. Kilpatrick claims (*Origins*, 110) that the αὐτῶν in Mark 1. 23 and 39; Luke 4. 15 should be omitted as later textual assimilation to Matthew. But the textual evidence he cites for the omissions is slight.

[2] See Chapter 15 of this book for details.

(b) Since the Sermon contains a minimal Christology and no sign of a Cross-Resurrection theology, the soteriology of this source differs considerably from the evangelist's (pp. 92 and 152-53). But this observation is valid only if we accept as an axiom that Matt 5–7 has been taken intact from a pre-Matthean source. If removed from the context of the whole gospel, many other sections of Matthew contain little Christology and no sign of a Cross-Resurrection theology.

(c) Betz claims that the distinctive eschatology of 7. 21-23 offers strong support for his hypothesis concerning the origin of the Sermon. Betz insists that in this passage Jesus is portrayed as advocate, and not, as elsewhere in Matthew (16. 27; 19. 28; 24. 30-31; 25. 31) as 'Son of Man-judge' (p. 147). This exegesis of 7. 21-23 runs counter to the almost universally accepted view that in this passage Jesus is the judge. As Betz himself notes, 7. 22-23 depicts in briefest scope proceedings at the last judgment (p. 127). Verses 21-23 are set out so tersely that it is not easy to decide whether Jesus is assumed to be advocate or judge.

But even if we allow that Betz's exegesis is just possible, there are difficulties with his view. He has to claim that Luke 6. 46 is not the source for Matt 7. 21-23; if it were, these verses could be seen more readily as a Matthean development of a Q tradition rather than as part of a pre-Matthean source which comprised the whole of the Sermon on the Mount. But there is such a concentration of Matthean vocabulary in 7. 21-23 that it is difficult to avoid the conclusion that the evangelist has developed considerably a Q logion. We noted above the following as Matthean words and phrases: βασιλεία τῶν οὐρανῶν, θέλημα, πατὴρ ἐν τοῖς οὐρανοῖς; to this list we may add πᾶς (often used redactionally) and the threefold pattern in v 22.

Betz refers to Matt 10. 32-33 as a parallel passage in which Jesus appears as 'advocate and witness for his own followers' (pp. 142-43). He recognizes that the case for seeing 7. 21-23 as un-Matthean and therefore part of a pre-Matthean Sermon is weakened if there is an important un-Matthean parallel in the Q tradition in 10. 32-33. So he boldly suggests that Matt 10. 1-42 is also a source which Matthew has taken up into his gospel! The mission discourse is 'a work that resembles the pre-Matthean Sermon in many respects' (p. 142). But if the Sermon on the Mount and the mission discourse are both pre-Matthean, are the discourses in 13, 18, (23) 24-25 also pre-Matthean? What has happened to the Q hypothesis? It is easy to pour scorn on some of the arguments which have been used in the past to support Q, but the hypothesis remains much more plausible than any of its rivals.

It is much more preferable to see Matt 7. 21-23 and 10. 32-33 as Matthean developments of Q traditions. The evangelist would not have been concerned about an apparent contradiction in viewing Jesus in some eschatological scenes as advocate and in some as judge; logical rigour was not the hallmark of the Jewish apocalyptic tradition to which he was indebted.

Betz has been unable to show that the Sermon contains a distinctive un-Matthean theology. Although it must remain possible that some Q traditions were expanded and perhaps combined with 'M' traditions before the evangelist Matthew composed these chapters, it is not easy to suppose that the Sermon as a whole is pre-Matthean. In Matt 5–7 the evangelist has woven together skilfully his sources into sections which have thematic and structural unity, just as he has done in his other four discourses.

An integral part of Matthew's gospel

The case for isolating the Sermon from the rest of Matthew's gospel is far from compelling. As we have seen, Matt 5–7 contains a large number of the evangelist's redactional words and phrases. But there are further reasons for insisting that neither the origin nor the purpose of the Sermon differs from the other discourses. In the paragraphs which follow we hope to show that in all the discourses the same methods of composition are used, many of the prominent themes of the Sermon are found, and the same *Sitz im Leben* is presupposed.

Most scholars accept that all five Matthean discourses have been constructed in precisely the same way. Attention has frequently been drawn to the evangelist's careful composition. As examples we may note two points which have rarely been given sufficient attention. (i) Ulrich Luz has recently shown that Matthew frequently indicates his themes through 'key' verses which are accentuated through their position. They relate to a larger context; they are not simply headings, but are placed at the beginning or conclusion of a section as generalizations which often function as 'transitional' verses. Luz lists as examples. 5. 17, 20, 48; 6. 1; 7. 12, 21; 10. 16, 26; 18. 10, 14.[1] To this list we may add 6. 33; 10. 34, 40. This technique is clearly particularly important and prominent in the Sermon, but it is also found in some of the other discourses.

(ii) Matthew not only re-interprets the sayings of Jesus found in his sources by rearrangement and modification; he often elucidates them with extra phrases or even (on occasion) whole verses which he himself has composed. The following may be noted as examples: 5. 10, 13a, 14a, 16; 6. 10b and c, 13b; 7. 12, 19, 20, 21; 10. 8, 24-25, 41; 18. 10a, 14, 35; 23. 28, 32-34. The evangelist expounds his sources creatively both in the Sermon and elsewhere in his gospel.[2]

Neither of these techniques is unique to Matthew; they can both be found elsewhere in the gospels and in other writings of the time. But they are especially characteristic of the evangelist and strongly suggest that the five discourses in his gospel have been composed by the same hand.

We turn now from the evangelist's methods to his theological themes. Several of the main concerns of the Sermon on the Mount are found in other parts of the gospel. The opening four chapters provide a rich theological preface to the Sermon. Some of the themes of Matt 5–7 are then developed more fully later in the gospel. In short, Matthew's gospel is a theological story; the five discourses may break up the flow of the narrative but the evangelist develops his

---

[1] See Luz, *Matthäus* I, 21.
[2] For details, see Chapter 14.

main story line both in narrative and in discourse.[1] It has sometimes been said that the fourth evangelist is his own best interpreter: the same can be said *mutatis mutandis* of Matthew.

The chapters which precede and follow the Sermon are profoundly Christological. But *pace* H.D. Betz, the Christology of the Sermon itself is not minimal. (a) 5. 11 presupposes that disciples will have been persecuted on account of their commitment to the person of Jesus (ἕνεκεν ἐμοῦ). The same theme recurs in 10. 17-18: disciples of Jesus will be dragged before governors and kings 'for my sake' (ἕνεκεν ἐμοῦ). (b) In 5. 17 Jesus claims that he himself fulfils Torah – a profound claim which is elucidated in the antitheses (5. 21-48) which follow. The evangelist extends this theme in his introductions to his 'formula' quotations of Scripture, all of which comment on the fulfilment of the prophets in the life of Jesus. (c) As we have seen, in 7. 21-23 Jesus is almost certainly portrayed as the eschatological judge, as he also is in 16. 27; 19. 28 and 25. 31-46. In short, the Christology of the Sermon is not unrelated to the rest of the gospel.

If Christology is Matthew's primary concern, discipleship (ecclesiology) is not far behind. The Sermon is clearly addressed to disciples. Peter, Andrew, James and John are called immediately before the opening of the Sermon. But both at the beginning and the end of the Sermon reference is made to the presence of crowds (οἱ ὄχλοι). Why are both disciples and crowds mentioned as the audience of the Sermon? Is this a 'loose end'? Are the crowds referred to in 7. 28 simply because Matthew has returned to his Marcan source at this point?

The 'dual' audience envisaged is quite deliberate. Similar reference to a 'dual' audience is made in two of the other discourses. The discourse in chapter 23 is also addressed to 'crowds and disciples'; in its continuation in chapters 24 and 25 Jesus speaks to the disciples in private. Similarly in chapter 13: the parable discourse is addressed to the crowds

---

[1] See J.D. Kingsbury, *Matthew as Story*. Kingsbury, however, does not discuss the Sermon on the Mount in detail.

and the disciples (13. 2, 10, 34), though part of it is addressed to disciples alone (13. 36-52).

In these three discourses the evangelist seems to hint that while all the teaching of Jesus in the five discourses is directed to his disciples, some parts are appropriate for a wider audience. This is confirmed in the closing verses of the gospel. The disciples are told by the Risen Lord to teach those who have been 'discipled' from the nations to keep all that Jesus has commanded (28. 18-20). Once again the Sermon is an integral part of the gospel.

In one of the 'key' verses in the Sermon, disciples are told that their ethical conduct must exceed that of the scribes and Pharisees (5. 20). In a related 'key' verse, 5. 48, disciples are told to be perfect or wholehearted (τέλειοι). In the verses which follow immediately in 6. 1-18, their conduct is contrasted starkly with that of the 'hypocrites' (6. 2, 5, 16) whom the reader naturally assumes to be none other than the scribes and Pharisees of 5. 20.

These same points are developed in chapter 23. The crowds and disciples are urged not to follow the example of the scribes and Pharisees (23. 2-3) who are then referred to explicitly as 'hypocrites' six times. There is even some verbal correspondence between 6. 1, 5 and 16 on the one hand, and 23. 5 and 28 on the other. Both in chapters 5 and 6 of the Sermon and in chapter 23 the evangelist uses the scribes and Pharisees as a foil: disciples are called to 'superior' ethical conduct.

In Matthew Christological and ecclesiological concerns are often interrelated. In 4. 15-16, immediately before the Sermon Matthew cites Isa 9. 1-2 in order to portray Jesus as the promised φῶς for Galilee of the Gentiles. At an important point in the structure of the Sermon, disciples are portrayed similarly: they are called to be φῶς τοῦ κόσμου (5. 14). This correspondence between Jesus and the disciples is all of a piece with the evangelist's insistence that the preaching and healing activity of the disciples is patterned closely on that of Jesus himself (10. 1, 7, 8).

Matt 5. 14 is part of a section in the Sermon where Matthew's universalist theme is present, a theme already set out in the genealogy,[1] in the coming of the magi, and in the reference to Galilee of the Gentiles at 4. 15. Disciples are called to be φῶς τοῦ κόσμου. In illustration of this, disciples are likened to a πόλις: the πόλις is not Jerusalem, for the article would then surely have been used.[2] The lamp in the further illustration which follows in 5. 15 gives light for all (πᾶσιν) in the house, a trait not present in the underlying Q logion.

The Sermon on the Mount and the other discourses presuppose the same *Sitz im Leben*. The evangelist's community still felt seriously threatened by Jewish opposition at the time the gospel was written: alongside 5. 10-12 we may set 10. 17-23 and 23. 34 and 37.[3] Immediately after the reference to opposition and persecution in 5. 11, disciples are warned that the persecution endured by the prophets of old is experienced anew by Christian prophets in the evangelist's own day. This point is made much more explicitly and vigorously in 23. 34, where once again the evangelist's own hand can be traced.

While 5. 11 does not name the opponents, by 5. 20 the reader is left in no doubt as to their identity. By insisting on a superior righteousness, the Matthean community is defining itself over against the scribes and Pharisees. It is characteristic of sectarian groups to call in question the integrity of the group from which they have separated. This is precisely what is happening in 5. 20, and also in 6. 1-18, where 'hypocrites' are referred to three times. The reader of 5. 20 knows full well that the 'hypocrites' of 6. 1-18 are the scribes and Pharisees whose religious practices are being gently mocked in order to establish the superiority of the religious practices of the Matthean community. This theme is, of course, extended considerably in chapter 23.

The references to persecution and the polemical passages in the Sermon and in the rest of Matthew reflect a Christian community coming to terms with the trauma of separation

---

[1] For a thorough discussion, see R.E. Brown, *The Birth of the Messiah*, Garden City 1977, 71-74.

[2] So U. Luz, *Matthäus*, I, 223, with reference to G. von Rad.

[3] See D.R.A. Hare, *Jewish Persecution*, 80-120.

from Judaism and with the perceived continuing threat of hostility and persecution. Matthew's denunciations of the scribes and Pharisees represent in part anger and frustration at the continuing rejection of Christian claims and at the continuing hostility of Jews towards the new community.[1] Both the Sermon and other passages in Matthew suggest that the evangelist and his readers were very much at odds, not only with contemporary Judaism, but also with the Gentile world. In the Sermon there are derogatory references to Gentiles in 5. 47; 6. 7 and 6. 32. In 10. 18 and 22 the disciples are told to expect hostility from Gentiles as well as Jews. And in 18. 7 and 17 there are two further negative references to the Gentile world 'outside' the Matthean community.[2]

We have seen that the Sermon and the rest of Matthew presuppose the same *Sitz im Leben*. We have also seen that a number of the evangelist's distinctive words, phrases and themes are found both in the Sermon and in the other parts of the gospel. Indeed, the evangelist has taken pains to link the Sermon closely to the rest of his gospel. Matt 5–7 is an important part of a major section which runs from 4. 23 to 9. 35. Chapters 5–7, which portray Jesus as 'Messiah of Word', are a diptych set opposite chapters 8 and 9, which portray Jesus as 'Messiah of Deed'. These five chapters are introduced and concluded by strikingly similar summaries, 4. 23-25 and 9. 35-36, which have been composed by the evangelist himself.

Although the Sermon is often singled out as the centre-piece of Matthew's gospel, or even as containing the 'essence of Christianity', for the evangelist it is only the first of five discourses to which he attaches equal importance. This is made clear at 26. 1, the verse which follows the final discourse. At the end of the earlier discourses (7. 28; 11. 1; 13. 53; 19. 1) there is a 'transitional' verse: 'when Jesus had

---

[1] For a fuller discussion, see Chapters 5 and 6.

[2] Here I am in agreement with Betz who notes that in the Sermon 'assimilation to pagan culture is sharply rejected throughout,' *Essays*, 93, and see also 19 n. 6. Betz also refers to Matt 5. 47; 6. 7 and 6. 32, but fails to note 10. 18 and 22; 18. 7 and 17 which reflect the same *Sitz im Leben* outside the Sermon.

finished these sayings. . .'. At 26. 1 the pattern recurs, but πάντας is added. Jesus has now finished all five discourses; the Passion drama unfolds.

The importance Matthew attaches to his five discourses is seen in two further ways. First: at 7. 21 we read, 'Not everyone who says to me 'Lord, lord,' will enter the kingdom of heaven, but he who does the will of my father in heaven'. In the underlying Q logion (Luke 6. 46) it is the words of Jesus which are to be obeyed; Matthew reshapes the logion by using one of his own favourite turns of phrase: 'the one who does the will of my Father in heaven'. For Matthew, the Q reference to 'carrying out the words of Jesus' can be paraphrased by 'doing the will of my Father.' For the evangelist the words of Jesus are that important.

And secondly, the five discourses are designed as a giant chiasm. The first discourse may be said to correspond to the last; they are both of similar length and much longer than the other discourses. Chapters 10 and 18 are related: chapter 10 instructs and encourages the community in mission, while chapter 18 considers the internal life of the community. Chapter 13 is central in every sense![1]

The Sermon is part and parcel of Matthew's gospel. The evangelist has drawn extensively on Q and other traditions, but he has reshaped and re-interpreted them considerably. Only when the Sermon is wrenched from its present context in Matthew can its theological concerns be contrasted with the evangelist's own. For Matthew the first of his five discourses is but one part of his attempt to set out the story and teaching of Jesus for the life of his own community. The interpreter of the Sermon who ignores the rest of Matthew's gospel misunderstands the evangelist's intentions and fails to do justice to the breadth of the evangelist's theological vision. In the Sermon and in the gospel as a whole, grace and demand are linked inextricably. For Matthew, the Jesus of the Sermon on the Mount is the Son of God through whom God

---

[1] See J.C. Fenton, 'Inclusio and Chiasmus in Matthew,' *Studia Evangelica* I, ed. F.L. Cross, Berlin 1959, 174-79; P. Gaechter, *Das Matthäus-Evangelium.*

is acting for mankind: it is his demanding teaching which is to be central in the life of the community and in its discipling of the nations.[1]

---

[1] H.D. Betz has published several essays on the Sermon on the Mount since this study was first printed in 1987. See the Bibliography, p. 398 for details.

Chapter Fourteen

Matthew as a Creative Interpreter
of the Sayings of Jesus

For many decades now the great literary and theological skill of Matthew has been recognized. The evangelist repeats key points several times; he abbreviates Mark's verbosity and improves his clumsy Greek style; he clarifies many of the Marcan theological enigmas – even if, in so doing, he creates a few new puzzles for his readers. He reshapes, rearranges and often conflates his two main sources, Mark and Q; he supplements them with additional material from a variety of sources (whether oral or written), and thereby creates a masterpiece of careful design. Even if there is still little scholarly agreement on some of the details of the distinctive themes of the evangelist, nearly four decades of redaction critical studies have shown that Matthew has placed his own stamp firmly on the traditions he uses.

In this chapter I shall discuss one particular phenomenon to which insufficient attention has been given: the points at which the evangelist himself has *expanded* the traditions of the words of Jesus to which he has had access.

Matthew is often seen as a revised and enlarged edition of Mark. This may well be an over-simplification, but the evangelist has been influenced very strongly indeed by Mark's narratives.[1] Equally important for the design of the

---

[1] In *Midrash and Lection* M.D. Goulder claims that apart from a very small number of oral traditions, Matthew depends on no source other than Mark; on his view Matthew has used midrashic techniques in order to expand Mark very considerably and to create the discourses.

gospel as a whole, and for our appreciation of the evangelist's intentions, however, is Matthew's presentation of the *sayings* of Jesus, only a relatively small proportion of which are taken from Mark. On any view the five grand Matthean discourses in chapters 5–7; 10; 13; 18; and 24–25 (with, perhaps, 23 as part of the fifth discourse) are most impressive. These discourses (and, to a lesser extent, several shorter collections of the sayings of Jesus) have a greater thematic unity and a more carefully worked out structure than any similar collections in Mark, Q or Luke.

Matthew has often been seen as an anthologist, an evangelist who has retained with relatively few modifications the sayings of Jesus he found in Mark and in Q and elsewhere. The evangelist's creativity is seen by most scholars to lie primarily in the *rearrangement* of the sayings of Jesus in his traditions. W.G. Kümmel, for example, claims that Matthew changes 'almost nothing in the sayings of Jesus he has taken over from Mark'.[1] Studies of the Q material often conclude that while the original order of the Q material is usually retained by Luke, it is Matthew who (on the whole) retains more carefully than Luke its original wording. D.E. Garland has recently insisted that

> Matthew's redaction of his material respected in most cases the formulation of an earlier time, but his rearrangement and his juxtaposition of independent units of tradition gave them a significance which they did not previously possess. The result reflects Matthew's theology and intention, for an insertion of traditional material into a different context overrides the original connotation of that material . . . He thus imposed his own message on traditional material by arranging it into a montage and creating a new context.[2]

While he has certainly exaggerated his case and has also failed to demolish the Q hypothesis, some of his observations on the extent to which Matthew has been influenced by Mark are valuable.

[1] *Introduction to the New Testament*, E.tr. London, 2nd ed. 1975, 107.

[2] *The Intention of Matthew 23*, Leiden 1979, 22f. Garland is referring primarily to the composition of ch. 23.

These observations are accurate – and similar comments have been made by other redaction critics – but they by-pass the phenomenon to which I wish to draw attention: Matthew's creativity lies not just in the modifications he makes to individual sayings and in his rearrangement of them into new contexts, but also in his own *expansion* of a number of sayings of Jesus. I hope to show that careful attention to this phenomenon sheds important light on the evangelist's methods and purposes.

In a study of the ways Matthew expands the sayings of Jesus, there is an obvious difficulty which must be faced immediately. How can we tell whether the expansion (or, to use a more neutral expression, the addition) comes from the evangelist's own hand or from tradition to which he had access? Redaction criticism can come to our aid at this point; with its help the evangelist's distinctive vocabulary and style can be detected fairly readily.[1]

I shall consider first of all what I take to be some examples of Matthean expansions of sayings of Jesus in Mark. If a fairly consistent pattern emerges, it will then be possible to turn to the Q material with greater confidence; finally, two passages in which the evangelist is dependent neither on Mark nor on Q, but on traditions not found elsewhere in the gospel (i.e., so-called 'M' traditions) will be examined.

Marcan traditions

1. *Matt 9. 13a, b (cf. Mark 2. 17) and Matt 12. 7 (cf. Mark 2. 26f.)*
In these two passages the wording of the quotation from Hosea 6. 6, ἔλεος θέλω καὶ οὐ θυσίαν and part of the introduction, τί ἐστιν, is identical. While the quotation is too short to determine whether it is more closely related to the LXX than

---

[1] Where there is general scholarly agreement that the logion or phrases under discussion come from Matthew himself, a detailed redaction critical analysis will not be undertaken here.

to the MT[1] (and thus more probably comes from the evangelist) the emphasis on mercy is found in several other passages in Matthew and is certainly typical of the evangelist.[2]

In Matt 9. 12 the reply of Jesus to the trenchant criticism levelled at him for eating with tax collectors and sinners is taken from Mark 2. 17. The comment added by Matthew in his next verse strengthens the reply of Jesus by appealing to Scripture: Jesus can associate freely with sinners because God is gracious and merciful.[3]

Matt 12. 1-8 is a more difficult pericope. While it is possible that verses 5-7 may all stem from the evangelist, verse 7 is almost certainly part of the evangelist's own addition to and interpretation of Mark 2. 23-28.[4] Matthew is stressing that God is merciful and that the Sabbath commandment should be considered in the light of his kindness. The Sabbath commandment is not abolished; it is subordinated to the kindness and mercy of God. In this way the conduct of the disciples is defended.[5]

This presentation in both passages of Jesus' attitude to the law and the use of the OT is quite consistent with Matthean teaching elsewhere. In both passages the evangelist himself creates 'new' words of Jesus as part of his elucidation and exposition of the Marcan pericopae. As in the other passages where the OT is quoted, Matthew is not reinterpreting Scripture in the light of Jesus, but rather citing Scripture in order to interpret the actions and teaching of Jesus.

---

[1] So, for example, K. Stendahl, *The School of Matthew*, 128, and W. Rothfuchs, *Die Erfüllungszitate des Matthäus-Evangeliums*, 25.

[2] See *Tradition*, 26 and 257.

[3] πορεύομαι is used 28 times in Matthew, but not at all in Mark. μανθάνω is used only here, at 11. 29 (in a phrase which I take to be a Matthean redactional addition - see below) and at 24. 32 (= Mark 13. 28, the only use in Mark).

[4] It is surely significant that Matthew inserts the same quotation of Hosea 6. 6 into two almost adjacent Marcan pericopae (Mark 2. 13-17 and 2. 23-28) even though he alters the Marcan order at this point.

[5] So also G. Barth in *Tradition*, 81 ff.

2. Matt 10. 5-6 (Mark 6. 6bff.) and Matt 15. 24 (Mark 7. 24ff.)
These passages should be considered together. In the latter passage Jesus explains to his disciples the reason for his apparent rejection of the Canaanite woman. 'I was sent only to the lost sheep of the house of Israel.' The words τὰ πρόβατα τὰ ἀπολωλότα οἴκου Ἰσραήλ are also used as part of the instruction given by Jesus to his disciples, 'Go nowhere among the Gentiles . . .' (Matt 10. 5).

The use of identical wording as part of an expansion of Marcan traditions and the way the evangelist underlines carefully (as elsewhere in the gospel) that the disciples act (and teach) in the same way as Jesus himself both point clearly to the evangelist's hand.

Many exegetes, however, have taken a rather different view. R. Bultmann's claim that Matt 15. 24 arose from discussions in the Palestinian church about the Gentile mission is often quoted.[1] R. Hummel takes Matt 10. 5f., 15. 24 and 5. 18f. as Jewish Christian material which Matthew consciously inserts into his gospel and reinterprets.[2]

But I am convinced that in Matt 15. 24 the evangelist is simply attempting to clarify the rather puzzling Marcan pericope. There is no suggestion in Matthew's interpretation of the incident that a strict 'Jewish Christian' restriction of mission to Israel is modified.[3] Matthew is stating as clearly as he can what he believes (following Mark) was the attitude of Jesus to the 'lost sheep' and to non-Jews. For Matthew, Israel's rejection of her Messiah at the end of the life of Jesus leads to acceptance of the Gentiles.[4]

---

[1] R. Bultmann, *The History of the Synopic Tradition*, E.tr. Oxford, 1963, 167.

[2] R. Hummel, *Auseinandersetzung*, 167. See also J.P. Meier, *Law and History*, 27.

[3] If Matt 5. 18 represents a strict Jewish-Christian attitude to the law, 5. 17 and 5. 18d (ἕως ἂν πάντα γένηται) make it clear that for the evangelist this view has been modified.

[4] So also W. Trilling, *Das Wahre Israel*, 105. (Trilling also takes 15. 24 as the creation of the evangelist.) Similarly, G. Strecker, *Der Weg*, 196, though he refers with approval to R. Bultmann' s view of the origin of the saying.

In the introduction to his account of the sending out of the disciples, Mark's reference in 6. 34 to the crowds as 'sheep who do not have a shepherd' is expanded with 'they were harassed and helpless' (9. 36). This Matthean addition is surely in line with τὰ πρόβατα τὰ ἀπολωλότα in 10. 6 and 15. 24: the 'sheep' are 'lost' because those responsible for guiding them have failed.[1]

In neither case do we need to assume use of a Jewish Christian tradition.[2] The evangelist is entirely consistent with his emphases elsewhere in the gospel. Once again Matthew is expanding his Marcan traditions in order to expound them.

3. Matt 21. 41c and 43 (cf. Mark 12. 9 and 11f.)
The reason for the evangelist's additions in the two passages just considered becomes even clearer in the light of his modifications to the Marcan parable of the wicked husbandmen. Matt 21. 43 is now widely accepted as the evangelist's own conclusion to the parable.[3] This is perhaps the clearest indication in the gospel that the Matthean community saw itself as a separate and quite distinct entity over against Judaism.[4]

In the light of 21. 43 Matthew has made expansions of Mark earlier in the parable at verses 34 and 41c. In verse 34 καιρός and καρπός are taken from Mark but linked together

---

1 See H. Frankemölle, *Jahwebund und Kirche Jesu*, 137f.
2 G.D. Kilpatrick, *Origins*, 27, even refers to the evangelist's *written* source.
3 See the detailed discussion of the individual words and phrases in W. Trilling, *Das Wahre Israel*, 58ff. Strecker (*Der Weg*, p. 164 n.4) however, is not convinced and insists that it is not possible to decide whether the evangelist has drawn on independent tradition or has composed the verse himself. Some of the evidence used by Trilling is not decisive, but in the light of the cumulative evidence for the evangelist's expansion of his sources given in this chapter, I am convinced that Matthew composed 21. 43 himself.
4 See D.R.A. Hare, *Jewish Persecution*, 153. Hare rejects Trilling's view that Matthew's community sees itself as the 'true' Israel: the transfer is from Israel to another people, 'non-Israel'.

in the phrase ὁ καιρὸς τῶν καρπῶν; in verse 41c τοὺς καρποὺς ἐν τοῖς καιροῖς αὐτῶν is an important expansion of Mark 12. 9. In these verses, as in 21. 43, the evangelist is drawing out what he takes to be the point of the Marcan parable. Although 21. 43 is a sharper and clearer statement of the rejection of Israel than is found in any part of Mark 12. 1-12, it is intended by Matthew to be his elucidation of verses 9-11, especially καὶ δώσει τὸν ἀμπελῶνα ἄλλοις and the citation of Psalm 118. 22f.

4. Matt 24. 10-12, 26 (cf. Mark 13. 13 and 23)

Although Matthew abbreviates Mark's eschatological discourse at several points, there are some significant additions. At 24. 24 the evangelist follows Mark 13. 22 almost *verbatim*. 'For false Christs and false prophets will arise and show great signs and wonders, so as to lead astray, if possible, even the elect.' In three places Matthew develops the theme of this verse in his own insertions into Marcan material. At 24. 5 he makes Mark 13. 6 refer more explicitly to false Christs. Matt 24. 11 has no direct parallel in Mark, but it is a repetition of part of 24. 24. At 24. 26 the 'false Christs' theme is taken up again in a verse which the evangelist himself adds to Mark – but this verse is simply an expansion of 24. 23 and 24.

There is little doubt that at 24. 10-12 all three logia stem from the evangelist and have been inserted into the Marcan context by him.[1] Almost every word of 24. 10 is taken from Mark 13. 9-13. The next verse comes from Mark 13. 22. While 24. 12 is not linked to Marcan phraseology, this logion is thoroughly in line with Matthean emphases elsewhere. The 'false prophets' theme is of special concern to the evangelist, as his redactional additions at 7. 15, 21-23 confirm.

These additions are not the only ones made by the evangelist in chapter 24, but they show clearly how in his additional sayings of Jesus he is often simply elaborating themes found already in his sources: very often those themes

---

[1] For a good detailed discussion see J. Lambrecht, 'The Parousia Discourse', in *Matthieu*, 320f., notes 28 and 29.

are underlined by the evangelist himself elsewhere in the gospel.

5. *Matt 26. 52-4 (cf. Mark 14. 47ff.)*
In these three verses words of Jesus have also been inserted by the evangelist into a Marcan context. At several points Matthew expands phrases found in the immediate context in Mark. D.P. Senior has shown convincingly that there is a 'homogeneous conception behind Matthew's redactional intervention'[1] in these verses: since their vocabulary and themes are thoroughly Matthean there is no need to consider use of a special source.

These five passages all show that Matthew has creatively added 'new' sayings of Jesus into Marcan traditions. But his redactional work is not arbitrary: in all five examples his intention has been to expound and elaborate his traditions. These conclusions can also be supported by a study of Matthew's additions to Marcan *narratives* – see, for example, 14. 28-31; 16. 12; 17. 6-7, 13.[2]

Q traditions

There are a number of passages in Matthew where the evangelist seems to have expanded Q traditions of the sayings of Jesus. In some cases it is of course possible that Matthew had access to a fuller form of Q than Luke; in some cases the evangelist may have expanded a logion with an independent piece of tradition. But there do seem to be

---

[1] D.P. Senior, *Passion Narrative*, 148. Senior provides a detailed discussion of Matt 26. 52-4 on 130-48.

[2] Cf. H.J. Held's conclusions on the basis of his study of Matthew's use of Mark's miracle stories: ' . . the retelling is in many cases fashioned in the light of a saying of Jesus in the pericope and brings it firmly into prominence. Thus the guiding thought in the interpretative retelling is already in the tradition itself.' *Tradition*, 298. See also D.P. Senior, *Passion Narrative*, 335 f., '. . . in the Passion narrative Matthew is not an innovator but a creative redactor.'

several passages which are entirely consistent with the way Matthew has expanded Marcan sayings of Jesus in order to underline his own emphases. If, in an apparently expanded Q tradition, the additional phrases (or a complete logion) seem to be designed to *expound* the tradition to which they are related, and if Matthean vocabulary or themes are in evidence, then we may be fairly confident that the evangelist himself is responsible for the 'new' words of Jesus.

1. *Matt 6. 9-13 (cf. Luke 11. 2-4)*
The addition to the opening address and the two petitions which are found only in the Matthean version of the Lord's Prayer probably come from Matthew rather than earlier tradition. For Matthew the coming of God's kingdom should mean that his will is done on earth, a point the evangelist stresses in his own additions to a logion (cf. Luke 6. 46) at 7. 21.[1] The addition to the final petition (ἀλλὰ ῥῦσαι ἡμᾶς ἀπὸ τοῦ πονηροῦ) can readily be seen as a 'filling out' of καὶ μὴ εἰσενέγκῃς ἡμᾶς εἰς πειρασμόν: it is certainly in line with the Matthean interpretation of the parable of the sower (where at 13. 19 ὁ πονηρός replaces Mark's ὁ σατανᾶς) and the Matthean interpretation of the parable of the weeds (where οἱ υἱοὶ τοῦ πονηροῦ at 13. 38 is almost certainly from the evangelist).

2. *Matt 7. 12, 15-20 (cf. Luke 6. 31 and 43-5)*
In the final sections of the Sermon on the Mount Matthew summarizes, repeats and develops a number of themes from earlier parts of the Sermon. At 7. 12 the Q version of the 'Golden Rule' is introduced by the Matthean πάντα ὅσα (cf. 28. 20) and the additional words οὗτος γάρ ἐστιν ὁ νόμος καὶ οἱ προφῆται are surely the evangelist's own composition, which recall 5. 17, a strongly redacted logion.

---

[1] In several redactional passages the evangelist carefully 'balances' heaven and earth: 6. 19-20; 6. 25, 28; 16. 19; 18. 18; 28. 18. Matt 5. 5 may have been created by the evangelist to expand and 'balance' 5. 3. See now, G. Schneider, 'Im Himmel – auf Erden', eine Perspektive matthäischen Theologie', in *Studien zu.n Matthäusevangelium* (FS W. Pesch) ed. L. Schenke, Stuttgart 1988, 285-97.

7. 13-20 contains excellent examples of Matthew's carefully balanced and easily memorable representation of Q logia. There are a number of expansions which sharpen the point of the original logia. At 7. 19 an additional logion which repeats Matt 3. 10 (Q, cf. Luke 3. 9) is inserted. The final verse, 7. 20, is a typical Matthean concluding summary.

3. *Matt 7. 21 (cf. Luke 6. 46)*

Here the evangelist has expanded considerably a Q logion. The Matthean version recalls 5. 20 which is a 'bridge' verse composed by the evangelist as a summary of 5. 17-19 and as an introduction to verses 21-48. The final clause of 7. 21 recalls, as we have seen, Matthew's own expansion of the Lord's Prayer.

But there is an even more important modification in this verse. Whereas Luke 6. 46 ('Why do you call me Lord, Lord, and not do what I say?') and 6. 47 ff. (the house built near a stream) both refer to carrying out the teaching of Jesus, Matthew reshapes Luke 6. 46 and makes it refer to 'doing the will of my Father in heaven'. In so doing he makes it quite clear that to hear and obey the words of Jesus is to do the will of the heavenly Father. Precisely the same Christological point is made at the end of the second major discourse: at 10. 40 (Matthean redaction of Q, cf. Luke 10. 16) the disciples are told 'he who receives me receives him who sent me'; the preceding context has made it clear that 'receiving' (δέχεσθαι) means 'accepting the teaching of' (cf. Matt 10. 14 where the phrase τοὺς λόγους ὑμῶν, which is added by Matthew to Mark 6. 11, makes this point).

4. *Matt 10. 1-42*

There are several significant expansions of Q (and Marcan) traditions in Matthew's 'mission' discourse. At 10. 8 the Q reference to healing (cf. Luke 10. 9) and the Marcan reference to healing and exorcisms (Mark 6. 12f.) are expanded by Matthew with references to raising the dead and cleansing lepers (cf. Matt 11. 5, Q) in order to emphasize that the disciples act in exactly the same way as Jesus himself.

At 10. 24-25 Matthew expands considerably a Q logion (cf. Luke 6. 40). This passage is probably recalled at 23. 34 where the fate of those sent is related to the crucifixion. The disciple is not above his master: if Jesus suffers crucifixion, it can also be expected by his disciples.[1]

The final three verses of chapter 10 reveal Matthew's literary and theological skill particularly clearly. 10. 41 has been composed by the evangelist: his distinctive vocabulary is clearly in evidence. This additional logion is not an arbitrary creation for it is an expansion and development of 10. 40 and 42. This important passage paves the way for the grand conclusion to Matthew's fifth discourse where, in the evangelist's interpretation of the 'great assize', his community is told that acceptance or rejection of Christian missionaries by 'all the nations' will be seen in the final judgement as acceptance or rejection of the Son of Man.[2] At the end of both the second and the fifth discourses the Matthean community is told that Jesus continues to be 'with' them in the closest possible way – the very theme with which the evangelist concludes his gospel at 28. 20.

5. *Matt 18. 10a, 14 (cf. Luke 15. 3-7)*

In Luke the parable of the lost sheep is a response to the critical comments of the scribes and Pharisees who are outraged by the way Jesus associates with tax collectors and sinners. God's acceptance of the 'undeserving' is proclaimed. But in Matthew the parable is addressed explicitly to the disciples and it is used to exhort the community to seek out the straying Christian 'lost sheep' of the evangelist's own day.

The Matthean interpretation results partly from the new setting but also partly from the words of Jesus added by the evangelist as an introduction and conclusion to the parable. 18. 14 includes several examples of the evangelist's distinctive vocabulary and it almost certainly comes from Matthew himself. At 18. 35 there is a further example of a thoroughly

---

[1] So also D.E. Garland, *The Intention of Matthew 23*, 177.

[2] See the discussion of this passage below, 342-4.

Matthean logion which has been added by the evangelist as a concluding summary to a parable.

Matt 18. 10a is probably the evangelist's own introduction to the parable. The phrase εἰς τῶν μικρῶν τούτων is used by the evangelist four times: at 10. 42 (which, as we have seen, is part of an important redactional passage); at 18. 6 (where Mark 9. 42 has been expanded in order to state explicitly that the 'little ones' believe *in Jesus* – the only time such a phrase is used in the synoptic traditions)[1] and at 18. 10, 14 where there are no parallels. The phrase, then, derives ultimately from Mark, but it has been developed considerably by Matthew: as in numerous other passages, the evangelist takes tradition as his starting point.[2]

Matthew's use of the phrase 'one of these little ones' is thoroughly in line with the observations we have made on the passages considered so far in this chapter. But it can hardly be claimed that in his interpretation of the parable *as a whole* the evangelist is simply developing, elucidating or expounding the Q tradition as it is found in Luke.

Do our observations on the methods used by the evangelist need to be modified considerably in the light of this passage? I do not think so. The Lucan setting may not be original. There is a characteristically Lucan conclusion to the parable (Luke 15. 7) and the present introduction in 15. 1-3 may well have been added to the parable either by Luke or at an earlier stage. It is probable that *both* evangelists have interpreted the parable by setting it in quite different contexts. By its very nature parabolic and metaphorical language lends itself readily to reinterpretation; a new context can easily alter the thrust of a particular tradition even if the original words are retained.

---

[1] A number of mss. do have εἰς ἐμέ at Mark 9. 42, but I take this reading to be a harmonisation of the Matthean tradition.

[2] The origin of Matt 18. 10b is more difficult to determine. This logion has no parallels elsewhere in Matthew, or in Mark or Luke.

6. Matt 5. 13a, 14a, 16 (cf. Mark 9. 49-50; 4. 21; Luke 14. 34-5; 8. 16 and 11. 33)

This passage is a further example of Matthean expansion of metaphorical or parabolic traditions. For convenience we shall consider it at this point even though it contains Marcan as well as Q traditions. It is extremely difficult to reconstruct the history of these enigmatic traditions which the evangelist has developed, but there is general scholarly agreement that Matthew has provided the parallel introductions ὑμεῖς ἐστε τὸ ἅλας τῆς γῆς in 5. 13a and ὑμεῖς ἐστε τὸ φῶς τοῦ κόσμου in 5. 14a as well as the whole of 5. 16. This latter logion can be compared with 18. 14 and 35: in each case a Matthean οὕτως logion summarizes and applies the preceding parable (or metaphor) to the community. Matthew has reinterpreted his traditions partly by juxtaposing the 'salt', 'city set on a hill' and 'lampstand' sayings, and partly by adding his own introduction and conclusion.

In so doing the evangelist stresses themes prominent elsewhere in the gospel.[1] G. Eichholz draws attention, surely appropriately, to Schlatter's observation: the task given to the disciples in this passage is quite simply, 'Make disciples of all nations.'[2] The ethical conduct of the disciples is stressed in 5. 16: τὰ καλὰ ἔργα is almost synonymous with δικαιοσύνη at 5. 20.

In this passage there is an example (which is rarely noted) of a pattern found elsewhere in Matthew. The disciples follow after Jesus: his coming to 'Galilee of the Gentiles' is a 'great light' (4. 23); they are to be the 'light of the world' (5. 14).

7. Matt 23. 28, 32-4 (cf. Luke 11. 44, 47 f.)

It is extremely difficult to isolate the evangelist's sources in Matt 23: at times he uses traditions not found elsewhere (the so-called M traditions); at times he uses Q traditions and in several places he seems to have composed logia himself. 23.

---

[1] See G. Bornkamm, Tradition, 16.

[2] G. Eichholz, Auslegung der Bergpredigt, 2nd ed. 1970, 58f. See also the interesting (but not completely convincing) discussion of this passage by M.J. Suggs, Wisdom, Christology and Law, 123ff.

28 is a good example of an expansion of Q traditions by the evangelist. Once again a οὕτως logion (cf. 5. 16; 18. 14, 35 discussed above) elucidates the preceding simile in the sixth woe; this verse may well be intended by the evangelist to summarize the previous woes.[1]

Matt 23. 32 also develops the Q tradition: this logion has probably been composed by the evangelist as a summary of the seventh woe and as a transition to the verses which follow.[2] Verse 33 parallels very closely the Q tradition applied by Matthew to the Pharisees and Sadducees at Matt 3. 7. The phrase γεννήματα ἐχιδνῶν is also found at 12. 34 in Matthew's reshaping of a Q tradition (cf. Luke 6. 45). The evangelist has added this verse here on the basis of Q traditions and his own modifications of them elsewhere.

In verse 34, in addition to important modifications of a Q logion (cf. Luke 11. 49) which cannot be discussed here, the second half of the logion, καὶ σταυρώσετε καὶ ἐξ αὐτῶν μαστιγώσετε ἐν ταῖς συναγωγαῖς ὑμῶν (καὶ διώξετε) ἀπὸ πόλεως εἰς πόλιν has been added by the evangelist.[3] But once again he repeats phrases used elsewhere in the gospel.[4] These verses confirm our earlier observations. The evangelist has added 'new' words of Jesus to his Q traditions, but his intention is to elucidate, apply and summarize his traditions rather than to supplement them with sayings which he has created *de novo*.

---

[1] So also D.E. Garland, *Intention*, 158 n. 29; R. Bultmann, *Synoptic Tradition*, 113.

[2] D.R.A. Hare, *Jewish Persecution*, 87, notes that it cannot be demonstrated that the diction of this verse is particularly characteristic of the evangelist and leaves open the possibility that it has been composed by Matthew. But since this logion functions in a similar way to other Matthean logia which expand and 'sum up' a preceding piece of tradition used by the evangelist, we may be reasonably confident that Matthew has supplied this verse.

[3] καὶ διώξετε is found in Luke 11. 49 (Q).

[4] μαστιγόω is found as a Matthean redaction of Mark 13. 9 at 10. 17; in the same verse Matthew adds αὐτῶν to ἐν ταῖς συναγωγαῖς (cf. Matt 4. 23; 9. 35 - the evangelist's own summaries); the phrase ἀπὸ πόλεως εἰς πόλιν recalls Matt 10. 23.

'M' traditions

There are a number of important sayings of Jesus and parables of Jesus in Matthew which are not found elsewhere in the gospels. Exegetes often reached quite divergent conclusions about their origin: some have claimed that many of these passages have been composed by the evangelist, while others have appealed to the use of independent tradition. If the cumulative argument of this chapter is sound, we may expect to find that the evangelist is closely dependent on his sources, but that he has not hesitated to expand them in order to repeat or develop his own redactional themes. This view can, I think, be advanced as a plausible hypothesis. A full defence of it is not possible here, but a brief examination of two passages will confirm that the evangelist has used and expanded at least some so-called M traditions of sayings of Jesus in the same way as Marcan and Q sayings.

1. Matt 11. 28-30
There is now general scholarly agreement that this passage has not been taken from Q. In its present context it refers to the disciples, though the original tradition may have had a much wider audience in mind. Many of the words in these verses are not found elsewhere in the gospel, but two clauses seem to me to be Matthean additions: καὶ μάθετε ἀπ᾽ ἐμοῦ, ὅτι πραΰς εἰμι καὶ ταπεινὸς τῇ καρδίᾳ. The original tradition which was expanded by the evangelist may have been as follows:

a   δεῦτε πρός με πάντες οἱ κοπιῶντες καὶ πεφορτισμένοι,
b   κἀγὼ ἀναπαύσω ὑμᾶς.
a¹   ἄρατε τὸν ζυγόν ἐφ᾽ ὑμᾶς.
b¹   καὶ εὑρήσετε ἀνάπαυσιν ταῖς ψυχαῖς ὑμῶν.
c   ὁ γὰρ ζυγός μου χρηστὸς καὶ τὸ φορτίον μου ἐλαφρόν ἐστιν.

The first four lines are well-balanced and are undergirded by the 'reasoning' of the fifth and final line. The clauses which have the clearest Matthean parallels (either in vocabulary or thought) καὶ μάθετε ἀπ᾽ ἐμοῦ, ὅτι πραΰς εἰμι καὶ ταπεινὸς τῇ καρδίᾳ break up the flow of the 'argument' in this section and seem to come from the evangelist's own hand.[1] This must now be demonstrated briefly.

The words 'learn from me' recall numerous passages in the gospel where Jesus (and not Moses or the scribes and Pharisees) is the *one* teacher par excellence.[2] The disciples must learn from Jesus for they are to teach all nations all that Jesus has commanded them (28. 20).

Jesus as the 'meek and lowly one' is also a Matthean theme. In his account of the entry of Jesus into Jerusalem the evangelist deliberately modifies Zech 9. 9 in order to allow the paradox of Jesus the *humble* one who is king to stand at the very centre of the fulfilment citation in 21. 4 ff.: 'Behold your king is coming to you, humble (πραΰς), and mounted on an ass . . .'

This very theme is central in two further fulfilment citations. At 12. 15 ff., the longest of all Matthew's citations from scripture, he has again reshaped the text to suit his own purposes and has emphasized the role of Jesus as humble servant. 'Here is my servant, whom I have chosen, *m y beloved on whom my favour rests . . .'* At this point the evangelist has modified Isa 42. 1 ff. in order to bring the phraseology into line with his account of the heavenly voice at the baptism of Jesus (3. 15) and at the Transfiguration (17. 5). Clearly this 'servant' citation from Isa 42 is a most important passage for the evangelist.

There is a further interpretative modification to be seen in this citation of Isa 42 in chapter 12. Matthew's phrase at the beginning of 12. 19 οὐκ ἐρίσει, can be explained neither from the MT nor from the LXX, but it can readily be related to the evangelist's concerns. At the end of the immediately preceding account of the healing of the man with the withered arm,

---

[1] For a fuller discussion see Chapter 16, 369-70. The analysis offered there differs slightly from that given above. I am grateful to A. Dihle for the suggestion that καὶ μάθετε ἀπ' ἐμοῦ may also have been a Matthean insertion. R. Guelich has pointed out to me that F. Filson's article, 'Broken Patterns in the Gospel of Matthew', *JBL* 75 (1956) 227ff. is relevant at this point.

[2] See D.E. Garland, *Intention,* 58, though he does not refer to Matt 11. 29.

Jesus withdraws deliberately in the face of Pharisaic opposition. He is the one who 'will not strive, he will not shout, nor will his voice be heard in the streets . . .'

At Matt 8. 17 the healing ministry of Jesus, which Matthew emphasizes strongly, is seen as a fulfilment of another 'servant' passage, Isa 53. 4: 'He took away our illnesses and lifted our diseases from us.'

So who is issuing the invitation in Matt 11. 28-30 as the passage now stands, with the evangelist's additions? It is not so much Jesus as Sophia (a theme which the evangelist barely hints at in his gospel), but Jesus as the humble Servant of God on whom God's Spirit rests, the Servant whose healing acts reveal his compassion for those in need.

I take 'all who are weary and heavy laden' to refer primarily to the costly and demanding nature of discipleship. Several verses earlier in chapter 11, as well as many in chapter 10, have stressed that disciples are to expect opposition and rejection. By linking 11. 28-30 on to the preceding pericope Matthew makes the end of this important discourse in chapter 11 become a word of encouragement to hard-pressed disciples – the very theme he emphasizes at the end of the discourses in chapters 10 and 25.

2. Matt 25. 31-46

This pericope is Matthew's grand climax to his presentation of the teaching of Jesus. As these verses now stand in the gospel they pick up and develop themes Matthew has emphasized. Judgement is associated with the Son of Man in two redactional passages, 19. 28 and 24. 30. Provision of hospitality is a mark of acceptance, 10. 11ff. Those who reject the disciples will be judged and punished, 10. 15 and, implicitly, 10. 42. The punishment is so severe that it is clear that persecution is in mind. Earlier in the final discourse, in a redactional addition, persecution by Gentiles is mentioned explicitly at 24. 9: 'Men of all nations will hate you for your allegiance to me.'

By now it will be clear how I interpret this much-disputed pericope.[1] The Matthean community is committed to evangelism among all nations. Rejection, opposition and persecution have been experienced. Quite naturally Matthean Christians have asked, 'Why does God allow his enemies to play havoc with the new people who do bear the proper fruit (cf. 21. 43)?' The evangelist's answer is that at the end all men will be judged, rewarded and punished on the basis of their acceptance or rejection of those who have taught all nations all that Jesus has commanded. This passage functions as a final note of consolation and encouragement to the Matthean community.

This very theme is prominent in Jewish apocalypses written about the same time as Matthew – about A.D. 90 Following the triumph of the Romans in 70 there was bound to be bewilderment and confusion and this is reflected in 4 Ezra and 2 Baruch. 4 Ezra 7. 37 and 2 Baruch 72. 2 provide very instructive parallels to the interpretation I have proposed.

This approach to 25. 31-46 depends heavily on taking πάντα τὰ ἔθνη in verse 32 in a Matthean sense as 'all non-Christian nations' and on interpreting ἑνὶ τούτων τῶν ἀδελφῶν τῶν ἐλαχίστων in verse 40 (and in verse 45) as a Matthean phrase which refers to members of the Christian community. These phrases are redactional Matthean additions elsewhere; they have almost certainly been added by the evangelist to this tradition here.[2]

On this interpretation Matt 25. 31-46 is a further example of a passage which Matthew has expanded and reinterpreted in the light of his own concerns elsewhere. Here the evangelist's reinterpretation is probably very considerable, for the original tradition may well have stated that judgement of *disciples* would be on the basis of their acceptance or rejection of all sorts and conditions of men in need. The evangelist's reinterpretation is bold, but it should not be seen as completely arbitrary. Parabolic language, which lends itself

---

[1] See the full discussion in Chapter 9.
[2] See J. Friedrich, *Gott im Bruder?* 258-70 for details.

readily to reinterpretation, has been set in a new context and applied, as so often in Matthew, to the needs of the evangelist's community.

From a wide range of examples (which is by no means an exhaustive list) a consistent pattern has emerged. The evangelist has expanded (often considerably) sayings of Jesus in Mark, Q and 'M'. There are a surprisingly large number of additions – and we have not considered sayings which Matthew has repeated. In the expansions we almost invariably find themes which the evangelist has himself emphasized elsewhere.

At the beginning of this chapter I referred to D. Garland's use of the analogy of a montage to illustrate the evangelist's methods. This analogy helpfully underlines the extent to which Matthew's gospel is both *more than* and *other than* the sum of the individual traditions which have been incorporated. The evangelist has reinterpreted his traditions by reshaping and 'tidying' them, and by setting them in new contexts – often by juxtaposition with originally unrelated traditions. For all of this, the analogy of a 'montage' is appropriate. But this analogy does not do justice to the extent to which the evangelist has himself *expanded* individual narrative and sayings traditions. Again and again we have seen that Matthew is creative but not innovative: he is committed to the traditions at his disposal, but he endeavours to elucidate them for his own community.

The evangelist's interests are varied. In the sayings we have considered discipleship and community themes are prominent, but so too are Christological and eschatological concerns. It is a mistake to try to decide which of these themes is *primary* for the evangelist, for in the context of the whole gospel they are intertwined and interdependent.

If these observations are valid, there are two implications which are of some importance. If, as I have argued, the evangelist is constantly attempting to draw out the significance of his *traditions,* then it is unlikely that he intended to modify radically Mark's presentation of the story and significance of Jesus.

The interpretative methods used by Matthew can be traced (though less clearly and less extensively) at other stages in the transmission of gospel traditions.[1] I am convinced that at all stages the creation *de novo* of sayings of Jesus was a relatively rare phenomenon. Much greater development of the traditions took place as they were set, elucidated and expounded in new contexts. On the whole the words of Jesus were transmitted with great care by the very earliest post-Easter communities. Discussions of the role of Christian prophets in the development of the synoptic tradition often overlook this point. The expansions we have observed are not the work of a Christian prophet, but of an 'exegete'.[2] Matthew insists that the words of Jesus are to be treasured carefully; they are elucidated by the evangelist so that they can be appropriated by his community and used in its proclamation (28. 18-20).

---

[1] See, for example, J. Wanke, ' "Kommentarworte", Älteste Kommentierungen von Herrenworten', *BZ* 24 (1980) 208-33.

[2] For a wide-ranging discussion of this point, see M. E. Boring, *Sayings of the Risen Jesus*, Cambridge 1982. With the exception of Matt 28. 18-20, Boring is rightly cautious about claims that individual sayings found in Matthew originated as words of Christian prophets. I do not think that 28.18-20 is an exception. Even this passage should be seen as an expansion and summary (in a new context) of themes the evangelist has stressed earlier in the gospel. These verses are not so much the key (so O. Michel) which unlocks the whole gospel (i.e. a new *revelation*) as a *grand finale* in which the evangelist summarizes his main points.

Chapter Fifteen

Matthew's Use of the Old Testament

Quotations and allusions to Old Testament passages are even more prominent in Matthew than they are in the other three gospels. Matthew's gospel includes a set of quite distinctive 'formula' quotations which have long intrigued scholars. These quotations are all theological 'asides' or comments by the evangelist. They have dominated discussion of Matthew's use of the OT and have frequently been appealed to in attempts to elucidate the origin and purpose of the gospel. In addition, there is a further important aspect of the use of the OT in Matthew which has often been neglected: the evangelist's modifications of the quotations found in his sources and the additional references he includes without using his 'introductory formula'. The OT is woven into the warp and woof of this gospel; the evangelist uses Scripture to underline some of his most prominent and distinctive theological concerns.

Some of the unusual features of Matthew's use of the OT were observed in the early church. In his *Dialogue with Trypho* Justin is well aware that Matthew's interpretation of Isa 7. 14 in Matt 1. 13 is open to Jewish objections that it is based on mistranslation of the Hebrew (see chaps 77-8 which quote Matthew 1 and 2 extensively; also 67; 71; 84). In their commentaries on Matt 27. 9, Origen and Jerome both try to explain why the evangelist attributes to Jeremiah a citation which is taken from Zech 11. 13. In two of his letters (20 and 130) Jerome notes that in the quotations of the OT in Matt 2. 15; 2. 23 and 12. 17-11, the evangelist prefers the Hebrew text to the LXX. This latter observation raises a question which has haunted all modern students of Matthew's use of the OT. Why do some of the evangelist's quotations of the OT seem to reflect use of the Hebrew text and some use of the LXX?

Massebieau (1885, pp. 93f)[1] seems to have been the first to point to a distinct group of passages in Matthew which show knowledge of the Hebrew text. He claimed that they are all 'citations apologétiques' which have been formulated according to the same principles in order to present the main events of the life of Jesus as fulfilment of OT prophecy. It soon became customary for scholars to distinguish between Matthew's formula quotations (known in German as *Reflexionszitate*) which seemed to come from a source, and his other references to the OT which are linked more firmly to their immediate context in the gospel (*Kontextzitate*) and seemed to come from the evangelist himself.

There are, however, sound reasons for calling in question these distinctions and for considering carefully the terminology used. As we shall see, some of the 'formula' quotations are linked very closely indeed to their immediate context. And it is by no means clear that they have all been taken either from a testimony book or source of any kind, or from pre-Matthean tradition; some of them, at least, seem to have been chosen by the evangelist himself.

Rothfuchs (1969) has suggested that since the most striking feature of the formula quotations is Matthew's emphasis on the 'fulfilment' of Scripture in the life of Jesus, the term *Erfullüngszitate* should be used in place of *Reflexionszitate*. (The latter term cannot easily be translated into English; 'formula quotation' has been widely used over the last 100 years.) This suggestion has been accepted by U. Luz (1985) in what is now the standard commentary in German; some scholars writing in English also use 'fulfilment quotations'. While there is much to be said for focusing attention on the 'fulfilment' theme, the term 'fulfilment quotation' is also

---

[1] For the full details of the abbreviated references to the literature which are given in the main text of this chapter, see the Bibliography on Matthew's use of the Old Testament, pp. 399-401.

appropriate for some quotations which imply that Scripture is being fulfilled but which are not introduced by Matthew's usual 'formula' (e.g. Matt 3. 3; 11. 10), and for some which are not comments by the evangelist himself (e.g. 9. 13; 12. 7 and 15. 8-9). It would be possible to overcome these difficulties by using 'fulfilment formula quotations', but this is an unacceptably clumsy term. Hence we shall use the term 'formula quotations', even though for Matthew the 'fulfilment' theme is more important than the 'formula' used to introduce the quotation.

With some additions made in individual cases to fit the immediate context, Matthew's introductory formulae all include the words ἵνα (ὅπως) πληρωθῇ τὸ ῥηθὲν διὰ τοῦ προφήτου λέγοντος. At this point it is worth noting that the first edition of the New English Bible (1961) overlooked the importance of this formula in Matthew's gospel. A variety of phrases was used, including (twice) 'to make good the prophecy of. . .'. In the second edition (1970) the translators made very few changes, but they were more consistent and used either 'fulfil' or 'fulfilment' for all Matthew's formula quotations.

There are ten quotations which can be considered together as a group: Matt 1. 22-3; 2. 15; 2. 17-18; 2. 23; 4. 14-16; 8. 17; 12. 17-21; 13. 35; 21. 4-5; 27. 9. They share three characteristics: they are all introduced by the 'formula' just noted; their text form is mixed, but it is less close to the LXX than the other references to the OT in Matthew; they all function as 'asides' of the evangelist and are not placed on the lips of Jesus or of other participants in the evangelist's story.

Matt 2. 5-6 should probably be added to this list as a marginal case: a pre-Matthean quotation seems to have been partly assimilated by the evangelist to the other formula quotations (so, for example, Soares Prabhu, 1976, p. 40). Three other possible candidates are now generally excluded. Matt 26. 54 and 56 both include the passive of πληρόω which is found in all the introductory formulae, but neither verse introduces a quotation from the OT; the former verse is a rhetorical question on the lips of Jesus and not a comment by the evangelist. Matt 27. 35b is not part of the original text of

Matthew: it is an interpolation in some later manuscripts from John 19. 24.

On any reckoning the quotation of Isa 6. 9f in Matt 13. 14-15 is unique: its introductory formula ἀναπληροῦται αὐτοῖς ἡ προφητεία Ἡσαΐου ἡ λέγουσα is not found elsewhere in Matthew – and neither the verb nor the noun is used elsewhere in the gospels or Acts; the quotation is not an 'aside' of the evangelist but is placed on the lips of Jesus; it comes rather awkwardly immediately after an allusion to Isa 6. 9f in the preceding verse; its text form is almost identical to the LXX. For these reasons it is taken by most exegetes to be a later interpolation, perhaps on the basis of Acts 28. 26-7 where a very similar version of Isa 6. 9f is cited. Segbroeck (1972, p. 126f) has, however, mounted a cautious defence of its authenticity, claiming that this citation is very appropriate at this point in Matthew 13.

Although the extent and the characteristics of this important group of formula quotations are now widely agreed, their origin and function are keenly contested. Do they stem from the evangelist himself? Or are they taken from a source, perhaps from an early Christian collection of OT passages – a testimony book? What theological purposes do they serve? Answers to these questions have been used to support widely differing views of the origin and purpose of Matthew's gospel.

Recent research

In order to clarify the issues, it will be helpful to consider several of the more influential modern studies. On the basis of careful analysis of the form of the textual traditions, Stendahl (1954) confirmed the results of several earlier studies. He claimed that whereas the formula quotations had a mixed text form, the other citations followed the LXX fairly closely. In other respects his own suggestions broke quite fresh ground. He claimed that in the formula quotations the biblical text is treated in somewhat the same manner as in the Habakkuk scroll discovered at Qumran. Matthew contains a number of examples of *pesher,* a special type of biblical interpretation which presupposes an advanced study of the Scriptures (in the 'school' of Matthew) and familiarity with the Hebrew text and the traditions of interpretation known to us from the versions.

Partly because Stendahl's monograph was one of the first books by a NT scholar to utilise the Dead Sea Scrolls, his work attracted a good deal of interest. Although his detailed study of the individual quotations in Matthew retains its value, his conclusions have not gone unchallenged. Gärtner (1954) denied that the Habakkuk scroll was produced by the artificial *ad hoc* exegesis which Stendahl had proposed for Matthew and claimed that the formula quotations did not originate as scholarly desk work but from the ordinary techniques of preaching. Gärtner also stressed that Matthew's quotations of the OT differ in an important respect from the methods of interpretation of Scripture found in the Qumran writings. Whereas *pesher* exegesis is an exposition of a continuous text, Matthew, on the other hand, relates a consecutive story and refers here and there to words of Scripture which will show to the reader that Jesus has fulfilled the messianic prophecies. Hence it is inaccurate to refer to Matthew's quotations as pesher exegesis. These important points were developed further by Rothfuchs (1969) who emphasised that Matthew does not intend to comment on OT passages, but rather to use them to comment on the life of Jesus.

In the preface to the second edition of his book Stendahl (1968) noted that research completed since he wrote his monograph has shown that both the Hebrew and the Greek textual traditions were very much more fluid in the first century than had been earlier supposed. He referred especially to Cross's work and stressed that the manuscript evidence now available pointed to a series of attempts to bring the Greek Bible into conformity with a changing Hebrew textual tradition. (The relevant essays have been brought together in F.M. Cross and S. Talmon, ed., *Qumran and the History of the Biblical Text,* Cambridge, MA 1975.) Stendahl readily conceded that some of his own results were called in question by more recent advances in our knowledge of OT textual traditions:

> New data are about to allow new and better founded hypotheses about text forms available in the first century A.D. Such a promising yet unfinished state of affairs both hinders and helps further progress in the study of the Matthean quotations. It makes more probable that readings found in Matthew could witness to text forms actually available in Greek, prior to Matthew. It makes the recourse to testimonies less compelling as an explanation of textual peculiarities. (1968, p. iv)

The importance of this continuing research on OT textual traditions for the student of Matthew's gospel can hardly be overestimated, but it has not yet been taken seriously in Matthean scholarship. One partial exception is Brown (1977, p. 103) who, in his study of the infancy narratives, referred briefly to the multiplicity and fluidity of Hebrew and Greek textual traditions in the first century, as well as of Aramaic targums. 'When we add to these the possibility of a free rendering by the evangelist himself, the avenue of deciding what citation is Matthean and what is pre-Matthean on the basis of wording becomes uncertain.' Surely this observation is correct. We shall return to it a little later.

While Stendahl emphasised, as have most modern scholars, that the 'mixed' text form of the formula quotations differs markedly from the other largely Septuagintal citations of the OT in Matthew, he failed to account clearly for the differing form of these two groups of traditions. The formula quotations are said to be the result of the exegetical work of Matthew's school – to which the evangelist himself presumably belonged. But surely the evangelist was also responsible for the other quotations? Stendahl wrote just a few years before the emergence of redaction criticism, so perhaps it is hardly surprising that he failed to address this important question.

In one of the first major redaction critical studies of Matthean theology, Strecker (1962), unlike Stendahl, did differentiate sharply between the two groups of quotations. He argued that although the formula which introduces Matthew's formula citations contains the evangelist's own turns of phrase, the citations themselves could not be the work of the evangelist. They do not contain Matthean words or phrases and their wording has not been influenced by the context in which they are set in the gospel. The evangelist has taken them from a distinct source – a collection of prophecies which reached him in written form (p. 83). These quotations, Strecker insisted, do not shed light on the interests of the evangelist, for they have been taken rather pedantically from a source. In Strecker's view they are used to set the history of Jesus back in the past as a chronologically and geographically distant event. The evangelist himself was not a Jewish Christian familiar with Jewish exegetical techniques and Hebrew or Aramaic textual traditions. Evidence which seems to point in that direction comes from earlier tradition which the evangelist has simply taken over. Strecker claims that Matthew was a Gentile who 'historicised' the life of Jesus as the central period in the history of salvation.

Although nearly all Strecker's conclusions have been challenged, his sharp distinction between the formula quotations which came from a source and the other references to the OT which bear the marks of Matthean redaction set the agenda which has been followed by most more recent scholarly work. Gundry's monograph (1967), is, however, a notable exception. Although his book was published several years after Strecker's major study, it made no reference to Strecker's work since it had largely been completed in 1961. Gundry attempted to refute the view that the text form of Matthew's formula quotations is distinctive, a view widely accepted since the work of Massebieau (1885). Gundry argued that the text forms of the formula quotations are mixed. That was no surprise, but his claim that this mixed text form is found in *all* parts of the synoptic gospels was a novel proposal. Gundry insisted that it is the close adherence to the LXX found in the Marcan quotations used by Matthew which is out of line with the rest of the synoptic material. He also claimed that if we set aside the strongly septuagintal Marcan quotations, the other references to the OT in the synoptic gospels (including Matthew's formula quotations) can all be traced back ultimately to the apostle Matthew who was his own targumist and drew on his knowledge of the Hebrew, Aramaic and Greek textual traditions of the OT. The evangelist used his own 'body of loose notes' made during the ministry of Jesus (p. 172). On this view, then, the formula quotations are no longer the most distinctive feature of the use of the OT in Matthew's gospel.

Gundry claimed that earlier scholars had mistakenly overlooked the *allusions* to the OT in the synoptic gospels: their text form is mixed and they should be set alongside the formula quotations in Matthew and all other non-Marcan quotations in the synoptic gospels. Gundry's careful presentation of the Hebrew, Aramaic and Greek textual traditions which are relevant for study of references to the OT in Matthew is still unrivalled. But his hypotheses concerning the authorship of Matthew's gospel and the origin of the gospel traditions raise more questions than they answer. His strong reliance on allusions to the OT turns out to be an Achilles' heel, for the text form of allusions which rarely consist of more than two or three words is necessarily elusive! Where a writer does not indicate explicitly that he is quoting Scripture, there must be at least a good possibility that he is drawing on his memory.

Was the LXX Matthew's Bible?

At this point we must return to the question which has dominated discussion of Matthew's use of the OT. Are there two quite distinct groups of OT quotations in Matthew's gospel? It has often been urged that one group shows no traces of the evangelist's own hand and has mixed text forms (the formula quotations); the other group of quotations (some of which are taken from Matthew's sources and some of which are added redactionally) confirms that the LXX was Matthew's Bible. If this analysis is correct, then we seem to have little option but to accept the view pressed vigorously by Strecker (but shared by other scholars) that the formula quotations have been taken over by the evangelist from an earlier source. This is the conclusion reached by Luz (1985) in his impressive commentary, although he rejects Strecker's claim that the evangelist was a Gentile, and he quite rightly questions whether the formula quotations could ever have belonged together in some kind of testimony book. Luz does, however, still insist that the formula quotations stem from pre-Matthean tradition.

But this conclusion can be challenged. It is by no means clear that the LXX was Matthew's Bible. Although Kilpatrick (1946, p. 56) accepted the view of several earlier writers and claimed that 'agreement with the LXX is regularly made more exact', Stendahl (1954, p. 148) was less dogmatic and referred to 'a slight but obvious tendency to greater fidelity to the LXX'. But the four passages Stendahl does list as closer to the LXX in Matthew than in Mark turn out, on closer inspection, to provide little or no support for this conclusion. (1) In Matt 19. 18f it is just possible that the citation of the decalogue has been assimilated to the LXX. In Mark 10. 9 the prohibitions are expressed with μή plus the subjunctive; in Matthew οὐ plus the future indicative is used. But the decalogue is found in several different forms in both the OT and the NT. So the variation in Matthew is probably purely stylistic: the changes may have been made in order to balance more precisely the negative commandments with the positive commandment ἀγαπήσεις τὸν πλησίον σου ὡς σεαυτόν which the evangelist adds here, the wording of which corresponds exactly both with the MT and with the LXX of Lev 19. 18. (2) At Matt 21. 9 Jesus is addressed as 'Son of David'. This is an important Matthean Christological addition, but it is unrelated to the LXX. (3) At Matt 22. 32 εἰμί is added to ἐγὼ ὁ θεός in Mark 12. 26. This may perhaps be classed as a Septuagintal addition, but it is more likely to be simply a Matthean stylistic improvement. (4) At Matt 24. 30 phrases from Zech. 11. 10 and an additional phrase from Dan. 7. 13, τοῦ οὐρανοῦ, are added to Mark 13. 26. But in neither case is there clearly closer conformity to the LXX.

Although most recent studies of Matthew's use of the OT have concentrated on the formula quotations, the evangelist's redaction of the quotations in Mark and Q is particularly instructive. There is little doubt that it undermines confidence in the widely accepted view that the LXX is Matthew's Bible. In a dozen or more passages Matthew retains, with little or no alteration, Mark's strongly Septuagintal quotations. This is not surprising since throughout his gospel he usually follows his sources closely. Matthew does make some modifications, but they can be shown to be closely in line with the redactional changes he makes to his sources elsewhere.

The two examples noted above are important. Matthew's additional reference to 'love of neighbour' in 19. 19 is characteristic: in 7. 12b and 22. 40 'love of neighbour' is emphasised redactionally as the essence of the law and the prophets. And Matthew's reference to Jesus as 'Son of David' in 21. 9 in a Marcan OT quotation underlines one of the evangelist's most distinctive Christological themes; this title is used redactionally in six passages.

Further examples of Matthew's redaction of references to Scripture in his sources confirm that his modifications are consistent with the redactional changes he makes to his main sources.

(i) In Matt 16. 9 the citation of Jer 5. 21 against the disciples in Mark 8. 18 ('Having eyes do you not see, and having ears, do you not hear?') is dropped completely, as are the preceding harsh words of Jesus, 'Do you not understand; are your hearts hardened ?' These changes form part of a consistent pattern: the evangelist omits or 'softens' all the Marcan passages which refer to the disciples' lack of understanding.

(ii) In Matt 21. 13, πᾶσιν τοῖς ἔθνεσιν, part of Mark's citation of Isa 56. 7 is omitted. Although several redactional passages in Matthew imply acceptance of the Gentiles, in this case reference to the Gentiles is left out as part of Matthew's sharpening of polemic against the Jewish leaders: they are not using the temple properly for prayer. In Mark the quotation is introduced by, 'Is it not written?'; in Matthew it

355

becomes, 'it is written', a firm accusation against the Jewish leaders.

(iii) The enigmatic allusion to Dan 12. 11 and 11. 31 in Mark 13. 14, 'the desolating sacrilege', is clarified by Matthew in 24. 15 and made into an explicit citation of Scripture by the addition of τὸ ῥηθὲν διὰ Δανιὴλ τοῦ προφήτου. τὸ ῥηθὲν διὰ τοῦ προφήτου is found in all the introductions to Matthew's ten formula quotations; only the element of 'fulfilment' is missing here. τὸ ῥηθέν is also found in two other Matthean redactional additions (3. 3 and 22. 31) but it does not occur elsewhere in the NT. So there can be little doubt that these additional words stem from the evangelist himself; they also suggest that he is responsible for the introductions to the formula quotations. This is made still more probable by our fourth example of Matthew's redaction of a Marcan quotation.

(iv) In Matt 26. 47-56 the evangelist sets out a more carefully structured version of Mark's account at 14. 43-52 of the arrest of Jesus. In Matt 26. 54 a reference to the 'fulfilment of the scriptures' is added by the evangelist. Two verses later he makes a second important modification to Mark. The words of Jesus in Mark 14. 49c, ἀλλ᾽ ἵνα πληρωθῶσιν αἱ γραφαί are an ellipse. Matthew clarifies this clause by expanding it and turning it into his own comment – a comment which closely resembles the introductions to two of Matthew's formula quotations:

Matt 26. 56: τοῦτο δὲ ὅλον γέγονεν ἵνα πληρωθῶσιν αἱ γραφαὶ τῶν προφητῶν.

Matt 1. 22: τοῦτο δὲ ὅλον γέγονεν ἵνα πληρωθῇ τὸ ῥηθὲν ὑπὸ κυρίου διὰ τοῦ προφήτου λέγοντος.

Matt 21. 4: τοῦτο δὲ γέγονεν ἵνα πληρωθῇ τὸ ῥηθὲν διὰ τοῦ προφήτου λέγοντος.

The words πληρωθῶσιν αἱ γραφαί are taken over from Mark. The phrase τῶν προφητῶν instead of the usual phrase διὰ τοῦ προφήτου comes as no surprise since Matthew does not cite a particular passage at this point. His intention is clearly to stress that the events which have just been recounted are to be seen as fulfilment of the Scriptures as a whole. This redactional verse contains two of the three characteristics of Matthew's formula quotations noted above. There is a declaration that the prophets have been fulfilled in the life of Jesus, and the verse is a comment of the evangelist – a theological 'aside' which informs the reader of the deeper significance of the preceding events.

In this pericope the evangelist is following his Marcan source closely. But the changes he makes in 26. 54 and 56 confirm that the introductions to his ten formula quotations come from his own hand: as in numerous other passages in the gospel, Matthew has developed Marcan traditions in his own characteristic way.

(v) In 9. 13 and 12. 7 Matthew has introduced into two Marcan passages an identical reference to Hos 6. 6: ἔλεος θέλω καὶ οὐ θυσίαν. The quotation could have been taken either from the LXX or the MT. In both cases Jesus is in dispute with Pharisees. The quotations are introduced in similar ways: πορευθέντες δὲ μάθετε τί ἐστιν (9. 13) and εἰ δὲ ἐγνώκειτε τί ἐστιν (12. 7). Since πορεύομαι is a favourite Matthean word and is used with an imperative six times (four of which are redactional) the introduction almost certainly comes from the hand of the evangelist himself. The emphasis on ἔλεος is certainly Matthean and is linked to the prominence given to the love commandment by the evangelist. As in several of the formula quotations, Matthew makes an essentially Christological comment: Jesus acts in accordance with Scripture – and with God's will.

(vi) In Matt 3. 3 there is a further interesting example of Matthean redaction of an OT citation which he found in his sources. The evangelist has carefully avoided Mark's citation of Exod 23. 20 + Mal 3. 1 which is mistakenly said to be from Isaiah. Once again Matthew's introductory words are significant: οὗτος γάρ ἐστιν ὁ ῥηθεὶς διὰ Ἠσαΐου τοῦ προφήτου λέγοντος. With the exception of a reference to 'fulfilment' (which is reserved for the story of Jesus), all the elements of Matthew's introductory formula are here. As in those ten formulae, ὁ ῥηθείς and διά point to God's attestation, for he has spoken through the prophet. In Mark (and in Luke) the quotation from Isa 40. 3 is linked to John's baptising activity in the wilderness, but in Matthew the emphasis falls squarely on the person of John the Baptist: his proclamation is attested by God. This is in line with the changes Matthew has made to Mark in the preceding verse: there he takes pains to make the message of John correspond exactly with the proclamation of Jesus (cf. 3. 2 and 4. 17). John and Jesus both herald the coming of the kingdom; both are attested by God in Scripture, but Jesus alone is its fulfilment.

Since Matthew usually follows his sources closely, it is no surprise to find that he takes over with little modification many of the Old Testament citations found in his sources, principally Mark. By and large they are Septuagintal, so he retains them in that form. However, in numerous passages Matthew does abbreviate, expand and modify Mark and Q in line with his own stylistic and theological concerns. As we have seen, he treats the OT quotations found in his sources in the same way as he treats the sources themselves. *Matthew's primary allegiance is to the textual form of the quotations in his sources rather than to the LXX as such.*

Matthew's formula quotations

If Matthew's own hand can be traced so clearly in the modifications he has made to citations of Scripture in his Marcan traditions, is this also the case with the formula quotations with their mixed text form which sometimes seems to reflect use of the LXX, sometimes the MT? Or should the formula quotations be set aside as a quite distinct group of pre-Matthean traditions? Their very different mixed text form seems to point in the latter direction. But if, as I have tried to show above, the LXX was not necessarily the evangelist's own Bible, it is at least possible that he himself is responsible for the mixed text form of some of the formula quotations.

It has become customary to assume that the formula quotations must all have originated in the same way: scholars have debated keenly whether they were all taken from a source or from earlier tradition, or whether the evangelist himself is responsible for them all. But the evangelist's own phraseology and emphases are so pervasive in his gospel that if we did not have Mark and Luke we should find it difficult or even impossible to unravel his sources. Some of his formula quotations have probably been taken by the evangelist from earlier tradition and fitted into his story with little or no adaptation. Perhaps he himself is responsible for some (such as the citation of Isa 9. 1f in Matt 4. 14-16 and of Isa 42. 1ff in Matt 12. 17-21) where the quotation and the context have more clearly been adapted to one another.

If there is still some uncertainty about the origin of the formula quotations, there is no doubt at all about the origin of the introductory formulae. As we have seen above, two of the three elements of the formulae can be seen in Matthew's redaction at 26. 54, 56 of Mark 14. 49c: as in numerous other passages, Matthew has taken a Marcan phrase and developed it considerably. Both Rothfuchs (1969) and Soares Prabhu (1976) have examined the individual words and phrases of the formulae meticulously and have shown that Matthew himself is responsible for the 'basic formula' which he has adapted slightly to fit individual contexts. In two cases, 1. 23 and 2. 15, the introductory formula mentions explicitly that it is God's word spoken through the prophet which has been fulfilled in Jesus; this is clearly implied by the use of τὸ ῥηθὲν διὰ τοῦ προφήτου in all the formulae.

The formula quotations are not spread evenly throughout the gospel. Four are in the infancy narratives; a fifth quotation, 2. 5-6, functions in a very similar way, even though 'fulfilment' is not mentioned explicitly. Four more occur in the central chapters, 4. 14-16; 8. 17; 12. 17-21; 13. 35. The final two are linked with the 'triumphal' entry of Jesus into Jerusalem (21. 4-5) and the death of Judas (27. 9). Why is there such a concentration of quotations in the infancy narratives and why are there so few in the passion narratives? There is no obvious answer, though it has been suggested that the evangelist was well aware that whereas Mark had already set the passion narratives against the backdrop of Scripture, traditions concerning the birth and infancy of Jesus had not yet been interpreted in this way.

Nearly all the evangelist's distinctive themes are found in chapters 1 and 2: the infancy narratives form a theological prologue to the gospel as a whole. Three factors strongly suggest that the formula quotations have been added by the evangelist himself to earlier traditions to which he had access. (i) Matt 1. 18 – 2. 23 can be read without the formula quotations – indeed, the story line flows rather better! Only in the (marginal) formula quotation at 2. 5-6 is the scriptural reference woven into the plot. (ii) Five of the six formula quotations outside the infancy narratives have clearly been added to Marcan traditions by the evangelist. So this is also likely to have happened in chapters 1 and 2, even though we cannot trace with certainty the extent of earlier traditions. (iii) The OT passages referred to are not quoted elsewhere in the NT. With the exception of the citation of Isa 7. 14 in Matt 1. 13 (and, perhaps, of Micah 5. 1 + 2 Sam 5. 2 in the 'marginal' formula quotation in Matt 2. 5-6), it is difficult to envisage just how these passages might have been used by earlier Christians. It seems likely that Matthew himself was the first to see their relevance in a Christian setting.

As in all the formula quotations, the text form is puzzling. There seem to be signs of dependence on both Greek and Hebrew textual traditions, and perhaps also of Aramaic targumic traditions. Given the evangelist's penchant for the text form used by his sources, the fluidity of textual traditions in the first century, and the possibility that some passages have been quoted from memory or adapted to fit the context, perhaps this is not surprising. There is little doubt that in two cases Matthew himself has adapted the wording of the quotation to fit its context in his infancy narratives. (i) In Matt 1. 23, against all the textual traditions, the third person plural καλέσουσιν is used. Since Jesus was not literally called 'Emmanuel' and since Joseph had just previously been told to call Mary's son 'Jesus' (1. 21), the evangelist has used this form of the verb in order to indicate that it is the 'people saved from their sins' (1. 21) – Christians in his own day – who will call Jesus 'Emmanuel'. (ii) By the addition of οὐδαμῶς in 2. 6, the original sense of Micah 5. 1 has been transformed: an unimportant village has now become (from

Matthew's perspective) supremely important on account of the birth of the Messiah.

To what extent have the formula quotations led to the adaptation or even the creation of the traditions to which they have been attached? This seems to have happened only on a limited scale. Perhaps the phrase καὶ ἐν πᾶσι τοῖς ὁρίοις αὐτῆς has been added in Matt 2. 16 in order to make the reference to Ramah in 2. 18 just a little less awkward. In fact the quotations in 2. 15; 2. 18 and 2. 23 all fit their present contexts so awkwardly that it is difficult to suppose that the traditions have been created on the basis of the quotations.

In two cases, however, the quotations chosen seem to have encouraged the evangelist to modify his own introductory formula. In two of the ten formula quotations the word υἱός occurs (1. 23 and 2. 15): in both verses (and only here) an explicit reference to the Lord (κύριος) as the one who has spoken through the prophet has been added to the introductory formula. Since this is hardly a coincidence, Matthew intends to make a Christological point: Jesus is the Son of God.

At first sight the quotations in chapter 2 seem to have been chosen to give scriptural undergirding to the geographical places mentioned: Bethlehem (2. 6), Egypt (2. 15), Ramah (assumed to be near Bethlehem, 2. 18) and Nazareth (2. 23). But the evangelist's concerns are primarily Christological. Jesus is to be called Emmanuel – God with us (1. 23), a theme echoed in the closing verse of the gospel where the risen Christ promises to be with his disciples (μεθ' ὑμῶν) until the close of the age. At 2. 6 Jesus is portrayed as the one who will shepherd God's people Israel. As we have seen, at 2. 15 Jesus is God's Son. Although the final two quotations in chapter 2 have long baffled exegetes, there is little doubt that in 2. 17-18 Matthew intends to link the story of Jesus with the Exodus and the Exile experiences of Israel: just as the machinations of the opponents of God's people were thwarted of old, so too will Herod fail to overturn God's purposes. In 2. 23 Jesus is called Ναζωραῖος; the most likely explanation of this apparently odd designation is that Jesus is seen as the messianic *neser* or 'branch' and the *nazîr* or 'holy one' of God.

The quotation of Isa 9. 2 in 4. 15-16 also functions similarly. The opening of the ministry of Jesus in Galilee, and in Capernaum in particular, is seen as the fulfilment of Scripture. But the evangelist's choice of this quotation is dictated by other considerations: in numerous passages in his gospel he stresses that the 'story' of Jesus is ultimately of significance for Gentiles as well as Jews. The reference (albeit indirect) to the coming of the φῶς is also related to Matthew's concerns. Jesus is here called (indirectly) φῶς for Γαλιλαία τῶν ἐθνῶν; his disciples will shortly be called to be τὸ φῶς τοῦ κόσμου (5. 14). As elsewhere, the evangelist draws attention to the ways in which the disciples (and Christians in his own day) continue the ministry of Jesus.

Two further formula quotations, 8. 17 and 13. 35, are linked to summary passages and stress that both the healing activity and parabolic teaching of Jesus are to be seen as fulfilment of Scripture. The longest quotation, of Isa 42. 1-4 in 12. 17-21, is also linked to a summary. Although the attempts of Cope (1976) and Neyrey (1982) to show that this quotation has influenced the themes and structure of the whole of Matthew 12 are only partly successful, there is little doubt that the quotation and its context have influenced one another to a greater extent than in the other formula quotations. There is also little doubt that once again Matthew's concerns are primarily Christological: Jesus is the servant who exercises his ministry in obedient lowliness and mercy. Even if he has overstated his case, Neyrey has shown that this lengthy quotation is also related to Matthew's apologetic concerns – to the conflict of Jesus with the Pharisees which dominates this part of Matthew's gospel.

Van Segbroeck (1972) has noted that four of Matthew's formula quotations are introduced with an explicit reference to Isaiah – and they all fall within chapters 4-13, chapters which Matthew has redacted particularly strongly. This may be a coincidence, but van Segbroeck believes that Matthew is especially interested in Isaiah since no prophet is as preoccupied with the salvation of Israel, even though Isaiah underlines in his preaching that his work is fruitless.

Zech 9. 9 is the only one of Matthew's formula quotations which is cited elsewhere in the NT. Although this passage is linked to the 'triumphal' entry of Jesus into Jerusalem both at Matt 21. 4-5 and at John 11. 14-15, the form of the quotation differs so markedly that a direct link between the two gospels is most unlikely. The Zechariah quotation seems to have led Matthew to introduce two animals into the Marcan tradition and to have supposed that Jesus rode on both at the same time. Although exegetes have been forced to exercise great ingenuity in their explanations of this passage, once again Matthew's concern is primarily Christological. Jesus enters Jerusalem as the humble (πραΰς) king, a theme which has interested the evangelist at 5. 5 and 11. 29.

By a curious coincidence there are also ten 'fulfilment' quotations in John's gospel. But the differences are more striking than the similarities. The introductory formulae in John are much more varied. Whereas only one of Matthew's formula quotations is found in his passion narratives (27. 9, the burial of Judas), the first does not occur in John until 12. 38. Only half the Johannine quotations are comments of the evangelist. Rothfuchs (1969, p. 176) has correctly noted that whereas the Johannine citations set the 'world's' hostile reaction to Jesus and his work in the light of prophecy, the Matthean quotations portray the person Jesus and the nature of his sending.

In this chapter I have tried to show just how closely Matthew's use of the OT is related to his distinctive theological themes. Although the evangelist usually retains with little modification OT quotations in his main sources, Mark and Q, some have been carefully adapted in line with his own concerns. But his most distinctive contribution is his use of ten OT passages with their carefully phrased introductions: they all comment on the story of Jesus and draw out its deeper significance by stressing that all its main features are in fulfilment of Scripture. While some of his quotations may have been used and transmitted orally by earlier Christians, Matthew himself is almost certainly responsible for the choice and adaptation of many of them.

Chapter Sixteen

Matthew 11. 28-30: Comfortable Words?

For many Christians today Matthew's version of the Lord's Prayer is probably the most familiar passage of scripture. But Matt 11. 28 may well be a close second. 'Come unto me all you who are weary and heavy laden and I will give you rest' has been prominent in many liturgies since the sixteenth century. This verse is the first of the 'comfortable words' which come immediately after the Absolution in the Book of Common Prayer Communion service:

> Hear what comfortable words our Saviour Christ saith unto all that truly turn to him:
> Come unto me all that travail and are heavy laden, and I will refresh you.

The 'comfortable words' go back to Cranmer's 1549 Prayer Book. His decision to include Matt 11. 28 as the first of four verses of scripture seems to have been influenced by the outcome of Hermann's important *Consultatio* at Cologne in 1545. This was attended by Melanchthon and Bucer, among others, and it led to the inclusion of five verses of scripture between the Confession and the Absolution. Hermann intended that one of the five verses would be selected for use in a Communion service. Matt 11. 28 was only the fourth verse in this list.[1]

---

[1] See J. Gunstone, 'The Art of Penitence', in *The Eucharist Today*, ed. R.C. D. Jasper, London 1974, 78.

As far as I can discover, Matt 11. 28 was first used in a Communion service by Zwingli in 1523. This seems to have been the first time in the sixteenth century that any additional verse of scripture was introduced into the liturgy. In Zwingli's 1523 service Matt 11. 28 was said immediately before the distribution of the bread with the words, 'The Body of our Lord Jesus Christ'.[1] It was probably this Zwinglian practice which led Cranmer to promote Matt 11. 28 to the top of the list of scriptural verses which he inherited from Hermann.

This verse is found in different positions in various liturgies and its function and its theological significance differ accordingly. In the Church of Scotland Book of Common Order (and in many liturgies influenced by it) Matt 11. 28, with v. 29 added, is part of the general invitation at the very beginning of the Communion liturgy. The emphasis is clearly upon 'Come unto me'. When Hermann placed this verse between the Confession and the Absolution it was being used to give scriptural authority for the forgiveness of sins; the emphasis was upon the promise of 'rest' to the weary and heavy laden. For Cranmer Matt 11. 28 becomes part of the pre-Communion devotion. In Zwingli's liturgy this verse comes at the very climax of the service and 'rest' is associated closely with the reception of the elements. In spite of the different ways Matt 11. 28 functions in these liturgies, in every case it is being understood as a soteriological saying, at least in the broad sense of that term. It is a 'comfortable word', even in liturgies which do not use Cranmer's phrase.

In the German theological tradition Matt 11. 28-30 is often referred to as the *Heilandsruf*, the invitation of the Saviour. This is the heading used in Huck's *Synopsis* and it is retained in Heinrich Greeven's substantially revised edition which has recently been published. The term *Heilandsruf* is used almost as frequently as *Jubelruf*, the traditional German way of summarizing the preceding verses, 11. 25-27, Jesus' thanksgiving to the Father.

---

[1] F. Schmidt-Clausing, *Zwinglis Liturgische Formulare*, Frankfurt 1970, 26.

Are these verses 'comfortable words' in their present setting in Matthew? Is this passage intended by the evangelist to be the 'call of the Saviour'? Or does the exegete have to concede that its use in liturgies and the traditional German summary are both far removed from Matthew's intentions? If the evangelist did intend these verses to be understood in a broadly soteriological sense, how do they relate to his other theological emphases? After all, many parts of Matthew are not in any sense soteriological and there are passages in the gospel which are certainly not 'comfortable words'!

Matthew 11. 28-30 and Sirach 51

It is now fashionable to stress that these verses are part of Matthew's Christology rather than his soteriology. M. Jack Suggs claims that one of the most distinctive features of Matthew's Christology is his identification of Jesus as Sophia-Wisdom; our passage is an important part of his evidence.[1] He insists that for Matthew Jesus is the *incarnation* of Sophia and of Torah.

The first steps along this path were taken by D.F. Strauss who published the first important modern study of Matt 11. 25-30 in 1863.[2] He noted the interesting parallels between this passage and Sir 51, but he also stressed the differences. Strauss suggested that the identification of Jesus with Wisdom (Sophia) might have been the first step towards a Logos Christology. In the first decades of the twentieth century several scholars followed up these observations with major studies of this passage. Although they differed in their conclusions, they all accepted that 11. 28-30 formed the third part of 11. 25-30, a block of traditions which stood together in Q

---

[1] M.J. Suggs, *Wisdom, Christology and Law in Matthew's Gospel*, Cambridge, Mass. 1970.

[2] I owe this point to H.D. Betz who includes a brief survey of the history of interpretation of this passage in his important article, 'The Logion of the Easy Yoke and of Rest', *JBL* 86 (1967) 10-24.

and were to be related to Sir 51 and to other parts of the Wisdom tradition.

Eduard Norden's analysis was particularly influential.[1] He claimed that Matt 11. 25-30 and Sir 51 were both constructed on the same basic three-fold pattern. Sir 51 is seen as a long hymn-like prayer which is divided into three sections:

1. Sir 51. 1-12, a prayer of praise to God; cf. Matt 11. 25-26.
2. Sir 51. 13-22, the seeking and finding of Wisdom; cf. Matt 11. 27
3. Sir 51. 23-30, the appeal to the ignorant; cf. Matt 11. 28-30.

Norden claimed that this block of Q and Sir 51 owed their structure and leading ideas to a schema which could also be traced behind other 'mystical theosophical writings'. Although this approach cannot now be defended – for reasons which will be mentioned in a moment – there is an interesting modern ring to his insistence that Q was compiled by a theologian and an author. 'Just like the evangelists (especially Matthew) the author of Q grouped together sayings into longer discourses for didactic and literary reasons.'[2] These words were written in 1913, but they might have come from a recent textbook on the gospels.

The scholars who followed up Norden's work modified many of his conclusions but they all accepted that Matthew 11. 25-30 originally belonged together as a unit in Q. As a result they all tended to play down or ignore the present setting of these verses in Matthew's gospel and to see the evangelist as an anthologist rather than as a theologian or writer, thus overlooking Norden's emphasis on the creative role of the evangelist.

Rudolf Bultmann was the first scholar to challenge the unity of 11. 25-30 as a Q passage.[3] He stressed the absence of 11. 28-30 from Luke and noted that these verses are different in character from v. 27. Whereas v. 27 promises *revelation*,

---

[1] E. Norden, *Agnostos Theos*, Berlin 1913, 276-308.

[2] E. Norden, *Agnostos Theos*, 306.

[3] *The History of the Synoptic Tradition*, E.tr. Oxford 1972, 159.

in 28-30 the 'teacher' makes his appeal and promises rewards for obedience to his commandments. More recently Bultmann's analysis has been strengthened by the discovery of an earlier form of Sir 51. 13ff. at Qumran, 11Q Ps^a 21ff., which has a decidedly erotic flavour now missing in Sir 51. And in an important manuscript of Sir 51 a Psalm is introduced into the text after 51.12.[1] In other words it is now clear that the structure of Sir 51 is by no means as rigid and as firmly based on a traditional three-fold schema as Norden maintained: the authors of Sir 51 and Matt 11. 25-30 are themselves responsible for the present ordering of their material.

Most scholars now accept that it is almost impossible to explain why Luke would have omitted 11. 28-30 if these verses had stood in Q. Many accept Bultmann's hypothesis (which in fact goes back to Strauss) that 11. 28-30 come from a lost Jewish Wisdom writing. Whatever their origin, we can be confident that it was the evangelist Matthew who linked 28-30 onto 25-27. Once this is recognized, we can consider the evangelist's intentions. Why did Matthew place 11. 28-30 at this point in his gospel? How closely are the verses related to his other themes?

Before I set out what I take to be the evangelist's primary concerns in this passage, I want to try to show that the repeated attempts from Strauss to Suggs to link these verses closely with Sir 51 are probably misguided.

Bultmann saw Matthew's portrait of Jesus as that of the wisdom teacher making his appeal to his hearers to embrace Sophia. Suggs takes a further step. He insists that in Matthew Jesus is not merely a wisdom teacher, Sophia's representative or emissary (as in Q), but Jesus is himself Sophia:

> The invitation which Jesus offers is the old invitation of Wisdom and the yoke which is offered is the yoke of Wisdom, the yoke of the Torah. . . We should be very clear that in the Matthean setting what is offered by Jesus is *not*

---

[1] See M.J. Suggs, *Wisdom, Christology and Law in Matthew's Gospel*, 77ff., and D. Lührmann, *Die Redaktion der Logienquelle*, Neukirchen-Vluyn 1969, 67.

an alternative to the yoke of the Torah. Jesus speaks *as* Sophia, and in such a saying that means *as* Torah as well.[1]

Suggs's exposition of Matthew's Wisdom Christology has been very influential, but the very first steps in his argument (as well as some of the later ones which cannot be discussed here) seem to me to be less secure than many recent writers have supposed.

(a) The verbal links between Matt 11. 28-30 and Sirach are in fact quite slender. Only two words, 'toil' and 'yoke', and one phrase, 'find rest', from these three Matthaean verses are found anywhere in Sirach. The verb 'toil' is found twice with reference to the search for Wisdom, but at Sir 6. 18 and 51. 27 the sense is very different: the emphasis is not on the toil needed to find Wisdom, but on the *ease* of the task.

(b) There is nothing in Sirach quite comparable with *two* of the most important clauses in Matt 11. 28-29, the group addressed as 'all who toil and are heavy laden' and the reference to Jesus as 'meek and lowly in heart'.

The portrait of Jesus as 'meek and lowly' is difficult to square with the portrait of Sophia which we find in the Wisdom writings. At Sir 24. 1, which introduces the so-called Sophia myth, Sophia speaks with *pride*. In Prov 1. 20ff. and again at 8. 1ff. Sophia lifts her voice and cries aloud. She stands by the gate and calls aloud in a rather arrogant manner.

It is, I think, not a coincidence that at the *very point* in 11. 28-30 where we seem to be a long way from the Wisdom tradition, we can see, in all probability, the evangelist's own hand. Many of the words in 11. 28-30 are not found elsewhere in the gospel, but 'meek' and 'lowly' are used by the evangelist and, as we shall see in a moment, they accord well with his portrait of Jesus. So the words 'for I am meek and lowly in heart' may well be Matthew's own addition to his source. As is well known, elsewhere Matthew does add interpretative phrases and clauses to his sources: there are classic

---

[1] M.J. Suggs, *Wisdom, Christology and Law in Matthew's Gospel*, 106.

examples in his version of the Lord's Prayer and the Beatitudes.[1]

In support of this suggestion we may note that v. 28 and v. 29a and c are parallel statements:

> Come unto me, all who labour and are heavy laden, and I will give you rest.
> Take my yoke and learn from me, and you will find rest for your souls.

Both statements are undergirded by the 'reasoning' of v. 30:
For my yoke is easy and my burden is light.
It is verse 29b, 'for I am meek and lowly in heart', which breaks up the flow of the 'argument' in this short section, and which seems to come from the evangelist's own hand.

If this proposal is correct, the evangelist's redactional addition runs directly *counter* to the Wisdom tradition. But even if this specific suggestion is not accepted, it is clear that 'I am meek and lowly in heart' is out of character with the portrait of Sophia in the Wisdom writings, but very much in line with Matthew's portrait of Jesus, as will be shown below.

(c) I find it difficult to see how either Matthew or his readers could make the jump from v. 27 where Jesus is presented as 'the Son' to v. 28, where, it is alleged, Jesus is Sophia/Wisdom. It is not just that Wisdom is a feminine noun in both Hebrew and Greek. In the Wisdom tradition Sophia is always portrayed in strongly female terms. Those who search and seek after her are always men: sexual imagery lies just beneath the surface in many passages. A similar point is made by M.D. Johnson when he insists that 'it would have been as incongruous to ancient Jewish sensibilities as it is to ours to speak of "Lady Wisdom" being incarnated as the "Son" '.[2]

In short, it is not at all clear that Matthew identifies Jesus as Sophia. The use of some Wisdom themes in 11. 28-30 is

---

[1] See Chapter 14, 334.
[2] M.D. Johnson, 'Reflections on a Wisdom Approach to Matthew's Gospel', *CBQ* 36 (1974) 61f.

not being disputed, but they do not seem to be the key to the passage as it now stands in Matthew's gospel. Whatever may have been their origin, the evangelist has redacted these verses, probably by adding his own portrait of Jesus as 'meek and lowly in heart', but certainly by placing them in their present position within his gospel.

Four questions

We can now ask four questions of this passage without any assumption that answers will necessarily be in terms of Wisdom. Who is issuing the invitation? Who is being addressed? What are they being called to do? What is the promise or reward to be given to them?

(i) It is not Jesus as Sophia who issues the invitation, but Jesus the meek and lowly one. In his account of the entry of Jesus into Jerusalem the evangelist deliberately modifies Zech 9. 9 in order to allow the paradox of Jesus the *humble* one who is king to stand at the very centre of the fulfilment citation in 21. 4ff.: 'Behold, your king is coming to you, humble, and mounted on an ass . . .'. And this very dissonance is prominent not only in Matthew's Passion narrative, but also right through the gospel.

This very theme is central in two further fulfilment citations. At 12. 15ff., the longest of all Matthew's citations from scripture, he has again reshaped the text to suit his own purposes and has emphasized the role of Jesus as humble servant. 'Here is my servant, whom I have chosen, *my beloved on whom my favour rests*. . .' At this point the evangelist has modified Isa 42. 1ff. in order to bring the phraseology into line with his account of the heavenly voice at the baptism of Jesus (3. 15) and at the Transfiguration (17. 5). Clearly this 'servant' citation from Isa 42 is a most important passage for the evangelist.

There is a further interpretative modification to be seen in this citation of Isa 42 in chapter 12. Matthew's phrase at the beginning of 12. 19 οὐκ ἐρίσει, he will not strive (NEB) or wrangle (RSV), cannot be explained either from the MT or

371

from the LXX, but it can readily be related to the evangelist's concerns. At the end of the immediately preceding account of the healing of the man with the withered arm, Jesus *withdraws* deliberately in the face of Pharisaic opposition. He is the one who 'will not strive, he will not shout, nor will his voice be heard in the streets . . .'. How unlike the traditional portrait of Sophia is this portrait of Jesus as the 'humble and lowly one'.

At Matt 8. 17 the healing ministry of Jesus, which Matthew emphasizes strongly, is seen as a fulfilment of another 'servant' passage, Isa 53. 4: 'He took away our illnesses and lifted our diseases from us.'

So who is issuing the invitation in 11. 28-30? It is not so much Jesus as Sophia (a theme which the evangelist barely hints at in his gospel), but Jesus as the humble Servant of God on whom God's Spirit rests, the Servant whose healing acts reveal his compassion for those in need.

(ii) Who are the 'weary and heavy laden' who are being addressed? This is the most difficult of the four questions with which we are concerned. There are two possibilities: those in need of acceptance or forgiveness, or the disciples. As noted earlier, the Wisdom traditions offer no help at this point. So we have no option but to examine the evangelist's emphases elsewhere in his gospel.

The careful reader of Matthew soon discovers that the evangelist has a particular interest in both the disciples and the crowds. But unfortunately we are not told whether the disciples or the crowds (or both, as in chapters 5–7, 13 and 23) overhear the words of Jesus in 11. 25-30. At 11. 7 Jesus speaks to *the crowds* concerning John, but the crowds are already in the underlying Q tradition and are in any case presupposed by the context. At 11. 20 Jesus upbraids unrepentant Chorazin, Bethsaida and Capernaum, but at 11. 25 there is no explicit indication of the audience, for Jesus is addressing the Father. V. 27 is no longer addressed to the Father and implies an 'audience', as does v. 28.

Does the evangelist have in mind the crowds or the disciples? Or is this an artificial distinction? In a number of passages Jesus acts compassionately towards the needy crowds. At 4. 16 the citation of Isa 9. 1-2 is used to introduce the ministry of Jesus: 'the people who sat in darkness have seen a great light, and for those who sat in the region and shadow of death light has dawned.' The coming of Jesus is 'light' for those in need; in the verses which follow the evangelist stresses that Jesus healed the sick and those with all kinds of physical and mental disabilities (4. 23ff.). This redactional summary is repeated and expanded at 9. 35ff. which concludes the evangelist's carefully constructed first presentation of the words (chapters 5–7) and deeds (chapters 8–9) of Jesus. In this second summary Jesus has compassion on the crowds 'because they were harassed and helpless, like sheep without a shepherd'. Is this the same group as the 'weary and heavy laden' in 11. 28?

If so, we should probably add 'the poor' to whom the good news is preached (11. 5) and perhaps 'the broken' of 12. 20. In this latter passage Isa 42. 1ff. is cited: 'He will not break a bruised reed or quench a smouldering wick.' This might be taken as a reference to the sick mentioned at 12. 15, the verse onto which this citation is firmly attached. But because of the next line (where the evangelist's hand can be seen) 'until he brings justice to victory', the thought cannot be *only* of the sick. In his commentary David Hill notes that the evangelist is concerned with 'the saving work of Jesus, directed towards the weak, the lost and the broken. . . . For this reason the Gentiles will have cause to hope in his name.'

With these passages in mind we might readily conclude that the 'weary and heavy laden' whom Jesus addresses in 11. 28 are the crowds rather than the disciples – all those in desperate need to whom Jesus shows compassion. If this is the correct interpretation, then 11. 28 is indeed for the evangelist 'the call of the Saviour' and a 'comfortable word'.

This approach is attractive. It is supported by J. Jeremias and F. Christ, among others.[1] But there are grounds for caution. It is not clear why 'the crowds' are toiling (the

---

[1] J. Jeremias, *New Testament Theology* I , London 1971, 112 (see also 159); F. Christ, *Jesus Sophia, Die Sophia-Christologie bei den Synoptiken*, Zürich 1970, 111.

present participle is used) and heavy laden. Exegetes often refer to the burden of Pharisaic legalism from which Jesus promises release. But as we shall see, this is almost certainly not a strongly anti-Pharisaic passage.

In addition, if we take the 'needy crowds' as the 'weary and heavy laden', the link between 11. 25-27 and 11. 28-30 becomes very awkward. In v. 25 Jesus gives thanks that revelation ('these things') has been granted not to 'the wise', but to 'babes'. And v. 27 speaks of those to whom the Son chooses to reveal knowledge of the Father. The evangelist seems to envisage disciples rather than 'needy crowds' as the audience in 25-27. And since he himself linked vv. 28-30 onto 25-27, we must conclude that in all probability in 28-30 it is *disciples* who are being addressed. But does this alternative interpretation make sense?

In numerous passages the evangelist stresses that discipleship is costly and demanding. Nowhere is this clearer than in the missionary discourse in chapter 10. In his brilliant essay on discipleship in Matthew, Ulrich Luz has shown that as the chapter unfolds it becomes clear that the evangelist not only has the disciples of the historical Jesus in mind but also Christian disciples his own community in his own day.[1] Although the evangelist does not use κοπιάω (labour or toil) or πεφορτισμένοι (heavy laden) elsewhere, κοπιάω is used by Paul and other early Christian writers to refer to the exertion involved in Christian service. So, 'all who labour and are heavy laden' probably refers primarily to the costly nature of discipleship; several verses earlier in this chapter, as well as many verses in chapter 10, have stressed that disciples are to expect opposition and rejection.

But a hard and fast line should not be drawn between crowds and disciples in Matthew. The evangelist seems to have both in mind in the Sermon on the Mount (cf. 5. 1f. and 7. 28). The image of 'harassed sheep' is used both for the crowds on whom Jesus has compassion (9. 36) and for the

---

[1] U. Luz, 'Die Jünger im Matthäusevangelium', ZNW 62 (1971) 141-171; E.tr. in *Matthew*, ed. G.N. Stanton, London and Philadelphia 1983.

disciples who are sent out to preach and to heal exactly as Jesus had done (10. 16).

(iii) The group addressed in 11. 28 is asked to take the yoke of Jesus and learn of him. The yoke of Jesus is often contrasted with the yoke of the law or the burden of Pharisaic legalism. Since controversy stories follow this passage in chapter 12, an anti-Pharisaic thrust cannot be ruled out at the end of chapter 11. But this does not seem to be primarily an anti-legalism passage. If we take it in that sense we run into difficulties with v. 30. The evangelist cannot be saying that the 'torah' of Jesus is easier to keep and less burdensome than Pharisaic torah, for he is no antinomian and in the very important verse 5. 20 he insists that the demand of Jesus is *greater* than that of the scribes and Pharisees.

Once again some exegetes have been bemused by alleged parallels with Sirach and have concluded too readily that the yoke of Jesus is being contrasted with the yoke of the law. 'Yoke' is also used in Jewish writings in a much wider sense in phrases such as 'the yoke of heaven', 'the yoke of God'; the term expresses a relation of absolute dependence.

The 'yoke of Jesus' is the yoke of discipleship. The call of Jesus in v. 28, 'Come unto me', is immediately followed by 'learn of me'. 'Come unto me' is almost on all fours with the first call of Jesus to the disciples at 4. 19, 'Come after me . . .', where Matthew retains Mark's turn of phrase. And for Matthew discipleship involves teaching, preaching and healing which is modelled precisely on the actions and words of Jesus himself. In the final verse of the gospel the disciples are told by the Risen Jesus to teach men to observe all the commandments Jesus has given to them. They are to retain the words of Jesus and to proclaim their continuing importance. For Matthew call and demand are inextricably interwoven.

(iv) How can the disciples be promised in v. 30 that the yoke of Jesus will be good to bear and his load light, especially if we take 'all who labour and are heavy laden' to refer to the costly nature of discipleship? If this seems to be paradoxical, we need do no more than recall 10. 39, 'He who finds his life will lose it, and he who loses his life for my sake will find it.'

Those who accept the yoke of discipleship are twice promised 'rest'. This term is to be taken, as in many OT passages, in a wide sense. Since the evangelist clearly has discipleship in his own day in mind, we can suggest that for Matthew costly and demanding discipleship turns out, paradoxically, to be a delight rather than a burden because of the promise of the presence of the Risen Christ in the closing words of the gospel: 'Lo, I am with you every day to the end of the age.'

I have suggested that Matt 11. 28-30 should be set alongside several other passages within the gospel rather than seen as closely influenced by Sir 51. The closing verses of the gospel are particularly important. At 28. 18 it is not 'Come to me', but 'Go, make disciples of all nations'. In both cases it is the authoritative teaching of Jesus which is central: 'learn from me' (11. 29) and 'teach them to observe all that I have commanded you' (28. 20). In chapter 11 the demand of discipleship is tempered with the promise of rest; in chapter 28 the promise to those engaged in the task of making disciples of all nations is the presence of the Risen Christ.

Can our passage be seen as 'comfortable words' and is its use in eucharistic liturgies appropriate? Although the evangelist does emphasize forgiveness of sins through Jesus at 1. 21 and at 26. 28, it is not primarily Christ's gracious acceptance of the needy or the sinful which is in view in 11. 28-30. These verses are 'comfortable words' for hard-pressed disciples. But 'salvation' in the broadest sense is *indirectly* in view as it is part of Matthew's understanding of discipleship. For the evangelist insists that disciples of Jesus in his own day are to continue the proclamation of Jesus, which Matthew sees as good news for those who know their need of God. 'This gospel of the kingdom will be proclaimed throughout the earth as a testimony to all nations' (24. 14). Like Jesus, disciples are to preach, teach and heal; they are light for all the world (5. 14), just as the coming of Jesus is light for those who sit in darkness (4. 16). It is the disciples (not Jesus as in Mark 6. 34) who are to act as shepherds to the crowds who are 'harassed and helpless like sheep' (9. 36ff.). In short, for Matthew discipleship involves proclamation of salvation.

But this is not the way Matt 11. 28 is usually understood when it is used in a liturgy today. If we wish to be more faithful to the evangelist's intentions we should not use 11. 28 in isolation from vv. 29 and 30, for v. 28 is just the first part of a carefully worked out argument; 'Come unto me' and 'take my yoke and learn of me' are parallel statements which should be held together.

Perhaps this passage should be moved away from the invitation at the opening of the communion liturgy, or from any of the other places where it has traditionally been placed. Some parts of it (but obviously not 'Come unto me') might be linked with phrases from 28. 18-20 to form a 'Matthean' dismissal: the disciple who has taken the cup of salvation 'for the forgiveness of sins' (which is the evangelist's own addition at 26. 28) is called to take the yoke of Jesus in costly and demanding discipleship; he is promised 'rest' and the presence of the Risen Christ and told to go and make disciples of all nations.

But a liturgical dismissal constructed along these lines would be clumsy and verbose. In any case it is not necessary to use Matthew's own formulation of the words of Jesus in order to be faithful to the evangelist's intention and his important theological insights.[1]

---

[1] In addition to the literature on this passage which has been cited above, see T. Arvedson, *Das Mysterium Christi. Eine Studie zu Mt 11, 25-30*, Uppsala 1937; J.B. Bauer, 'Das milde Joch und die Ruhe, Matt. 11, 28-30', *BZ* 17 (1961) 99-106; L. Cerfaux, 'Les Sources scriptuaires de Mt. xi, 25-30' in *Recueil Lucien Cerfaux* III, Gembloux 1962, 139-159; S. Légasse, *Jésus et L'Enfant*, Paris 1969, 129-37 and 235-46.

Since this article was published the following literature has appeared: D.C. Allison, 'Two Notes on a Key Text: Matthew 11, 25-30', *JTS* 39 (1988) 477-85; Celia Deutsch, *Hidden Wisdom and the Easy Yoke*, JSNTSS 18, Sheffield 1987; Celia Deutsch, 'Wisdom in Matthew: Transformation of a Symbol', *NovT* 32 (1990) 12-47.

Conclusions: A Gospel for a New People

Matthew wrote his gospel as a 'foundation document' for a cluster of Christian communities, probably in Syria in the mid 80s. The evangelist and the original recipients of his gospel saw themselves as a 'new people', minority Christian communities over against both Judaism and the Gentile world at large.

The gospel contains a whole series of 'legitimating answers' for the 'new people'.[1] It responds both directly and indirectly to polemic from the parent body,[2] and it defends vigorously its own distinctive convictions and self-understanding. In short, in many respects it is an apology.

Matthew's gospel legitimates the recent painful separation of Matthean communities from Judaism by providing divine sanction for the parting of the ways: as a result of the hostility of the Jewish leaders to Jesus and his followers, *God himself* initiated the rupture and transfered the kingdom to the 'new people' (21. 43; 8. 12; cf. also 15. 13-14).

The evangelist repeatedly re-enforces Christian convictions concerning the significance of Jesus which shaped the community life of the 'new people'. *God himself* has disclosed to the 'new people' that Jesus is the Son of God (3. 17; 11. 25-7; 16. 17; 17. 5). Jesus was sent on *God's initiative* (1. 20; 10. 40; 21. 37). Through Jesus, *God is present with his people*

---

[1] P.L. Perger and T. Luckmann note that 'not only children but adults "forget" the legitimating answers. They must ever again be "reminded". In other words, the legitimating formulas must be repeated'. *The Social Construction of Reality: a Treatise in the Sociology of Knowledge*, New York and London 1966, 31.

[2] See the summary in the Conclusions to Part II, 280-1.

(1. 23; 8. 23-7; 14. 22-33; 18. 20; 28. 20); these verses have deep roots in Old Testament references to the presence of God with his people: an old theme is transposed into a new key.

One of Matthew's 'legitimating answers' is particularly prominent. He includes as part of his story a sustained defence of open and full acceptance of Gentiles. This is carried out with such literary skill that it is highly likely that this was a matter of continuing importance for the 'new people'. Even if the principle was largely accepted when Matthew wrote, it was still necessary to repeat the explanation of how this step had been taken, a step which ultimately proved to be crucial for the parting of the ways with Judaism.

At first the evangelist does no more than hint that the story of Jesus has implications for Gentiles as well as Jews. The opening line of the gospel refers to Jesus Christ as a son of Abraham; Matthew does not need to explain that in Scripture Abraham is portrayed as the father of many nations (cf. also 3. 9). The four references to women in the genealogy would have taken the initial recipients of the gospel by surprise; many would have known that the four were considered to be non-Jews. The magi who pay homage to the child Jesus come from right outside the Jewish world. Scripture is cited twice as divine sanction for a mission to the Gentiles (4. 15; and 12. 18-21). This theme is developed further in the references in the Sermon on the Mount to the disciples as 'salt of the earth' and 'light of the world' (5. 13-14), in Jesus' acceptance of the faith of the Gentile centurion (8. 10), and in the broad hint that followers of Jesus will be rejected not only by Jewish households and towns, but also by Gentiles (10. 18). Before the end comes, 'this gospel of the kingdom' (i.e. Matthew's gospel itself, see p. 17) 'will be proclaimed throughout the earth as a witness to all nations' (24. 14; cf. also 26. 13). In the final command of the Risen Jesus (28. 18-20) earlier hints become a clarion call: 'Go, make disciples of all nations' countermands the insistence by Jesus earlier in the story that he was sent 'only to the lost sheep of the house of Israel' (15. 24), as were the disciples themselves (10. 5-6).

The evangelist's juxtaposition of 'particularist' ('go only to the house of Israel') and 'universalist' ('go to all nations') strands has baffled many modern readers, but as a 'foundation document' the gospel would have been read and listened to 'with awareness' by the original recipients.[1] They would have known instinctively which parts of the story belonged to past history, and which parts were important for their on-going Christian community life. For example, they would have known that it was both impossible and inappropriate for them to offer gifts at the temple altar (5. 23-4), and to carry out the teaching of the scribes and Pharisees (23. 5-6). They would also have known that although the opening of the mission discourse (ch. 10) is set firmly in the lifetime of Jesus, the main part of the discourse was addressed directly to them as both exhortation and as consolation.

In Part I of this book three chapters are devoted to questions of method; conclusions are set out on pp. 108-110. In Part II I have argued that Matthew's gospel was written *partly* as a response to the social setting of the first recipients. The most striking features of that social setting are summarised in the conclusions to Part II (pp. 278-81) and are not repeated here. Two particular points, however, need to be stressed.

(i) Right at the outset of this book (p. 3), I emphasized that Matthew does not have *one* over-riding concern which provides the key to every pericope in his gospel. The more narrowly his purposes are defined, the less compelling are the explanations. Matthew writes with *broad* catechetical and pastoral concerns: he sets out the story and significance of Jesus in order to assist Christians to come to terms with their identity as communities distinct from Judaism.

(ii) Many writers have noted that the circumstances of the first recipients of this gospel determined, at least in part, several of the evangelist's strongest emphases. But few, if any have noted that the social setting of the recipients has shaped

---

[1] Similarly, the Qumran community would have known whether references to 'Damascus' in CD, their 'foundation document', were to a geographical location or to their own community.

one of the most distinctive features of Matthew's Christology: his *sharp contrast* between the humility and meekness shown in the recent past by Jesus, the 'chosen servant' who is the Son of David, and the glory of his future coming as Son of Man and judge. Unlike most of Matthew's Christological emphases, this theme is barely hinted at in his sources. On pp. 185-91, I suggested that this aspect of Matthew's Christology is an early form of the 'two parousias' schema which contrasts the first coming of Jesus in humility with his future coming in glory.

The Matthean form of this Christological pattern reflects (in part) the self-understanding of the communities for which Matthew wrote his gospel: Christology and ecclesiology are inter-related. In a series of redactional passages Matthew's Christian readers are encouraged to live by the conviction that since their Lord who was sent by God is also the humble servant of God (11. 29 [MtR – see pp. 340-1, 369-70]; 12. 17-21; 21. 5) who was confronted at every turn by his opponents, they themselves must carry out that role. Their message and ministry are the same as those of Jesus himself (10. 7-8). They are 'the little ones' (10. 42; 18. 6, 10, 14; 25. 40), 'the poor in spirit', 'the meek' (5. 3, 5), 'the simple unlearned ones' (11. 25) who must face fierce opposition and rejection (5. 10-12; 10. 11-42; 11. 28 [see pp. 374-6]; 23. 34). But just as Jesus himself was vindicated by God, their cause will be vindicated at the future coming of the Son of Man himself (25. 31-46 [see pp. 207-30]; and cf. 5. 12; 10. 41-2).

Matthew intended that his biography of Jesus, with its many strong Christological themes, would shape the convictions and lives of the recipients of his gospel. The reverse has also taken place: the circumstances and self-understanding of the 'new people' have shaped Matthew's contrast between the two 'comings' of Jesus. But in making this suggestion I am not claiming that Matthew's Christology as a whole is the product of a particular social setting. Most of his major Christological themes are deeply embedded in the Marcan and Q traditions on which he drew; they have been sharpened and extended (but not created *de novo*) in the light of the social circumstances of the evangelist's day.

Many of the other distinctive themes of this gospel also have their roots in the sources on which Matthew drew and were also developed by him to meet the needs of the first recipients. The evangelist strengthens both the anti-Jewish polemic and the apocalyptic motifs found in his sources (see pp. 146-68). Sayings of Jesus are re-shaped and extended creatively, but nearly always as an interpretation of earlier traditions (see pp. 326-45). The ten 'formula' introductions to Matthew's 'set-piece' quotations of Scripture have a Marcan base (see pp. 356-7). Matthew has taken over and extended the Q beatitudes (see pp. 299-300). The sixfold antithetical structure of 5. 21-48 is found in embryonic form in Q (Luke 6. 27a [see p. 301]). Matthew's use of the rhetorical strategy of comparison is a considerable development of Q traditions (see pp. 81-3). Even Matthew's distinctive phrases 'their synagogue(s)', 'your synagogues', have a Marcan root (see p. 128).

The evangelist's crowning achievement in his 'foundation document' for the 'new people' is undoubtedly his provision of five major and several shorter carefully arranged discourses. Here too there is good precedent in Matthew's sources: all the evangelist's discourses are considerable extensions of Marcan and Q collections of the sayings of Jesus.

Matthew has taken great care over the composition of the discourses because he values the sayings of Jesus highly. The sayings of Jesus are to be prominent in the missionary proclamation and catechetical instruction of the 'new people' (28. 18-20). The closing verses of the Sermon on the Mount emphasize strongly the importance of hearing and acting on the words of Jesus (7. 24-7). For Matthew 'the will of the heavenly Father' is equated with carrying out the sayings of Jesus (7. 21, cf. Luke 6. 46 [see p. 335]).

Matthew's gospel provided the 'new people' with a new set of authoritative traditions to be set alongside the law and the prophets. The evangelist does not spell out as clearly as his modern interpreters would like the precise relationship of 'new' and 'old'. Matthew's Jesus does not repudiate the law:

its continuing importance is affirmed very strongly (5. 17-19), and Mark's more radical traditions are toned down (cf. especially 15. 1-20 and Mark 7. 1-23). The love commandment of Jesus is singled out as expressing the very essence of Scripture (7. 12; 22. 37-9), but in no way does this contradict the law, any more than do the so-called antitheses in 5. 21-48 (see p. 302). Matthew hints – but no more – that the sayings of Jesus are the criterion for the interpretation of Scripture, but his primary emphasis is on the ways the sayings of Jesus strengthen and fulfil the law and the prophets.

In some respects, however, the sayings of Jesus (and Matthew's gospel as a whole) must *in practice* (though not in theory) have taken priority over the law and the prophets in the community life of the 'new people'. The gospel provided the 'new people' with a prayer of Jesus (6. 9-13) which probably became central in their worship quite soon; this is strongly suggested by *Didache* 8. 3, written just a generation or so after Matthew's gospel and deeply dependent on it. With even more confidence we can affirm that the traditions in Matthew concerning baptism (28. 19), the eucharist (26. 26-8, which reflects liturgical shaping of the Marcan tradition), and community discipline (16. 19; 18. 16-18) were central in the life of Matthean communities. Above all, Matthew's gospel provided the 'new people' with a story which was *new*, even though it had deep roots in Scripture.

In these ways Matthew paved the way for later developments. John's gospel provided the building blocks on which the doctrinal tradition of the church was eventually based. Luke's gospel influenced the development of ecclesiastical structures and the church year. But it was Matthew's gospel which won even wider and speedier acceptance, and which shaped the ethical tradition of the church. Matthew's strong emphasis on the importance of 'hearing and obeying' the words of Jesus encouraged many diverse Christian communities in the second century to set this gospel alongside the law and the prophets as 'Scripture', as a *new* set of authoritative traditions which in due course had to be distinguished from the 'old'.

Bibliography

(i) Books and Articles on Matthew: a Select List

Anderson, Janice Capel, 'Double and Triple Stories, the Implied Reader, and Redundancy in Matthew', in *Reader Response Approaches to Biblical and Secular Texts* (= *Semeia* 31), ed. R. Detweiler, Decatur 1985, 71-89.

– , 'Matthew: Gender and Meaning', *Semeia* 28 (1983) 3-27.

Bacon, B.W., 'The "Five Books" of Moses against the Jews', *The Expositor* 15 (1918) 56-66.

– , *Studies in Matthew*, London 1930.

Barr, D.L., 'The Drama of Matthew's Gospel: a Reconsideration of its Structure and Purpose', *TD* 24 (1976) 349-59.

Barta, Karen A., 'Mission in Matthew: the Second Discourse as Narrative', in *SBL 1988 Seminar Papers*, Atlanta 1988, 527-35.

Barth, G., 'Matthew's Understanding of the Law', in *Tradition*, 58-164.

Bauer, David R., *The Structure of Matthew's Gospel: a Study in Literary Design*, JSNTSS 31, Sheffield 1988.

Beare, F.W., 'The Mission of the Disciples and the Mission Charge. Matthew 10 and Parallels', *JBL* (1970) 1-13.

– , 'The Sayings of Jesus in the Gospel according to St. Matthew', *Studia Evangelica* IV, TU 102, Berlin 1982, 31-9.

Blair, E. P., *Jesus in the Gospel of Matthew*, New York 1960.

Bonnard, P., 'Matthieu, éducateur du peuple chrétien', *Mélanges bibliques en hommage au R. P. Béda Rigaux*, eds. A. Descamps and A. de Halleux, Gembloux 1970, 1-7.

Bornkamm, G., 'Die Sturmstillung im Matthäusevangelium', *Wort und Dienst*. Jahrbuch der Theologischen Schule Bethel 1 (1948) 49-54. E.tr. in *Tradition*, 52-7.

– , 'Enderwartung und Kirche im Matthäusevangelium', *The Background of the New Testament and its Eschatology* (FS C.H. Dodd) eds. W.D. Davies and D. Daube, Cambridge 1956; E.tr. *Tradition*, 15-51.

– , 'Der Auferstandene und der Irdische. Mt. 28, 16-20', *Zeit und Geschichte* (FS R. Bultmann) ed. E. Dinkler, Tübingen, 1964; E.tr. *The Future of our Religious Past*, ed. J.M. Robinson, London 1971, 203-29.

– , 'Die Binde - und Lösegewalt in der Kirche des Matthäus', *Die Zeit Jesu* (FS H. Schlier) eds. G. Bornkamm and K. Rahner, Munich 1970; E.tr., *Jesus and Man's Hope* I, ed. D.G. Miller et al., Pittsburgh 1970.

– , 'Der Aufbau der Bergpredigt', *NTS* 24 (1978) 419-32.

Bornkamm, G., Barth, G., and Held H.J., *Tradition and Interpretation in Matthew*, E.tr. London 1963.

Broer, I., *Freiheit vom Gesetz und Radikalisierung des Gesetzes. Ein Beitrag zur Theologie des Evangelisten Matthäus*, SBS 98, Stuttgart 1980.

Brooks, S.H., *Matthew's Community: The Evidence of his Special Sayings Material*, JSNTSS 16, Sheffield 1985.

Brown, R.E., Donfried, K.P. and Reumann, J., eds., *Peter in the New Testament*, Minneapolis/New York 1973.

Brown, R.E., and Meier, J.P., *Antioch and Rome. New Testament Cradles of Catholic Christianity*, New York 1983.

Brown, R.E., *The Birth of the Messiah*, New York 1977.

Brown, S., 'The Two-Fold Representation of the Mission in Matthew's Gospel', *ST* 31 (1977) 21-32.

– , 'The Mission to Israel in Matthew's Central Section', *ZNW* 69 (1978) 73-90.

– , 'The Matthean Apocalypse', *JSNT* 4 (1979) 2-27.

– , 'The Matthean Community and the Gentile Mission', *NovT* 22 (1980) 193-221.

Burger, C., *Jesus als Davidssohn. Eine traditionsgeschichtliche Untersuchung*, Göttingen 1970.

– , 'Jesu Taten nach Matthäus 8 und 9', *ZNW* 70 (1973) 272-87.

Burnett, F.W., *The Testament of Jesus Sophia: a Redaction Critical Study of the Eschatological Discourse in Matthew*, Washington DC 1979.

– , 'Prolegomenon to Reading Matthew's Eschatological Discourse: Redundancy and the Education of the Reader in Matthew', in *Reader Response Approaches to Biblical and Secular Texts* (= *Semeia* 31), ed. R. Detweiler, Decatur 1985, 91-110.

Butler, B.C., *The Originality of St. Matthew*, Cambridge 1951.

Casalini, Nello, *Il vangelo di Matteo come racconto teologico. Analisi delle sequenze narative*, Jerusalem 1990.

– , Nello, *Libro dell'origine di Gesù Cristo. Analisi letteraria e teologica di Matt 1–2*, Jerusalem 1990.

Clark, K.W., 'The Gentile Bias in Matthew', *JBL* 66 (1947) 165-172.

Combrink, H.J.B., 'The Macrostructure of the Gospel of Matthew',. *Neotestamentica* 16 (1982) 1-20.

– , 'The Structure of the Gospel of Matthew as Narrative', *TB* 34 (1983) 61-90.

Cope, O.L., *Matthew: A Scribe Trained for the Kingdom of Heaven*, CBQMS 5, Washington 1976.

Cothenet, E., 'Les prophètes chrétiens dans l'Évangile selon saint Matthieu', *Matthieu*, 281-308.

Crosby, H., *House of Disciples. Church, Economics and Justice in Matthew*, Maryknoll, N.Y. 1988.

Dahl, N.A., 'Die Passionsgeschichte bei Matthäus', *NTS* 2 (1955-56) 17-32; E.tr. in *Matthew*, 42-55.

Davies, W.D., *The Setting of the Sermon on the Mount*, Cambridge 1966.

Davison, J.E., 'Anomia and the Question of an Antinomian Polemic in Matthew', *JBL* 104 (1985) 617-35.

Deutsch, Celia, *Hidden Wisdom and the Easy Yoke. Wisdom, Torah and Discipleship in Matthew 11: 28-30*, JSNTSS 18, Sheffield 1987.

Devisch, M., 'Le Document Q, source de Matthieu. Problématique actuelle', in *Matthieu*, 71-98.

Didier, M., ed., *L'Evangile selon Matthieu. Rédaction et Théologie*, BETL 29, Gembloux 1972.

Dobschütz, E. von, 'Matthäus als Rabbi und Katechet', *ZNW* 27 (1928) 338-48; E.tr. in *Matthew*, 19-29.

Donaldson, T.L., *Jesus on the Mountain. A Study in Matthean Theology*, JSNTSS 8, Sheffield 1985.

Donfried, K.P, 'The Allegory of the Ten Virgins (Matt. 25:1-13) as a summary of Matthean Theology', *JBL* 93 (1974) 415-28.

Duling, D.C., 'The Therapeutic son of David: an Element in Matthew's Christological Apologetic', *NTS* 24 (1978) 392-409.

Edwards, R.A., *Matthew's Story of Jesus*, Philadelphia 1985.

– , 'Uncertain Faith: Matthew's Portrait of the Disciples', in *Discipleship in the New Testament*, ed. Fernando F. Segovia, Philadelphia 1985, 47-61.

Ellis, P.E., *Matthew: His Mind and His Message*, Collegeville, Minn. 1974.

Farrer, A.M., 'On Dispensing with Q', in *Studies in the Gospels*, ed. D.E. Nineham, Oxford 1955, 59-88.

Fenton, J.C., 'Inclusio and Chiasmus in Matthew', *Studia Evangelica* I, TU 73, ed. F.L. Cross, Berlin 1959, 174-79.

– , 'Matthew and the Divinity of Jesus: Three Questions Concerning Matthew 1. 20-23', *Studia Biblica* 1978, II, ed. E.A. Livingstone, Sheffield 1980, 79-82.

Filson, F.V., 'Broken Patterns in the Gospel of Matthew', *JBL* 75 (1956) 227-31.

Fowler, R.M., 'Reading Matthew Reading Mark: Observing the First Steps Toward Meaning-as-Reference in the Synoptic Gospels', in ed. K.H. Richards, *SBL 1986 Seminar Papers*, Atlanta 1986, 1-16.

France, R.T., *Matthew: Evangelist and Teacher*, London and Grand Rapids 1989.

Frankemölle, H., 'Amtskritik im Matthäus-Evangelium', *Biblica* 54 (1973) 247-62.

– , *Jahwebund und Kirche Christi*, NTAbh 10, Münster 1974.

Freyne, Séan, 'Vilifying the Other and Defining the Self: Matthew's and John's Anti-Jewish Polemic in Focus', in *"To See Ourselves as Others See Us", Christians, Jews, "Others" in Late Antiquity*, eds. J. Neusner and E.S. Frerichs, Chico, Calif. 1985, 117-144.

Gaechter, P., *Die literarische Kunst im Matthäus-Evangelium*, SBS 7, Stuttgart 1965.

Garland, D.E., *The Intention of Matthew 23*, NovTSup 52, Leiden 1979.

Gärtner, B., 'The Habakkuk Commentary (DSH) and the Gospel of Matthew', *ST* 8 (1954) 1-24.

Gaston, L., 'The Messiah of Israel as Teacher of the Gentiles', *Interpretation* 29 (1975) 25-40.

Gerhardsson, B., 'Jésus livré et abandonné d'après la passion selon saint Matthieu', *RB* 76 (1969) 206-227.

– , 'Gottes Sohn als Diener Gottes. Messias, Agape und Himmelsherrschaft nach dem Matthäusevangelium', *ST* 27 (1973) 25-50.

– , *The Mighty Acts of Jesus according to Matthew*, Lund 1979.

Gibbs, J.M., 'Purpose and Pattern in Matthew's Use of the Title "Son of David"', *NTS* 10 (1964) 446-464.

– , 'The Son of God as Torah Incarnate in Matthew', *Studia Evangelica IV*, TU 102, Berlin 1968, 38-46.

Giesen, Heinz, *Christliches Handeln: eine redaktionskritische Untersuchung zum δικαιοσύνη - Begriff im Matthäus-Evangelium*, Frankfurt 1982.

– , *Glaube und Handeln I: Beiträge zur Exegese und Theologie des Matthäus -und Markus-Evangeliums.*, Frankfurt 1983.

Gnilka, Joachim, 'Die Kirche des Matthäus und die Gemeinde von Qumran', *BZ* 7 (1963) 43-63.

Goodspeed, E.J., *Matthew, Apostle and Evangelist*, Philadelphia 1959.

Goulder, M.D., *Midrash and Lection in Matthew*, London 1974.

– , *Luke: a New Paradigm*, 2 vols., Sheffield 1989.

Green, H.B., 'The Structure of St Matthew's Gospel', in *Studia Evangelica IV*, TU 102, ed F.L. Cross, Berlin 1968, 47-59.

Greeven, H., 'Die Heilung des Gelähmten nach Matthäus', *Wort und Dienst* 4 (1955) 65-78.

Haenchen, E., 'Matthäus 23', *ZThK* 48 (1951) 38-63.

Hagner, D.A., 'Apocalyptic Motifs in the Gospel of Matthew: Continuity and Discontinuity', *Horizons in Biblical Theology* 7 (1985) 53-82.

– , 'The *Sitz im Leben* of the Gospel of Matthew', in *SBL 1985 Seminar Papers*, 243-69.

Hare, D.R.A., and Harrington, D.J., '"Make Disciples of all the Gentiles" (Mt. 28. 19)', *CBQ* 37 (1975) 359-69.

Hare, D.R.A., *The Theme of Jewish Persecution of Christians in the Gospel According to St. Matthew*, SNTSMS 6, Cambridge 1967.

Harrington, D.J., 'Matthean Studies since Joachim Rohde', *HJ* 16 (1975) 375-88.

Held, H.J., 'Matthew as Interpreter of the Miracle Stories', in *Tradition*, 165-300.

Hill, D., 'The Figure of Jesus in Matthew's Gospel: a Response to Professor Kingsbury's Literary-Critical Probe', *JSNT* 21 (1984) 37-52.

– , 'Son and Servant: An Essay on Matthean Christology', *JSNT* 6 (1980) 2-16.

Hoffmann, P., 'Der Petrus-Primat im Matthäusevangelium', in *Neues Testament und Kirche* (FS R. Schnackenburg) ed. J. Gnilka, Freiburg 1974, 94-114.

Houlden, J.L., *Backwards into Light. The Passion and Resurrection of Jesus according to Matthew and Mark*, London, 1987.

Howell, David B., *Matthew's Inclusive Story. A Study in the Narrative Rhetoric of the First Gospel*, JSNTSS 42, Sheffield 1990.

Hubbard, B.J., *The Matthean Redaction of a Primitive Apostolic Commissioning: An Exegesis of Matthew 28. 16-20*, SBLDS 19, Missoula 1974.

Hummel, R., *Die Auseinandersetzung zwischen Kirche und Judentum im Matthäusevangelium*, BEvT 33, Munich, 1963; 2nd ed. 1966.

Johnson, M.D., 'Reflections on a Wisdom Approach to Matthew's Christology', *CBQ* 36 (1974) 44-74.

Käsemann, E., 'The Beginnings of Christian Theology', in E. Käsemann, *New Testament Questions of Today*, E.tr. London 1969.

Kilpatrick, G.D., *The Origins of the Gospel According to St. Matthew*, Oxford 1946.

Kingsbury, Jack Dean, *The Parables of Jesus in Matthew 13*, London 1969.

–, 'The Composition and Christology of Matt. 28: 16-20', *JBL* 93 (1974) 573-84.

–, 'The Title "Son of David" in Matthew's Gospel', *JBL* 95 (1976) 591-602.

–, *Matthew: Structure, Christology, Kingdom*, London 1976.

–, 'The Verb *Akolouthein* as an Index of Matthew's View of his Community', *JBL* 97 (1978) 56-73

–, 'The Figure of Peter in Matthew's Gospel as a Theological Problem', *JBL* 98 (1979) 67-83.

–, 'The Figure of Jesus in Matthew's Story: a Literary-Critical Probe', *JSNT* 21 (1984) 3-36.

–, 'The Figure of Jesus in Matthew's Story: a Rejoinder to David Hill', *JSNT* 25 (1985) 61-81.

–, 'The Parable of the Wicked Husbandmen and the Secret of Jesus' Divine Sonship in Matthew', *JBL* 105 (1986) 643-55.

–, *Matthew as Story*, Philadelphia 1986; 2nd ed. 1988.

–, 'The Developing Conflict between Jesus and the Jewish Leaders in Matthew's Gospel: a Literary Critical Study', *CBQ* 49 (1987) 57-73.

–, 'On Following Jesus: the 'Eager' Scribe and the 'Reluctant' Disciple, Matthew 8:18-22', *NTS* 34 (1988) 45-59.

–, 'Reflections on "the Reader" of Matthew's Gospel', *NTS* 34 (1988) 442-60.

Köhler, W., *Die Rezeption des Matthäusevangeliums in der Zeit vor Irenäus*, WUNT 24, Tübingen 1987.

Krentz, E., 'The Extent of Matthew's Prologue', *JBL* 83 (1964) 409-414.

Kretzer, A., *Die Herrschaft der Himmel und die Söhne des Reiches*, SBS 10, Stuttgart 1971.

Künzel, G., *Studien zum Gemeindeverständnis des Matthäus-Evangeliums*, Calwer theologische Monographien, Reihe 1, Stuttgart 1978.

Lambrecht, J., 'The Parousia Discourse: Composition and Content in Mt. XXIV-XXV', *Matthieu*, 309-342.

Lange, J., *Das Erscheinen des Auferstandenen im Evangelium nach Matthäus*, Forschung zur Bibel 11, Würzburg 1973.

– , ed., *Das Matthäus-Evangelium*, Wege der Forschung 525, Darmstadt 1980.

Légasse, S., 'L'antijudaïsme dans l'Évangile selon Matthieu', *Matthieu*, 417-428.

Levine, A.J., *The Social and Ethnic Dimensions of Matthean Salvation History*, Lewiston 1988.

Lincoln, A.T., 'Matthew - a Story for Teachers?', in *The Bible in Three Dimensions*, eds. D.J.A. Clines, S.E. Fowl, S.E. Porter, Sheffield 1990, 103-26.

Lohr, C. H., 'Oral Techniques in the Gospel of Matthew', *CBQ* 23 (1961) 403-435.

Luz, U., 'Die Jünger im Matthäusevangelium', *ZNW* 62 (1971) 141-71; E.tr. in *Matthew*, 98-128.

– , 'Eine thetische Skizze der matthäischen Christologie', *Anfänge der Christologie* (FS F. Hahn) ed. C. Breytenbach and H. Paulsen, Göttingen 1991, 221-35.

Marguerat, Daniel, *Le Jugement dans l'évangile de Matthieu*, Geneva 1981.

Massaux, E., *Influence de L'Évangile de saint Matthieu sur la littérature chrétienne avant saint Irénée*, Louvain 1950; revised ed. BETL 75, Leuven 1986.

Matera, F., 'The Plot of Matthew's Gospel', *CBQ* 49 (1987) 233-53.

McConnell, R. S., *Law and Prophecy in Matthew's Gospel*, Basel 1969.

Meeks, W.A., 'Breaking Away: Three New Testament Pictures of Christianity's Separation from the Jewish Communities', in *"To see Ourselves as Others See Us": Christians, Jews, "Others" in Late Antiquity*, eds. J. Neusner and E.S. Frerichs, Chico Calif. 1985, 93-116.

Malina, Bruce and Neyrey, Jerome H., *Calling Jesus Names: the Social Value of Labels in Matthew*, Sonoma Calif. 1988.

Meier, J.P., *Law and History in Matthew's Gospel*, Analecta Biblica 71, Rome 1976.

– , 'Nations or Gentiles in Matthew 28. 19?', *CBQ* 39 (1977) 94-102.

–, 'Two Disputed Questions in Matt. 28. 16-20', *JBL* 96 (1977) 407-24.

–, *The Vision of Matthew: Christ, Church and Morality in the First Gospel*, New York 1979.

–, 'John the Baptist in Matthew's Gospel', *JBL* 99 (1980) 383-405.

Michel, O., 'Der Abschluß des Matthäusevangeliums', *EvT* 10 (1950-1) 16-26; E.tr. in *Matthew*, 30-41.

Minear, P.S., 'False Prophecy and Hypocrisy in the Gospel of Matthew', *Neues Testament und Kirche* (FS R. Schnackenburg) ed. J. Gnilka, Freiburg 1974, 76-93.

–, 'The Disciples and the Crowds in the Gospel of Matthew', *Anglican Theological Review*, Supplementary Series 3 (1974) 28-44.

Mohrlang, Roger, *Matthew and Paul: a Comparison of Ethical Perspectives*, SNTSMS 48, Cambridge 1984.

Moule, C.F.D., 'Matthew's Gospel: Some Neglected Features', *Studia Evangelica* II, TU 87, Berlin 1964, 91-9.

Mora, Vincent, *Le Refus d'Israël. Matthieu 27, 25*, Lectio Divina 125, Paris 1986.

Neirynck, F., *The Minor Agreements of Matthew and Luke against Mark*, BETL 37, Leuven 1974.

–, *Evangelica. Collected Essays*, BETL 60, Leuven 1982.

–, *Evangelica II. Collected Essays 1982 – 1991*, BETL 99, Leuven 1991.

Nellessen, E., *Das Kind und seine Mütter*, SBS 39, Stuttgart 1969.

Nepper-Christensen, P., *Das Matthäusevangelium – ein judenchristliches Evangelium?* Acta Theologica Danica 1, Aarhus 1958.

–, 'Die Taufe im Matthäusevangelium', *NTS* 31 (1985) 189-207.

Neusner, J., and Frerichs, E.S., eds., *"To See Ourselves as Others See Us", Christians, Jews, "Others" in Late Antiquity*, Chico 1985.

Nolan, B., *The Royal Son of God: The Christology of Matthew 1-2*, Orbis Biblicus et Orientalis 23, Göttingen 1979.

Orchard, B., and Riley, H., *The Order of the Synoptics. Why Three Synoptic Gospels?* Macon, Georgia, 1987.

Orton, D.E., *The Understanding Scribe*, JSNTSS 25, Sheffield 1988.

Overman, J.A., *Matthew's Gospel and Formative Judaism*, Minneapolis 1990.

Pesch, W., *Matthäus, der Seelsorger*, SBS 2, Stuttgart 1966.

Phillips, Gary A., 'History and Text: the Reader in Context in Matthew's Parable Discourse', in *Reader Response*, ed. R. Detweiler, 111-40.

Przybylski, B., *Righteousness in Matthew and his World of Thought*, SNTSMS 41, Cambridge 1980.

– , 'The Setting of Matthean Anti-Judaism', in *Anti-Judaism in Early Christianity*, eds. P. Richardson and D. Granskou, Waterloo, I 1986, 181-200.

Riches, J., 'The Sociology of Matthew: Some Basic Questions Concerning its Relation to the Theology of the New Testament', *SBL Seminar Papers* (1983) 259-71.

Rist, J.M., *On the Independence of Matthew and Mark*, SNTSMS 32, Cambridge 1978.

Rohde, J., *Rediscovering the Teaching of the Evangelists*, E.tr. London 1968.

Sand, A., *Das Gesetz und die Propheten: Untersuchungen zur Theologie des Evangeliums nach Matthäus*, Biblische Untersuchungen 11, Regensburg 1974.

Schaberg, Jane, *The Father, the Son and the Holy Spirit. The Triadic Phrase in Matthew 28. 19b*, SBLDS 61, Chico 1982.

Schenk, Wolfgang, *Die Sprache des Matthäus: Die Text-Konstituenten in ihren makro- und mikrostrukturellen Relationen*, Göttingen 1987.

Schenke, L., ed. *Studien zum Matthäusevangelium* (FS W. Pesch) Stuttgart 1988.

Schlatter, A., *Die Kirche des Matthäus*, Beiträge zur Förderung christlicher Theologie 33, 1, Gütersloh, 1930.

– , *Der Evangelist Matthäus. Seine Sprache, sein Ziel, seine Selbständigkeit*, 6th ed., Suttgart 1963.

Schweizer, E., 'Observance of the Law and Charismatic Activity in Matthew', *NTS* 16 (1969-70) 213-30.

– , 'The "Matthean Church"', *NTS* 20 (1974) 215.

– , E., *Matthäus und seine Gemeinde*, SBS 71, Stuttgart 1974.

Scott, J.W., 'Matthew's Intention to Write Story', *WJT* 47 (1985) 68-82.

Senior, D.P, *The Passion Narrative According to Matthew*, BETL 39, Leuven 1975.

– , *What are They Saying About Matthew?* New York 1983.

Shuler, P.L., *A Genre for the Gospels: the Biographical Character of Matthew*, Philadelphia 1982.

Slingerland, H.D., 'The Transjordanian Origin of Matthew's Gospel', *JSNT* 3 (1979) 18-28.

Stanton, G.N., 'The Origin and Purpose of Matthew's Gospel: Matthean Scholarship from 1945 – 1980', *ANRW* II. 25.3, (1985) 1889-1951.

– , ed., *The Interpretation of Matthew. Issues in Religion and Theology 3*, Philadelphia and London 1983.

Stendahl, K., *The School of St. Matthew and its Use of the Old Testament*, Lund and Copenhagen 1954; 2nd ed. Philadelphia 1968.

Strecker, G., *Der Weg der Gerechtigkeit*, FRLANT 82, 1st ed. Göttingen 1962; 3rd ed. 1971.

– , 'Das Geschichtsverständnis des Matthäus, *EvT* 26 (1966) 57-74.

Suggs, M, J., *Wisdom, Christology and Law in Matthew's Gospel*, Cambridge Mass. 1970.

Suhl, A., 'Der Davidssohn im Matthäus-Evangelium', *ZNW* 59 (1968) 57-81.

Thompson, W.G, *Matthew's Advice to a Divided Community: Matthew 17:22 – 18:35*, Rome 1970.

Thysman, R., *Communauté et directives / éthiques: la Catéchèse de Matthieu*, Recherches et Synthèses, Sect. d'Exégèse 1, Gembloux 1974.

Trevett, C., 'Approaching Matthew from the Second Century: the Under-used Ignatian Correspondence', *JSNT* 20 (1984) 59-67.

Trilling, W., *Das Wahre Israel*. Studien zum Alten und Neuen Testament 10, 2nd ed. Leipzig, 1961; 3rd ed. Munich, 1964.

– , 'Amt und Amtsverständnis bei Matthäus', *Mélanges bibliques en hommage au R. P. Béda Rigaux*, eds. A. Descamps and A. de Halleux, Gembloux 1970, 29-44.

Tilborg, S. van, *The Jewish Leaders in Matthew*, Leiden 1972.

Verseput, D.J., *The Rejection of the Humble Messianic King. A Study of the Composition of Matthew 11-12*, Frankfurt 1986.

Viviano, B.T., 'Where was the Gospel According to Matthew Written?', CBQ 41 (1979) 533-546.

Vögtle, A., *Messias und Gottessohn, Herkunft und Sinn der matthäischen Geburts- und Kindheitsgeschichte*, Düsseldorf 1971.

Waetjen, W.C., 'The Genealogy as the Key to the Gospel according to Matthew', *JBL* 95 (1976) 205-230.

Walker, R., *Die Heilsgeschichte im ersten Evangelium*, FRLANT 91, Göttingen 1967.

Weaver, Dorothy Jean, *Matthew's Missionary Discourse: A Literary Critical Analysis*, JSNTSS 38, Sheffield 1990.

Wilkins, M.J., *The Concept of Disciple in Matthew's Gospel*, Leiden 1988.

Zumstein, J., *La Condition du croyant dans l'évangile selon Matthieu*, Orbis Biblicus et Orientalis 16, Fribourg & Göttingen 1977.

(ii) Major Commentaries since 1900

Albright, W.F., and Mann, C.S., *Matthew*, Anchor Bible 26, New York 1971.

Allen, W.C., *A Critical and Exegetical Commentary on the Gospel according to S. Matthew*, ICC, Edinburgh 3rd ed. 1912.

Beare, F.W., *The Gospel According to Matthew*, San Francisco and Oxford 1981.

Benoit, P., *L' Évangile selon S. Matthieu*, Paris 1950; 4th ed. 1972.

Bonnard, P., *L'Évangile selon saint Matthieu*, Neuchatel 1963; 2nd ed.1970.

Carson, D.A., 'Matthew', in *The Expositor's Bible Commentary* 8, ed. F. Gaebelein, Grand Rapids 1984, 3-599.

Davies, W.D. and Allison, D.C., *A Critical and Exegetical Commentary on the Gospel according to Saint Matthew*, ICC, Edinburgh I, 1988; II, 1991.

Filson, F.V., *A Commentary on the Gospel according to St. Matthew*, London 1960.

France, R.T., *The Gospel according to Matthew*, Leicester 1985.

Gaechter, P., *Das Matthäus-Evangelium*, Innsbruck 1963.

Gander, G., *Évangile de l'Église. Commentaire de l'Évangile selon Matthieu*, Aix en Provence 1967-70.

Gnilka, *Das Matthäusevangelium*, HThK, Freiburg I, 1986, II 1988.

Green, H.B., *The Gospel according to Matthew*, New Clarendon Bible. Oxford 1975.

Grundmann, W., *Das Evangelium nach Matthäus*, ThHK Berlin 1968; 4th ed. 1975.

Gundry, R.H., *Matthew: a Commentary on his Literary and Theological Art*, Grand Rapids 1981.

Hill, D., *The Gospel of Matthew*, New Century Bible. London, 1972.

Klostermann, E., *Das Matthäusevangelium*, Handbuch zum NT. Tübingen, 2nd ed., 1927, 3rd ed. 1938.

Lagrange, M.-J., *Évangile selon Saint Matthieu*, Paris, 1927; 7th ed., 1948.

Lohmeyer, E., *Das Evangelium des Matthäus* (ed. W. Schmauch), KEK, Göttingen 1956.

Loisy, A., *Les Évangiles Synoptiques*, Bd. I, Ceffonds 1907

Luz, U. *Das Evangelium nach Matthäus*, EKK, Zürich I 1985; II 1990; E.tr. Edinburgh I 1989.

M' Neile, A.H., *The Gospel According to St Matthew*, London 1915.

Maier, G., *Matthäusevangelium*, 2 vols., Neuhausen-Stuttgart 1979.

Michaelis, W., *Das Evangelium nach Matthäus*, I, 1948, II, Zürich 1949.

Patte, Daniel, *The Gospel According to Matthew. A Structural Commentary on Matthew's Faith*, Philadelphia 1987.

Plummer, A., *An Exegetical Commentary on the Gospel according to St Matthew*, London 1909.

Radermakers, J., *Au fil de l'Évangile selon saint Matthieu*, 2 vols., Heverlee-Louvain 1972.

Robinson, T.H., *The Gospel of Matthew*, London 1928.

Sabourin, L., *L'Évangile selon saint Matthieu et ses principaux parallèles*, Rome 1978.

Sand, A., *Das Evangelium nach Matthäus*, Regensburg 1986.

Schlatter, A., *Der Evangelist Matthäus*, Stuttgart 1929; 6th ed., 1963.

Schmid, J., *Das Evangelium nach Matthäus*, Regensburg, 1965.

Schnackenburg, R., *Matthäusevangelium*, I, Würzburg 1985; II, 1987.

Schniewind, J., *Das Evangelium nach Matthäus*, NTD, Göttingen 1956.

Schweizer, E., *Das Evangelium nach Matthäus*, NTD, Göttingen 1973; E.tr. *The Good News According to Matthew*, Atlanta 1975, and London 1976.

Stendahl, K., 'Matthew', in *Peake's Commentary on the Bible*, ed. M. Black and H.H. Rowley, London 1962.

Trilling, W., *The Gospel according to St Matthew for Spiritual Reading*, 2 vols., London 1969

Wellhausen, J., *Das Evangelium Matthaei*, Berlin 1904; 2nd ed., 1914.

Zahn, T., *Das Evangelium des Matthäus*, Leipzig 1903; 4th ed. 1922.

(iii) The Sermon on the Mount

Banks, R.J., 'Matthew's Understanding of the Law: Authenticity and Interpretation in Matthew 5: 17-20', *JBL* 93 (1974) 226-42.

Berner, U., *Die Bergpredigt: Rezeption und Auslegung im 20. Jahrhundert*, Göttinger theologische Arbeiten 12, Göttingen 1979.

Betz, H.D., *Essays on the Sermon on the Mount*, Philadelphia 1985.

– , 'The Sermon on the Mount and Q: Some Aspects of the Problem', in *Gospel Origins and Christian Beginnings* (FS James M. Robinson) eds. J. Goehring et al., Polebridge 1990, 19-34.

– , 'The Problem of Christology in the Sermon on the Mount', in *Text and Logos: The Humanistic Interpretation of the New Testament* (FS Hendrikus W. Boers), ed. T.W. Jennings, Jr, Atlanta 1990, 191-209.

– , 'The Sermon on the Mount in Matthew's Interpretation', in *The Future of Early Christianity* (FS H. Koester), eds. B.A. Pearson et al., Minneapolis 1991, 258-75.

Bornkamm, G., 'Der Aufbau der Bergpredigt', *NTS* 24 (1977-8) 419-32.

Broer, I., *Die Seligpreisungen der Bergpredigt. Studien zu ihrer Überlieferung und Interpretation*, BBB 61, Bonn 1986.

Carlston, C.E., 'Betz on the Sermon on the Mount – a Critique', *CBQ* 50 (1988) 47-57.

Davies, W.D., *The Setting of the Sermon on the Mount*, Cambridge 1964.

Dupont, J., *Les Béatitudes*, Paris, I, 2nd ed. 1969; II, 1969; III, 2nd ed. 1973.

Grant, R.M., 'The Sermon on the Mount in Early Christianity', *Semeia* 12 (1978) 215-31.

Guelich, R. A., ' "Not to Annul the Law Rather to Fulfill the Prophets": An Exegetical Study of Jesus and the Law in Matthew with Emphasis on 5: 17-48', Diss. Hamburg, 1967.

– , 'The Matthean Beatitudes: Entrance Requirements or Eschatological Blessings?' *JBL* 95 (1976) 415-34.

– , *The Sermon on the Mount: a Foundation for Understanding*, Waco 1982.

Hamerton-Kelly, R. G., 'Attitudes to the Law in Matthew's Gospel: A Discussion of Matthew 5: 18', *Biblical Research* 17 (1972) 19-32.

Hendrickx, H., *The Sermon on the Mount*, London 1984.

Hengel, M., 'Zur matthäischen Bergpredigt und ihrem jüdischen Hintergrund', *ThR* 52 (1987) 327-400.

Hill, D., 'False Prophets and Charismatics: Structure and Interpretation in Matthew 7. 15-23', *Biblica* 57 (1976) 327-48.

Jeremias, J., *The Sermon on the Mount*, Facet Books, Philadelphia 1963.

Keck, L., 'The Sermon on the Mount', in: *Jesus and Man's Hope* II, ed. D.G. Miller et al., Pittsburgh 1971.

Kissinger, W.S., *The Sermon on the Mount: A History of Interpretation and Bibliography*, ATLA Bibliography Series 3, Metuchen 1975.

Lambrecht, J., *The Sermon on the Mount*, Wilmington 1985.

Kingsbury, J.D., 'The Place, Structure, and Meaning of the Sermon on the Mount within Matthew', *Interpretation* 41 (1987) 131-43.

Strecker, G., 'Die Makarismen der Bergpredigt', *NTS* 17 (1970-1) 255-75.

– , 'Die Antithesen der Bergpredigt', *ZNW* 69 (1978) 36-72.

– , *The Sermon on the Mount: an Exegetical Commentary*, E.tr. Edinburgh 1988.

Syreeni, Kari, *The Making of the Sermon on the Mount. A procedural analysis of Matthew's redactoral activity.* Helsinki 1987.

Wrege, H.-T., *Die Überlieferungsgeschichte der Bergpredigt*, WUNT 9, Tübingen 1968.

Tilborg, S. van, *The Sermon on the Mount as an Ideological Intervention*, Van Gorcum 1986.

(iv) Matthew's Use of the Old Testament

Brown, R.E., *The Birth of the Messiah*, New York 1977.

Cangh, M. van, 'La Bible de Matthieu: Les citations d'accomplissement', *EThL* 6 (1975) 205-11.

Cope, O.L., *Matthew: A Scribe Trained for the Kingdom of Heaven*, CBQMS 5, Washington 1976.

France, R.T., 'The Formula Quotations of Matthew 2 and the Problem of Communication', *NTS* 27 (1981) 233-51.

Gärtner, B., 'The Habakkuk Commentary (DSH) and the Gospel of Matthew ', *ST* 8 (1954) 1-24.

Goulder, M.D., *Midrash and Lection in Matthew*, London 1974.

Gundry, R.H., *The Use of the Old Testament in St. Matthew's Gospel with Special Reference to the Messianic Hope*, NovTSup 18, Leiden 1967.

Hartman, L., 'Scriptural Exegesis in the Gospel of St. Matthew and the Problem of Communication', in *L'Évangile selon Matthieu, Rédaction et Théologie*, ed. M. Didier, BEThL 29, Gembloux 1972, 131-52.

Hill, D., 'Son and Servant. An Essay in Matthean Christology', *JSNT* 6 (1980) 2-16.

Kilpatrick, G.D., *The Origins of the Gospel According to St Matthew*, Oxford 1946.

Kingsbury, J.D., *The Parables of Jesus in Matthew 13*, London 1969.

Luz, U., *Das Evangelium nach Matthäus*, EKK 1/1, Zürich and Neukirchen-Vluyn, I, 1985. Excursus: 'Die Erfüllungszitate', 134-80.

McConnell, R.S., *Law and Prophecy in Matthew's Gospel*, Basel 1969.

Massebieau, E., *Examen des citations de l'Ancien Testament dans l'évangile selon saint Matthieu*, Paris 1885.

Neyrey, J.N., 'The Thematic Use of Isa 42. 1-4 in Matthew 12', *Biblica* 63 (1982) 457-83.

Pesch, R., 'Der Gottessohn im matthäischen Evangelien-prolog (Mt 1-2). Beobachtungen zu den Zitationsformeln der Reflexionzitate', *Biblica* 48 (1967) 395-420.

Rothfuchs, W., *Die Erfüllungszitate des Matthäus-Evangeliums*, BWANT 88, Stuttgart 1969.

Sand, A., *Das Gesetz und die Propheten. Untersuchungen zur Theologie des Evangeliums nach Matthäus*, BU 11, Regensburg 1974.

Smith, D.M., 'The Use of the Old Testament in the New', in *The Use of the Old Testament in the New and Other Essays*, ed. J.M. Efird, Durham NC 1972, 3-65.

Soares Prabhu, G.M., *The Formula Quotations in the Infancy Narrative of Matthew*, AnBib 63, Rome 1976.

Stendahl, K., *The School of St. Matthew and its Use of the Old Testament*, 1st ed. Lund and Copenhagen, 1954; 2nd ed. Philadelphia 1968.

Strecker, G, *Der Weg der Gerechtigkeit*, FRLANT 82, 1st ed. Göttingen 1962; 3rd ed. Göttingen 1971.

Trilling, W., *Das Wahre Israel*, SANT 10, 2nd ed. Leipzig 1961; 3rd ed. Münich 1964.

Van Segbroeck, F., 'Les Citations d'Accomplissement dans l'Évangile selon Matthieu d'après trois ouvrages récents', in *L'Évangile selon Matthieu. Rédaction et Théologie*, ed. M. Didier, BETL 19, Gembloux 1971, 107-130.

(v) Matthew 25. 31-46

Agbanou, V.K., *Le Discours eschatologique de Matthieu 24-25: Tradition et rédaction*, EB 2, Paris 1983.

Bonnard, P., 'Matthieu 25, 31-46. Questions de lecture et d'interpretation', *Foi et Vie* 76 (1977) 81-7.

Brandenburger, Egon, *Das Recht des Weltenrichters. Untersuchung zur Matthäus 25, 31-46*, SBS 99, Stuttgart 1980.

Brandt, W., 'Die geringste Brüder. Aus dem Gespräch der Kirche mit Matthäus 25, 31-46', *Jahrbuch der theologischen Schule Bethel* 8 (1937) 1-28.

Brown S., 'Faith, the Poor and the Gentiles: a Tradition-Historical Reflection on Mathew 25: 31-46', *Toronto Journal of Theology* 6 (1990) 171-81.

Catchpole, D.R., 'The Poor on Earth and the Son of Man in Heaven. A Re-Appraisal of Matthew xxv. 31-46', *BJRL* 61 (1979) 355-97.

Christian, P., *Jesus und seine geringsten Brüder: Mt 25, 31-46 redaktionsgeschichtliche untersucht*, Erfurter Theologische Schriften 12, Leipzig 1975.

Cope, L., 'Matthew xxv. 31-46 – "The Sheep and the Goats" Reinterpreted', *NovT* 11 (1969) 32-44.

Court, J.M., 'Right and Left: the Implications for Matthew 25. 31-46', *NTS* 31 (1985) 223-33.

Cranfield, C.E.B., 'Diakonia. Matthew 25, 31-46', *London Quarterly and Holborn Review* 186 (1961) 275-81.

Donahue, J.R., 'The "Parable" of the Sheep and the Goats: A Challenge to Christian Ethics', *TS* 47 (1986) 3-31.

– , *The Gospel in Parable*, Philadelphia 1988, 109-25.

Friedrich, J., *Gott im Bruder? Eine methodenkritische Untersuchung von Redaktion, Überlieferung und Traditionen in Mt 25, 31-46*, Stuttgart 1977.

Furnish, V., *The Love Command in the New Testament*, London 1973, 79-84.

Gray, Sherman W., *The Least of My Brothers: Matthew 25: 31-46: a History of Interpretation*, SBLDS 114, Atlanta 1989.

Haufe, G., 'Soviel ihr getan habt einem dieser meiner geringsten Brüder . . .' in *Ruf und Antwort* (FS E. Fuchs) Leipzig 1964, 484-93.

Ladd, G.E., 'The Parable of the Sheep and the Goats in Recent Interpretation', in *New Dimensions in New Testament Study*, eds. R.N. Longenecker and M.C. Tenney, Grand Rapids 1974, 191-9.

Lambrecht, J., 'The Parousia Discourse: Composition and Content in Mt XXIV–XXV', in *Matthieu*, 309-42.

– , *Once More Astonished: the Parables of Jesus*, New York 1983, 196-235.

Lohse, E., 'Christus als Weltenrichter', in *Jesus Christus in Historie und Theologie* (FS H. Conzelmann) ed. G. Strecker, Tübingen 1975, 474-86.

Maddox, R., 'Who are the "Sheep" and the "Goats"? A Study of the Purpose and Meaning of Matthew xxv: 31-46', *Australian Biblical Review* 13 (1965) 19-25.

Mánek, J., 'Mit wem identifiziert sich Jesus (Matt. 25: 31-46)?' in *Christ and Spirit in the New Testament* (FS C.F.D. Moule) eds. B. Lindars and S.S. Smalley, Cambridge 1973, 15-25.

Marguerat, D., *Le Jugement dans l' Evangile de Matthieu*, Geneva 1981, 481-520.

Michaels, J.R., 'Apostolic Hardships and Righteous Gentiles. A Study of Mt. 25: 31-46', *JBL* 84 (1965) 27-37.

Robinson, J.A.T., 'The "Parable" of the Sheep and the Goats', *NTS* 2 (1955-6) 225-37.

Wikenhauser, A., 'Die Liebeswerke in dem Gerichtsgemälde Mt 25: 31-46' *BZ* 20 (1932) 366-77.

Wilckens, U., 'Gottes geringste Brüder - zu Mt 25, 31-46', in *Jesus und Paulus* (FS W.G. Kümmel) eds. E.E. Ellis and E. Grässer, Göttingen 1975, 363-83.

Winandy, J., 'La scène du jugement dernier (Mt. 25, 31-46)', *ScEccl* 18 (1966) 169-86.

Index of References

Index of Modern Authors